Other SIGNET Non-Fiction Titles
You Will Enjoy

THE BOSTON STRANGLER

GEROLD FRANK

BETTI'S BOOK SHOP
108 Clinton St.
Charlevoix, Mich.
Sold & Exchanged

547-6814

A SIGNET BOOK from
NEW AMERICAN LIBRARY
TIMES MIRROR

SIGNET TRADEMARK REG. U.S. PAT. OFF. AND FOREIGN COUNTRIES
REGISTERED TRADEMARK—MARCA REGISTRADA
HECHO EN CHICAGO, U.S.A.

SIGNET, SIGNET CLASSICS, SIGNETTE, MENTOR AND PLUME BOOKS
are published by The New American Library, Inc.,
1301 Avenue of the Americas, New York, New York 10019

FIRST PRINTING, AUGUST, 1967

PRINTED IN THE UNITED STATES OF AMERICA

For Amy and John

A NOTE TO THE READER

This book, which has taken on a shape and a direction I could not anticipate when I began, has been an extraordinary experience for me. I have lived it as well as written it.

I first became interested in what was taking place in Boston in the late summer of 1963. At that time there had been a series of murders of single women, most of whom were middle-aged, under circumstances as baffling as any in fiction. Each woman had been strangled in her apartment. There were no signs of forcible entry. Around the necks of the victims were knotted nylon stockings or other articles of their apparel. Each woman had been sexually molested or assaulted. No clues were found; nothing had been stolen; there was no discernible motive. The victims were, so far as could be determined, modest, inconspicuous, almost anonymous women, leading blameless lives. Beyond the mystery of their deaths, there was something terribly sad and pathetic about these victims who apparently either knew or were unafraid of their murderer, and let him into their apartments and did not even put up a struggle before they were finished off. It was obvious that the murderer—or murderers—was insane. As a result, Boston was a city near panic.

As a young reporter I had had my fill of crime. I had covered electrocutions in Sing Sing prison, and had never gotten over the sight of murderers in the electric chair, nor the sense that we, the spectators, were outraging decency by witnessing the last private moments of these men. Later, as a foreign correspondent, I had reported riots, revolutions, and political assassinations. Sudden death was not unknown to me and I was not particularly eager to explore the subject again. My interest, therefore, was not so much in writing a book about the Boston stranglings as it was to write about what happens to a great city when it is besieged by terror—terror stemming from a horrifying explosion of the violence that seems more and more a part of contemporary life. How do people behave in a climate of fear? What defenses do they put up? To what extremes are they driven? How does rationality cope with irrationality, common sense with hysteria?

The city, then, was to be my subject—and the victims. For if these murders were, as it appeared, utterly senseless, why should these women have been chosen to die? What brought them to this place, at this moment in time, so that their lives met that of their assailant, moving about the city tortured by some private anguish of his own—Death incarnate?

But it turned out that this was only the prologue. I could not know then that for the next three years I would be possessed—and obsessed—by this story as it grew and unfolded under my hand, as murder succeeded murder and new victims were strangled even while I was on the scene. I found myself, without having planned it, becoming the historian of a singular chapter in American social history: one of the world's greatest multiple murders, one of the most exhaustive manhunts of modern times, and finally, what is surely the most extraordinary and sustained self-revelation yet made by a criminal.

As the only writer completely involved with the case, I was given the fullest cooperation—not only in Boston but in the neighboring towns where the stranglings and other crimes also occurred. The result is that everything that is in this book is based on fact. In some instances the identities of certain persons have been disguised but these persons were and are real. What appears in the following pages comes not only from my research and from hundreds of hours of personal interviews with the principal actors in the drama, and with scores of other participants, but also from the actual documentation—the police and court records, the medical and psychiatric reports, the transcripts of interrogations (some under hypnosis and hypnotic drugs), and the letters, diaries, and other source papers.

In short, the words and thoughts of the hunters and the hunted are not my invention but are, within the limits of human error, true. Unavoidably, errors will have crept in; mistakes in emphasis and interpretation will have been made; but in all instances I have done my best to mirror faithfully what went on in Boston in the time of the Boston Strangler.

GEROLD FRANK

New York, August, 1966

THE DEAD

JUNE 14, 1962	Anna Slesers, fifty-five 77 Gainsborough Street, Boston
JUNE 30, 1962	Nina Nichols, sixty-eight 19 ( ) Commonwealth Avenue, Boston
JUNE 30, 1962	Helen Blake, sixty-five 73 Newhall Street, Lynn
AUGUST 19, 1962	Ida Irga, seventy-five 7 Grove Street, Boston
AUGUST 20, 1962	Jane Sullivan, sixty-seven 435 Columbia Road, Boston
DECEMBER 5, 1962	Sophie Clark, twenty 315 Huntington Avenue, Boston
DECEMBER 31, 1962	Patricia Bissette, twenty-three 515 Park Drive, Boston
MAY 6, 1963	Beverly Samans, twenty-three 4 University Road, Cambridge
SEPTEMBER 8, 1963	Evelyn Corbin, fifty-eight 224 Lafayette Street, Salem
NOVEMBER 23, 1963	Joann Graff, twenty-three 54 Essex Street, Lawrence
JANUARY 4, 1964	Mary Sullivan, nineteen 44A Charles Street, Boston
	AND
JUNE 28, 1962	Mary Mullen, eighty-five 1435 Commonwealth Avenue, Boston
MARCH 9, 1963	Mary Brown, sixty-nine 319 Park Avenue, Lawrence

Dates are the original police estimates.

THE VICTIMS OF THE BOSTON STRANGLER

1. **June 14, 1962 • Anna Slesers, fifty-five**
   77 Gainsborough Street; Boston

2. **June 30, 1962 • Nina Nichols, sixty-eight**
   1940 Commonwealth Avenue, Boston

3. **June 30, 1962 • Helen Blake, sixty-five**
   73 Newhall Street, Lynn

4. **August 19, 1962 • Ida Irga, seventy-five**
   7 Grove Street, Boston

5. **August 20, 1962 • Jane Sullivan, sixty-seven**
   435 Columbia Road, Boston

6. **December 5, 1962 • Sophie Clark, twenty**
   315 Huntington Avenue, Boston

7. **December 31, 1962 • Patricia Bissette, twenty-three**
   515 Park Drive, Boston

8. **May 6, 1963 • Beverly Samans, twenty-three**
   4 University Road, Cambridge

9. **September 8, 1963 • Evelyn Corbin, fifty-eight**
   224 Lafayette Street, Salem

10. **November 23, 1963 • Joann Graff, twenty-three**
    54 Essex Street, Lawrence

11. **January 4, 1964 • Mary Sullivan, nineteen**
    44A Charles Street, Boston

    And

12. **June 28, 1962 • Mary Mullen, eighty-five**
    1435 Commonwealth Avenue, Boston

13. **March 9, 1963 • Mary Brown, sixty-nine**
    319 Park Avenue, Lawrence

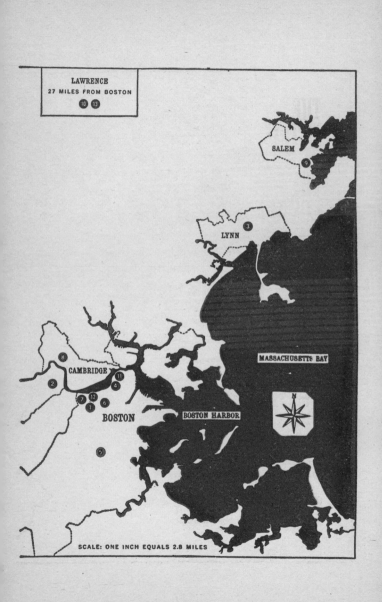

LAWRENCE
27 MILES FROM BOSTON
⑩ ⑬

SALEM
⑨

LYNN
③

MASSACHUSETTS BAY

CAMBRIDGE
⑧
②
⑪
④
⑦ ⑫ ⑥
①
BOSTON
⑤

BOSTON HARBOR

N

SCALE: ONE INCH EQUALS 2.8 MILES

PART ONE

1

This is a story about Boston. It is a true story, about the people in it, what happened to them, and the strange and implausible events that took place there in a time which is today and—man being the creature he is—may again be tomorrow.

It begins on Thursday, June 14, 1962.

That day, under a sky that threatened rain but never carried out its threat, Bostonians went about their business—concerned with their private or public affairs, legal or illicit, generous or self-serving, history-making or utterly unimportant. Yet if we hold a microscope to it it becomes something of a special day.

In Cambridge, across the Charles River, Harvard University was holding its 311th Commencement, and in the Yard thousands of students, alumni, and guests were gathering about the buffet tables set up under canvas, heavy with the traditional chicken salad and beer. At 4:15 P.M., the sun came out from behind the clouds: since Boston had known only rain these last few days—it had forced cancellation of the Harvard-Yale baseball game the day before—that was a signal for everyone to break out in a mighty song, "Fair Harvard." The ancient bells of Memorial Church chimed in, echoing across the campus.

At that time, through the Back Bay and downtown districts of the city itself, some 100,000 Bostonians lined the streets cheering Commander Alan B. Shepard, Jr., the nation's first astronaut. The man who had ridden the nose of a rocket more than a hundred miles above the earth a year before had come to his home town, nearby Derry, New Hampshire, to receive a New England Aero Club award and be guest of honor on that day—Flag Day—at ceremonies on Boston Common. He stood in the back of a convertible, a shining, handsome man, and as he rode by the applause rippled up the street.

That was a cheerful scene. A stone's throw away in State Street—Boston's Wall Street—the scene was anything but cheerful. The stock market had fallen violently for the fourth consecutive day. This time the Dow-Jones averages, made up of thirty blue-chip stocks, had plunged below the floor set two weeks earlier on May 28—Black Monday—which had seen the sharpest one-day drop since the crash of 1929. Something close to panic was in the air. Although the market closed at 3:30 P.M. as usual, the tape was late and it wasn't until some time later that statisticians could announce that American industry was then worth 5.6 billion dollars less than when the market had opened at 10 A.M. that morning.

By six o'clock, however, all this was history. Then the microscope held to the city would have revealed a curious process under way. Boston is a town whose population swells and decreases by half every twenty-four hours. At 8 A.M., as workers pour into the city from the surrounding suburbs, it becomes a metropolis of 1,500,000; but at dusk as they flow back to their homes, it shrinks to a town half as populated, tenanted only by those who live there.

Among these was Mrs. Anna E. Slesers, fifty-five, a divorcée for more than twenty years, who had come to this country with her son and daughter in 1950 as a displaced person from Latvia. As dusk fell over the city, Mrs. Slesers was preparing her bath in her small, third-floor apartment at 77 Gainsborough Street, in the Back Bay area of Boston. Gainsborough Street is an old-fashioned, tree-lined, lamplit street of identical bay-windowed, four-story red brick homes, each with its cement stoop and low picket fence guarding a miniature lawn. Once these buildings, each a town house, had a certain elegance; now, remodeled into small apartments, they housed mainly students, transients, and elderly couples living on modest pensions.

For Mrs. Slesers, a small woman with a petite face and large dark eyes who looked much younger than her age, this Thursday had been leisurely. Little of the excitement elsewhere in the city had touched her. Trade had been slack at Decorator Fabrics, Incorporated, where she worked as a sixty-dollar-a-week seamstress. She had been sent home at 1 P.M. the day before and told not to report again until Monday. A long weekend stretched before her. On Thursday she had shopped until nearly five o'clock, and then returned to cook a frugal dinner for herself and await her son Juris, twenty-five. He was to come by at seven o'clock to drive her to memorial services at the Latvian Lutheran Church in nearby Roxbury. For Latvians, June fourteenth is a national day of mourning for thousands of their countrymen, deported to Siberia when the Russians overran Latvia in World War II.

Mrs. Slesers took her time moving about the neat little apartment. She baked a pan of muffins for Juris, and put them to cool on the kitchen table. Then, at a small desk in the living room, she made out a few checks—gas, telephone, electricity. From where she sat she could see the heavy ropes supporting a scaffolding just below her front window. Men had been working there, painting and pointing up the brick exterior. But because of the constant rain and because today, too, threatened rain, the scaffolding had hung empty and deserted for days. Mrs. Slesers sealed the envelopes and left them on her desk. Then she undressed in her bedroom and, in robe and slippers, entered the bathroom and turned on the taps. From the living room a high fidelity set, an FM radio-record-player assembly put together by Juris, who was expert in such matters, filled the apartment with the strains of *Tristan und Isolde*. Music was one of Mrs. Slesers' chief joys. As a matter of fact, after Juris had suggested a few weeks before that maybe they should take separate apartments because they were beginning to get on each other's nerves (her daughter Maija had married a few years before and lived in Maryland), she had chosen 77 Gainsborough Street because she could walk to Symphony Hall around the corner on Huntington Avenue. The music swelled; in the bathroom the water poured into the tub. If there was any noise attendant upon what took place in Apartment 3F in the next half hour or so, it is quite possible that the music and running water drowned it out.

A few minutes before seven o'clock Juris, a slight, bespectacled young man with a crew cut, a research engineer at the M.I.T. Lincoln Laboratories in suburban Lexington, drove up and parked. He climbed to the third floor and rapped on the door of his mother's apartment. Juris had been up early that morning because each Thursday before driving to his job he spent the hour from 7 A.M. to 8 A.M. with his psychiatrist* in

---

* He had been having such sessions since the first of the year, once a week. Nothing particularly serious, save a general feeling of depression. Because of the supportive therapy given him, he had been able to suggest to his mother that they live apart. Common sense dictated that, too: she wanted to live in Boston, but why should he, when he worked fifteen miles away in Lexington?

Cambridge. After work he'd been busy, taking a pair of shoes to be repaired, returning a library book, cooking dinner for himself in the room he'd taken in Lexington. Then it was time for the half-hour drive to Boston to pick up his mother. He was a little tired.

Juris knocked again. He pressed his ear to the metal door: all was quiet within. Could she have gone out for a last minute's shopping? He descended the narrow stairs to the street, sat on the cement stoop, and waited, annoyed. He hadn't really wanted to take her to the services. When she telephoned him the night before, he had agreed to drive her to a public memorial gathering at 8:15 P.M. But then she had called him back to say she had been on the telephone with her pastor who said a church service would be held at 7:30, preceding the meeting. Would Juris pick her up earlier so she could make that, too? "I don't particularly want to go to both," he had said, but she had pleaded and he finally agreed. Now he had come earlier, he was waiting—he'd even brought her a little Latvian flag—it was already 7:15, and no sign of her. Maybe she'd been in the bathroom and hadn't heard him, he thought; he went up again and this time knocked even louder. Still no answer. He tried the door; it was locked.

Impatient, he went down into the street again and as he passed through the dark little vestibule with its dull, cream-colored wainscoating, he noticed the white gleam of mail in his mother's box. She must have forgotten to take it up. He waited on the sidewalk, pacing back and forth, expecting her to appear any minute; then he went up again. This time he pounded. Still no answer. The thought that she might have done something to herself flashed through his mind. She had sounded depressed on the phone. She had said, when he finally agreed, speaking in her sad, mother's voice, "Now, you're sure I won't be imposing on you—"

"No, no, it's quite all right," he had said, guiltily.

Perhaps at this very moment she was lying sick inside—

It was 7:45. He would break the door down. He put his shoulder to it once, backed up, rammed it hard a second time—it sprang open. The apartment was quite dark, but there was a faint light in the kitchen. Nevertheless he almost stumbled over a chair directly before him. The door must have struck against it, placed unaccountably in the very middle of the hallway. His mother was not in the living room; he hurried into the bedroom. She was not in there, but the dresser drawers had been left open, which was not like her. Then he retraced his steps down the hallway, past the curiously placed chair, toward the kitchen . . .

• • •

It was 7:49 P.M. when Officers Benson and Joyce, cruising in Police Car fifteen a few blocks away, heard the dispatcher's rasping voice: "Fifteen A—go to Seventy-seven Gainsborough Street, report of an alleged suicide." Three minutes later Juris, who had waited for them outside the building, led them upstairs. Shock seemed to have driven all emotion from him. His mother had committed suicide. She had been depressed. She had hanged herself on the corner of the bathroom door with the cord of her bathrobe; her body had fallen to the floor. She lay in the hall next to the bathroom. He had been about to touch her, but then he had realized she was dead, and instead he had telephoned the police and then called his married sister in Maryland.

Almost automatically he had placed the little Latvian standard on his mother's desk, and now he sat quietly on the sofa while the apartment filled with those assigned by society to take over in time of sudden death: the doctor who pronounced her dead, the medical examiner who ordered her body to the morgue for autopsy to determine the cause of death, the photographer to record what met the eye in every room, the artist to draw every object to scale, the fingerprint man dusting tables, doorjambs, and toilet seats, the men from Homicide, who live with murder, to examine and question, and the police stenographer to take down statements.

Cruising on Commonwealth Avenue, Special Officer James Mellon and Sergeant John Driscoll of Homicide heard the dispatcher's message over their radio. Mellon swung the car around. "They'll want us over there anyway, may as well go now." A moment later the order came sending them to 77 Gainsborough Street, too. A few minutes after eight o'clock Officer Mellon walked into Apartment 3F. As he came through the door he found himself in a tiny foyer; directly before him the living room desk with a lamp, a telephone, and the tiny Latvian flag. Mellon's first impression was of neatness. The very floor gleamed. A policeman was seated near the desk making out his report. Mellon glanced automatically to the left, toward the rear, bedroom section of the apartment. "Where's the body?" he asked.

The other gestured in the opposite direction, toward the kitchen. "Nothing to it—suicide," he said.

Mellon turned to the right and found himself staring directly at the body of a woman. He was always to remember his first sight of Anna Slesers' body, its sheer, startling nudity, the shockingly exposed position in which it had been left. She lay outstretched, a fragile-appearing woman with brown bobbed hair and thin mouth, lying on her back on a gray runner. She wore a blue taffeta housecoat with a red lining, but it had been spread completely apart in front, so that from shoulders down she was nude. She lay grotesquely, her head a few feet from the open bathroom door, her left leg stretched straight toward him, the other flung wide, almost at right angles, and bent at the knee so that she was grossly exposed. The blue cloth cord of her housecoat had been knotted tightly about her neck, its ends turned up so that it might have been a bow, tied little-girl fashion under her chin. There was a spot of blood under her head.

The tub, he saw, was one-third full of water; next to it, her gray knitted slippers, left neatly as she had stepped out of them. In that first swift glance Mellon saw a pair of dentures soaking in a glass of water on the pantry shelf, a kettle on the four-burner stove, a pan of muffins on the kitchen table, next to it a change purse partly open, and a pair of steel-rimmed glasses; near the body, on the runner, a white pocketbook open, some of its contents beside it—Kleenex, cigarettes, matchbook, comb. Near the threshold of the kitchen stood a wastebasket in which someone had rummaged, for odds and ends of trash were strewn on the floor about it.

Mellon was a tall, blond man of thirty-four. Thoughtful, resourceful (for the last half dozen years he had eked out his limited policeman's salary by working after hours as a housing contractor), he was a man unafraid of facts. Holy Christ, he thought, how can you call this a suicide? Obviously the woman had been hit over the head in the tiny bathroom, placed upon the runner, dragged into the hall, probably raped, then strangled.

He walked back into the living room. "Did you look at the body?" he asked the policeman. Juris, sitting immobile on the sofa, seemed almost invisible, half-melted into the background.

The policeman nodded.

"You call that a suicide?" demanded Mellon, angry despite himself. He could not forgive Juris for not covering the body with a sheet.

"I'll bet you five dollars it's suicide," said the other, still working on his report.

"I'll be stealing your money, but you've got a bet," said Mellon. "I say it's definitely murder."

He sat down next to Juris and had him repeat what he had

told the policemen. "I'll have to take you to Homicide and take a statement from you," Mellon told him. "We'll want your fingerprints, too, for purposes of elimination." By this time Detective Lieutenant John Donovan, Chief of Boston's Homicide Division, had arrived with other men and it was Mellon's duty to join in a door-to-door questioning of tenants. But before he left the apartment, he could not help asking, "Juris, how come you can walk into a situation like this, see your mother in that position, and not cover her body?"

Juris thought for a long moment. "I saw she was dead," he said dully.

Mellon looked at him, then turned away and went down to the first floor. For nearly a decade Mellon had been assigned to night duty, from 4 P.M. to 2 A.M., covering on foot and by car an area of ten square miles of the Back Bay area, and he knew this neighborhood and the people in it. In the building lived a man well known to the police. He made a practice of corresponding with women belonging to a Lonely Hearts Club, inviting them to come to Boston and stay with him on pretext of marriage. After a week or so he would announce he'd changed his mind and send them home. Perhaps a dozen women had been involved, but only two or three had complained to the police, and all had been too embarrassed to prosecute. Now he swore he knew nothing of what had happened in Apartment 3F, but his name was put down for further checking.

In the apartment directly below Anna Slesers' apartment lived an interior decorator. He had come home just before six o'clock and lain down for a nap. Suddenly he was awakened by a loud *bump! bump! bump!* overhead. He looked at his watch—he had no idea how long he'd dozed off—it was 6:10. Only ten minutes. The noise, he said, sounded like someone was moving furniture—or perhaps dancing. He had stared up at the ceiling, thinking angrily, "What do I have living upstairs now, a dancer?" A lady had moved in only two weeks ago and he knew nothing about her. The noise had subsided and then it seemed to him—he explained that his bedroom was immediately next to the stairwell—that he didn't so much hear as *feel* that someone was sneaking down the stairs. No creaking of the steps: he could only say he "felt" it. After a few minutes he heard someone mounting the stairs, heavy footsteps, and a loud knocking at the door of the Slesers apartment. Then, footsteps descending again. He had rolled off his bed and looked out the window onto Gainsborough Street. He saw a thin young man in glasses and crew haircut pacing back and forth, then reentering the building;

he heard him go up the stairs once more and knock again on the door.

In Apartment 4F, just above the Slesers apartment, the tenant turned out to be a forty-two-year-old student at Boston University. He, too, had heard the knocking. "Someone was pounding on that door like he was trying to wake the dead," he said.

Mellon said, "That's what he was trying to do—it was his mother and she was strangled."

The other said, shocked, "You're kidding me!"

"It's not part of our job to kid people," said Mellon, and returned to the Slesers apartment and took Juris in his police car to headquarters to learn a little more about Anna Slesers and who would have wanted to kill her, and why.

He was still troubled by Juris. Sitting next to him in the car, he said slowly, watching the other in the dashboard mirror, "Whoever did this will be living with it the rest of his life. He'll be doing it over and over again in his dreams as long as he lives." Juris's face disclosed nothing; he said nothing.

When they entered police headquarters, Mellon let Juris mount the stairs ahead of him, and listened carefully. Was his tread light or heavy? It seemed to Mellon that it was light. If so, why did Juris make so much noise going up and down the stairs at 77 Gainsborough Street? Or was he imagining things—as perhaps the interior decorator in the apartment below had been imagining things?

Boston has some fifty murders each year, and so the death of Anna Slesers became one more statistic. Few of the details of the scene or the manner of her dying were made public. Two days later Lieutenant Donovan, through his right-hand man, Detective Lieutenant Edward Sherry, announced that more than sixty persons had been questioned—neighbors, friends, fellow employees, building maintenance men, the painters, the contractors who had hired them, the mailmen, delivery men, and the like—without yielding any clue as to the identity of the assailant or how he got into the apartment. Would Mrs. Slesers, shy and retiring, open her door to a stranger or even to a friend while in her robe and without her dentures?

The ransacking indicated that burglary might be the motive. Mrs. Slesers had suffered head injuries, either from a blow or a fall, but she had been strangled, no doubt of that. And though there was no evidence of rape, she had been sexually assaulted. As one detective put it, a routine housebreaking—with complications. Presumably, the assailant broke into the apartment to rob, came upon Mrs. Slesers disrobing for her bath—a woman appearing much younger than her age—was seized by an uncontrollable urge, and then strangled her fearing she might recognize him in the future.

Whatever the case, it seemed obvious the motive was not to be found in her own background. Her days were bounded by her work, her church, her music, and her son and daughter. The husband she had divorced two decades ago in Latvia had remarried long since and now lived in Canada. She had no known men friends. At work she was described as a conscientious woman who kept to herself and did not associate with other employees. No one there knew anything of her friends or her social life.

The information Juris supplied about her past in Latvia was equally unrewarding. His mother had graduated from a university as an agronomist, worked as a bookkeeper; then the war came and tossed them about until they found themselves in a displaced persons' camp in Germany. She worked there as a kitchen helper until they came to the United States and settled in Michigan, where relatives lived. Mrs. Slesers had worked to send Juris through the University of Maryland. After his sister Maija married two years before, he and his mother had lived together until a month ago, when Juris had taken his room in Lexington. On June 1 Mrs. Slesers had moved into Apartment 3F.

Housebreaking—with complications. The complications privately troubled the police. Had the apartment really been ransacked? Or had it been made to appear so? The bedroom dresser drawers had all been pulled open, their contents disturbed, but they had not been pushed completely shut again: instead, they had been left to describe a pyramid, the lowest drawer two inches out, that above it an inch and a half, that above it once inch . . . A case of color slides had been carefully placed on the bedroom floor—certainly not dropped. This was no hasty search. The record player was still on, though it was silent. Mrs. Slesers could not have turned it off because Juris had fixed the master switch inside the player itself. Whoever had turned it off had actually turned off only the amplifier. Someone had taken time to do this, and to set a scene of apparent robbery—perhaps. A small gold watch was left untouched on a shelf above the tub; other modest pieces of jewelry remained in a jewel box on the dresser. If robbery had been the motive, why weren't these taken?

The Anna Slesers file was kept open. In the Homicide Division on the second floor of Police Headquarters Lieutenant

Donovan and Lieutenant Sherry, though busy with other homicides—fights, drunken shootings, and the like—studied the photographs taken in Apartment 3F and the reports still filtering in. Although 90 percent of murders are solved, experience has shown that unless a murderer is caught in the first two weeks it is unlikely that he will ever be caught. There were no clues here. The life of an inoffensive woman had been suddenly and violently snuffed out and only because of the manner of her death would more than a handful of people know that she had ever existed.

One week, two weeks, passed.

Late Saturday afternoon, June 30, Nina Nichols, an energetic woman who with her gray bobbed hair and blue tennis sneakers looked younger than her sixty-eight years, hurried into the elevator of 1940 Commonwealth Avenue, bags in both hands. She had just spent three days with friends out of town and was due that evening—it was now just after five o'clock—for dinner and an overnight visit at the home of her sister, Mrs. Chester Steadman, in nearby Wellesley Hills.

It was a swelteringly hot day. Even at five, the thermometer showed nearly ninety degrees. Mrs. Nichols, once inside her fourth-floor apartment, took only enough time to throw open the windows, pull off her dress and replace it with a comfortably thin housecoat before telephoning her sister to say she was back in town and would be there around six o'clock.

As they talked, Mrs. Nichols suddenly interrupted herself. "Excuse me, Marguerite, there's my buzzer. I'll call you right back." At the other end Mrs. Steadman, too, had heard it: someone buzzing Nina from the lobby. She hung up and went about her dinner preparations.

But Nina did not call back. Six o'clock came and went. Chester Steadman, an attorney who was also president of the Boston Bar Association, dialed his sister-in-law's number. There was no answer. She must have decided not to call back and was on her way, delayed by weekend traffic.

When she did not arrive by seven-thirty, Steadman telephoned the apartment house and asked the janitor, sixty-five-year-old Thomas Bruce, if he'd look out the window and see if Mrs. Nichols' car was still in the parking lot behind the building. When Bruce said it was, Steadman asked if he would please go up and check her apartment and see if she was all right. Maybe she'd been taken ill. Bruce went upstairs, rapped loudly on the door, finally opened it with his master key, stared for a shocked moment, hurriedly slammed it shut, and ran back to his telephone.

What the janitor saw from where he stood was an apartment that obviously had been burglarized: drawers pulled open, possessions strewn about the floor. The bottom drawer of the chifforobe was open showing, surprisingly enough, sterling silver neatly arrayed and apparently untouched. As he raised his eyes, he saw the open bedroom door and on the bedroom floor, directly in his line of vision, her feet toward him, the legs spread, the nude body of Nina Nichols. She lay dead, her eyes wide open, on a hooked rug. Her pink housecoat and white slip had been pulled up to her waist so she lay exposed; about her neck, twisted together like a rope, tied so tightly that they cut a groove into her flesh, were two nylon stockings knotted under her chin. The ends of the stockings had been arranged on the floor so they turned up on either side like a grotesque bow. Her watch was on her left wrist; on her feet were her blue sneakers.

Nina Nichols had been strangled with a pair of her own stockings, an act done in a frenzy from the look of it, and she had been criminally molested. The killer had apparently gone through the apartment in the same fury, searching, ransacking, pulling everything apart, tossing clothes and possessions wildly in all directions. Her bags had been torn open, their contents strewn about. There was her expensive camera, still in its leather case; an eight-by-ten photograph of a favorite dog; her opened black purse; a Pan American traveling bag and hatbox awry on a sofa. A photo album had been ripped apart, its leaves everywhere. A copy of that morning's Boston *Herald* with the headline CIVIL RIGHTS STIR FIGHT was half buried in the disorder on the sofa. Her dress lay across the bed, on it her steel-rimmed eyeglasses as she must have left them. At the foot of the bed, a leather attaché case and a blanket folded neatly. But everywhere else—even the small drawer in the telephone stand had been pulled out and ransacked. Her address book lay open, her correspondence had been gone through.

Why? Searching for what? Money? There was less than five dollars and change in her purse. She rarely had cash in the apartment; she was reputed to pay even her newsboy by check. And though 1940 Commonwealth Avenue was still impressive, still fashionable, it was not the address of affluence it had been many years before.

A quick run-through of Nina Nichols' background only added to the mystery. A widow for many years, she had been chief physiotherapist at Massachusetts Memorial Hospital until her sixty-fifth birthday three years ago. She had also been Secretary of the American Physiotherapy Association. Now semiretired, living on a modest income from stocks and insurance, she contributed two mornings a week to elderly charity patients at St. Patrick's Manor, and for the last few years had also been treating a private patient, a seventy-year-old man in Webster. Her hobbies were photography and music; she spent nearly every weekend either in Duxbury, where she'd been this last week, or with other friends, women of long acquaintance, in Nonquitt, Massachusetts. (She was also a guest in Florida each winter and Maine each summer.) Her husband had died twenty years ago. She was never seen with a man. Indeed, with the exception of her brother-in-law Chester Steadman, the only man ever known by neighbors to have set foot inside Mrs. Nichols' apartment was the painter who had worked in it when she moved in three years ago.

Until long after midnight Lieutenant Sherry and fellow detectives remained on the scene. Sherry, a gentle, gray-haired bachelor in his fifties, whose chief interest for the last twenty-three years had been his work, had been sitting down to dinner in his apartment a few streets away when the call came. He had hurriedly driven over and arrived just as Medical Examiner Dr. Michael Luongo completed his examination. What Sherry looked for most hopefully was evidence that something had been stolen—a valuable watch, a camera, a ring—that could be traced to a pawnshop. But it appeared that nothing had been taken. Her camera was worth at least three hundred dollars, and among the most easily pawned of all objects. Yet if not robbery, why the disorder?

The detectives went from door to door asking questions, but the only clue was the mysterious sound of the buzzer. According to Mrs. Steadman, it sounded in her sister's apartment at 5:10; when she hung up she'd glanced at the clock to gauge her dinner preparations. Had her sister let up whoever had buzzed her from below? Would she have been expecting him? There were no signs of forcible entry. "We don't know whether she admitted him or he used a master key," said Sherry. "There is no indication that he broke in." Would Nina Nichols, eminently respectable, living a life devoid of male friends, have allowed a strange man to enter her apartment while she was wearing only a thin flannel robe over her slip?

Although it was nearly 3 A.M. Sunday before Sherry got to bed, he was at Homicide at 8 A.M. that morning going over the Nichols and Slesers cases with Donovan. Sixteen days apart but in a five-mile-square area, two elderly women stran-

gled and sexually molested, their apartments ransacked . . .
Police Commissioner Edmund McNamara, whom Mayor
Collins had appointed less than two months before to revital-
ize the city's police force, called a conference of department
heads for the next day, Monday, July 2.

For Mrs. Annie Winchell, seventy-five, and her next-door
neighbor, Margaret Hamilton, seventy, of Lynn, Massachusetts, a town several miles north of Boston, Monday was a
troubling day. Both lived on the second floor of 73 Newhall
Street, a bay-windowed, red brick apartment house that had
known better times. Mrs. Winchell lived in Apartment 8,
Mrs. Hamilton in Apartment 10. Their neighbor across the
hall in Apartment 9 was Helen Blake, sixty-five, a retired
practical nurse. The morning really began for the women
when they heard their mail dropped before their doors. Then,
in their dressing gowns, they would open their doors, pick up
the mail, and stand in their doorways exchanging gossip and
news of the day. They looked forward to their morning meetings almost like young girls in a dormitory. But this Monday,
though Annie and Margaret had collected their mail and
talked together for nearly ten minutes, Helen had not appeared.

Come to think of it, they hadn't heard or seen her since
early Saturday. They had been tenants a long time here; the
sounds of their neighbors getting ready for the day were familiar to them. Helen's door had opened twice Saturday
morning, that was certain: just before eight o'clock, when
she'd gone down the hall taking rubbish to the incinerator—her businesslike footsteps sounded clearly coming and
going on the linoleum-covered corridor—and then, some fifteen minutes later, when she took in the milk. A moment before they'd heard the milkman, Mr. Lennon, and the clank of
the two bottles he put down before her door, and then his
footsteps vanishing.

As Monday wore on they discussed Helen's absence, more
and more worried, and finally confided in Mrs. Mabel
O'Malley, who lived on the first floor just below Helen. No,
Mrs. O'Malley had not heard or seen anything of her over
the weekend. But she recalled that Helen had gone about her
household duties Saturday morning with her usual vigor. No
one looking at Helen Blake, sturdy, bob-haired, and energetic, would have taken her to be sixty-five. Mrs. O'Malley
particularly remembered that Helen had flung open her bedroom window and shaken out a rug or two just above her
own bedroom window—this just after 8 A.M. And about 8:30

she heard the sound of Helen moving furniture about as she housecleaned.

All that activity early Saturday—and nothing since . . .

By 5 P.M. the two women could contain themselves no longer. They obtained a key from the super to Helen's apartment and opened the door. They peeked in to see a scene of disarray. Every drawer in the bureaus was open. This was not like Helen, the soul of neatness. Too frightened to go inside, they locked the door again.

When Lynn police arrived, and with them Detective Lieutenant Andrew Tuney, of the Essex District Attorney's office, who lived in neighboring Georgetown, they found Helen Blake dead. She lay face down on her bed, her legs apart, nude save for the tops of her pajamas which had been pushed up over her shoulders. A nylon stocking had been twisted with ferocious strength around her neck and knotted just at the nape: her cotton brassiere had been looped under the stockings, and then its ends brought forward and tied in a flamboyant bow under her chin. She had been sexually assaulted.

Someone had searched the apartment thoroughly. A footlocker was found across the arms of an easy chair in the bedroom, a piece of kitchen knife broken in its lock: the killer apparently had attempted to pry it open and failed. The broken knife was found under the bed. The drawers in the bedroom had been rummaged through; the living room desk drawer had been placed on the floor, as if the killer had crouched there and carefully examined what it held; letters, stationery, rubber bands, a religious medal, and curiously enough, one of a pair of dice. In the kitchen, on top of the refrigerator, were two quart bottles of milk, quite sour.

Helen Blake had been of modest means, but she did own two small diamond rings. Marks on her fingers indicated that she might have been wearing them and the killer might have pulled them off. There was a rumor among neighbors, too, that she was about to inherit $45,000. Perhaps the killer knew that and thought she had already received it, for a metal strongbox she kept under her bed had been pulled out and someone had tried to pry it open. He must have been someone she knew, John P. Burke, Essex District Attorney, told reporters: it was difficult to imagine how anyone got into the apartment unless Miss Blake herself had admitted him since the door had a chain, a bolt, and a firm Yale lock on it. There was no sign of forced entry. With so many ears about, no one heard her voice raised or even sounds of a struggle.

She was not the sort of woman who would have succumbed easily.

Yet the idea that Helen Blake, in pajamas, would have allowed a man to come into her apartment was ridiculous to those who knew her. No one could remember having seen her with a man: she had been married briefly, but her marriage had been annulled more than thirty-five years before. She lived a quiet life, accepting a private nursing case now and then; she enjoyed entertaining her friends by telling their fortunes with cards; she loved music, played the piano well, and attended many evening concerts in Lynn and Boston. There was nothing here to grasp hold of.

Little more was turned up in the door-to-door investigation. Mr. Lennon, the milkman, had been in the building only long enough to deliver his bottles. This was confirmed by the janitor who had been taking an old bed out to the street at the time, and had seen him come and go.

As far as police could determine, she had been strangled in the kitchen, then carried into the bedroom, where she had been assaulted. It must have taken a strong man: Miss Blake weighed more than 165 pounds.

When had death struck? One friend had telephoned Helen at 10 A.M. Saturday, and several times later without result. Two others had called her Saturday afternoon, again without an answer. She had failed to keep a dinner engagement Saturday evening; and calls made to her Sunday received no response. On her bedroom wall hung a calendar that required one to tear off a page a day: it showed Friday, June 29. Friday evening's newspaper was in the apartment. All of this seemed to fix the time of death between 8:15 A.M. Saturday, when she picked up the milk, and 10 A.M., when she did not respond to her telephone.

Or had it really been Helen whom Annie and Margaret heard open her door at 8:15 and take in the milk? If so, would she not have put the bottles in the refrigerator, not on top of it? Had her killer slipped in when she went to the incinerator at 8 A.M. and had he been behind her door, waiting, when she returned? Was she already dead at 8:15 A.M. when the milk was delivered and had it been he who opened the door and brought in the bottles lest their presence in the hall cause suspicion? Had he placed them on top of the refrigerator and then continued his strange search for whatever he sought? The sounds Mrs. O'Malley in the apartment below heard at 8:30 A.M. might actually have been the footlocker and the trunk being moved about by him. And when he was finished and departed, he might simply have allowed the door to lock itself after him, which would explain why the bolt had not been drawn and the chain not fastened.

Helen Blake, a woman of sixty-five, sexually assaulted and strangled to death in Lynn between 8 A.M. and 10 A.M. Saturday, June 30.

Nina Nichols, a woman of sixty-eight, sexually assaulted and strangled to death in Boston, less than an hour by trolley from Lynn, between 5 P.M. and 6 P.M. the same day.

Police Commissioner McNamara, a former Holy Cross star fullback who later became an FBI agent, was winding up his late Monday conference on the Anna Slesers and Nina Nichols stranglings when Detective Lieutenant Donovan told him about Helen Blake's body just found in Lynn. As the details were unfolded, he put into words an anxiety he would not admit to the press. "Oh, God," he said, "we've got a madman loose!"

Commissioner McNamara had no idea that Helen Blake's death, already the third murder by strangulation in a two-week period, was only the beginning. In the next eighteen months eleven women in Greater Boston would be found strangled and sexually attacked without a single clue as to their killer; Boston—melodramatic as it may sound—would become a town besieged by terror. Not since Jack the Ripper murdered and dismembered women in the gaslit streets of London three quarters of a century before had anything comparable been experienced.

Boston could not know that these stranglings, each more bizarre than the one before, would give rise to the greatest manhunt in the history of modern crime, using every technique of detection, natural and supernatural: computers, clairvoyants, "sensitives," men and women claiming ESP powers, psychiatrists armed with hypnotic drugs, hallucinating agents and truth serums, specialists in anthropology, graphology, forensic law. Here was a city laid siege to by a killer whose insanity was equaled by his cunning, who apparently could materialize within locked apartments and not only kill but do fearful things to the women he killed—without leaving a clue.

The search would cut through social and political strata. It would involve the Attorney General of Massachusetts and the FBI; the police on all levels, and the press, crusading and competitive; through it would run local political jealousies and national political hopes. It would affect the citizenry itself, setting wives against husbands, neighbor against neighbor, translating the sexual frustrations of men and women into acts astonishing and bizarre, bringing into the open an incredible cast of true life actors. Under the pressure of the Strangler, whether a man or men, and the search for him, an entire city would be stripped bare.

McNamara acted. All police leaves were cancelled. All detectives were immediately assigned to Homicide. A roundup was ordered of all known sex offenders, a check made on every man between eighteen and forty released in the last two years from mental institutions. "Special attention should be paid to persons suffering from a paranoia of mother-hate," read one sentence of the order. McNamara and Donovan would have been the last to claim themselves experts on Freud, but the implication was clear: a deranged man, suffering from delusions of persecution, young rather than middle-aged, hating all older women because he hated his mother, therefore attacking them because each symbolized his mother.

The police appealed to women: keep your doors locked, allow no strangers to enter, report all prowlers or anyone behaving peculiarly, especially in areas where women lived alone. An emergency number—DE 8-1212—was published in all newspapers and broadcast, to be called day or night. From the apartments of the three victims, carpets, runners, linen, blankets, floor sweepings of the most minute nature were sent to police laboratories to be examined—a thread from a man's suit, a button, a single human hair. (In the Lindbergh baby kidnapping case a piece of wood had led them to Hauptmann.)

In the midst of this, on July 11, at 10 A.M.—nine days after Helen Blake had been found—a chambermaid entered a room in a cheap hotel to clean up. A moment later she ran screaming from the room.

A nude woman lay dead across the bed. She had gray hair. She had been strangled. Her killer had choked her to death with his hands, as the autopsy later disclosed. Draped over a nearby chair were her clothes, all identification marks removed. She and a man, both drunk, had registered the night before as Mr. and Mrs. Byron Spanney. The man had been unable to write his address; the woman finally gave it to the nightclerk as 315 The Riverview, Roxbury. Sherry discovered the names were fictitious, and the address turned out to be a Catholic convent. Later the woman was identified as Mrs. Margaret Davis, sixty, a widow, of Roxbury. She had told a partial truth: nuns at 315 The Riverview had been trying to help her control her drinking. All this pointed to a run-of-the-mill homicide such as every large city knows—a derelict man and woman, a hotel assignation, a drunken fight, and a drunken murder. The police relaxed a little.

But the very absence of a pattern in this strangling—no apartment, no article of clothing used as a ligature, no obvious positioning of the body—made Lieutenant Sherry aware that there *was* a pattern. As he was to say, "The seed was planted when I stood in that hotel room and looked at the body and realized I was looking for *something* . . ." For the first time, against his common sense, his long experience which taught him that super-criminals exist only in fiction, he began to think, What's going on here?

Then Ida Irga was found.

2

There are people who say that there are aspects of Boston that remain essentially unchanged since the days of Salem witchburnings: a belief that only extreme rectitude and immediate recognition of sin can cope with the evil inherent in men. Some of Boston still lives in the times of the early Lodges and Cabots and Bradfords. For all its superb educational system, Boston is one of the few cities in the United States that still permits physical punishment of children. Even today, in this fountain of intellectuality, teachers may rattan unruly boys in the elementary and junior high schools.

Later there would be those who said it was not the stranglings that shocked Boston so much: it was the abhorrent sexual aspect that summoned to mind in Bostonians deep lurking fears of Sodom and Gomorrah. Such acts would have caused a strong impact anywhere; but Boston was especially vulnerable. It could not avoid its double legacy of Calvinist Puritanism, reflected in the Yankee Protestant population, and Jansenist repression, reflected in the newer Irish Catholic immigrant population. The city that produced a Watch and Ward Society was still a city that prided itself on its conservatism; where one had difficulty buying "pornographic" literature (one had to go across the Charles River into Cambridge even to see a copy of *Lolita* when that book first came out); where producers of plays had to delete lines found acceptable elsewhere; and where bars closed at 1 A.M. forcing the thirsty to search out an "after hours" club if they wanted to drink. College students in such places as Berkeley or Ann Arbor might live by sexual codes that dismayed their parents; but in Boston, as recently as 1964, students at Boston College hung in effigy a novelist who dared advocate bigamy. Taking a page out of Hawthorne, they strung their straw man up bebetween two poles, painted a scarlet *A* on his chest, and marched with him through Boston Common carrying banners proclaiming LET'S KEEP BOSTON CLEAN!

Yet had the Strangler—if the Strangler it was—ceased after three women, it is quite possible that the deaths of Anna Slesers, Nina Nichols, and Helen Blake might slowly have been absorbed in the general stream of daily life. In the course of a year in Boston nearly 20,000 crimes of all kinds occur; in June 1962, excluding the three women, many other murders had taken place with hardly more than a paragraph in the newspapers. Most were sordid affairs, mainly in the Bowery-like South End.

Though Precinct No. 4, which commands this area, was at times the busiest police precinct in the United States, it still remained one of the least publicized. Violent death might carry a kind of horrid glamour in New York or Chicago, but it was a facet of life that Bostonians characteristically preferred to keep swept under the rug.

Horrifying as the stranglings were, they might also have been crowded out of the public mind by the transformation the city itself was undergoing. For that summer of 1962, things were at last looking up in Boston. A Boston man was in the White House, the Speaker of the House of Representatives was a Bostonian, the ranking member of the Senate Foreign Relations Committee was from Boston. Matching this coming to power on the national scene was a stirring within Boston itself. After more than thirty years of stagnation, the city was beginning to struggle to its feet. Boston had been the only large city in the United States to lose population in the postwar boom. In half a century it had dropped from the fourth largest city in the country to the thirteenth. For nearly three decades there had been no new construction of any consequence. Now, suddenly, enormous projects that would change the face of one fourth of the city had finally gotten off the planning boards. Estimated to embrace some billion dollars in new construction, they included the $200,000,000 Prudential Insurance Company complex, the new $200,000,-000 sixty-acre Government Center, the $100,000,000 waterfront development program, and some fourteen separate slum clearance programs. Surrounding the city were the growing space-based electronic industries; soon to come were the multimillion-dollar National Aeronautics and Space Administration installations. In downtown Boston the first girders were already rising to support a fifty-two-story office building, the tallest skyscraper outside New York and the heart of the Prudential complex.

Perhaps because a Boston man *was* in the White House,

and because of that beneficent influence, for the first time the two great disparate elements in Boston—the old Protestant Yankee families representing wealth, and the new Irish Catholic families representing political power—had joined hands. They had joined forces under a newly elected Mayor, John F. Collins, a man of energy and ambition, to back these ventures. The result was that a New Boston was in the making—a renaissance was under way. And that was the moment—the very moment that this hideous series of crimes broke out to hold up a completely different picture of the city to the shocked attention of the world.*

Among the most embarrassed was Police Commissioner McNamara. He had been appointed to eliminate graft, for his predecessor had resigned under fire after CBS presented a television documentary, "Biography of a Bookie Joint," which showed a suspicious connection between the police and horsebetting parlors. He was also expected to streamline the force so it could cope more efficiently with crime. And now, in his first weeks in office, he already faced three unsolved and particularly dreadful sex slayings of women. McNamara appealed for it all to be played down while he threw every available man into the search. One man might have done them all, but there was no proof. And any publicity given a crime always brought out imitators. Everyone knew that if you printed news about suicides, you would invariably read a few days later of one or two poor, sick human beings who had followed suit. There was every reason not to talk or speculate publicly about a strangler or stranglers.

In a kind of desperation McNamara turned to the FBI and asked for a specialist in sex crimes to conduct a seminar as soon as possible—preferably within the next month—to which he would send fifty chosen detectives. They would attend lectures from 9 A.M. to 4 P.M. and, after completing their course, he would assign them to the stranglings.

At this point, early July, a measure of relief unexpectedly came from two directions. Two brooches and a necklace were found missing from Anna Slesers' apartment. Sketches drawn of them by Juris were sent to all police departments in the state. Every pawnshop in a fifty-mile radius was checked. If the missing jewelry meant anything, it supported robbery as a motive—which took a great deal of the fearful mystery out of Anna Slesers' slaying. Shortly after, police seized a

* The Chamber of Commerce's campaign for "every individual and business organization" in the city to promote the "New Boston" was announced on June 14, 1962—the day Anna Slesers was strangled.

dazed man, his face scratched, who had been seen leaving the Hotel Roosevelt a few hours before Margaret Davis's body was found. It appeared likely that her strangling stood on its own and was not linked to the others.

Sooner or later the Slesers, Nichols, and Blake crimes might fall into a saner perspective. Police reluctance to accept the idea of a Strangler was understandable—"All those cops and they can't catch one man!"—but behind it lay a far more serious fear. A city is quick to panic: forgetting the public image and the anguish of Chambers of Commerce, the fact remained that the spectacle of a homicidal maniac on the loose, preying on women living alone, could utterly demoralize a city like Boston, having a large concentration of single women and women living alone.

The police exhibited caution. When Anna Slesers' missing jewelry turned out to have been in her apartment all the time, thus eliminating robbery and returning her to the pattern, they kept this depressing news to themselves. The public was apprehensive enough: telephone calls and letters conveying tips, suspicions, and alarms deluged police headquarters. Truth or fantasy, each had to be checked out. One of the first calls to DE 8-1212 came from Mrs. Helen Bigelow who lived in Apartment 25 on the fourth floor of 1940 Commonwealth Avenue, down the hall from the tragic Nina Nichols. There was something she had been keeping to herself. Looking out her window onto the small parking lot, Mrs. Bigelow had noticed on three successive days—Thursday, Friday, and Saturday, June 28, 29, and 30, ending on the Saturday Miss Nichols was killed—a man, about forty, in a white sportshirt, sitting from 10 A.M. to noon each day in the front seat of a gray sedan, staring up at the windows of the apartment house. Nina Nichols' windows? Mrs. Bigelow hadn't thought it important then, but now . . .

At eleven o'clock the next night police rushed to an apartment house on Charlesgate East, not far from Anna Slesers'. A twenty-two-year-old girl sat huddled in a chair, crying hysterically. Walking home from a movie a little while before, she had heard footsteps behind her: she walked faster; the footsteps kept pace; she began to run until she reached her apartment house. Fumbling desperately for her key, she felt a presence and turned in time to see a tall man silently looping a piece of wire about her neck. She screamed, ducked out of his arms, and broke away. Someone at that moment emerged from the apartment house; she fled inside, the man vanished. Imagination? Hallucination? Police found a four-foot length of telephone wire on the sidewalk. A few minutes later they seized a man lurking nearby. He denied everything. Unfortunately the girl could not identify him.

At the Golden Nugget in downtown Boston a forty-five-year-old woman met a young man who said he was an ex-Marine. After the bar closed he invited her to his apartment where they could continue drinking. Instead, he forced her into the basement, seized her by the throat, raped her, and whispered, "I like to choke older women."

A sixty-year-old widow of a physician was watching television about 9 P.M. when a knock sounded on her front door. She opened it. A man stood there, his features indistinct in the gloom of the porch. "Your husband, the doctor, told me to look you up," he said. The woman's scalp prickled: her husband had been dead ten years. The man's voice, boyish, pleasant, persuasive, went on, "He was telling me—" She slammed the door which locked automatically, called DE 8-1212 and waited, trembling, for the police. Not far away at the YWCA on the busy corner of Stuart and Clarendon Streets, the manager of the cafeteria reported a strange young man who repeatedly tried to strike up friendships with elderly ladies eating alone. What upset the manager was that on six different occasions, after the young man had finished his meal and left, the bus girl found razor blades folded in his napkin.

Boston homicide received a telephone call: a twenty-one-year-old girl had just reported that the man, about thirty-two, with whom she had been living, had tried to strangle her six months before. "He's in Lynn and Boston often," she said. "He gets vicious and then blacks out. One night he smashed up all our furniture and next day didn't remember a thing. Once he grabbed me around the throat and shouted, 'I'll choke you until your eyes pop out!' " She thought it only a bad joke then. Now she slept with a butcher knife under her pillow.

When the FBI Sex Seminar got under way in early August, FBI Agent Walter G. McLaughlin of Philadelphia lectured his class of fifty on the varieties of sexual perversion (some astonishing even to veteran detectives), their relationship to different categories of sex crimes, the personalities of sex criminals, and the symptoms of their illness, the deep compulsions that could drive them, often despite themselves, to such acts. Lieutenant Sherry, a methodical man, took more than ninety pages of notes which he mimeographed for others in the department. Much as he knew, he had learned a great deal more. He hadn't realized that many sex crimes are progressive, that for example, the man who began by exposing himself to children might later, needing more and more stimulation (like a drug addict) ultimately go on to rape and then murder. The fifty detectives emerged from the lecture room shaken, but with one certainty: never trust appearances, never overlook the kindly old man living next door; anyone, *anyone—including yourself*—could be the one. The evil lay in every man. God help him in whom it got out of control. One detective, father of a teen-age daughter and himself a Catholic, walked from the final lecture thinking wildly, *we are all suspects; the day the Pope left Rome, he became a suspect.*

The fifty were assigned to check released sex offenders and ex-mental patients, to question neighbors and friends, to go over records; now, with their specialized knowledge, a detail dropped about a neighbor, a visitor, a stranger, would alert them. For Lieutenant Donovan and Lieutenant Sherry, for Special Officer Mellon, and Detective Phil DiNatale, who cruised the Back Bay area with Mellon, and for scores of other detectives, these were busy days, nights, weekends. Sergeant John P. Harrington, specialist in administering lie detector tests, spent hours as suspects were taken out of a parade of protesting men brought in, examined, freed—and watched thereafter.

Then on August 21, Ida Irga, a quiet, inoffensive woman of seventy-five, so retiring as to be all but invisible to any outside her immediate family, was found strangled in her locked apartment.

She lived on the top floor of 7 Grove Street, a five-story brick apartment house in Boston's West End, an area fashionable thirty-five years ago when she first moved there with her husband. Now it was the wrong side of Beacon Hill; rundown and shabby, it had become a Bohemian district frequented by students, artists, and homosexuals.

Mrs. Irga had been dead about two days. She had been strangled by human hands; then one of her own pillow cases had been tightly tied about her neck. She had been sexually molested. A short, stocky woman with iron-gray hair, widowed for more than thirty years, she lived quietly and cautiously. She shopped daily for her small needs and had been making weekly visits for a skin ailment to Massachusetts Memorial Hospital. She rarely went out after dark except to walk to a concert in the nearby Esplanade. Her three-room apartment had been searched, but her purse, containing money, was untouched on a bookcase, as were a gold watch and pin. Save for the disorder in the drawers and closets, the apartment was spotlessly clean. There were no signs of forcible entry.

She had last been seen Sunday—two days before—taking the sun with a woman friend on Boston Common. Just before dusk she had left—"I want to get home before dark," she had said—and returned to her apartment. At 1 P.M. Sunday, she had telephoned her sister, Mrs. Ronya Brooks of Dorchester, to say she would give her part of a chicken she'd prepared so Ronya wouldn't have to cook in such hot weather. Ronya, however, heard nothing from her on Monday. When she telephoned Ida early Tuesday evening and got no answer, she called the caretaker of the building. He sent his thirteen-year-old son with a passkey—and the boy had come back to stammer out what he had found.

So far, all too familiar. But the manner in which Ida Irga's body was left pointed with awful emphasis to the pattern, now even more bizarre. Police Sergeant James McDonald, first on the scene, began his report in this manner: ". . . . Upon entering the apartment the officers observed the body of Ida Irga lying on her back on the living room floor wearing a light brown nightdress which was torn, completely exposing her body. There was a white pillowcase knotted tightly around her neck. Her legs were spread approximately four to five feet from heel to heel and her feet were propped up on individual chairs and a standard bed pillow, less the cover, was placed under her buttocks . . ." He did not write that the ankles were locked into position between the vertical wooden rungs of the backs of two dining room chairs and that the body had been so placed, in this grotesque parody of the obstetrical position, feet facing the entrance of the apartment; that this was the sight that struck one brutally, almost like an assault on one's eyes, that one could not escape seeing the moment one opened the door.

These appalling details were not made public: only that she had been strangled and criminally attacked. The rest was withheld. Not only was it too shocking to print, but the police desperately wanted to be in possession of facts known only to themselves and the killer. It gave them something to watch for, a slip of the tongue, a detail dropped that only the guilty man could know. The impact of Ida Irga's strangling—now the fourth such murder—struck Boston with accumulative force.

Wild stories began to circulate, whispered by one woman to another, told authoritatively by cabdrivers to curious out-of-town passengers, stories which vaguely approximated the truth: that the bodies were left exhibited in obscene positions, that the killer did not rape his victims—this was frightful enough—but assaulted them with a "foreign object," attacking them in death or as they lay dying . . . Chilling reports appeared in the press. The Strangler was a man "of animal strength in his hands and arms" (a heavy belt, such as that used on suitcases, had been found almost torn in two next to Nina Nichols' body), who "scaled the apartment house walls to reach open windows." His great strength might explain why no victim had ever been heard to scream—he worked so quickly, garroting them with his hands or the crook of his arm so powerfully that he rendered them unconscious instantly.

Women all but barricaded themselves in their apartments.

Donovan's men had to question Ida Irga's neighbors on Grove Street through closed doors. Even their badges handed through the gap between door and jamb, open only as much as a safety chain would allow, would not admit them. Gas meter readers, telephone installers, delivery boys were frustrated; Avon and Fuller Brush sales plummeted; political candidates for state senate and house, canvassing for votes, were brusquely turned away. There were runs on door locks and locksmiths; the demand for watchdogs, for dogs of any kind, cleaned out the Animal Rescue League pound minutes after it opened each morning. Elderly widows living alone arranged for their married children to phone them three times a day. With the frightening stories of what the Strangler actually did to his victims came reports of weird experiences throughout the city: a nurse who telephoned the police about a prowler received a doll in her mail a week later with a miniature nylon stocking twisted about its neck, and a scrawled note, THE POLICE CAN'T WATCH YOU FOREVER. Women, many in tears, called the police to complain of obscene calls: men murmuring unprintable suggestions over the phone, or simply breathing heavily on the other end, and then hanging up without a word.*

Other women were receiving calls from a physician unknown to them saying, "I want to check your heart," and demanding, almost imperiously, "When is the best time for me

---

* Individual reaction to these calls was surprising. Many girls and women felt an inexplicable sense of guilt. Had they brought it upon themselves? Were they encouraging men without knowing it—as though something secretly shameful, wanton, in them made itself known to men? How did the caller get their number? Had he followed them home, seen them remove their mail, looked them up in the telephone book? The idea that a mysterious stranger—perhaps even the Strangler himself—might have been watching them all this time, keeping them under surveillance without their knowledge, was all but intolerable.

to call?" One woman, in near hysteria, reported that she had seen a man, rouged and lipsticked but clearly a man, wearing women's clothes and high heels, dressed all in brown with long white kid gloves, riding up and down a self-service elevator in her apartment house, not far from where Nina Nichols had lived.

Amid the panic came intense speculation. One strangler—or more? If one, what kind of a man and how could he, as the police put it, "cajole his victims into inviting him into their apartments?" Did they know him? Did he choose them? Was he a homosexual? Someone like the strange, demented young man played by Tony Perkins in the Hitchcock horror film *Psycho*, who suffered from a mother complex and a murderous hatred of women? A man outwardly normal, inwardly psychotic, deranged, hallucinating? Perhaps—and this might explain how the killer got doors to open—perhaps a *woman?*

Among those caught up in speculation was a forty-three-year-old free-lance advertising copywriter who shall be called Paul M. Gordon, who in his spare time bred tropical fish, practiced weight lifting, and dabbled in hypnotism and psychic phenomena. He had satisfied himself and his wife that he possessed ESP—extrasensory perception. He had been in correspondence with Dr. J. B. Rhine at Duke University, foremost authority on the subject, but had declined Dr. Rhine's invitation to come to Duke for testing, on the ground that he was not a performer and had no need to prove his gift to anyone.

Working at his typewriter in his comfortable apartment in downtown Boston, listening to radio reports of the stranglings, Gordon allowed his mind to play with the identity of the Strangler. Who was he? What would lead him to commit such crimes? Vague images of man began to appear in his consciousness, as he was to say later. He did not summon them; they simply appeared, and with them an idea of the man's history and personality. With the Ida Irga killing, the image became so clear that Gordon telephoned a friend who was also his attorney.

The lawyer had great respect for Gordon's ESP ability. Some time before he had been faced by an unsolved arson case. Gordon had casually remarked that a boy had done it, and described him. A few days later the arsonist was caught: it was a boy who matched Gordon's description. The lawyer had been impressed. Now he listened with interest as Gordon talked. "I see the Strangler as a man in his late twenties, lonely, troubled, misunderstood, always searching for his dead mother." He told him how, in the images that came to him, he saw the Strangler enter the Anna Slesers apartment, and vaguely what happened there. "I don't know how I get this," said Gordon. "I just asked myself the kind of questions anyone might ask, and led myself through this experience . . ."

He had thought about offering his help to the police, he said, but he recalled his experiences two years before, after a housewife had disappeared from her home in a suburb of Boston. He had offered to help find her but the police dismissed him as a crackpot. He said now, "No, I guess I'll just do nothing."

In her bedroom on the top floor of an apartment house on Commonwealth Avenue, a woman who shall be called Mrs. Margaret Callahan, thirty-eight, pencil and notebook in hand, sat with her ear pressed to the wall, listening to what was going on in the adjoining apartment. For several weeks now Mrs. Callahan had been keeping a record of the activities of one of her neighbors, Dr. Lawrence Shaw, as he shall here be known. Dark-eyed, his prematurely gray hair crew-cut, about forty, he was unmarried, a sober, methodical, intelligent man, and she had become familiar with his comings and goings, the almost clocklike routine by which he lived. Therefore, she could not help noticing when this pattern changed sharply. Then, to her surprise, he showed evidence of drinking; he appeared depressed, disorganized; he came and went at odd hours; through the thin walls she frequently heard women's voices; when she passed him on the stairs he seemed not to recognize her. These states could last a month. She began jotting down dates in her notebook.

The first had begun June 11 and ended July 12. For several weeks he was himself again. But on Monday, August 20, around midnight, she heard him leave his apartment. She jumped out of bed, threw on a robe, and ran up one flight to the roof to see which way he went. He was walking slowly, down the deserted street, in a trancelike state, and he disappeared around the corner. The next day, August 21, she passed him on the stairs. He appeared ignorant of her presence. She noticed his right arm was bruised below the elbow.

She discussed his strange behavior with her niece who lived with her. What could it mean? Could there be a connection between it—and the stranglings? In the period June 11 to July 12, when Dr. Shaw was in one of his "states," Anna Slesers, Nina Nichols, and Helen Blake had been strangled. Now

Ida Irga—and again Dr. Shaw was acting strangely. Were these only coincidences?

Mrs. Callahan promised herself to learn all she could about Dr. Shaw and keep the closest watch on him. Her niece, too, would help. Quietly, Mrs. Callahan alerted two or three neighbors. They were frightened, but they would watch, too.

To calm Bostonians, three days after Ida Irga was found the Boston *Herald* published an editorial, "Hysteria Solves Nothing."

"For the rest of the population there ought to be some comfort in statistics," it read. "If it may be fairly said the police are looking for a needle in a haystack, it may be said with equal validity that a given person's chances of becoming a victim of the killer or killers are almost nil."

All this meant little six days later. Jane Sullivan, sixty-seven, a nurse who lived alone, was found strangled in her first-floor apartment at 435 Columbia Road, Dorchester, the other side of Boston from Ida Irga. A heavyset woman with gray bobbed hair, she worked the 11 P.M. to 7 A.M. shift at Longwood Hospital, where she was known as reserved, efficient, and having nothing to do with men. She had recently moved to No. 435, a red brick building with bay windows, because she feared the long nightly walk she had to take to her bus from her previous residence. At 435 Columbia Road, the bus stopped directly in front.

She had been dead more than a week. Her body was discovered placed in a half-kneeling position, face down in the bathtub, her face and forearms submerged in six inches of water so that her buttocks were exposed. Her cotton housecoat was pulled up over her shoulders, her girdle pushed above her waist, her underpants pulled down about her ankles. She had been strangled with two of her own nylon stockings tied together. Evidence indicated the crime had taken place in another room and she had been carried to the bathroom and placed in the tub afterwards. She was found at 4:30 P.M. Thursday, August 30. The time of death was estimated about ten days earlier—August 20—which would mean that she and Ida Irga had been strangled within the same twenty-four-hour period. It was assumed she had been sexually assaulted but the condition of her body was such that this could not be definitely ascertained. Her apartment had been searched, but apparently nothing had been taken.

Ida Irga's son, Joseph, thirty-nine, reading the news, stared at the accompanying photograph of Jane Sullivan, taken a few weeks before her death. "It's so strange," he exclaimed. "For a moment I thought it was my mother. They look so much alike."

Boston knew a dreadful Labor Day weekend.

3

Three months followed without a strangling.

But Boston was like a city created by a mad playwright for the Theater of the Absurd.

A long-haired man known as Psycho Charlie was arrested in the act of prying dimes out of a parking meter. Several women immediately claimed he was the man who had been running down the halls of their apartment houses slipping obscene notes under their doors. In the rear of a movie house an usher seized a dapper, moustached twenty-six-year-old youth. He indignantly identified himself as a student at the New England Conservatory of Music, but at precinct headquarters his name went on the record with the notation: "The above man apparently suffers from a form of sexual deviation; he has a climax from seeing the open toes of women in theaters or beaches; he carries a pen flashlight so he can see them in darkened theaters." Police answered an alarm on Columbia Road, not far from Jane Sullivan's building. A woman had seen a smiling, nattily dressed man coming toward her. Only after he passed did she realize that peeping out of his breast pocket was not the white edge of a handkerchief but unmistakably the tip of a nylon stocking.

Elderly women were awakened at two and three in the morning by the ringing of their telephone. "Darling," a husky voice whispered, "can I come over now?" In Brockton a housewife, awaiting a friend, opened her door to a knock: a strange man stood there. She fell dead of a heart attack. The stranger was selling encyclopedias.

Working women hurried home before dusk—the time the Strangler usually struck—and slammed their doors locked, only to discover hours later that in their panic they had left the keys on the outside of the door. Some found themselves in agonies of indecision the moment they arrived in their apartments. To lock the door at once might mean locking themselves in with the Strangler, waiting in a closet to pounce on them: yet they didn't dare leave the door unlocked while they looked about to see if anyone was hiding . . .

The "Mad Strangler" and "Phantom Strangler" and "Sunset Killer" took over the newspapers. From London came special dispatches comparing Boston's Strangler with Jack the Ripper. There were parallels but differences, too. Though seventy-five years had passed since Jack the Ripper killed seven women in the slums of London, his file still remained open at Scotland Yard. He had never been caught. He did not strangle his victims; he cut their throats, then dismembered them with the skill of a surgeon. He chose only prostitutes—as if carrying out an awful moral judgment of his own—and after each murder sent Scotland Yard taunting letters signed "Jack the Ripper." (Some were fiendish beyond belief: in one he enclosed a human kidney, and wrote, "I ate the other one: it was delicious! Yours in Hell, Jack the Ripper.")

Even as the newspaper reported these parallels, attempts were made to reach out to the Strangler. The Boston *Advertiser,* remembering the success of a public appeal to the "Mad Bomber" who had terrorized New York in the 1940's and 1950's, printed a front page APPEAL TO THE STRANGLER.

"Don't kill again," it began. "Come to us for help . . . You are a sick man. You know it . . ." It paid tribute to him as "a clever man smart enough to have avoided detection by the shrewdest detectives in the community," and went on, "This appeal is to you the man you were before this terrible urge overwhelmed you. YOU don't want to kill again, but you know you will unless you give yourself up."

No reply came.

Two days after Labor Day Dr. Richard Ford, Chairman of the Department of Legal Medicine at Harvard University, called together state and Boston law enforcement officials, medical examiners, and psychiatrists to "exchange ideas." Some way must be devised to meet this siege by a maniac. Boston, with its great universities, its law and medical schools, its hospitals, clinics, and diagnostic centers, its NASA installations, surely possessed as formidable a concentration of human intelligence as anywhere else in the world. It was ironic that this community which called itself the Athens of America, which prided itself upon its rationality, should find itself—as it did now—at the mercy of a supreme irrationality.

"Since robbery is not the motive, we are dealing with a demented man," Dr. Ford said flatly. As chief Suffolk County

Medical Examiner, he was familiar with the autopsies of the victims. Beyond his initial statement he would not go. It might be one man, it might be many. "There is nothing to tie these crimes together, no single proof," he said. "The more such things happen, the more are likely to happen because—and you can quote me—because the world is full of screwballs and there are so many around we just couldn't begin to round them all up." He and his associates were looking for "a common denominator," perhaps to be found "in how and when these women met their deaths, or in something about the places in which they lived, or in something relating to their mode of living. All we know is that we are looking for one or more insane persons."

If one eliminated Margaret Davis, was there a common denominator? Music? Association with a hospital? Helen Blake and Jane Sullivan were nurses. Nina Nichols was a physiotherapist. Anna Slesers and Ida Irga had both recently been outpatients. Had the killer met his victims at a concert or in a hospital, ingratiated himself and so prepared the way for his fatal visit? Was he even now to be found seated quietly in a concert audience, or working in a hospital as an attendant, an orderly, or even a physician?

The ransacking of apartments might also be a common denominator. What was the killer searching for? He searched carefully, and obviously he wore gloves, for no fingerprints had ever been found. Why had he gone through his victims' possessions, pulled out drawers, emptied pocketbooks, even thumbed through appointment books and personal letters? Was it to learn all he could about the woman he had killed? If—as many theorized—he attacked these elderly women because each in his deranged mind represented his mother whom he hated yet loved, he might be searching for a clue—an object, a talisman, something—to link her with himself, to identify her as *his* mother. Or it might be fetishism. He could be a man so terrified of women that he was driven to hunt for a handkerchief, an article of feminine apparel that would give him the essence of femininity without its menace.

And why did he leave his victims in obscene positions, as if deliberately to debase and degrade them, why the grotesque "decoration" about their necks, the streamers, the bows, the knots? And what about the mysteriously incomplete "sexual assault" or "sexual molestation"? Was the killing incidental to the assault, or the assault incidental to the killing? Most rape-murder cases were easily reconstructed. An attractive young woman, a discarded suitor or workman who saw her, or a burglar who came upon her by accident, or a rapist who followed her—then murder in a moment of panic to silence her or prevent her from identifying him. None of these patterns appeared likely here, although all were within the realm of possibility.

Psychiatrists tried to analyze the Strangler. Dr. Philip Solomon, Psychiatrist in Chief at Boston City Hospital, suggested that he might be a Dr. Jekyll–Mr. Hyde personality—a man who worked at a menial job, perhaps in a hospital; a man who might seem quiet and well-adjusted when actually he was a "psychotic sex pervert suffering from the most malignant form of schizophrenia," a disease in which the victim lives in a world of fantasy which he thinks is real. If not caught such a man would kill again. His obsession would give him no peace. But the forces driving him would sooner or later cause him to make a slip so he could be caught.

Dr. Robert W. Hyde, Assistant State Commissioner of Mental Health, agreed that the Strangler might look like any other person on the streets of Boston. Neither his manner nor his habits would call attention to him. He probably had a routine nine-to-five job. That would explain why many stranglings occurred just before dusk—he probably committed them on the way home from work. No absence from his job during the day, no absence from his home during the night, to give fellow employees or neighbors reason to suspect him. That would also explain his "phantom" quality—he *was* invisible because he melted into the sea of faces in which everyone lived and moved without causing a second glance.

At the Homicide Division on the second floor of police headquarters, concealed behind a screen in a small room, rested a perforated wooden board. A length of rope had been brought through each hole and a knot tied in it. If the board were turned about, one saw that name tags had been attached to each knot: Anna Slesers, Nina Nichols, Helen Blake, Ida Irga, Jane Sullivan.

Each was a replica of the knot found in the ligatures about the women's necks. But whether housecoat cord, nylon stocking, or pillowcase, the knot was the same: a granny knot, a square knot with a double half hitch. Lieutenant Sherry, sick at heart, stared at them. He had not seen the body of Anna Slesers because the crime took place on his day off; nor that of Helen Blake, because it occurred in Lynn, outside his jurisdiction. When he saw Nina Nichols' body, he had shaken his head; the lack of pattern in the drunken Margaret Davis killing had first planted the idea that it might be one man;

when he saw the body of Ida Irga he had thought, What a terrible death for an old woman; at the sight of Jane Sullivan, stripped of all human dignity, he had turned away.

He stared at the knots, wondering whether this type of knot was peculiar to any one occupation, whether it pointed to a sailor, a surgeon, a warehouse packer, a stock clerk, a grocery clerk, a newspaper wrapper, a shoe salesman. And he checked these ideas against the suspects, with no definite results.

New suspects were rounded up daily; some were men whose names had been sent in by anonymous informants, others were part of a pathetic cache of souls brought in by the police net—loiterers, Peeping Toms, housebreakers who stole only women's undergarments, alcoholics who turned themselves in fearing they might have strangled women during their blackouts.

In an adjoining room on the second floor three men spent their days examining thousands of handwritten records turned in daily over the past two years by Boston's six thousand cabdrivers, checking for pickups and drops made at the five addresses, then eliminating all but the five victims, seeking to determine to what destinations they went, from what addresses they returned, whom they knew unknown to their friends and relatives.

At the Massachusetts Bureau of Identification, at 1010 Commonwealth Avenue, headed by Robert Roth, compilators worked on lists of bank and stockbrokers' statements, names on checkstubs, medical, dental, and legal bills, laundry and dry-cleaning marks, department store bills, clothing labels, exterminators, mailmen, delivery truck drivers, building up a file of establishments to check, names of clerks, tellers, salesmen, and other employees to interrogate.

Each day plainclothesmen rode the buses and subways used by the five women at the hour they used them, watching the people who got on and off, studying the faces of passengers, trying to read answers from the very buildings passing by, searching, searching, searching . . .

Wednesday, December 5, 1962, was a wet and nasty day. On Tuesday night it had snowed. Wednesday it rained, and the rain transformed the dirty snow into mud-colored slush, making walking difficult. At 12:30 P.M. Sophie Clark, an attractive Negro student of twenty, left the Carnegie Institute of Medical Technology for her apartment, which she shared with two other girls, Audri Adams and Gloria Todd, both hospital technicians. The apartment was on the fourth floor of 315 Huntington Avenue, a crowded, commercial street in the Back Bay area. Two blocks away was Gainsborough Street, where Anna Slesers had lived.

Sophie, a popular but reserved girl, was to have waited at school until two o'clock for a class photograph. No one knew why she left earlier.

What is known is that a few minutes before 2:30 P.M. she was in her apartment writing a letter to her fiancé in Englewood, New Jersey, her home town. He was to visit her the following weekend. She wrote:

My Dearest Chuck:
May this letter find the man I love well. How is that cold of yours? I feel fine, especially after you called me last night—you're the kind of medicine I need—you can make a person feel well without putting forth any effort. What would you like to have next weekend? Naturally I thought of chicken, but perhaps you're tired of that. Do you have any suggestions? That's the least I can do for you, darling, and I want you to have a good meal while you're here . . .
Today is a nasty day. I do hope the weather is better next week for our sakes. Audri just called from work. It's going on 2:30 now. I'll start my homework when I finish this letter, then I'll shift over to the kitchen and cook supper. We're going to have liver tonight cooked in onions and gravy along with mashed potatoes and a vegetable, I guess. Maybe this weekend I'll get around to making some pizza . . . Darling, I hope you don't take this long to write again. You know how I get when I don't hear from you. I . . .

Here the letter stopped.

At 5:30 P.M. when Audri came home, she found Sophie lying dead on the living room rug. She had been strangled with three nylon stockings—her stockings—twisted together so tightly about her neck that they were almost lost in her flesh. They were knotted under her chin. Her killer had twisted her white slip and a white elastic belt about her neck, too. A gag had been stuffed into her mouth. She lay nude on her back, in the middle of the room, her blue bathrobe flung open in front. Her legs, in black stockings neatly held up by a garter belt, were extended and spread wide apart. She still wore her black loafers; her bra had been torn off with great violence, her glasses broken; both lay near her. She had been sexually assaulted. There was evidence of a struggle. The bureau drawers had been searched, their contents left in disorder. The killer had even gone through her collection of classical records in a corner of the living room.

To enter the apartment that afternoon Audri had to unlock the double lock on the door. After the Strangler first appeared in Boston, Sophie had insisted on a second lock. She never opened the door, even to friends, until she was certain who they were. She was so cautious that if she still doubted a voice, she would ask, "What kind of car do you drive?" Yet there were no signs of forcible entry. Sophie herself must have opened the door to her murderer.

There were some differences between this crime and the earlier stranglings. Sophie was twenty; the other victims had been elderly women. She was a Negro, and she did not live alone. But most of the elements of the crime were only too familiar. There was one fact: when the chemical analysis came back from the police laboratory, it bore the notation: "Seminal stains found on rug next to body." The Strangler had not left such a calling card before.

There were other puzzling aspects of the crime. That morning, at coffee with a classmate in the school cafeteria, Sophie had said, "I'm so afraid of the Strangler." The remark stuck in the friend's mind. After all, three months had passed since a strangling, and in any event the Strangler chose only elderly women. Why should Sophie have said this? And on this day?

Meanwhile, police questioned neighbors, among them Mrs. Marcella Lulka, twenty-nine, who lived in Apartment 2B on the second floor of the building adjoining Sophie's, which shared her entrance lobby. Mrs. Lulka told them that about 2:20 that afternoon, she had answered a knock on her door. A man stood there, about twenty-five or thirty, of average height, with honey-colored hair, in a dark waist-length jacket and dark green slacks. "My name's Thompson," he said. "The super sent me to see about painting your apartment."

Mrs. Lulka said uncertainly, "We're not due for a painting," but the man walked by her, looked about the living room, walked into the bathroom—he seemed to know how the apartment was laid out—and returned to her. "We'll have to fix that bathroom ceiling," he said. Then, unexpectedly, "You know, you have a beautiful figure. Have you ever thought of modeling? With your form—"

Thinking quickly, Mrs. Lulka put her finger warningly to her lips.

Mr. Thompson grew angry. "What's that for?" he asked roughly.

She whispered, lying, "My husband is sleeping in the bedroom."

The man completely changed character. "Maybe I have the wrong apartment—perhaps it's the one down the hall." He left hurriedly, almost colliding with her five-year-old son who was running in the door.

Was it the Strangler?

While police pondered the question, their investigation of the Clark case continued along other lines as well. They studied the victim's personal life, as they had done in the earlier cases.

Sophie Clark, very much in love, rarely dated anyone in Boston. She was a girl of regular habits. School until 1 P.M., then back to the apartment where she drew the shades, turned on the lights, exchanged her laboratory gown for a housecoat, and studied. About four o'clock she would begin to prepare supper for herself and her two roommates. Audri had called her that afternoon; and at 4:40, Gloria, too, telephoned her, to ask if a letter she expected had arrived and the telephone had not been answered.

The cold wintry twilight fell. At that hour—the Strangler's hour—fifty handpicked men, members of Commissioner McNamara's newly created, specially trained Tactical Patrol Force, were spread out through the Back Bay, combing the very streets through which the killer must have made his way to and from Sophie's apartment.

Early next morning her two roommates moved away, telling no one their destination. Amid Sophie's possessions handled by her murderer—left flung open on the floor—was a photo album with a snapshot of a pajama party clearly showing Gloria and Audri, standing arm in arm with Sophie. That terrified them, and that was not the only thing. Suppose it had not really been Sophie who had been marked for death, but one of them? It had been Sophie's fate to return early, and thus she was in the apartment when the sun began to go down that wintry day, and twilight came, and out of the growing darkness, the Strangler . . . They dared not spend another day—or dusk—at 315 Huntington Avenue.

Mrs. Margaret Callahan, keeping close watch on her neighbor, Dr. Lawrence Shaw, could hardly contain herself. For the past two weeks he had been in one of his "states." One afternoon, visiting her—through it all, Mrs. Callahan had maintained neighborly relations—his attention had been caught by a print of a young Negro girl on her wall. Dr. Shaw had been absolutely fascinated by it; he sat staring almost as if in a trance. Once or twice Mrs. Callahan spoke to him. He did not hear her. After he left she telephoned a friend who taught high school psychology. "Something's going to happen," Mrs. Callahan predicted, "You watch, Mary—there's going to be a murder of a Negro girl."

Now, Sophie Clark's strangling! Mrs. Callahan spent days trying to get Lieutenant Donovan himself on the telephone. Finally, on December 13, two men from Homicide, Detective William McCarthy and Sergeant Thomas Gavin, agreed to see her. Taking the utmost precautions, Mrs. Callahan and her niece met them in a private room at the Hotel Vendome in downtown Boston. Mrs. Callahan told all she knew. She had done more than watch and listen. On August 30—was this not the day Jane Sullivan's body had been discovered?—she had followed Dr. Shaw to Cambridge. He had walked into a bookstore in Harvard Square and bought a copy of *The Scientific Study of Crime*. Once, she recalled, he had recommended a book to her and had loaned it to her from his library: all the erotic passages—and there were shockingly many—had been underlined in red ink. She had checked further on her neighbor. Sophie Clark lived at 315 Huntington Avenue. And Dr. Shaw's office, to which he had recently moved, was also on Huntington Avenue, only a ten-minute walk away!

Detective McCarthy and Sergeant Gavin listened courteously, but it seemed obvious to her that they were not particularly impressed.

Mrs. Callahan began assembling witnesses. She hired a lawyer. Her dossier on Dr. Shaw grew, page by page.

In his office Lieutenant Sherry was talking soothingly over the telephone. "Now, you thought it was in connection with the Strangler—right away you thought of the worst. . . . All I can tell you is that someone wrote us a letter about your husband and we questioned him about information in the letter . . . We're simply checking it. We don't know if it's someone's idea of a joke, or something done in spite, or what . . . Now, now, there's no need to be so upset." He spoke very gently to the weeping woman on the other end. "Just because the police question someone doesn't mean he's guilty. If he's not involved he's got nothing to worry about. No, this won't get into the papers—that only happens on TV. Please don't be upset. I told your husband to call me in two days and I hope we'll have it all cleared up by then . . ."

He listened for a moment. "I don't feel you need a lawyer—why pay lawyer's bills? We haven't done anything to abuse your husband. No, he's not under arrest—we have to decide if whoever wrote that letter is worthy of belief . . . Believe me, your husband isn't the first man we've talked to. I could show you drawers filled with names—do you know how many people are writing us? And we must check them all out—" He continued to speak reassuringly. "I know it's just a routine investigation to us and it's a heartache for you, but please don't be upset—if you are, give me a ring, will you? Sure, sure, you can leave the house—of course you and your husband can go to a movie tonight . . ."

He hung up, thinking, This woman and her husband have to go through all this because of some son-of-a-bitch who might as easily write my name or anyone else's name in an anonymous letter . . .

Lieutenant Sherry had come to be surprised at little in his job, particularly during those terrible days. Many of the wives and mothers he had spoken to had been weeping. But on the other hand, more than one anonymous letter identifying a specific man as the Strangler had turned out to come from the man's own wife, wanting to punish him for having an affair. She knew he was not the Strangler, of course, but a session or two with the police would give him a bad few days and serve him right. People, Lieutenant Sherry thought, are complicated creatures.

Now he sat back and tried to make sense of the material on his desk. For six months homicide detectives armed with mimeographed questionnaires had gone from house to house, street to street, interrogating women, moving in ever widening circles outward from each strangling scene. "Did you know the deceased? Did you see anyone suspicious in this neighborhood at the time of the crime? Have any friends told you anything out of the ordinary? Have you had any unusual incidents while living here?"

On his desk lay the completed questionnaires. Nothing to seize upon save the response to the last question. At least half a dozen women had reported that a Dr. Jonathan Logan—in some cases, Dr. John Logan—had telephoned them in the evening. The stories were similar.

In each case, Dr. Logan said over the phone that he had met the woman some time before at a cocktail party "on the Hill"; he had been struck not only by her appearance but by how intelligently she expressed herself—he had made a mental note to look her up soon. Now—he hoped she would forgive this unorthodox approach—he was taking the liberty of calling her to say he'd love to pick up their conversation where they'd left off. What was she doing right now? Might he drop by for a drink?

None of the women could remember having met a Dr. Logan. Yet, it was possible. What girl hadn't at one time or another gone to a party on Beacon Hill? The Hill was like one vast sorority house. Thousands of students, secretaries, and career girls lived in the small apartments made over from the great town houses, and the social activity was intense. Although some of the women he telephoned had cut him short, many had allowed Dr. Logan to "drop by." They were embarrassed to admit it—the information came reluctantly and only after repeated questioning—but he turned out to be a *most* charming gentleman, and. . . . In six months, Sherry estimated in some awe, the mysterious Dr. Logan must have met and bedded forty to fifty women. Once he achieved a conquest, the girl never saw him again. Nor had any of them been able to find his name in the telephone book or in any medical directory. Only this curious fact led them to disclose so personal an experience. . . .

Lieutenant Sherry could only marvel at human nature— that these sophisticated career girls could allow a stranger to walk into their apartment and make love to them when an entire city lay paralyzed with fear of a sex-mad strangler known for his ability to talk his way into the homes of his victims. . . . Sherry determined to set a trap for the extraordinary Dr. Logan. He had little hope of coming up with the Strangler himself—none of Dr. Logan's conquests had complained of odd or psychotic sexual behavior on his part. But how *could* this happen, now, in these tense days, in Boston?

Indeed, how was one to cope with it all—the grotesque, the comic and awful, the appalling varieties of human behavior coming to light? For even while Dr. Logan was plying his art, young girls recently arrived from Ireland in search of domestic jobs were receiving telephone calls from a man who identified himself as a doctor on the staff of the United States Immigration Service, taking them to task for failing to report for their "three-year physical."

Three-year physical?

The doctor would explain, with some annoyance, that United States laws required all immigrants to have a physical examination every three years.

Oh, she hadn't known, the girl would say apologetically. When might she make an appointment to come down?

"You're too late for that now, we'll just have to do it over the phone," the voice would reply briskly. "Remove your dress and brassiere, please." As she disrobed, he asked her to report each step to him; then, to test her reflexes; and then, to her dismay, to follow other instructions he gave her. Standing at the telephone, one girl had stripped herself nude and on the verge of tears was carrying out his orders when her mother walked in on her, managed to slam the receiver on its hook, and called the police.

Three weeks after Sophie Clark's killing, on Monday morning, December 31, the last day of that terrible year of 1962, Patricia Bissette, twenty-three, was found dead in her locked apartment at 515 Park Drive. It was the same Back Bay area, that of Anna Slesers and Sophie Clark. Patricia, dark-eyed and capable, was a secretary at Engineering Systems, Incorporated, across the street from the famous Lahey Medical Clinic. In her living room a Christmas tree stood, still glittering with the decorations she had hung on it. In the adjoining bedroom Patricia lay face up on the bed, a white coverlet drawn up snugly to her chin. She lay peacefully, her eyes closed, her head turned a little to the right as if she had just lain down for a moment's nap.

When Dr. Michael Luongo, the medical examiner, removed the coverings he saw the nylon stockings tightly twisted about her neck. There were three of them—Patricia's own stockings—knotted and intertwined with her white silk blouse. She wore only the tops of her imitation leopard-skin pajamas, and these had been pushed up to her shoulders. She was naked from the breasts down. There was evidence of recent sexual intercourse. Her apartment had been searched. There was no sign to show how her killer had gained entrance.

The last time Patricia had been seen was 3:30 P.M. Saturday. She had taken her wash down to the laundry room of the adjoining building, No. 509. Superintendent Christian Von Olst had passed by as she was pouring in the soap powder. She was humming to herself, gave him a cheery smile, turned on the washer, and hurried out. At 4:30 P.M. Von Olst passed through the laundry room again. The machine was empty. Patricia had evidently returned and picked up her wash.

Curious, thought Dr. Luongo as he made his notes. Patricia was not only covered, but her arms had been placed neatly along her sides, her legs placed together, almost as if her killer had tenderly arranged her body and as tenderly drawn up the covers to hide her nakedness. Dr. Luongo, who at forty-six had conducted several thousand autopsies, had seen this "compassionate" setting before. One usually came upon it when a man killed his wife or mistress and, already remorseful a moment after his act, painstakingly rearranged her clothes, and cleaned up the room before turning himself in to the police.

The police wondered, too. Patricia, they learned, had been having an affair. This might explain the signs of recent intercourse and the fact, soon determined, that Patricia was one month pregnant. Could her lover have killed her?

Another possibility occurred to them. The Strangler could have been hidden in the closet while Patricia and her lover were together, and waited for the lover to leave before carrying out his insane compulsion, now intensified by a Godlike wrath. In this case he might have slipped into the apartment when Patricia was in the basement picking up her wash. She might have left the door ajar to avoid the bother of unlocking it with her arms full of laundry.

Whatever the case, the fact was that twenty-three-year-old Patricia Bissette had been strangled and sexually assaulted, and decorated in the Strangler's fashion, in her locked apartment, in the Strangler's area, at the Strangler's time.

What was one to say to the people of Boston?

Until now elderly women living alone had met this awful death. Now the Strangler, if there were a Strangler (and could one actually believe there were two or three such insane men on the loose in Boston, each imitating the other), now the Strangler had begun to choose young women, career girls; and age no longer mattered.

On this final day of the year of 1962, after six appallingly similar sex stranglings, not a single sound clue had been found by a force of nearly twenty-six hundred men working twelve and fourteen hours a day. Not only that, but in the midst of this search, the greatest manhunt in history, a seventh strangling had taken place.

All that could be said now was, no woman in Boston, young or old, living alone or with others, was safe.

4

The morning after Patricia Bissette's murder, Jack Mc-Lean, the mild-looking but energetic city editor of the Boston *Record American*, Boston's large circulation morning tabloid, called two reporters to his desk. Both were women, in their early thirties, married, with young children. He wanted them to drop everything they were doing and, working together as a team, retrace the steps of the Strangler—or stranglers.

One of the two was Jean Cole, thirty-four, who had won several awards for her ability and resourcefulness as an investigator. The other was Loretta McLaughlin, thirty-three, who, like Jean, had earned recognition, and frequently worked on medical stories. At that time, Jean was in the midst of an exposé of Massachusetts nursing homes, a *Record American* campaign that Managing Editor Edward Holland had begun some years before. Jean, dressed in a nurse's uniform and posing as a nurse's aide, had managed to get employment in several nursing institutions, and had worked in each one long enough to emerge with firsthand reports of fire hazards, primitive facilities, and lack of proper nursing help. Her stories caused a furore.

Meanwhile, Loretta had become deeply interested in the stranglings. She had been particularly unable to get Ida Irga out of her mind, a seventy-five-year-old woman killed so senselessly. She had gone up to McLean the day after Mrs. Irga's body had been found. "Look," she had said. "I'd like to write a series of articles on the stranglings. Try to pull them together, to put them in perspective—"

At that time, McLean had been unenthusiastic. "What are you going to build a story on? Their names mean absolutely nothing—they're nobodies. Who'd be interested in them?"

"That's just it," Loretta said. "Why should four nobodies

be murdered? Every woman in the city can identify with a woman in no way set apart from another. I couldn't identify with them if they were celebrities, but if they're like the rest of us they're sisters under the skin to every woman who reads the paper."

It was the dog days of August, many people were away on vacation, the editorial rooms were hot and uncomfortable. What better way was there to deal with a restless reporter? McLean shrugged his shoulders. "Okay," he said.

Loretta had written a series of four articles emphasizing the common links of music and hospital association, the fact that each of the four women was retiring, methodical, fastidious, frugal. She had interviewed doctors and psychiatrists and tried to learn what she could from the police. The police had been tight-lipped, which she thought understandable, even though she did not know that a basic tenet laid down during the FBI Seminar on Sex Crimes had been: Gentlemen, your No. 1 enemy is the newspaper reporter, because you may reveal something to him that will tip over your case.

But that had been before young career girls were numbered among the victims. Now that new possibilities had appeared in the Strangler's crimes, McLean thought it time for a new series. He had discussed the idea with Executive Editor Win Brooks and Managing Editor Holland. Both men were in their fifties, both were fathers of daughters, and both were native Bostonians who had come to the *Record American* nearly thirty years before. They had watched the stranglings mount with increasing concern. These, as Holland put it, were not the usual riffraff murders, the violent, suddenly fatal quarrels of the slums, squalid killings that went all but unnoticed because they were part of a sociological problem common to all large cities, and had little impact upon the community. These stranglings, however unhappy the police felt about publicity, could not be cursorily dismissed. The two editors tried not to overplay the story, but they would not ignore news that Bostonians were legitimately entitled to know—for their own protection, among other reasons.

Something ought to be done. Brooks and Holland immediately approved the idea. Jean and Loretta were assigned to "go out and do some old-fashioned newspaper work and see what you come up with."

In the midst of their investigation came the strangling of sixteen-year-old Daniela Maria Saunders, whose body was found in an alleyway on January 5. It was to be solved two weeks later when a fifteen-year-old boy living nearby admitted killing her because she refused him a kiss, but the discovery of her body, only five days after Patricia Bissette's, led to the loudest public outcry so far. A beleaguered Commissioner McNamara met the press in his office seventy-two hours later. "The responsibility is mine," he said. "If there is any onus attached to an individual because the murders remain unsolved, it should fall on me." It was difficult, he went on, to imagine what else the police could do. He cited statistics. They had checked over five thousand Massachusetts sex offenders, screened every inmate at the Center for The Treatment of Sexually Dangerous Persons at Bridgewater State Hospital, interviewed thousands of persons, questioned four hundred suspects—which meant investigating every detail of their alibis, an almost endless task—they had checked out hundreds of written and telephoned tips, letters, and suggestions coming from as far away as Australia. The heel of a hand print had been found on the door frame of Ida Irga's apartment. Whether it was her killer's, no one knew, but they had so far examined over half a million prints without matching it.

Governor Peabody had announced a five-thousand-dollar reward for information leading to the apprehension of the murderer or murderers, but the outcry continued. "If this rampant crime keeps up, the Mayor will fire McNamara as quickly as anyone else," a city councilman declared. In the House of Representatives, with memories of the bookie-police scandal months before, there were demands for an investigation of the police department as well as its methods of crime detection.

Doggedly, McNamara insisted that everything human intelligence could do was being done. Every man on his force, the eighth largest in the United States, would continue to work around the clock, "using every good, known, and solid law enforcement technique" to discover "the persons responsible for the murders."

Although McNamara several weeks before at a closed session of the City Council had admitted that three or four of the stranglings might be connected, now he spoke only in the plural—"the persons responsible." There were too many "dissimilarities" to make one man responsible. He would not disclose what they were, but "they indicate more than one killer." He would not speculate beyond this.

The result was that the public was terrified not only of what it knew, but also by what it didn't know. Women now carried pepper and ammonia in their purses, tear gas bombs in their pockets, hatpins stuck in their coat sleeves; and some had even taken up judo and karate. The fear was such that when a woman came upon a bundle of six used laundered doctor's coats tossed into a corner rubbish can, panic descended on the area. Police spent two days investigating before they found that the coats had been routinely discarded by a neighborhood physician.

Holland told Jean and Loretta: "Go back to the Anna Slesers case, talk to friends and neighbors, get into the apartment. The same with the second and third strangling and right through to Patricia Bissette's. We'll print the facts: maybe these murders do fit a pattern and the pattern will point the way to the killer." He no longer cared what McNamara or anyone else thought, whether the police believed it was one or a dozen stranglers. "Now we ourselves want to know." The girls were to work together in a team of two, as did detectives, so one would always be a witness for the other.

They had unexpected difficulties. Repeatedly, a Mrs. Margaret Callahan telephoned them to insist they investigate her neighbor, Dr. Lawrence Shaw. She had considerable material on Dr. Shaw she was prepared to show them, if they had sense enough to recognize facts as clear as the noses on their faces—something the Boston police obviously lacked. The girls received crank letters and obscene telephone calls until finally both obtained unlisted numbers.

Each night, after their investigations on the scene, and after they cooked supper and put their children to bed, each sat behind locked doors in her home in suburban Boston—Jean in Weymouth, Loretta in Braintree—and wrote her story. Loretta worked late at night at her typewriter on the dining room table under an old-fashioned Tiffany chandelier that cast its kaleidoscopic colors on her paper to make the grotesque events she described even more unnerving. Several times she went upstairs to wake her husband Jim and insist he come down and sit by while she wrote. Both her own and Jean's photographs appeared with each article: their only safety lay in their assumption that neither of them was the Strangler's type.

How, how could it have happened? Jean and Loretta asked themselves. How *must* it have happened? Time and again they were overcome by the conviction—irrational as it was—that the dead women, killed and violated so brutally, were trying to break though, to speak from the grave to them, to help them so that they would suddenly realize. Of course! Of course, this is the way it was! That's how he got in, that's why there's never been a scream, that's how he leaves no clues—this is how it had to be!

Working on the basis of several autopsy reports they obtained through leaks in the Medical Examiner's offices, they printed a number of unpublished details. The police were indignant. Good journalism or not, Lieutenant Donovan felt it was sabotage and ordered no information given out beyond routine releases.

In these first months of 1963 a public feud got under way, between those supporting the police and those attacking them. Sides were chosen. Blake Ehrlich, Science Editor of the Boston *Herald,* retraced the crimes in a series of articles that stressed the enormous amount of police work done. The girls meanwhile charged that some written autopsy reports were still not available to the very detectives working on the cases.

At Harvard Medical School Dr. Richard Ford, Senior Medical Examiner, also read the *Record American* series with annoyance. No question of it: printing those details furnished Boston's lunatic fringe with a *modus operandi.* Now housebreakers and rapists who might have left their victims alive could silence them forever, decorate them with nylon stockings, leave them in exhibitionist poses, and go off confident the crimes would be ascribed to the Strangler.

Among the detectives themselves there was an even greater bitterness. Reporters were meddling in police work. Jim Mellon refused to read the articles. "I don't want to be confused between fact and fiction," he told a friend. "I want to be sure that what I know comes from the case itself, not from someone's typewriter."

The girls' series of twenty-nine daily articles was brought to an end in early February. Both Jean and Loretta felt that the reason was, in part, police pressure. But their conclusions were clear:

There *was* a clear linking of the stranglings. There *was* a pattern in the choice of victims, a pattern in the crimes. Each victim was "orderly, well-groomed, self-sufficient, respectable"; each crime was "marked by a strangling, using a personal article of the victim"; each murder was committed in the victim's dwelling and each aftermath of death revealed "time spent in inspecting the victim's belongings"; and each sexual assault was "peculiarly incomplete." *

They summarized psychiatric opinion: the Strangler was a man, intelligent, psychopathic, suffering from some form of sex deviation. The entire crime—strangling, assault, ransack-

---

* What could not be revealed in their articles was that the actual wounds were nearly all similar lacerations which might have been caused by an instrument such as a speculum, used by gynecologists in examination of their patients, or by some other object.

ing of apartment—was all part of the strange sexual urge he could not suppress. He would not become so deranged as to give himself away, and would be "more likely to continue his crimes than to stop."

But all that brought no one closer to the Strangler.

The city waited.

A moment of comic relief came for the police when Lieutenant Sherry's net pulled in the elusive "Dr. Jonathan Logan." He had made the error of calling a nurse whom he had taken out before: she had been warned to notify police, and when he walked into her apartment that evening, two detectives greeted him.

Dr. Logan turned out to be a slight, pleasant-faced man in his late twenties with the courteous manners of a hotel clerk. He was not a doctor but a wholesale pickle salesman. He was married, with two children and a third on the way. A little black address book in his pocket held the names of some five hundred women he had telephoned in the past year and a half: he had taken out at least one hundred of them, and his proportion of successes was remarkable. How had he found the time for these affairs? "I'd tell my wife I was going to Buffalo on a selling trip," he said calmly. He would go to Buffalo for three or four days, call her from there to establish his alibi, then return to Boston with three full days and nights to play Casanova before reporting home again. He had never met any of his conquests at a party "on the Hill." He chose the girls' names at random from the telephone directory, or followed a pretty girl home to learn her address and then telephoned her. He was anything but guilt-stricken, and took his successes modestly. "I've found out if they'll smile, they'll talk, and if they'll talk—" He spread his hands deprecatingly. The detectives prevailed on several women to come to Homicide and identify him through a one-way glass. One woman, however, saw him in person. She approached him and pointed an accusing finger. "Oh, John," she said, "that you could be doing this after all that went on between us."

The pickle salesman looked at her blankly.

"Don't you even remember me?" she said, aghast.

He blushed. "There've been so many, ma'am—" he began, apologetically, but she burst into tears and fled.

Obviously, thought Sherry, this is not the Strangler. Yet, he had the opportunity to kill them—so, too, might the Strangler operate . . . "Dr. Jonathan Logan" was held on a charge of "open and gross lewdness," and after a thorough investigation, was given a suspended sentence and finally released to his wife and children.

It was a brief enough respite. In March, a Movietone News team arrived to make a documentary on the Boston Strangler. They could not have chosen a more inopportune time. On April 23, *Look* Magazine was to award Boston its All-American City Award in recognition of its civic revitalization. Nevertheless, the documentary was made. One saw Jack the Ripper in London washing his hands in the Thames, then in Boston the fog creeping over Beacon Hill, the white-faced crowds watching the body of Ida Irga taken away in an ambulance—nearly a thousand spectators had crowded the area that night while klieg lights from a local TV unit lit up the scene—Loretta and Jean working at their desks . . .

But it was never shown. The official reason spoke of "technical difficulties," but obviously the police and the news media were in a dilemma: should they publicize the Strangler so that everyone in Boston would be enlisted in the search, at the cost of the city's demoralization; or should they play him down hoping that he would be caught anyway, or simply vanish?

So it rested until 7 P.M. Wednesday night, May 8.

At that hour, thirty-three-year-old Oliver Chamberlin, Jr., hurried into a red brick apartment house at 4 University Road, Cambridge, and knocked sharply on the door of his fiancée, Beverly Samans. He was worried about Beverly, an attractive, dark-haired Boston University graduate student of twenty-three who looked forward to an operatic career. A few minutes before, Oliver had found a note in his room from Mary Vivien, the organist at the Second Unitarian Church in Boston's Back Bay. "I'm concerned about Bev," the note read. "She didn't show up for choir practice this morning or for rehearsal this afternoon." Beverly was to appear in a production of *Così fan tutti* later in the month. Oliver and Beverly had graduated together from a music conservatory three years before: they had remained close friends since. A warm, outgoing girl, Beverly had worked as a music therapist at the Walter E. Fernald School for Retarded Children in Waverly, and currently spent two days a week as a rehabilitation counselor at Medfield State Hospital.

Now, when there was no reply to his knock, Oliver used a key she had given him to open the door.

He saw her at once. He could not help seeing her. She lay directly within his line of vision, sprawled nude on her back on her convertible sofa bed in the combination living-bedroom, her legs apart, her right leg on the bed, her left hanging over the edge between bed and wall. Her wrists had been tied behind her with a gaily-colored silk scarf glittering with sequins. A blood-stained nylon stocking and two hand-kerchiefs tied together were knotted about her neck; there was blood on her chest and neck; a cloth was over her mouth; a lace blouse had been draped about her shoulders.

Almost paralyzed with horror, Oliver managed to walk to the bed and stand over her. Was she dead? He pulled away the cloth over her mouth. A second cloth had been stuffed into her mouth. He pulled that out. Her mouth was open; her eyes closed; her body lifeless.

Though it appeared that Beverly Samans had been stran-gled, death had come as a result of stabbing—twenty-two times, four in the throat, eighteen in the left breast where the stab wounds described an unmistakable bull's-eye design—a large circle enclosing a smaller circle with the final stab wound in the center. The "decorations" about her neck ap-peared to be precisely that. None of them had been tied tightly enough to cause death. A bloody knife with a four-and-a-half-inch blade was found in the kitchen sink. She had been dead for forty-eight to seventy-two hours, Police Cap-tain John Grainger of Cambridge said. Sunday's newspaper, dated May 5, was on a chair.

Sunday was the last day she had been seen alive. At 8 A.M., her neighbor across the hall heard Beverly practicing several arias; later that Sunday morning Beverly sang in the choir of the Second Unitarian Church as usual; in the after-noon, she attended a rehearsal of the opera in nearby Brook-line, drove home at 9 P.M., met a girl friend for a late snack in a neighborhood restaurant, and parted from her at eleven o'clock. No one had seen her since.

Beverly was to receive her master's degree in rehabilitation counseling in June. Then she intended to go to New York for a tryout with the Metropolitan Opera. In the small two-room apartment were many classical records, sheet music and tape recordings. In her portable typewriter, set up on a coffee table a few feet from where her body lay, was page eighteen of her master's thesis. It was entitled, "Factors Pertaining to the Etiology of Male Homosexuality."

The pattern was the same—the nylon stockings, the deco-rations, the body's position, the victim's background—music and hospital. Only the stabbing was different. Some detectives theorized that Beverly might have developed such powerful throat muscles from singing that the Strangler, unable to ren-der her unconscious at once, had seized a knife and stabbed her. Only that was different—and the fact that Beverly had been exploring a subject that might well have brought her into the world of the Strangler.

No notes were found on the coffee table nor on her desk. Could she have been writing her thesis without notes? She undoubtedly sat on the end of the bed when she typed. A chair stood nearby, facing the typewriter. Someone could have been seated there, giving her information for her thesis. Was it he who killed her and took her notes with him?

In Boston, detectives learned the news on the police teletype. Since the crime occurred in Cambridge, it was not in their jurisdiction. They could not help feeling something akin to relief. The Strangler had struck on the other side of the Charles River, and now their colleagues in Cambridge were caught up in the nightmare, too. As each day passed without a major development in the Beverly Samans case, the harassed men of Homicide went about their endless investigations in Boston proper with a kind of grim satisfaction. They were not the only detective force to be baffled, outraged, and made ridiculous before the press and the world by a madman.

5

That May of 1963, with the strangling toll at eight, Detective Phil DiNatale of Boston's Station Sixteen had dinner one evening at the home of his uncle and aunt, Dr. and Mrs. Peter DiNatale.

Detective DiNatale, who now worked the 8 P.M. to 3 A.M. shift in the Back Bay with his partner Jim Mellon, was one of the city's most skillful back-alley men—so called because he specialized in the back alleys, the dead end streets, the courtyards and backyards of apartment houses. In pitch darkness he knew his way in and out of basements, how to negotiate fire escapes, roofs, and parking lots: such was his knowledge of the Back Bay and of what routes a fleeing man might take that more than once, responding to an alarm of "B and E" man, mugger, or purse snatcher, while other police rushed to the scene, DiNatale raced through a back alley, vaulted a fence, and was standing, waiting in the shadows, for the thief to run into his arms.

A heavyset, earnest man of forty-three, DiNatale followed his calling with the fervor of the truly committed. Save for the time he spent with his family, he devoted every waking hour to his work. He had been one of the fifty detectives chosen to attend the FBI Sex Seminar; by now he considered the Strangler his personal enemy. "I can see him," he'd tell his colleagues; "he's sitting there, sneering at me, challenging me. 'Just try and catch me,' he's saying." Although Phil might talk of other matters to persons outside the department, the Strangler was rarely out of his thoughts.

Now, over coffee, his aunt turned to him.

"Phil, you're still on the strangulation cases, aren't you?"

Phil nodded.

She said, "Well, I think I know someone who knows who the Strangler is."

Phil stared at her, thinking, How could anyone know who the Strangler is and not once in all these months come forward and tell us? Aloud he said, "Who is it? Can you contact this person?"

Mrs. DiNatale promptly telephoned Mrs. George Stratton, wife of a psychiatrist at Boston State Hospital at Mattapan, a mental institution. Phil could hear the voice on the other end. "I don't know if this man will talk to your nephew, Grace. He tried to help the police once before, but they wouldn't listen—he won't have anything to do with the police anymore."

Phil said emphatically, "Tell her I'm willing to listen to anything he has to say."

Ten minutes later the phone rang. It was for Phil. On the wire was the friend and attorney of Paul Gordon, advertising copywriter and student of ESP phenomena. Yes, Mr. Gordon had been treated like "some kind of a nut" the last time he tried to help the police. Detective DiNatale could understand that he didn't particularly relish going through that again.

Phil said, "Look, anyone who can help us we're grateful to. I'll be at work tonight at seven-thirty. If Mr. Gordon could drop in, I'd really appreciate it."

"Well—" said the lawyer. "All right. He'll be there." He hung up.

How did his aunt know about this? Phil asked her. She explained that Mrs. Stratton was an old friend. The Strattons knew Gordon's lawyer. Some time ago while they were playing poker, the lawyer spoke to Dr. Stratton about his amazing friend who seemed to know all about the Strangler. Only the other day Mrs. Stratton happened to mention this to Mrs. DiNatale, and so she was now passing it on to him.

That night at seven-thirty Gordon's attorney arrived at Station Sixteen, police headquarters for downtown Boston, and introduced himself to Phil. Gordon, he explained, would be along later. Did DiNatale know anything about extrasensory perception? This was a kind of telepathy, he explained—no magic, no one sitting around burning incense—nothing silly like that. It was a special kind of sensitivity some people possessed—and Gordon had it to a great degree.

At eight o'clock when, as Phil surmised, he had been sufficiently briefed, Paul Gordon himself arrived. He turned out to be a short, heavyset man with huge shoulders and dark brown eyes. He was partially bald. He appeared to be in his early forties. He spoke with a perceptible lisp, but there was no hesitancy in his words.

"Now, before I begin, I want to make certain things clear," he said. "I'm not saying I can prove anything I'm going to tell you. All I can say is that I have ideas for which I don't have a normal, usual explanation. They come to me from some well in my mind—at first it seems I'm remembering them—but when I analyze it I realize I don't really know why I'm getting the ideas or how they come to me."

He smiled. "Now, maybe they don't make sense to me but they might make sense to you, and that's why I'm here." If he was asked point-blank, he added, he would have to say yes, he did have an idea who the Strangler was and what he looked like.

"Please tell us," said Phil.

Gordon nodded. "I picture him as fairly tall, bony hands, pale white skin, red, bony knuckles, his eyes hollow-set—I was particularly struck by his eyes. His hair disturbed me a little bit because he has a habit of pushing back a little curl of hair that falls on his forehead. He's got a tooth missing in the upper right front of his mouth." Gordon spoke easily. "He's in a hospital, as I see him, but I'm not sure if it is a hospital—it could be some kind of home." He described it, and Phil realized that Gordon was describing Boston State Hospital. "He's not confined, I know that, because I see him walking across a wide expanse of lawn. He can walk about, and he does a lot of sitting on a bench on the grounds."

The Strangler, Gordon went on, had "many problems. He used to beat up his mother cruelly—she was an idiotic, domineering woman—and his two sisters live unhappy lives. The family comes from Maine or Vermont. He's terribly lonely—when he's in the city I see him sleeping in cellars, but he likes to wander about the streets watching women, wanting to get as close as possible to them." He paused, and said, with surprising emotion, "You see, the poor fellow is in a continual search for his mother, but he can't find her because she's dead."

Phil listened without any comment. The three men were seated in the interrogation room where suspects were brought for questioning. Phil sat behind a large wooden desk while the two others sat side by side in front of it.

"How many murders do you think he committed?" Phil asked.

"Oh, not more than four, maybe five," Gordon replied.

Could Mr. Gordon tell him something about the stranglings? Say, the first one?

"Oh, yes," said Gordon. "That was Anna Slesers. I picture him standing about on the corner of Huntington and Gainsborough, with a sort of decrepit looking appearance—tan sweater with black and orange border, and brown work pants, and white sneakers. I had no idea why he was there when I first pictured him. It just seemed he was standing there hours at a time.

"Then, as his mental image began to develop, I saw him leaning against a tree in front of the building at 77 Gainsborough Street. An ice cream truck drives up, jangles its bell, and all the kids playing on the street run over to it. He takes this minute to dash into the building, up the stairs, and knock on Anna's door. She opens it; he thinks she's his mother; he goes to her with his arms out, he wants to hug her, to show her how sorry he is that he beat her; and as he goes toward her, she backs up, and resists his advances, and then he can't help it: he chokes her and kills her." Gordon paused.

"Then what happened?" Phil asked.

Gordon shook his head. "I can't tell you—I don't want to tell you—it's just too brutal." Then, "You must realize, Mr. DiNatale, that when I tell you this, it's very much an actual event to me, and I think I'm participating in it—I get ill, if you really want to know."

Phil looked at him. Then he opened the desk drawer and brought out six photographs. They were police photographs of men Phil had seized in the act of mugging people or breaking into buildings and shops in the Back Bay area. All six had turned out to have records as sex offenders, and Phil had kept their photographs. "Mr. Gordon," he said, "look at these." He spread them out on the desk. "Is the Strangler any one of these?"

Gordon studied them. He pushed one aside, and examined the others again. Then he sat back and pointed to the photograph he had selected. There was no doubt in his voice. "This is the man I see. Either he's the Strangler or he's his twin brother."

Phil looked at it. It showed an extremely tall, cadaverous young man in his twenties with hollow cheeks, a curl of black hair over his forehead, a lantern jaw—a man perfectly fitting the description Gordon had given him a few minutes before. On the back of the photograph was the name, Arnold Wallace.

Now, suddenly, Phil remembered. On August 19, 1962—two days before Ida Irga was found—he had collared Arnold Wallace (which is not his true name) breaking into a tea shop on Newbury Street. Brought into the light, Arnold was a frightening spectacle: over six feet two inches, skin the color of clay, a long lean face and enormously long arms that seemed to reach almost to his knees. He was twenty-six, a mental patient at Boston State Hospital. He had been committed by his family, but had ground privileges which meant he could leave his ward and stroll about. He had simply walked off a few days before, and had been prowling about the city, sleeping in the basements of apartment houses. His record had shown him to be "assaultive"—he had punched and beaten his mother—and to "brood about sex."

Phil had kept his prisoner in jail overnight and next morning took him in a van to court. On the way he tried to question him. It wasn't easy to communicate with Arnold. Sometimes he simply stared at Phil, without a word, no matter how many questions were asked. At other times he responded with a foolish grin—was it only foolish, or was it a little contemptuous?—and uttered a few noncommittal words. He showed interest only when Phil asked, "Arnold, tell me, do you like women? You like girls?"

At this Arnold rubbed his knuckles and nodded. "Oh, yes, I like women. I like them all very much."

"How about old ladies?"

Arnold's long face grew dreamy. "I like them too. I like to hug and kiss them—"

The court had ordered Arnold returned to the hospital, and Phil had added his photograph to his collection.

But now this man, this astonishing Gordon, had described Arnold Wallace with frightening accuracy—even to his habit of sleeping in cellars—and had done it *before* being shown the photograph.

Phil revealed nothing of what he thought. "Okay," he said. "How about some of the other stranglings. Sophie Clark, for example?"

He mentioned Sophie Clark because, like Anna Slesers, her murder had taken place in the Back Bay.

"That was different," said Gordon. "I picture Sophie's killer as a Negro, a big, husky man. He knocked on her door—Sophie knew him, knew his voice—and she opened it, and he just pushed his way past her. That's why there's no broken lock or chain. As he entered, his right leg struck a semicircular glass coffee table." Gordon spoke as if remembering, and went on to describe the hallway and living room: two sofas, one brown, one black, on one of which Sophie used to sleep; a telephone table and over it two prints hanging on the wall. The kitchen door to the back hallway had been nailed shut.

Phil listened impassively. He had been joined by his colleagues, Jim Mellon and Detective Frank Craemer, while Gordon talked. The detailed information Gordon poured out with such assurance was all but overwhelming. A Negro *was* a suspect in the Sophie Clark murder—a six-foot-three hand-some youth of twenty-four, to be called here Lewis Barnett, who considered himself a Don Juan—indeed, boasted that women often paid him for his favors. No one could have got-ten into Sophie Clark's double-locked and bolted apartment unless she admitted him. She knew Barnett. He had taken her out at least once. But she was deeply in love with her fiancé back in Englewood, New Jersey, and as she told her room-mates, Lew had to count her one of his few failures. He had dropped into the apartment once before; he could have done so this afternoon, forced himself on her, and when she re-fused him, become so enraged that he strangled her, perhaps even unintentionally.

Aloud, Phil asked, "What did the killer do to Sophie?"

"I don't want to go into that," Gordon said again. "I told you it makes me sick. I dream about the brutality; I can't sleep nights." He stopped, a little agitated. "I'll tell you after all this is all over."

When would that be?

"Oh, real soon." Gordon grew expansive. "Sooner than you think. When this whole thing is solved, Phil," he said ear-nestly, "and the Strangler has reached his climax, when he reaches the top of the world, he'll shout and put his arms out and will tell everybody, 'I'm the man who did it!' " Gordon jumped to his feet, threw his arms out, and cried, " 'I am the Strangler! I've reached my limit, and this is it! Now, what are you going to do about it?' And when this fellow confesses," Gordon went on excitedly, "it's going to be like a big carpet rolled out in front of you and all the answers will be so sim-ple you'll kick yourself for months at a time that you couldn't see it!"

He sat down and everyone stared at him.

Gordon himself broke the silence. "I have to get home, I have work to do," he said. "I was just thinking about those two girls attacked the other night. If you fellows could take me where it happened, I might be of some help."

About three weeks earlier, on April 9, two coeds at North-eastern University, returning separately to their dormitory, were attacked, one after the other, a few streets apart, not far from the Anna Slesers apartment by a man they described as very tall and "dirty, dirty, dirty," as though he had just "come out of a coal bin." The girls had been seized from be-hind, their scarves had been tightened about their necks, and they had been thrown violently to the ground. The man at-tempted to rape them, but their screams drove him away. Each girl had noticed a missing front tooth.

"That fits Arnold, and Lord knows, he's filthy enough, sleeping in cellars," said Gordon.

Phil thought, Who knows how far to go with this? Yet the man had picked out Arnold Wallace's photograph. "All right," he said. "Let's go." A moment later the group—Gordon, his attorney, Phil, Jim Mellon, and Frank Craemer, were driving to Westmorland Street, a long thoroughfare in Back Bay in the area where the two girls had been attacked. On Westmorland Street they left the car and continued on foot.

What took place that May evening was an extraordinary exhibition that none of the detectives would forget. As Gordon came near the scene, he seemed to bristle; he grew more and more excited. He increased his pace until he was trotting, the others hastening after him, darting to one side of the street, stopping short, absorbing the atmosphere about him, then suddenly to the other side, sniffing, listening, meanwhile talking urgently under his breath, "I'll hide here—the girl comes, I'll grab her—I'll wait for her here—" The others realized that Gordon was enacting the role of the Strangler. Now Gordon became the witness: "He grabs her—his pants are open, his penis is out—he throws her to the ground—she screams, lights go on, windows go up, students look out—he's scared now, he's running up the alley—he cuts across the street—"

Gordon raced to the other side. When the others caught up to him, he was portraying a terrified fugitive. "Where'll I go?" he moaned. "Where'll I go? I'll hide in this car—" He scurried to the parked police car. "He jumps inside, he thinks: 'I'll hide—I'll wait—I'll wait an hour, two hours—they'll go away . . . Oh, I can't stand those police sirens, they're getting louder—'"

Suddenly he wheeled and began running down the street again, the others behind him. After a few steps, Jim Mellon stopped short. He thought to himself, Are you nuts? Sweet Mother of Christ, if you go on with this, you're batty! He stood there for a moment. He saw Gordon's burly figure silhouetted in the lamplight as he ran, crouching. His lawyer and Frank Craemer trotted behind him and lumbering doggedly after them was Phil DiNatale. I've had it, Mellon thought. He turned on his heel, went back to the police car, made himself comfortable in the back seat, and waited.

Back in his office, Phil gave the subject of Paul Gordon some thought. DiNatale had grown up in a police family. His father, a detective, had been in the force forty-three years. His four brothers and his two uncles were police officers. Phil had listened and benefited from their experience, and he had learned one important rule: keep an open mind, no matter how strange a man or his story might seem. This Gordon might be a crackpot. Yet perhaps he *could* sense things as others could not. Phil had never heard of extrasensory perception. From what he could make out of the attorney's briefing, it was something like a woman's intuition. Phil made several calls that night and the next day—among them to a physician, a priest, and two nuns. Had they heard of ESP? The physician said he believed it did exist in some measure; the priest said it was most difficult to determine; one nun had studied it in college, the other knew nothing about it.

I'll go along with this fellow, Phil decided. I'll find out if he's worth while. If not, I'll drop him. But I'll stick with him, step by step. He would have to do it on his own time, Phil knew, because he wasn't sure what his superiors might think. I want to see what makes this fellow tick, he told himself. Why is he coming forth with this information? For the reward? Is he mentally sick? Is he a con man? Why does he stop his description just before the murder? Because he doesn't know? Or because he does know? *Could he be the killer himself?* He's big and strong enough. There's a reason Gordon is telling us all this, thought Phil, and I'm going to find out why.

A week later Gordon dropped in again. He gave a few more details of the stranglings. "Say, would you fellows take me to some of the murder apartments?" he asked. Impressions, he said, would be far more powerful on the scene.

Phil listened to this suggestion with more eagerness than he showed. He and Jim Mellon had been checking on Arnold Wallace. Gordon was uncannily close to the truth. Phil had found a former landlady with whom Arnold's mother roomed before her death in 1961. She recalled how Arnold fought with his mother, beating and punching her to give him her welfare checks. "Once I heard an awful crash," she said. "I ran out to see Mrs. Wallace in a heap at the foot of the stairs and when I looked up there was Arnold, standing at the top of the stairs, grinning. If that poor woman knew her son was coming over she'd run out screaming, 'He's going to murder me.'" Arnold might actually have had a hand in her death. She had undergone an operation at Boston City Hospital on April 14, 1961. Arnold visited her shortly after she came down from surgery. When a nurse entered her room a few minutes later, Arnold was gone, but his mother lay unconscious on the floor, the various tubes through which she had been fed and given plasma torn from her body. She died later that day without regaining consciousness.

Arnold insisted that she was sleeping peacefully when he left. If one wished, one could assume that she had convulsively thrown herself out of bed. But nurses said wooden sides had been fitted to it . . .

Important as that was in placing Arnold into the psychological pattern of the Strangler, more important was the fact that he had escaped from Boston State Hospital five or six times—*and each time coincided with a strangling!*

Was that coincidence only? thought Phil. Or had Gordon, with his ESP, actually zeroed in on the Strangler? There was no use questioning Arnold: he denied everything, but he was schizophrenic, and his answers made little sense.

Aloud Phil said, "That sounds like a good idea, Paul." Jim Mellon was not on duty that evening, but Detective Craemer and two other colleagues went along. They decided to go first to Sophie Clark's. The group drove there and parked near her apartment house at 315 Huntington Avenue.

Gordon spoke. "The killer first met Sophie in that drugstore." He pointed to the Gainsborough Pharmacy on the corner of Huntington and Gainsborough Street. Around the corner was Anna Slesers' apartment. "They had a cup of coffee together, and he got to know her. She'd shop at the A and P a few doors down the street there. He'd see her in the place, then walk home with her."

He led the others to the rear of 311 Huntington Avenue. He was about to go into the basement when Phil said, "Sophie didn't live in this building, Paul. She lived two doors down, at 315." Gordon brushed him aside. "I know, but the killer entered this cellar. You see, they all connect, like dungeons." Gordon was moving rapidly now, and the detectives were hard put to keep up with him as he hustled into the first building, out of it, into another, through service entrances, around furnaces and storage rooms, until they were in the basement of 315—Sophie's building.

Phil marveled, thinking, I'm eighteen years in the Back Bay, I know these places, but, by God, this character knows them as well as I do . . . Either he's a good bird dog, or that ESP really means something, or else he's been here before and memorized the place.

Gordon suddenly stopped. "See that door? The killer hid behind it for a couple of hours waiting for Sophie to come home. It was a wet slushy day; he was conscious he would leave wet footprints, so he rubbed his feet to dry them over there, and he was nervous, smoking cigarettes all the time.

You open that door and you'll find a pile of butts behind it. Chesterfields."

Dutifully Phil opened the heavy door: three or four butts lay on the cement floor. They did not appear to be stacked: rather they were spread over a five square foot area. But a man might have flipped them so they fell in that pattern. They were Chesterfields.

"Now, please follow me," said Gordon. He hurried up two flights of back steps. "We're coming to a door with plate glass on it," Gordon announced. Sure enough, around a turn in the stairs they came upon a glass-plated door. Now they were before Apartment 3C, directly under the Sophie Clark apartment. Gordon had become agitated; perspiration showed on his forehead; he was actually trembling.

"What's the matter, Paul?" Phil asked.

Gordon was pale. "There is something inside there that upsets me. It's making me ill."

"Well," said Phil casually, "you know, Paul, this isn't Sophie's apartment. Hers is one flight up—4C."

"Oh, oh!" said Gordon. "You see, when I get near it—"

They went up one more flight and stood at the door of 4C. Gordon seemed to have himself under control, his voice strong and eager. "As you go in the door, remember that coffee table I told you about. The telephone table, the prints on the wall, the two sofas I mentioned—one black, on the right side of the living room, one brown, on the other side. The killer sat in the brown one for a while. You'll find a bookcase in the right-hand corner near the window and a gray easy chair next to it."

The furnished apartment in which Sophie and her two roommates had lived had since been rented by two youths attending Boston University. One boy was home and let the men in. There was no indication that he knew what had taken place there before.

Astonishingly enough, the apartment was almost exactly as Gordon had described it. The bookcase was where he said it would be, the gray easy chair next to it. Only one sofa—a black one—was seen on the right side of the room. There was no telephone table, however, in the hall, and no prints on the wall.

While Gordon went about, touching and examining, Phil took the new tenant aside, talked with him softly, then came back to look at Gordon with renewed interest. There had been a brown couch when he rented the place, the boy said: the day they moved in, they put it down in the cellar. There had been a telephone table in the hall, and there might well have been two pictures on the wall, for the plaster showed the holes. And the back door, as Gordon had told Phil days before, was nailed shut.

How could Gordon know all this unless he had been in the apartment when the three girls lived there? Or unless he really possessed ESP?

Gordon led the way into the bathroom. "Look here," he said. He stared at the white medicine chest. "The killer looked through this for a razor. Why the hell would he want a razor?" Gordon seemed as puzzled as anyone as he went back to the living room. "I picture the killer sitting here on the brown sofa. Sophie is in the kitchen preparing supper. The phone rings—"

Phil almost started, but said nothing.

"Sophie comes out to answer it, but she has to pass by him to get to the telephone in the hall, and she's afraid because every time she tries to go by, he grabs at her. Finally she makes a break for it, he grabs her, they struggle, he strikes her on the side of the head, and she falls unconscious . . ."

Through Phil's mind ran the fact that Audri Adams, Sophie's roommate, had telephoned Sophie at two-thirty. She was O.K. then. Gloria Todd, her other roommate, telephoned her at four-thirty, to ask her about mail. The telephone rang and rang, without answer.

"Then I picture him—" Gordon was drawling his story, slowly, as one trying to remember. "—I picture him going into the bathroom and tearing up the shower curtains, maybe to use them to tie her up—and he sees he can't take them down because they're on hooks, and have to be unhooked, so he grabs at the door of the medicine cabinet—he's going to open it to get that razor—perhaps to cut her throat—then he realizes girls don't shave, no razor, so he doesn't even open the door. He's in a hurry—just breezes in and out of the bathroom. When he came back into this room, Sophie was just coming to—he began choking her, then he'd wait for her to come to consciousness, then choke her again—" He stopped.

"Then what happened?" demanded Phil.

Again Gordon evaded the question. "I can't tell you that—I don't care to, because when I get that close to the victim, in my mind, at least, I don't want to look at what happened. I don't want to see it. I'm telling you about the cigarettes and the rest because maybe that'll be helpful to you—that's all."

The men left the apartment. Phil suggested they drive around the corner to 77 Gainsborough Street, Anna Slesers' building. They parked in front of No. 77, and Gordon retold his story—Arnold leaning against the tree, the arrival of the ice cream truck . . . DiNatale, looking down this street of identical buildings, each with its huge, silent bay window, thought, People sit at those windows day and night looking out from behind their curtains. Old ladies sit there for hours. A thousand eyes were on this street the day the Strangler mounted the seven steps to the stoop, pulled open the door of No. 77—and no one saw anything. Nothing at all.

On the morning of May 20 Phil and Jim were suddenly summoned to Boston State Hospital, to find Paul Gordon and his attorney, a number of police officials, and Dr. Stratton and several other psychiatrists.

Everyone was in a state of excitement. Paul Gordon had identified Arnold Wallace as the man he had visualized as the Strangler.

Gordon had called upon Dr. Stratton the day before with a request: "Could I meet Arnold Wallace? I want to see if he and the man I see are the same person."

Dr. Stratton took Gordon into a reception room and sent an orderly for Arnold. As they waited, Gordon said, "When this fellow opens his mouth, you'll see a missing tooth here—" He indicated one of his own front teeth.

A few minutes later the tall figure of Arnold came into view down the corridor. Gordon whispered excitedly to Dr. Stratton: "That's your fellow!"

Dr. Stratton presented the two to each other. "Paul, this is Arnold Wallace. Arnold, this is Paul Gordon." Arnold looked at Paul, held out a limp hand. "Yes, I know," he said, surprisingly.

The three talked for a few minutes, then Dr. Stratton left for an appointment. Five minutes later Gordon emerged. Arnold had returned to his ward.

"Isn't that amazing!" Gordon exclaimed, when he found Dr. Stratton. "Arnold said 'I know' when you introduced us. That jarred me. He knows me."

How could he explain that?

"I've been concentrating on him so much, I've been visualizing him until I almost live in him," said Gordon. "Maybe it's given him a subconscious sense of having met me. If I can visualize him, maybe he can visualize me."

Would he consider Arnold a suspect?

"He's the man," Gordon said positively. "And that's not an easy thing for me to say, Doctor, because I have no real way of proving it."

Now, having identified Arnold, Gordon began telling the assembled group what happened in the Nina Nichols strangling; how Arnold walked into the lobby of 1940 Commonwealth Avenue that tragic Saturday afternoon, June 30, 1962, buzzed Nina Nichols from below—the buzz heard by her sister-in-law, Mrs. Chester Steadman, over the telephone—walked up the three flights of stairs, knocked, and went in. How he approached her as if she were his mother, how she backed away, paralyzed with fear, how he choked her half unconscious, placed her in a chair, shook her, pleaded with her as if she were his mother and finally killed her, not to kill her but to silence her so she would listen.

Lieutenant Sherry broke in. "Paul, I'm new at this ESP thing. You answer one question and I'll believe you. Tell me what happened to Nina Nichols. She knows, but she's dead: only the medical examiner and I know. Can you see what happened to Nina Nichols at the time she was being murdered?"

Paul Gordon opened his mouth, but his attorney leaped to his feet. "Wait a minute, Paul! Lieutenant Sherry, if he gives you that answer, does that mean you'll arrest Paul as the Strangler?"

Sherry looked at him, as if pondering his reply, but Paul spoke up, back to his original gambit. "I don't like to go into that, Lieutenant, but some day when you're not wearing a badge I'll call you and tell you what happened to Nina Nichols and the other women. Stuff like that makes me feel squeamish. I can't sleep nights, it's so real to me."

The meeting ended soon after.

Days later, Phil and Jim interviewed Dr. Stratton and came away more puzzled than ever. The psychiatrist knew little about Gordon. He had met him as Phil's aunt had explained. The poker game at which the attorney had mentioned Gordon's name to him had been in March. Gordon had come up to Boston State Hospital a few days later and introduced himself, said Dr. Stratton casually, and had come up twice since then to consult him about various personal matters. Dr. Stratton was understandably noncommittal.

All the two detectives could think of now was that Paul Gordon had visited Boston State Hospital in March—*before* he called on Phil DiNatale in May and identified Arnold Wallace's photograph among those on his desk.

Could Paul and Arnold have met on the hospital grounds in March? Arnold was not confined to a ward. Perhaps Paul had identified the photograph not because he possessed ESP, but because he had seen and even perhaps talked with the real Arnold. That could be why Arnold appeared to know him when Dr. Stratton introduced the two men. Was the whole thing a hoax?

Or was it possible that the two had never met and Arnold, in his confused mental state, thought he knew Gordon, perhaps mistook him for one of the many physicians about the hospital?

Why was Paul Gordon so *sure* that Arnold was the Strangler?

Was Arnold the Strangler?

In an attempt to throw light on this perplexing situation, a court order was obtained permitting the police to subject Arnold to a lie-detector test. Early in June Phil DiNatale and Jim Mellon took Arnold from the hospital to the offices of Charles Zimmerman, a private polygraph expert formerly associated with Interpol, the international detective agency. Zimmerman was frequently used by the Boston police because of his experience in the field.*

The two detectives waited in Zimmerman's anteroom. Arnold, tall, lanky, his long jaws blue with beard, in khaki chinos and an open-necked blue shirt, sat vacantly on a chair, the two detectives in chairs next to him. Mellon, thinking the sight of girls might start Arnold talking, picked up a movie magazine from a sofa opposite them and handed it to Arnold. The latter thumbed through it. He stopped at a page showing a Hollywood starlet in a bathing suit. He did not move. His face grew dreamy.

"Arnold," said Mellon. "What are you thinking of?"

Arnold looked at him. His voice was far away. He was holding the magazine in both hands on his lap. "I'm screwing this girl right now," he said. "I got her on that couch." His eyes closed, and he was lost in his private fantasies. He slowly relaxed. His eyes opened. Arnold glanced at the two detectives staring at him, and the same slow, vacant grin appeared on his face. "I do it in my mind," he said boastfully, almost like a little boy.

The lie-detector test, when he took it, was inconclusive.

Arnold Wallace had an I.Q. of between 60 and 70. The normal figure is 100 to 110. His low intelligence was one bar-

* The polygraph is an instrument that simultaneously measures and records changes in blood pressure, respiration, and electric resistance due to perspiration while a subject answers questions. These readings, interpreted by a highly trained examiner, are believed by many to be an almost infallible test of truth or falsehood. Lie-detector evidence, however, is not admissible as legal evidence in court.

rier to communication with him. Add to that his psychotic state and his ability to put himself into a world where fantasy and reality were one, and it seemed obvious that any conversation with him must be as inconclusive as the polygraph test. One could not believe his denials—or, for that matter, his confession, were he ever to confess.

The two men took him back to Boston State Hospital.

There was nothing to do but check and recheck circumstantial exidence, and try to make up their minds about the amazing Paul Gordon who knew so much and said he learned it telepathically from Arnold Wallace, the Strangler.

6

July, August, September, 1963.

The days ticked off through the hot summer. Each week that passed without a strangling was accepted gratefully. It seemed possible once more to buy newspapers without fear that the same headline would leap at one, and to become involved again in what took place outside Boston—Pope John's death and Pope Paul's election, the Soviet's achievement in sending a woman into space, the welcome given by millions to a Bostonian named John F. Kennedy during his tour of Europe, the extraordinary civil rights march on Washington, D.C.

On Sunday, September 8, people sunned themselves in the Public Garden or strolled on the green Esplanade on the banks of the Charles. Perhaps some may have remembered the tense Labor Day weekend just a year before, after the discovery of sixty-seven-year-old Jane Sullivan's body—and the realization that she and Ida Irga, a woman of seventy-five, had been strangled in the same twenty-four-hour period. Those grotesque crimes, indeed all the grotesque crimes before and since, seemed far away that peaceful summer day.

That morning, shortly before ten o'clock in suburban Salem, Mrs. Evelyn Corbin dropped in to have Sunday breakfast with her good friend, Mrs. Flora Manchester, sixty-six, who lived down the hall on the first floor of a five-story red brick building at 224 Lafayette Street. Mrs. Corbin was blond, blue-eyed, and vivacious, a petite divorcée of fifty-eight who looked nearly fifteen years younger. Few knew her real age. She had celebrated her birthday two days before: everyone assumed that it was at most her forty-fifth. She had a modest job in the lamp-assembly line at the Sylvania Electric Company, and had been going with Mrs. Man-

82

chester's son Bob, forty-one, for some time. The three were almost a family group.

It was the habit of the two women to take Sunday breakfast together, each still in nightgown and housecoat; then Mrs. Corbin would return to her apartment and dress for 11:30 A.M. Mass at nearby St. Theresa's Chapel. On her way out she would rap twice on Mrs. Manchester's door to signal her departure. Returning an hour or so later she would knock again to indicate she was back.

Bob, a sales engineer, had left at 9 A.M. for his office in Newton Highlands, twenty-five miles away, to catch up on work. The two women had one bit of gossip—someone had tampered with both their doors earlier that morning. Mrs. Manchester had no doubt of it. About 9:10, someone had tried a key in the lock, found it wouldn't work, and went away. She had been so upset that although Mrs. Corbin lived only a few yards down the hall, she telephoned her. "Someone just tried my door," she said. "Was it you?"

"No," said Evelyn. She sounded equally puzzled. "Someone tried mine only a minute ago." She had looked out, but no one was there.

Both women dismissed it from their minds, and Mrs. Corbin left about 10:35 for her own apartment to prepare for church.

Mrs. Manchester heard no double knock at 11:10, the usual time. When she had not heard it by 11:15, she telephoned Evelyn to warn her she'd be late for Mass. There was no answer. At 12:30 P.M., having heard neither the signal for departure nor return, Mrs. Manchester telephoned Eaten's Drug Store across the street, where Evelyn always picked up her Sunday paper on the way back from church. No, she had not been there yet.

A half hour later Mrs. Manchester, another neighbor at her side—Mrs. Manchester had a heart condition and wasn't sure she'd be up to handling things if Evelyn had taken ill—unlocked Mrs. Corbin's door with the key she had. They found Evelyn Corbin sprawled across her bed, still in the blue nightgown and gray housecoat, the white ankle socks and slippers, she'd worn to breakfast a few hours before.

She had been strangled with two of her nylon stockings, tied together at the throat, and knotted with the extra half hitch. The front of her housecoat had been ripped open with such violence that three buttons had flown off, exposing her left breast. Her night gown had been pushed up; her right leg extended on the bed, the other placed at almost right angles dangling over the side so that she lay nude and grossly exposed. Her killer had stuffed her underpants into her mouth as a gag, and tied a third nylon stocking in an elaborate bow about the ankle of her left foot, hanging motionless a few inches above the floor. The knot here, too, was the double half hitch—the Strangler's knot.

She had been sexually assaulted in a manner the newspapers found difficult to describe, save to say evidence indicated that her killer "had satisfied an unnatural sexual appetite in the commission of his crime."

Salem police had only to note a few other facts. The apartment had been locked. Mrs. Corbin's possessions had been searched. Two bureau drawers were half open. Apparently nothing had been taken. A jewelry tray had been removed and carefully set on the floor. Her empty purse was found on the floor beside the bed, its contents dumped on a couch nearby. She had recently visited friends in Salem Hospital. She was an accomplished pianist—sheet music lay on the bench before the baby grand in her living room.

Again there were no clues—or were there? There was the tampering with the doors that morning. Outside Mrs. Corbin's kitchen window, on the rear fire escape, police found a fresh doughnut. No doughnuts were found in the apartment, nor had any tenants tossed doughnuts from the windows above.

The terror was still at work, and if possible, even more awful. For a little while he had turned his attentions to younger women. Had he now come back to his first prey again? A year had passed since Ida Irga and Jane Sullivan, and more than a year since Anna Slesers and Helen Blake and Nina Nichols, and it had begun all over again.

On Friday, November 22, 1963, President John F. Kennedy was assassinated.

From one-thirty that afternoon—the hour of his death—a distrait Boston, its shops closed, its streets all but empty, sustaining a sense of loss more personal than any other city, for this had been his home, began the long mourning vigil. At 12:17 the next afternoon—Saturday, November 23—the people of Boston saw President Lyndon B. Johnson en route to St. John's Cathedral for memorial services, and then watched as the TV cameras moved to the White House to show dignitaries slowly entering the East Room where the casket of John Kennedy lay, banked with flowers.

And in the hours that immediately followed, between 12:30 P.M. and 3:30 P.M. that Saturday afternoon, as Boston and the rest of America sat numbly before its television screens, a quiet, retiring twenty-three-year-old girl named Joann Graff was raped and strangled to death in her locked apartment in suburban Lawrence, an hour's drive from Boston.

She was strangled with two nylon stockings intertwined with a leg of her black leotard, tied about her neck in an elaborate, flowing bow, like a circus clown's bow tie, and with the extra half hitch—the Strangler's knot. She lay diagonally across her bed, nude save for a pink blouse bunched up about her shoulders, her legs wide apart, the left extended directly forward, the other bent almost at right angles, dangling over the edge of the bed, a white slipper still on the foot. The front of her blouse had been ripped open with such violence that four buttons had popped off. There were unmistakable teeth marks on her left breast. Under her head was found the earpiece of her metal-rimmed glasses, surprisingly old-fashioned for a girl of twenty-three.

A Salem detective left the scene muttering, "It's like rerunning a film of Evelyn Corbin."

Joann's one-room apartment had been ransacked, but left untouched on the table was an envelope with her gas bill and several dollars. There was no sign of forced entry. A girl with few friends, she had come from Chicago five months ago after graduation from the Chicago Art Institute, and she taught sixth grade Sunday School at the Lutheran Redeemer Church in Lawrence. She was so conservative that she thought most print dresses too gaudy to wear. The firm for which she worked as a designer, creating motifs for automobile upholstery, tablecloths, and trays, was directly across the street from Lawrence General Hospital.

The time of death was carefully established. At 11:30 Saturday morning, Mrs. John S. Johnson of Andover, who had befriended Joann when she first arrived, telephoned to invite her to dinner that night. She had accepted gratefully. At 12:30 P.M., George Privetera, her landlord, came by to collect the fifteen-dollar weekly rent. He held Joann in high regard. Before she took the apartment she had asked innumerable questions—"Is it respectable? Will I be safe here?"—and she had insisted that he tell her about the other tenants. She kept the place spotless—often he found her on her knees scrubbing the floor—and her blinds were always drawn because she once glimpsed a Peeping Tom training his binoculars on her windows from a neighboring building. As she paid her rent (she never allowed him to enter, but kept him standing in the hall), he noticed through the partly opened door that she had done her breakfast dishes and had been studying a religious tract on her kitchen table. Later her fountain pen was found under it, as if her murderer might have surprised her as she made notes for next day's Sunday School class.

At 3:25 on the floor above her apartment, Kenneth Rowe, a twenty-two-year-old engineering student at Northeastern University, was alone, studying, when he heard footsteps outside in the hall. He would have paid no attention save that for two preceding nights his wife Sandra, twenty-one—now out at the neighborhood laundromat—had complained someone was "sneaking about" the halls. Rowe tiptoed to his door and listened.

The footsteps approached, and stopped. He heard someone knock on the door directly opposite theirs. Apparently no one was home: a moment later the knock sounded on his door. He opened it to see a man about twenty-seven with shiny pomaded hair, wearing a brown jacket, a dark shirt, and dark green slacks. "Does Joann Graff live here?" he asked. Rowe could not see his features clearly because the man's hand was rubbing his nose as he asked his question. He pronounced it "Joan," not "Jo-ann," as her friends did.

Rowe said, "No, she lives just below the apartment you were knocking on before."

The man mumbled thanks and was already walking down the corridor. He vanished at the turn of the stairs. A moment later Rowe heard a door open and shut on the floor below. He assumed Joann had opened her door and let her visitor in.

At 3:30, Mrs. Johnson telephoned Joann to say her husband would pick her up at 4:30. There was no answer. The Johnsons, who attended the same church, had met Joann through the minister, the Reverend Kirstips Valters, after Joann asked his help in introducing her to people in the congregation.* Repeatedly at fifteen-minute intervals Mrs. Johnson called, without an answer. At 4:40, Mr. Johnson decided to drive to Lawrence anyway. He hurried into Joann's building and rapped loudly on her door. All was silence. He did not know it, but death had preceded him.

The morning before—Friday, November 22—a neighbor down the hall from Joann heard someone outside her door. Suddenly her attention was caught by a piece of white paper

---

* Here one of the coincidences so often to appear in the search occurred: The Reverend Mr. Valters had been a displaced person from Latvia, like Anna Slesers. He had met Juris Slesers, her son, through the Talvija Club, a Latvian student group, and had accompanied Juris to his mother's funeral, although Mrs. Slesers attended another church.

being slipped under her door, perhaps two inches. Now it was slowly being moved from side to side. There was no voice. Was it a prank, or someone seeking to tantalize her into opening her door? Too terrified to move, she remained rooted where she stood, watching the paper move back and forth, like a person hypnotized, for what seemed an unendurable time. Suddenly it was withdrawn. She heard footsteps move away. Then, silence.

Had it really happened? Was it a delusion?

No one at 54 Essex Street knew more until the discovery Sunday of Joann Graff's body as she had been left murdered in her apartment that Saturday afternoon, November 23, 1963.

That the Strangler had struck at such an hour and at such a time when the entire world was in a state of shock at President Kennedy's assassination and its aftermath, was later characterized by one psychiatrist as the greatest act of megalomania in the history of modern crime.

What mind could conceive and carry this out, as if to proclaim "However shocked the world, I will shock it still more!"

Christmas 1963 came. People did their best to forget. It seemed there was a slow fading away of some of the horror in the excitement of the holiday season. Shortly after noon on New Year's Day 1964, nineteen-year-old Mary Sullivan, a gay, friendly girl who loved music and had once worked as a nurse's aide in a Cape Cod hospital, moved into a third-floor apartment at 44A Charles Street, on Beacon Hill. Recently arrived from Hyannis, she was delighted to have found Pamela Parker, eighteen, and Patricia Delmore, nineteen, who worked at Filene's and had been looking for a roommate to replace a girl who had left to be married two weeks before.

On Saturday, January 4, Pam and Pat came home from work, unlocked the door to their three-room apartment, and a moment later walked dazedly into the dusk of crowded Charles Street.

Mary was dead, strangled, but the manner of her death was such that it multiplied all the horror of the ten strangulations that preceded hers. Under a Utrillo reproduction on the wall showing a snowy Paris street scene, Mary's body—in the words of the police stenographer's report—was "on bed in propped position, buttocks on pillow, back against headboard, head on right shoulder, knees up, eyes closed, viscous liquid (seminal?) dripping from mouth to right breast, breasts and lower extremities exposed, broomstick handle inserted in vagina, steak knife on bed near brown straw end. . . . Seminal stains on blanket . . ."

Knotted about her neck were: first, a charcoal-colored stocking; over that a pink silk scarf tied with a huge bow under the chin; and over that, tied loosely, almost rakishly, so that one could admit one's hand between it and her neck, a bright pink-and-white flowered scarf. A gaily colored New Year's card reading "Happy New Year!" had been placed against the toes of her left foot.

Now the public clamor could not be silenced. Two weeks later Attorney General Edward W. Brooke, Jr., announced that the Attorney General's Office of the Commonwealth of Massachusetts, the highest law enforcement agency of the state, was taking over the investigation of all the stranglings, in and out of Boston.

The crime against the people of the Commonwealth had reached a point that was intolerable.

PART TWO

7

In the history of cities as well as that of peoples, one asks, What is the straw that breaks the camel's back? Why should the death of nineteen-year-old Mary Sullivan—the eleventh unsolved strangling in an eighteen-month period—have brought about an action that was not brought about by the tenth or ninth?

The fact was that no other strangling struck the city with such impact. It was not only Mary's youth—the youngest of the eleven—but also that she so typically represented a vast segment of Boston's population. Everywhere in Boston, crowding the trolleys and buses, hurrying home from their jobs as typists, clerks, salesgirls, sitting four at a table chattering in the cafeterias at lunch and the midafternoon coffee break, one saw thousands of Mary Sullivans—girls of Irish-Catholic background and modest economic condition, young, pretty, gregarious, full of life, who sooner or later would give up their jobs, marry, and move to the suburbs to raise their large families and live out their days uneventfully. When Mary Sullivan was struck down, the shock that went through Boston was not only the shock of horror but the shock of recognition.

Even more important was the essential awfulness of the crime, and the fact that more of its terrible details filtered through to the public than in any of the others. There had been veiled references in the newspapers and magazines to "molestation" and "assault by a foreign object." There had been carefully worded phrases such as "satisfying his unnatural sexual appetite" and "the victim had experienced the supreme intimacy." It was difficult in family publications to tell what one knew, even if dissemination of these details might lead one of the millions of readers to come up with a clue. A bottle had been found next to Nina Nichols' body. A broom had been found in a closet of Jane Sullivan's apartment—obviously placed there after her death. In Mary's case one almost saw the Strangler thinking, This time there'll be no doubt: I'll spell it out; then, like a demented stage designer, setting up his mad, maniacal production for everyone to see, adding a final, contemptuous taunt to the police—the card reading "Happy New Year!" There was no word to describe it but fiendish. And when detectives went over the apartment with every kind of microscopic and chemical test, they found a tiny sliver of tinfoil like that used to wrap film, suggesting that the Strangler, before departing, carefully photographed the scene to record his artistry.

What had been going on, as Attorney General Brooke characterized it, had reached beyond the point of endurance.

Now matters moved swiftly.

Even as Lieutenant Donovan and his men worked around the clock on the Mary Sullivan case, within forty-eight hours of Brooke's announcement, his new coordinating office—the Special Division of Crime Research and Detection—had begun work on the second floor of the gold-domed State House on Beacon Hill. Its powers would go far beyond that of any police department in the country.

Brooke, handsome and capable, a man of immense personal charm, was the nation's first Negro attorney general. No Negro had ever been elected to so high a political post. After Brooke, a Republican, had won a resounding victory in a strongly Democratic state—the Democratic registration in Massachusetts is almost double that of the Republican—many predicted he would be the first Negro governor in the United States. He had a brilliant career before him. There was no doubt that he risked much by stepping into this hornet's nest, the more so since 1964 was an election year. "As a politician I know I can be criticized by both police and public," he admitted. But he felt he had to do what had to be done. "This is an abnormal and unusual case and it demands abnormal and unusual procedures," he declared. In charge of the entire operation he was appointing Assistant Attorney General John S. Bottomly, head of the Eminent Domain Division in the Attorney General's office.

No onus was to be placed on the Boston police. This was not a take-over. It was a coordination. Greater Boston is a crazy quilt of independent municipalities; the city itself is a concentrated core of business and industry, surrounded for some fifty miles by nearly eighty "bedroom" towns. This circumstance, and the fact that each of these suburbs had its own police department, made the situation absolutely chaotic. In the eleven stranglings that began with Anna Slesers' there were now six separate police departments and three district attorneys involved.

To add to the confusion not only were the police keeping the more lurid details from the public, but frequently police of one city kept details from other police departments. Some of that was prudence—the fewer who knew, the less chance for leaks. Some of it was competitiveness. Some of it was because some officials believed that the crimes were not related, and that to assume they were would only further confuse the situation. And some of it was a consequence of genuine difficulties in communication.

The Boston *Record American* had charged, in a story by Jean Cole, that whatever the cause, failure to exchange all data by Boston, Cambridge, Lynn, Lawrence, and Salem made it impossible to solve the stranglings, and that "to date there has not been a single organized . . . effort by officials involved to trap the mad killer." Repeatedly the paper urged that a central "clearing house" be set up.

There were other problems. As things now stood, any detective could be pulled off work on the stranglings at any moment to deal with other crimes—murders, shootings, abortions, riot.* Brooke, in announcing his move, said he wanted skilled men to be assigned full time to the stranglings alone, and not only detectives. He would bring in pathologists, psychiatrists, psychoanalysts, sociologists, even anthropologists, to concentrate their skills on the search. The best brains in the country would be pressed into service. The only authority in the Commonwealth with the money and power to do this—and with sufficient prestige to command the help of specialists anywhere in the world—was the Attorney General.

"We start now," Brooke said.

In his green-walled office in the State House atop Beacon Hill, Assistant Attorney General John Bottomly, the man chosen to coordinate the search, sat studying the voluminous files before him. Outside it was dark: across Beacon Street, Boston Common and the adjoining Public Garden were still garlanded with Christmas lights, and, nearby, candles flickered in the high windows of the Park Street Church.

Where to begin—and how?

* At 1 A.M., January 5, a few hours after Mary Sullivan's body was found, a man walked into Station Three to announce that he had killed his wife. Lieutenant Donovan had to divorce Lieutenant Sherry completely from the Sullivan investigation to work on it.

It did not escape Bottomly that from this command post he was much like an Army general directing a vast military operation—save that his enemy was invisible. Even worse: he was an enemy of whom nothing really was known—his weaknesses, his strengths, his deployment of forces—nothing. The only proof that he existed at all was the wake of death behind him.

For Bottomly it was one more challenge. The man whom Brooke had selected was no austere detective of fiction. He had no experience in criminology. He was forty-two, a native of Boston, a graduate of Deerfield, Harvard, and Boston University Law School—a six-foot-four bespectacled attorney who threw himself with gusto into any job he tackled. Independently wealthy, he had a wide range of interests: finance, mining, ship salvage, professional sports, and politics, and he had settled on the law only after contemplating, one time or another, careers in medicine, the ministry, teaching, and farming. Politics and reform movements particularly fascinated him. He came by this interest naturally. His father, Robert J. Bottomly, an attorney who died in 1948, had been one of Massachusetts' most influential Republican leaders. He had served as Executive Secretary of Boston's Good Government Association which in 1912 ousted "Honey Fitz" John Fitzgerald, President Kennedy's maternal grandfather, from the Mayor's seat and replaced him with a reform administration.

John Bottomly had built an enviable reputation as chief of the forty-four attorneys in Eminent Domain. That department dealt with the condemnation of private property for public use—the taking over by the Commonwealth of land needed for highways, bridges, parks, and the like—and with the enormously complex litigation growing out of the subsequent damage claims. In little more than a year Bottomly had disposed of nearly a thousand cases that had cluttered the docket for almost a decade. He was chiefly an administrator, a man who could size up a chaotic situation, streamline it, and resolve it. He had made an equally fine record as Assistant United States Secretary to the Allied Control Authority set up in Berlin to rule Germany immediately after World War II. Here numerous committees funneled through him and he had managed to deal with explosive personalities and to keep order, channel information, and coordinate complicated data that might otherwise have overwhelmed the American, British, French, and Soviet generals in charge.

His task in his new position was clear. First, to assemble information on every strangling, every victim, every suspect, every piece of data obtained in each case in Boston, Cambridge, Lynn, Lawrence, and Salem; second, to organize it, which meant overcoming resistance from various quarters reluctant to give him what he wanted; and third, to analyze it. He was aware that in some Democratic circles—especially the police—there had been charges that Attorney General Brooke had leaped into the situation for political purposes. These rumors depicted Brooke as a Republican making a bid for power in Democratically controlled Boston, and trying to reap as much publicity out of it as possible. Interest in the Boston Strangler was worldwide: Mary Sullivan's death had received bigger headlines in London and Cape Town than it had in Boston.

Bottomly immediately pressed into service Michael Cullinane, the shrewd, fifty-eight-year-old acting Captain of State Detectives, to act as his liaison with police. Later Detective Phillip DiNatale, Special Officer Jim Mellon and Metropolitan Police Officer Stephen Delaney—men who had distinguished themselves by working on their own time on the various strangling cases—would join his investigative staff and concentrate full time on the search. In addition to a "Hot Line" telephone, he established a post office box to which everyone was urged to forward any leads of any kind: suspicions, suggestions, names of persons who might know more than they had told, with the assurance that the informants would be protected. (That was tantamount to inviting a correspondence with every eccentric in New England, but one had no idea where a valuable lead might come from.) He ordered copies made of every report on the stranglings in the files of every police force—some 37,500 pages. By the end of January these made a stack of paper ten feet high. That meant the hundreds of questionnaires detectives had filled out in the last eighteen months in Boston and its suburbs; every interview; every letter, telephone call, tip, complaint; all testimony given by every friend, neighbor, relative, fellow employee.

As additional material came in, as persons only mentioned in passing earlier were interviewed and in turn gave additional names who were in turn interviewed, these reports would grow until some—dealing with one strangling alone—added up to more than two thousand pages. Each of these became a loose-leaf casebook—eleven in all. Five copies were made of each one: a master one for Bottomly's safe; a second for his staff and investigators; a third for Donovan's Homicide Bureau; a fourth for Robert Roth's State Identification Bureau, involved on the computer program; and a fifth for Bottomly's newest creation, a Medical-Psychiatric Committee.

The last was composed of a gynecologist, a psychiatrist with a background in sex crimes, an internist, the medical examiners who had done autopsies on the eleven victims, and a physician with experience in clinical anthropology. Later other psychiatrists, a chemist, and a graphologist would be added as consultants.

The committee was headed by Dr. Donald P. Kenefick of the Law-Medicine Research Institute of Boston University. Its task was to evaluate the information in the casebooks, analyze evidence as it developed, and attempt to produce a "psychiatric profile"—a character-personality sketch—of the killer or killers. It was a job, Dr. Kenefick remarked, comparable to "trying to reconstruct a dinosaur."

Had the women been murdered because they happened to be on the scene when the assailant arrived? That had been the hope—if hope is the word—in the Anna Slesers case, the very first. But in view of the later stranglings, this hypothesis had come increasingly into question. Was it not plausible that each woman, whether young or old, had been chosen? Chosen to be assaulted? Chosen to be killed? Chosen to be left on display?

If this was the case, what made the killer select these women? Was it to be found in the women themselves? Or was it something that the murderer, in his insanity, fancied he saw in them?

One fact stood out startlingly. All but two stranglings took place on weekends. Anna Slesers' occurred on June 14, a Thursday. But June 14 was Flag Day, observed as a holiday in many states. Sophie Clark had been strangled on December 5—a Wednesday. However one might explain the date of Sophie's death, the murderer might be someone who came to the Boston area only on weekends and holidays—perhaps a student, who would be free at such times.

Bottomly knew the sharp cleavage between the two public points of view, one represented by Jean Cole and Loretta McLaughlin, that the stranglings were the work of one man—the other, by Lieutenant Donovan, Chief of Homicide, the hard-nosed professional police view that, until proved otherwise, these were separate murders with elements of imitation because of so much publicity, and should be treated as unrelated crimes even while police remained alert for similarities.

Donovan, a police official with twenty-three years' experience and himself the son of a police officer who had spent forty years on the Boston force, was a huge, taciturn man of forty-seven whose pale blue eyes rarely changed expression even when he smiled. He spoke out of knowledge of some three hundred homicide investigations. Of course, he asserted, the women were mainly living alone, because women living alone were the easiest prey. Of course there had been no screams, because the man who strangled them used the simplest, most universal method—the arm choke, or garrote, seizing them from behind about the neck in the crook of his arm.* Of course stockings, brassieres, and the like had been used, undoubtedly after the women had been rendered unconscious, because these natural ligatures were always available on the scene. As for gaining entry into locked apartments—in some cases the locks were faulty (Juris Slesers had forced open his mother's door with a shove of his shoulder), in others the assailant might have used a celluloid or plastic strip to slip the lock, and in still others, the women themselves might have opened their doors expecting a delivery boy or repairman. And police knew only too well, Lieutenant Donovan added, how surprisingly many woman, if they are rung from the vestibule below, simply press their buzzer to open the door and wait expectantly for whoever it might be.

What Bottomly had in mind, after discussion with police experts, was a reversal of usual detective practice. Generally, given a crime, police look for persons capable of committing it, persons who use a particular "M.O.," or method of operation. Criminals hold pretty much to their own specialties. The breakers-and-enterers—the "B and E" men—are burglars. They break into houses and shops. Some work only shops; some work only the first floor of houses; some work only second stories; some concentrate on apartments, specializing in entering via fire escapes and through roof trapdoors; some use keys, made by impression, or manage in other ways to force open locks; but however they operate, they restrict their activities to "B and E."

Similarly, purse snatchers and pickpockets hew to their own line. This explains why the victim of a pickpocket frequently finds his wallet returned a few days later, discovered by some passerby in the alley or ashcan where it had been tossed. The cash is gone, of course, but the valuable credit

---

* Dr. Luongo, the medical examiner who had performed most of the autopsies, had often stated privately—it was not something to be blared aloud—how easy it is to kill by strangling. In ancient times the Roman robber killed quickly, without much fuss, by exerting pressure on the neck arteries carrying blood to the brain. It brought complete incapacity in three seconds. Nor did it require great strength.

cards, personal blank checks and keys to car, office, and home have not been taken. The criminal has no interest in forgery, car theft, or burglary. He is a pickpocket.

Such certainties help immensely in crime detection for they enable police to concentrate their search.

But what was one to do about the Strangler?

A check showed that nearly five hundred sex offenders capable of such murders had been released in Massachusetts alone within the last year. Thousands more, certainly, had been freed in other states. Some idea of the scope of the sex offender problem could be gained by FBI figures issued only the year before: a sexual assault of one kind or another took place every twenty-eight minutes, day and night. Since in the Strangler murders one was dealing with a demented man, who might have no record as a sex criminal or might never have been arrested, the field was limitless. And as he obviously worked alone, and belonged to no criminal ring or gang, one could not turn to stool pigeons, disgruntled associates, or confidants who might in a drunken moment reveal information to a bartender who in turn could tip off the police.

In short, the usual procedures seemed to hold little hope.

But if one assumed that the women were not accidental victims but had been chosen, the thing to do was to work from the victims outward as well as to look among criminals for the assailant. That meant examining each victim's life back to her birth until every knowable fact had been ascertained about her. Every suspect would have to be examined similarly, with the same thoroughness, to determine if he possessed the psychopathology required to commit such a grotesque crime. The answers must be found either in the lives of the victims, or in the lives of the suspects, or both.

As all this material flowed into the casebooks, and the casebooks grew, they would be studied continuously by the Medical-Psychiatric Committee to determine what the victims had in common, as well as to paint a personality portrait of the killer or killers.

Once every fact was gathered, how were they to be correlated? Sometimes Bottomly thought his dream verged on the fantastic. Yet it was practicality itself. The data already gathered, and the additional data produced as investigators probed deeper and deeper into each case, could be fed into a digital computer. This would include every important date in the victim's life: every name in her address book; every place of employment; every restaurant she frequented, every concert she attended, every hospital in which she had been a patient, or worked, or in which she had visited friends. It would include the schools she attended, the names of her classmates, the church in which she was confirmed, the names of her teachers, the names of every clerk who waited on her in shops and department stores, her physicians, dentists, lawyers, and professional men, even the accountants who made out her income tax—in short, *every human contact in her life.*

Then the police would feed into the machine similar material relating to every suspect, hoping that at some juncture two facts, two numbers, two pieces of data would coincide: suspect and victim would have been at the same place at the same time. Or have a friend in common. Or have been served by the same salesman.

At least it would be one clue, one tiny, usable clue!

Bottomly suited action to the word. A computing firm in Concord that was involved in the nation's space program volunteered its services to work with Robert Roth, Director of the Massachusetts Bureau of Identification. As new pages were added to the casebooks, the information was transferred to punch cards, and experts began preparing it for the electronic brain. It meant, as of January 1964, beginning to process information from ten thousand source documents figuring so far in the investigation. Roth established other categories for the computer: the victim's race, religion, occupation and hobbies, clothing worn at time of attack, date and time of death, day of the week, position of body when found, where in room, type of room, window blinds up or down— every physical variable.

A second project would be devoted to suspects alone, emphasizing each man's environment, his relationship with his mother and with women in general, his sex habits, and any abnormal facet of his behavior.

The offer came from a well-known Boston industrialist who wished to remain anonymous. Why not make use of Peter Hurkos, the famous Dutch mystic, who had reportedly helped solve twenty-seven murders in seventeen countries? He was now in the United States. Police in half a dozen American cities had already made use of him. If Hurkos would accept the assignment, Boston should jump at the chance. There would be no cost to the Commonwealth, for the writer of the letter was so convinced of Hurkos' abilities that he and a group of friends would pay Hurkos' fee—perhaps a thousand dollars or so—and expenses. For eighteen months the police had tried everything they knew—in vain. Since orthodox measures had failed, why not try unorthodox measures? What had one to lose?

Why not? thought Bottomly. But there was a problem. To be accused of taking seriously seers, psychics, and others with "supernatural" powers, to accept their evidence against a citizen, smacked of witchcraft. And in Boston, of all places, which had never forgotten the Salem witch trials of the 1690's. Bad enough for Bottomly to risk certain criticism but to place Brooke in this position seemed unfair.

On the other hand, Bottomly, a rational and realistic man who possessed a strong vein of skepticism, had witnessed phenomena which made him think twice before dismissing anything in human experience as nonsense. Once, at a party in wartime London, a gray-haired woman had been introduced to him. She was a psychic, his host said, with a smile. She had shaken hands pleasantly with Bottomly, asked for his wallet, and holding it between her palms, proceeded in a heavy Hungarian accent to tell him facts about his early childhood that not even friends at home knew. He and the woman had never met before, nor was there any likelihood that their paths could have crossed. She was a refugee just escaped from Budapest; they had no mutual acquaintances. In any event, much of what she told him he had all but forgotten himself.

Putting that aside, he had long been intrigued by telepathic experiments conducted by friends in the National Aeronautic and Space Administration laboratories at Cambridge. It was known that the human brain generates a measurable electrical current. These scientists proceeded on the theory that if the brain could send forth such impulses, it was conceivable that it could also pick them up. Could not such emanations be produced by thought? And might not sensitivity to them be more developed in some persons than in others? In NASA files, he had been told, was a documented case of a human sender and receiver—that is, two men telepathically attuned to each other—who had worked together during a critical period in the war. One had been smuggled into occupied France, the other sent to London. A number of times, at a fixed hour, they had attempted to communicate. One, seated in his apartment on the outskirts of Paris, concentrated on sending a specific message; the other, seated in a London flat, concentrated all his powers on receiving it. Several times the message had come through. The team was not always successful but their rate of success far exceeded the wide range of mathematical probability.

On Bottomly's own staff, Detective Tommy Davis, an expert on electronic matters, had once reported a fascinating experiment in infrared phenomena. At eleven o'clock one night he photographed a parking lot filled with automobiles. At 1 A.M. when the owners had driven their cars away and the lot was empty, he took another photograph from the same vantage point, this time under infrared light. It showed the lot crowded with the automobiles that had been there two hours before! The images had remained—to be picked up by infrared rays. The two photographs were identical. The one taken under infrared was somewhat ghostly, but the negative was clear enough to discern the make of car and even the license numbers.

Who was to say what impressions—visual, psychic, the products of reality or men's thoughts—existed all about us, only waiting for an instrument sensitive enough to pick them up?

Now this man Hurkos . . .

A book entitled *The Door to the Future,* by Jess Stearn,* with a long chapter on Peter Hurkos, had been forwarded to Bottomly with other material on the Dutch mystic.

Bottomly glanced through its pages. Hurkos, he read, was known in occult circles as a psychometrist—that is, one who divines facts about an object or its owner by touching or being near the object. A man in his forties, he had originally been a house painter in Holland. In 1943 he fell thirty-five feet from a ladder, fractured his skull, and lay in a coma for three days. When he regained consciousness, he was in a hospital bed and a doctor was leaning over him. Hurkos' first words were, "Doctor, don't go! Something terrible will happen!"

The physician who, it turned out, had been planning to take a trip abroad, joked with Hurkos, then left the country—and was killed shortly after. During Hurkos' recuperation he began telling fellow patients and nurses about themselves; his fame grew after he left the hospital; he was called in to find one lost child, then another, then missing persons, stolen property—he had helped Scotland Yard find the stolen Stone of Scone, a national treasure—and finally, murderers. He was said to have solved one murder simply by pressing the victim's photograph against his forehead. Taken to the scene of a crime, Bottomly read, Hurkos often solved it, some speculated, because of his extreme sensitivity "to the auras, emanations, or odic life force clinging to that scene."

Bottomly read on. In Miami, in October 1958, a cabdriver had been shot to death in a downtown street. A few hours later, a Navy commander had been fatally shot in his apart-

* Doubleday and Company, New York, 1961.

ment not far away. Both had been killed by bullets from a .22 automatic. Hurkos had been sent for; he seated himself in the dead man's taxicab and at once described the murderer in detail to Detective Lieutenant Thomas Lipes, Chief of Miami's Homicide Squad.

Bottomly acted. He asked his Administrative Assistant, Bill Manning, to check at once with the police chiefs cited in the book, and especially with Lieutenant Lipes, known as a hard-headed, no-nonsense police official. When Manning reached him on the telephone, it was obvious that Lipes had been greatly impressed by Hurkos. "He helped us tremendously on two homicides," Lipes told Manning. "I know you people are skeptical up in Boston about things like this, but believe me, this man has something you and I haven't got."

Okay, thought Bottomly. We'll try him on condition that Commissioner McNamara and other police officials agree that Hurkos' work will not interfere with theirs. Bottomly himself was confident of that: all investigations would go on as before; this would simply be an added investigation. Brooke had promised the people of Boston that "everything humanly possible" would be done to find the Strangler. Even if Hurkos had no special powers, surely bringing into the search a new mind, an investigator accustomed to out-of-the-ordinary murder cases, a man who had worked with police throughout the world, should help. Even if Hurkos only succeeded in irritating Boston detectives so that they redoubled their efforts to prove him a fraud, the increased activity might be advantageous.

Bottomly strode into an outside room and tossed *The Door to the Future* on Bill Manning's desk. "Read up on this fellow Hurkos, and get hold of him," he said. "I want to talk to him."

Late Wednesday night, January 29, Detective Sergeant Leo Martin drove Bottomly to the Providence, Rhode Island, airport to pick up Peter Hurkos, arriving from California. Manning had traced him to the home of Glenn Ford, the actor, who, Hurkos said, planned to play him in a film based on his career as the world's best-known psychometric detective.

Bottomly had spoken to Hurkos, who had agreed to come to Boston on the condition that no publicity of any kind appear until he had completed his work and left town. Otherwise, he said, the crowds of curiosity seekers would constantly impede him.

Arranging this *sub rosa* visit to Boston had taken all of Bottomly's ingenuity. Though Police Commissioner Mc-

Namara doubted strongly—profanely would be a more accurate word—that Peter Hurkos could be of any help, he would not stand in the way. Bottomly had also managed to obtain a pledge of secrecy not only from local newspapers, radio, and television, but from *The New York Times* and the New York *Herald Tribune,* the Associated Press, United Press International, *Time,* and *Newsweek,* as well as from every correspondent of foreign newspapers and magazines. Save in time of war, so complete a blanketing of the world's communication media was unheard of: it had taken two days of meetings in Brooke's office to do it, but it had been done. And finally, lest Peter be recognized in Boston's busy Logan Airport, Bottomly had asked him to land at Providence, forty-four miles away.

The plane had arrived early: Hurkos had to be paged. In the corner of the terminal Bottomly and Sergeant Martin saw a giant of a man, some four inches taller than Bottomly—which meant at least six feet eight—wearing a huge cowboy hat, yellow cowboy boots and trousers, a wide leather belt, and a yellow-fringed leather shirt. The figure rose and bore down on them.

"I'm Jim Crane," he announced. He looked at them from a pair of suspicious blue eyes. "You got any identification?"

Bottomly knew of Crane. This man was a West Coast speculator who had taken Peter's advice on a gold mine investment, and had been so delighted with the result that he had appointed himself Peter's bodyguard. In a deep side pocket Bottomly made out the bulge of a revolver.

After satisfying himself as to their credentials, Crane vanished in the direction of the balcony restaurant to return with a heavyset, heavy-jowled man about six feet tall, with curly black hair and darting black eyes—the celebrated Dutch mystic himself. He turned out to be a very engaging man, completely uninhibited, who spoke sharp, quick sentences, impatiently, in bad English, with a thick Dutch accent.

It was now nearly midnight. Bottomly wanted to keep Hurkos out of sight as much as possible, and rather than have him and his bodyguard stay in Boston, plans had been made for them to register under false names at the Battle Green Motel in Lexington, about fifteen miles from Boston. As they drove, Hurkos explained that he had discussed the Boston assignment with Glenn Ford, as well as with Doris Day, who was to play opposite Ford in the film, and with actress Katherine Grayson. He had helped Miss Grayson search for a fortune in jewels stolen from her Palmer House suite in Chicago some weeks before. The three Hollywood stars urged him, Hurkos said, to accept the Boston assignment: he owed it to his talent to help the people of Boston.

En route to Lexington, they stopped for coffee. Sitting in the roadside restaurant, Peter suddenly looked up from his cup at Sergeant Martin, seated opposite him. "Who is Katherine?" he demanded.

Martin, taken aback, said, "That's my mother's name—that's the only Katherine I know."

"You tell her, take doctor's advice," said Peter. He slapped his legs dramatically. "I am worried about her legs. Very bad varicose veins—she should do what family says."

Leo stared at him, round-eyed. "That's just what we've been telling her!" he exclaimed. "But she won't go to the hospital. You're right, Peter, you're darn right." He continued to stare at him.

Peter nodded. "One good thing, Leo. It is good she got those glasses two months ago. That left eye, very bad."

Leo's mouth was open. "How'd you know that?" he managed to ask.

Bottomly thought, So this is how a seer operates. O.K. Let's say he worked up information about the men on my staff. But Leo's mother? And why Leo? How did he know Leo would come with me tonight?

Peter was away and running now. "Very religious woman, your mother, Leo. Mass every morning, Novenas every Wednesday—" Leo nodded wordlessly. Peter paused for a loud sip of coffee. Unexpectedly he bent over and jabbed his thumb into his own back. "Your wife," he said. "Bad back. Here. Hurts all the time. Right?"

Leo could only nod, look at Bottomly, then at Peter again.

"Know how she got it?" Peter asked conversationally. He obviously enjoyed the effect he created. Leo shook his head. "She's had it ever since I know her," he said. Peter said, "She little girl, five and a half, she fall down stairs on bottom of spine. Not break, but always hurt." He finished his coffee, and smiled affably. "I am ready now."

Bottomly helped the two men check into the motel. "Tomorrow one of my men will call on you," he told Hurkos. "He'll be my liaison with you, be with you all the time you're here, give you whatever you want, take you anywhere you want to go." Bottomly had decided that if he wanted to judge Peter Hurkos objectively, it would be better not to work closely with him, but receive reports from others. "His name is Julian Soshnick. I'll tell you what he looks like so you'll recognize him—"

"No, no," said Peter impatiently. "Not necessary. I tell

you." He described a dark-eyed, restless man of medium height, about thirty, who walked with his toes pointed out so that the back of his heels were worn down on the outside, "and never wears hat because it mix up his hair."

It was Bottomly's turn to stare. This was Assistant Attorney General Julian Soshnick to a T—even to the private little vanity about his hair. Why should Peter Hurkos know—how *could* he know—Soshnick? Even if one granted the improbable—that Peter, never before in Boston, had somehow familiarized himself with every member of his staff, as well as with the character, appearance, and ailments of their mothers, wives, and the rest—why should he know this man? For Julian was not a member of Bottomly's investigative team. He had not been working on the stranglings. He was one of the forty-four attorneys in Eminent Domain, he had come into the picture at the very last moment because he was capable, resourceful, and could be counted upon to cope with the unexpected. He lived in Lexington, and it had been he who arranged for Peter and Crane to stay incognito at the motel, which was owned by a friend of his.

But Bottomly had not decided to enlist Soshnick's help until a few hours earlier, at which time Peter Hurkos was already on the plane en route from California!

A Hollywood director might have been hard put to set up a more intriguing scene than the one that occurred the next afternoon in the large suite occupied by Peter Hurkos and his bodyguard, Jim Crane.

Hurkos sat on a chair, facing the bed, on which Julian Soshnick had arranged a dozen or more sets of photographs, face down. Next to him, hovering over a tape recorder, sat Detective Tommy Davis; next to him, attending another tape recorder—"for our own records"—sat Jim Crane; his revolver, a .44 Magnum, was prominently on hand on an adjacent end table. George Indignaro, police stenographer, sat at a desk nearby to make the official transcription.

Soshnick had driven up a few minutes before. He had brought, in the locked trunk of his car, two large boxes. One contained the nylon stockings, scarves, blouses—the "decorations"—used by the Strangler on his victims. The other held nearly three hundred eight-by-ten police photographs of the strangling scenes, in sets of from fifteen to twenty-five in each case. Peter had asked for both—objects he would use in his psychometry. The photographs, each set placed in an identical plain manila cnvelope, were handed to Soshnick that morning by Bill Manning who had himself taken them from the locked files in the Attorney General's office five minutes earlier. Soshnick removed them from the envelopes without looking at them and then carefully placed them in stacks, face down, on the bed.

"O.K., Peter," he said. "It's all yours."

Peter bent over the bed. On a coffee table to his left, he had a glass of Scotch on ice, which he had requested: throughout the afternoon he sipped at it from time to time. Now he moved his right hand, palm down, in quick circles about two inches above the photographs. Suddenly his hand slammed down on one stack. "This phony baloney!" he cried. "This not belong!"

Soshnick, with an embarrassed grin, picked up the set and turned over the photographs. He had included as a control a set of photographs of a solved murder case—a woman who had been strangled by her husband.

Peter looked at him fiercely for a moment, then burst into laughter. "Ah, you think, This Hurkos a faker. I show him up, eh?" He turned back to his work. His hand circled again, hovered over one stack, then came down hard on it. "This one, this top one, show dead woman, legs apart—I see her, one hand up, one down, funny way—Here, I show you." He got on the floor, rolled on his back, spread his legs, crooked one knee, put one arm up, one down, turned his head sideways with a slight grimace on his face. "That woman like this!"

Soshnick had marked the pile by placing a cigarette on it. Now he turned the top photograph right side up. It was of Anna Slesers photographed as she had been found. There were at least twenty photographs in the stack: only three were of the victim, the other seventeen showing apartment scenes, entrances and exits, the building's exterior. But the top one was, as Peter said it would be, that of a woman precisely in the position he described.

Peter scrambled triumphantly to his feet. Again he brought his hand down on a stack: again he demonstrated the posture . . . once more the photograph was that of a victim—this time, Beverly Samans as she was found on her bed in Cambridge, one leg extended, the other hanging over the edge—exactly as Peter now lay.

Repeatedly Peter did the same thing.

"O.K., give me stockings," he said. He moved them—the stockings, scarves, brassieres, and blouses—through his hands slowly, rubbing the cloth as though gauging the quality of a fabric. "I feel man who killed!" he cried. "I see him . . . he is not too big, five feet seven, eight—" he stopped long enough to whip out a pencil and make a mark on the wall "—he weigh a hundred and thirty or forty pounds." He had a "spitzy nose"—a sharp nose, Jim Crane interpreted, in a whisper—a scar on his left arm where he had been hurt by machinery. Peter thought he had worked with some kind of diesel engine. "Something wrong with thumb—no feeling, bad skin, something—" Peter spoke swiftly, in spurts. "I see pictures like television," he had said earlier. "They go by, I tell you as they go by." He paused. "I see girl, she love to dance, not old, young girl . . ." Then, in excitement, "I see man—he come from hospital, then down basement—he with stick, he use stick first to switch around room and break curtains, then put stick in vagina, and he masturbate. I not sure she dead yet. I see very bad damage inside. Maybe she unconscious from strangling? I not sure she dead . . ."

"Did he personally assault her?" a detective asked quietly.

"No, no, I see masturbation, sperm on blanket, on body. Man wild . . ."

No one spoke. Peter's eyes were focused on the far wall, his thumb and two fingers of his right hand testing the cloth as his left slowly drew it through his hand. There was no doubt of it. He was describing, as though he had been there when she was found, nineteen-year-old Mary Sullivan's body, with details known only to a handful of detectives. "One thing I not sure," Peter was saying. "He come in back or front door? But he know way. I see bandages . . . He have pain in head, he hear things, he put bandages on head for pain . . . It hurts, he put stocking on head, it hurts, it hurts, he is screaming out . . ." Peter almost shouted: "Give me towel, I show you—"

A detective dashed into the bathroom and returned with a bath towel. Peter seized it, tied it tightly about his forehead and down across his ears. "This is what he do!" He threw himself on the floor and thrashed about, flailing his arms, crying in a piercing voice, "Oh! Oh! Oh!" He got to his feet. "This is what I see so clear." Then, sharply, "What I don't see, I don't tell."

There was no sound save the hum of the tape recorder and Peter's heavy breathing after his exertion. Still looking into space, he ran his fingertips over a blouse. "This man—he not sleep in bed," he said. "No mattress, nothing. He sleep flat on floor." "Why?" someone asked. "God," Peter replied cryptically. "You mean to punish himself?" "I don't know, I don't know," said Peter. "What's his complexion?" he was asked. "Not a colored man. White," he said quickly. "But . . . he make it colored." A pause. "He love shoes. He love shoes."

Why did he love shoes? "I don't know," said Peter. "Maybe he masturbate in shoes. Something wrong with this man. He look in suitcase not for money but for shoes. The body walk on shoes. God don't walk on shoes. This is how man's mind works . . ." His words came swiftly. "When he kill her, she must have shoes on. But he must be clean to God. God walks barefoot, so he take off shoes, then kill her . . . He wash hands in toilet, never take bath, always wash in toilets, not sleep on bed, sleep on floor, after killing he sleep like God sleep, on iron, on steel, on pins—"

He stopped. "I need map."

Soshnick grabbed a Boston telephone directory and tore out the folded city map bound in back. Peter drew a small circle. "I see man live here . . . Yes, he is priest—" There was a gasp from the detectives. "I see priest . . . no, he is not priest, he doctor from hospital, no, no—not doctor, not priest, he look like priest, he dress like priest, I see him with many priests." He was speaking jerkily now. "I see him in white building, many windows—" The tip of his index finger moved again and again over the Newton-Boston area, in which were located Boston College, a Jesuit institution, the residence of Cardinal Cushing, and St. John's Seminary. "This man, he get soup, free soup, he no pay," came Peter's voice. "He speak French, English—I heard French accent—he talk like girl, like this—" Peter's voice became a falsetto. Suddenly his face changed. He began to curse. "God damn, this no good son of a bitch, he a pervert!" Peter's wrists went limp, and he imitated an obvious homosexual.

He tossed the map on the bed. "I stop now." He seemed utterly exhausted. Soshnick noted with surprise that though the room was not warm, Peter was soaked with perspiration. Now he slumped into a chair. Jim Crane produced a big Dutch cigar, and solicitously lit it for him. Someone else replenished his drink. Peter rested.

Soshnick had watched the man's remarkable exhibition with great interest. Having undergone twelve years of psychoanalysis, he felt qualified to face up to any type of human behavior. Now he thought, Careful. Don't be carried away. Don't attempt any value judgments. This man obviously has some type of sensitivity. Question: how far does it go? He knew nothing of Peter's feat the night before—describing him so accurately, sight unseen—because Bottomly had kept this to himself lest it influence Soshnick's objectivity.

At this point—it was now late afternoon—a detective arrived, apologetic for being late. His car had broken down on the way from Boston, he said. Peter perked up. He rose from

his chair, cigar in hand, walked up to the newcomer, and
pointed a deliberate finger at him. His voice was strong again.
"You not late because of car; you late because you get
fucked!"

The detective's jaw dropped.

"You think I kid you, eh?" Peter addressed himself to the
entire room. "I tell you what happened, you laugh. His boss
tell him two, three hour ago, 'You go to Lexington, work
with this fellow, this nut, this Hurkos.' He say, 'Gee, boss, I
got date, I don't want to work.' Boss say, 'You got to work.'
So, what you do?" He stared accusingly at the detective.
"You call girl friend and say, 'Honey, I got to work tonight, I
can't see you,' and she say, 'Aw, why you not come over on
way to work?' so you go to her house, she very pretty girl,
twenty-eight, twenty-nine, she divorce her husband, he give
her house, you say, 'I got to work with that mind reader, that
faker, that Hurkos guy.' Right? Right?"

The other's mouth hung open.

"She say, 'Before you leave, honey, you have cup of
coffee.' You go into kitchen with her, she bend down to get
coffeepot in cabinet, you grab her, you push her on kitchen
table and you fuck her. Then you come here. That why you
late. Right?"

There was absolute silence. Every man in the room seemed
frozen in his place, all staring at the detective. If only he
would laugh in Peter's face and walk away, so that all things
would be as they were before. But he was like a man in
shock. His eyes widened, and continued to widen until the
whites showed all around, as if someone had placed tooth-
picks between his lids. He managed to close his mouth, then
open it again to utter a choked "Ahhhhh . . . Ahhhhhh."

Peter looked at him. "That girly pretty damn good, eh?
You see, I no faker," and walked back to his chair.

It was almost half an hour before the detective could re-
cover. He sat in one corner, surrounded by fellow detectives,
repeating to every question dazedly, "That's right! That's
right!" He would not—or could not—say more.

Friday morning Soshnick and the detectives drove Peter
into Boston to discuss with Bottomly what was to be done
now. On the way, Peter, talking animatedly in the back seat,
leaped up as though he had been stung. "Terrible, awful terrible thing happen here! Murder!" Soshnick brought the car
to a screeching stop. They were on Commonwealth Avenue.
Davis jumped out, inspected the number of the apartment
house they had just passed, and returned. It was No.

1940—1940 Commonwealth Avenue. Nina Nichols had been strangled in this building.

The men drove the rest of the way in silence.

Bottomly, who had arranged to see them in his own law office, away from the State House, had not yet arrived and while they waited for him, Sergeant Leo Martin came in. "Peter, what do you make of this?" He handed him a letter.

Instead of reading it, Peter crumpled it in his fist, his eyes closed in concentration. Suddenly he sat bolt upright in his chair, and perspiration began to pour down his face. "By God, son of a bitch, he do it! This the one—he the murderer!"

Soshnick grabbed the crumpled letter and spread it flat. Everyone read over his shoulder. Printed in pencil and signed "Thomas P. O'Brien" (which is not his real name), it was addressed to the Boston College School of Nursing and dated a few days before. The sender's address, in the upper right-hand corner, was in the very area Peter Hurkos' finger had gone over again and again on the map.

It read:

Boston College School of Nursing
Boston College
Chestnut Hill
Newton 67, Mass.
c/o Nurse Director

Dear Madam:

I have a difficulty (please pardon this pencil script) perhaps you'll smile when you read about it; but I'm coming to you because I think you can help me.

I'm a BC grad, and when I look at the years I've been out of school, "I stroke my longish beard"; I've tried selling, off and on, for quite some time, and now I'm still in the selling field; I even made a do or die try to become a newspaper comic strip artist, only to fail, and before the year is out I hope to have another try at it: drawing a comic strip for kids, and such a comic strip that even grown-ups will like it.

My reason for writing now, is to say that I am a bachelor and for some long time I've wanted to meet a good Catholic nurse who might have graduated from nursing school about 1950; even an undergrad about that time would be O.K.; one who is working in or near Boston.

I've even had the idea of doing an article on this class,

interviewing as many as possible, to learn their opinions and experiences, in training and in the field since graduation; then offering some nursing publication such an article.

Perhaps while interviewing, I might see a nurse who might like me as much as I'd like her, and if so, we could begin a friendship that might lead to the altar.

Chances maybe, however, that very few nurses of the year 1950 (grads) are eligible, or might even consider me eligible. O.K. If there are such, maybe there is a better way to meet them than the way I have suggested above.

I'd be glad to call at the office to see you about this, if you wish; at any rate, may I hear from you? If you'd like to, you could call Dr. Richard H. Wright, of 1190 Beacon St., Brookline; he has known me for many years.

With every best wish,

I am,

Sincerely,

Thomas P. O'Brien

"Yes!" cried Peter. "He the man!"

The letter had come to Boston College, Sergeant Martin said, and they had turned it over to Boston police who had sent it to Homicide that very morning. Sergeant Martin had picked it up on his way over.

In the midst of the excitement, Bottomly, who only now had been able to get from under the mass of material pouring in on him at the State House, arrived. He immediately telephoned Dr. Wright, who was Cardinal Cushing's own physician. Yes, he knew O'Brien; he was a man in his fifties, with a history of mental illness; he had many problems. Bottomly put several men on the phones. The state police produced a record on O'Brien: as far back as 1962 someone had sent in an anonymous tip on him. A brother had attempted to persuade him to commit himself for treatment. O'Brien had briefly been in a monastic order—he had lived with the Trappist Monks at St. John's Seminary, but the discipline was too much for him. It was a French order; many spoke with a French accent; its members dressed like priests, they were fed bread and soup . . . Yes, he had worked as a salesman, a door-to-door salesman, of ladies' shoes. More specifically, nurses' shoes.

As each of these facts was elicited—mental illness, the French accent, the men like priests, the soup—those in the

room grew more and more tense. Now Bottomly and Soshnick looked at each other in an uneasy silence. Door-
to-door—this gave access to apartments. Nurses' shoes—was
this the long-sought hospital link? Would not the older victims at one time or another have worn nurses' shoes?

Both Bottomly and Soshnick are fast-triggered men, and it
was a question now which was the more excited. Soshnick
grabbed Bottomly's arm, "Jack, we may have something—"
Now half a dozen men were on the telephones. Soshnick was
pacing back and forth, muttering, "We've got to find some
way to pick him up, to have Peter see him—"

Bottomly assigned Detective Davis and Peter to call on
Thomas O'Brien—more than two men might frighten
him—and see what they could learn. They would say they
came in response to his letter. They found the address, a di-
lapidated rooming house, and rapped on a door on the second floor. After a moment, it opened little more than an
inch: they caught a glimpse of the wan face of a slight, middle-aged, pinch-nosed man. A pair of pale blue eyes peered
over the chain at them.

"Yes?" The voice was high-pitched and effeminate.

"Mr. O'Brien, you wrote to Boston College—" Davis
began.

"I don't want to see anyone," the man said, and shut the
door. They heard the bolt drawn, then the scrape of a chair
as it was jammed into place under the doorknob.

Peter could hardly contain himself as they went down the
steps. "Jesus Christ, he the man! He the murderer!"

Twenty minutes later they held council with Bottomly.
How could they question O'Brien? They could not arrest him.
There were no criminal charges against him. Soshnick suddenly leaped up. He had remembered a state statute that allowed a physician to commit any person acting oddly to a
mental institution—if the superintendent agrees—for ten
days' observation. Once O'Brien was hospitalized, they could
question him. Soshnick would also obtain a warrant to search
O'Brien's room for evidence that might link him with the
stranglings.

The machinery was set in motion. Peter, slumped in a
chair, seemed exhausted. Could he be driven back to his hotel
to rest the remainder of the day?

As they walked to his car later, Soshnick saw Crane beck-
oning him. He fell in step with the Californian. "When Peter's stimulated like this, he often talks in his sleep," the other
said. "You fellows might get something valuable—"

"Done!" said Soshnick. He decided he would stay that

night in Peter's suite, and set up a tape recorder at Peter's bed to take down anything he might say. He dropped back to chat with Peter, only to find himself violently shoved to one side. It was Jim Crane. Soshnick looked at him in amazement. "You were getting on his right, Mr. Soshnick," he said apologetically. Then he explained. Peter had asked the advice of three fellow psychics, two in Los Angeles, one in Chicago, before deciding to take the Boston assignment. His California colleagues saw nothing against it, but the Chicago seer felt troubled. "I see harm coming to you from the right," he told Peter. Peter had come anyway, but had Soshnick been observant, he would have noted that whenever Peter appeared in public, Crane always walked three steps ahead and to Peter's right, to shield him from whatever might menace him.

By this time Soshnick had given up attempting to make value judgments on Peter Hurkos. "Oh, I'm sorry," he said humbly. "I didn't know."

8

While Soshnick prepared for his all-night session with Peter Hurkos, Bottomly was poring over a report just brought to him entitled "David Parker." A dozen others lay on his desk, including the last-minute information from Donovan's men who had so far questioned hundreds of persons in connection with the Mary Sullivan murder.

At the moment, David Parker (which is not his name) intrigued Bottomly. What with Hurkos pursuing Thomas O'Brien, the shoe salesman, Detectives DiNatale and Mellon checking on Arnold Wallace and Paul Gordon, various committees—medical, computing, legal—already at work, Bottomly felt like a juggler trying to keep a dozen brilliantly spinning pinwheels in the air. But something had to be done immediately about Parker, because charges, however minor, had been brought against him. He was in police hands, and it would be possible, if one moved swiftly, to place him under psychiatric study.

The Parker story, as unfolded to Bottomly by Cambridge police, was as follows.

On Wednesday afternoon, January 22, Detective Sergeant Leo F. Davenport was typing notes at his desk at police headquarters, Cambridge, when he looked up to see Officer James Roscoe bring in a tall, slender, bearded youth in his early twenties. Bearded college students were no novelty in Cambridge, and this youth would have attracted no special attention save that his jet black hair, obviously dyed, was curled in ringlets pasted on his forehead; a large gold earring pierced his right ear; his face—his features were quite handsome—had been darkened by a suntan preparation, and he wore sandals on his bare feet—this in mid-January with the temperature well below freezing.

114

Davenport knew him as a brilliant former Harvard student who had caused Cambridge police trouble before.

"Hello, David," he said, and turned to Officer Roscoe. "What's it now?" Over the policeman's shoulder he could see in the anteroom a young girl, quite pregnant, watching nervously.

Roscoe, cruising through Harvard Square a few minutes before, had come upon a crowd watching David struggling to force a young lady—the girl in the other room—into his car. "Take your hands off this girl," Roscoe ordered him, whereupon David pulled her even more violently, shouting, "She's my wife and she'll go with me where I want her to go!"

His eyes looked dilated; he seemed like a wild man. The girl screamed, and as he fought with her his tweed jacket opened to reveal a dagger stuck in his belt. Roscoe grabbed him with one hand, pulled his gun with the other, and then took the dagger away. David loosed his grip on the girl and danced up and down in a very frenzy of protest. "Don't you dare stop me!" he cried. "I'm on my way to Hollywood."

The girl—it was his wife—managed to say, "Officer, I'm afraid of him—he's been acting strange for a long time."

Roscoe had arrested him on charges of disturbing the peace.

Sergeant Davenport was a sharp, lean, irreverent man in his early forties, who had twenty years' experience with Cambridge students behind him. He had spent months working—it was still his major task—on the murder of Beverly Samans. He was perhaps as well informed as any man on life in the Cambridge-Harvard area. It had not surprised him to discover that a woman living down the hall from Beverly, who had heard nothing the Sunday night of the murder, had been in bed with her boyfriend most of the evening, the TV turned up loudly so no one would suspect she was entertaining anyone; or that not far away lived a student from India who invited girls up to his room where, quoting Shakespeare on the ennobling qualities of suffering, he lashed them with a whip; or that Beverly herself (as Sergeant Davenport had determined) had a number of men friends, among them a distinguished professor known for the urbanity with which he had seduced several girls in his classes. Sergeant Davenport was accustomed to the many varieties of human behavior, and like his colleague Lieutenant Sherry in Boston, took much of it philosophically and even sympathetically.

Now he turned to Parker who had been listening to Roscoe's recital in high good humor.

"David, what the hell is the matter with you?"

"Nothing," said David lightly. "Why?" He was sitting on a wooden bench, drumming his fingers steadily on the side.

Sergeant Davenport looked at him. Only six weeks before David had been marched into the station house on the same charge—disturbing the peace. He had been going from house to house ringing doorbells, then careening through backyards, dancing and singing. He was under some kind of stimulant: his eyes seemed glazed, he rambled in his speech, he couldn't remember his address, he broke into sudden bursts of laughter. When asked his age, he retorted, "Last time I measured it, it was twenty-two." Once in his cell, he paced back and forth, laughing to himself.

At that time a check disclosed that he had been arrested two years before, in April 1961, while still a student at Harvard. Police had come upon him and four other boys "acting suspiciously." They searched them and found on David a homemade bomb—a foot-long piece of steel pipe, plugged at both ends and filled with gunpowder that he admitted he took from shotgun shells he had bought at Sears Roebuck. Attached was an ingenious battery device to detonate it. The other boys attended Harvard, too. According to one, David had been making bombs of this nature for weeks, giving them to students to explode at night on the Esplanade, the grassy walk bordering the Charles River, to startle the strollers and lovers under the trees.

At Harvard, David was regarded with awe as having an almost genius intelligence—his I.Q. ranged between 150 and 170.

Shortly after this, he was caught selling narcotics—including the dangerous mind-expanding drugs, mescaline and lysergic acid diethylamide, or LSD, the most powerful hallucinating compound known—to students in Harvard Square. He was promptly dropped from school. Then came his arrest six weeks ago, when he was dancing and singing in the streets; and now this altercation with his wife.

Something struck a chord of memory in Sergeant Davenport's mind. David's was not an ordinary beatnik costume. Then he remembered. More than twenty years ago, while stationed in the Navy in San Francisco, Sergeant Davenport had gone to see Paul Robeson, the Negro singer, in *Othello*. He had never forgotten Robeson's magnificent performance—nor his appearance.

There was no doubt of it—the dagger that was stuck in his waist, the earrings, the beard, the hair, the stuff on his face, and the sandals. "David," he said, "you look just like Othello."

David smiled broadly. "Bravo, Sergeant," he said. "You hit it. As a matter of fact, I'm living the part of Othello."

"Yes, you fit the picture perfectly, except for one thing—"

"I know," said David. "I don't put on enough Man-Tan to make my face as dark as the Moor's."

Why was he going about in public like this? David explained painstakingly he had formed a dramatic troupe. "We're getting ready to go to Hollywood," he said. "We're going to make a film showing why people should love policemen." He laughed.

Davenport said, "David, you don't have to go to Hollywood. You better go to a psychiatrist."

"I just did," said David with a smirk. "When I was arrested last month they sent me to Westborough Hospital but the doctors said I was sane."

Sergeant Davenport asked, "Why the dagger? That's carrying concealed weapons. You know it's against the law."

"Oh, it's just a stage prop," said David. "I carry it all the time so that when I display my talents I'll have it."

And the altercation with his wife?

"That's her fault," said David indignantly. "I'd just bought some champagne and cheese, I rented a sweet little car from Avis, and I wanted to take her out on a picnic. That's all."

"David," Sergeant Davenport said reasonably, "you know people don't go on picnics in January. It's too cold."

"It's never too cold to have fun," said David, impatiently. "She didn't want to come and I was trying to get her into the car." He stood up and danced a little hillbilly jig, at which point Sergeant Davenport decided there was no use in continuing the conversation, sent him to await court hearing, and turned to the girl.

She refused to come into the room until her husband had been led out. She was slight, which made her pregnancy seem even more advanced, and she was obviously terrified. "I'm scared to death of him," she said in a whisper. "He tried to strangle me once." She went on to tell how he had suddenly seized her in their bedroom and bent her back on the bed, both hands tightened on her throat . . . "It was awful!" she said. "His eyes were almost of one color, you could hardly tell the pupils from the whites, I think he was on LSD, his hands were actually around my neck—"

He had stopped as suddenly as he began. He pulled his hands back, stood up, said majestically, "I have decided I shall not strangle you," turned his back, and walked out of the room.

When had they been married? "Two weeks ago," she said,

without embarrassment. "January fourth." Automatically the date registered in Sergeant Davenport's mind. That was the day Mary Sullivan was strangled. The girl went on to explain that David believed the baby about to be born was not his but that of his closest friend. "And he insisted, just the same, on having him as his best man at our wedding. He's so strange!" She was too nervous to be questioned further and was permitted to go.

Sergeant Davenport thought, For a bride of two weeks, she's a long way gone—seven or eight months . . . In *Othello*, the Moor actually strangles his wife, thinking she betrayed him with his best friend . . . And David's more than a little hoppy, too . . .

He decided to check into David Parker. He ordered his court and probation records, and spent the next days interviewing the boy's former roommates and friends.

What Davenport had learned in this past week now held Bottomly's attention.

David was known as an oddball among his friends. He had studied drama, traveled to Europe, attended a school on karate. He told friends he took Methedrine, and more than once had tried LSD, which is far more potent and may cause psychoses in those who take it—sometimes permanent psychoses. When he was under the influence of these drugs, his friends actually feared him: one came upon him walking in circles in his room, striking his head against the walls, "speaking badly of himself." At Westborough Hospital where he had been sent a few weeks before, he had been found suffering from a "personality disorder," and after being given large doses of Thorazine, a powerful tranquilizer, had been discharged, although the court-appointed physician who recommended his hospitalization thought he was suffering from "acute schizophrenia."

There was a definite medical-hospital background. His father was a chemist, his mother a social worker. "He had a very strange childhood," one schoolmate said. "I don't think his father was around until he was three or so, and he was brought up by women, and nurses, and he hates them." He was known to be subject to wild fits of violence and intense anger.

Did David Parker possess the psychopathology of the Strangler? Bottomly wondered. Clearly this boy who not only sold but took dangerous hallucinating drugs, who experimented with deadly explosives, who married a girl he was convinced had betrayed him with his dearest friend, who hated women, who had once almost strangled his wife, whose I.Q. reflected superior intelligence, was emotionally disturbed—a dangerous and unpredictable man, especially when under the influence of drugs. Could he be capable of the Strangler's crimes? Could anyone but a man of superior intelligence have managed all that the Strangler had done without making a false step, or leaving a single clue, or betraying himself in any fashion?

What might be learned if David Parker could be carefully questioned and studied by a skilled psychiatrist without being aware that he was a suspect?

There was one door open to Bottomly and he used it. In Massachusetts any male over seventeen charged with a crime can, if his crime or his behavior warrant it, be sent for thirty-five days' psychiatric observation to the State Hospital at Bridgewater, Massachusetts, twenty-five miles from Boston. The hospital's role is to determine the defendant's competence to stand trial. Bridgewater deals almost solely with the courts: virtually every temporary patient behind its walls is a person under criminal indictment sent there for pretrial observation. On January 22, the day David was arrested, Judge A. Edward Viola in Cambridge had observed the strangeness of his manner (standing before him, David had leaped onto a table and begun his hillbilly jig) and had ordered him to Bridgewater.

Bottomly telephoned Ames Robey, Medical Director at the institution. Would Dr. Robey, himself a psychiatrist, give David Parker—and, in the future, any others who might be singled out by Bottomly—special attention? Would he and his colleagues examine and observe Parker with a view to eliciting material helpful in the strangling investigations?

Dr. Robey, precocious, pipe-smoking, scholarly, who at the age of thirty-five had been appointed to this important post only a year before, agreed. He and his associates would consider it part of their responsibility to the people of the Commonwealth. However, every safeguard would be taken to protect the civil rights of patients. (Dr. Robey was particularly interested in this, for one of his specialties was the legal aspects of psychiatry.) That meant if David Parker told Dr. Robey that he was indeed a murderer, this confession could not be used as legal evidence against him, particularly in the absence of a lawyer to advise Parker what to answer and what not to answer. Nor would Dr. Robey testify in court as to what he had learned during his examinations. He would deliberately make no detailed notes on his interviews to avoid any chance that these would be later used to deprive the patient of his rights.

What Dr. Robey, in effect, promised Bottomly was this:

If the persons you wish us to question are sufficiently lucid, or if by medication we can improve them so they can be lucid, we shall question them. If we elicit suspicious material, we shall forward it to you informally to guide you in your further investigations. If we find nothing suspicious, we shall report that as well. If, in our opinion, the suspect could not be capable of the stranglings, we shall say so. Our purpose is to help you find the guilty and eliminate the innocent.

Before Bottomly turned his attention to Peter Hurkos again, he sent Dr. Robey a long memo on the eleven stranglings, listing clues that might guide him and his associates in their interrogations. New facts were being elicited every day as both Lieutenant Donovan's Homicide Division and Bottomly's investigators pushed more deeply into each strangling. Dr. Robey would be kept up to the minute.

9

It was 4 A.M. Sunday, February 2, when Julian Soshnick, asleep in the room adjoining Peter Hurkos' in the Battle Green Motel in Lexington, suddenly awakened. Jim Crane was bending over him, flicking his ear. "He's started to talk," Crane whispered. "I've turned on the recorder—"

Soshnick tiptoed into the next room. Peter lay asleep, snoring gently. On his pillow, six inches from his face, rested the microphone leading to the tape recorder. Three detectives sat in the room, illuminated only by the cold moonlight filtering through a half-drawn window blind. Crane put his finger to his lips; the men waited.

Peter spoke. "Sophia morte . . . Sophia morte!" It was a deep, strained voice, then came five or six swift words in a foreign tongue. The voice did not sound like Peter's, nor had it any trace of his familiar Dutch accent. Then, the gentle snore again. No question of it, Peter was sound asleep. It was no act. He spoke once more. "Hallo, hallo!" A pause. "Engineero, engineero . . ." He began counting, "Una, dua, treya, Radio Internationale, W-two-D-K-one, W-two-D-K-one, hallo, hallo—" So would a radio ham announcer call out the letters of his station. Then again, slowly, sadly, the deep sepulchral voice, "Sophia mortica . . . Sophia mortica, Sophia—a—a . . ."

Soshnick tiptoed about making a quick whispered check. No one recognized the language. Soshnick himself knew a smattering of French, German, Latin, and Hebrew, and a little Spanish; it vaguely resembled Spanish, but whatever the tongue, the words obviously meant "Sophia dead" or "Sophia is dying" or "Sophia killed."

Sophia. Sophia. Although Soshnick was not too familiar with the individual stranglings, he had read up on the cases since being assigned to Peter. Sophia must refer to So-

121

phie—Sophie Clark, the Negro girl murdered on December 5, 1962, more than a year ago. Again, the gentle snores, interrupted by several short sentences in the same unfamiliar language.

"W-two-D-K-one, W-two-D-K-one, Radio Internationale, Radio Internationale," came Peter's words, intoned with almost metronomic precision. Suddenly his voice changed. It became high and feminine, almost whispery, a Boston voice speaking English with no trace of foreign accent: "I take the shoes off! Here is the body! I take the shoes off! I undress her! Oh, I go to church, I go to church. I do nothing wrong. I know what is right. I told you I do right." Almost petulantly, "I do right: I wash my hands in toilet."

Then, silence. His snores rose and fell. A detective gently picked up the microphone and whispered into it, for the record: "It is now four-fourteen A.M., February second, 1964. Peter Hurkos is sound asleep. He is talking in his sleep."

Peter began again, but now his voice dropped in pitch. It had almost a brogue, the heavy, matter-of-fact growl of a detective. "Yeah, you was right." Then, with a sigh, "No, I'm not mad at you. You wash your hands in toilet. I'm not mad." Soothingly, reassuringly: "Sure you go to heaven! Sure." He talked as if comforting a frightened child. Then, in a voice unexpectedly sly, cunning, almost like a man playing a children's game with children, "I find you through the toilets. I *find* you . . ."

A long silence. No one moved. Peter, the no-nonsense detective again: "You call this holy water? You're nuts! For the monks, eh? You are nuts!" Minutes passed. "And the monks don't like you? I don't blame them. Bring it to the monks, the toilet water? You make the cross in the toilet water?" Disgusted: "I tell you, you are nuts!"

The snores resumed, and he did not speak again.

After breakfast, Soshnick telephoned Bill Manning in Bottomly's office and reported what happened. Would Manning look through the Sophie Clark casebook and see if he could find anything bearing on this? Would he also check the call letters W2DK1? Julian was sending the tape into the office. Would they get a man from Berlitz to tell them what language Peter spoke—if it was a recognizable language—and translate what he said?

Later that day Manning reported back. "Julian, I won't comment on what I'm telling you. I am just telling it to you so you will know. Peter spoke Portuguese but the sentences were too fragmentary to make any sense except for the words

'Sophia dead.' Sophie Clark was a Negro, as you know, but we've learned that she was only half-Negro. Her father was Portuguese. There are no call letters W-two-D-K-one listed in any international registry we can find, but there is a small ham radio station in New Jersey with the call letters W-two-D-K. We made a little check on it. That's owned—" he paused, almost as if fighting to control his voice "—that's owned by a man who turned out to be Sophie Clark's cousin."

Soshnick looked at the receiver and hung up. If all that meant anything, it meant they must really give serious consideration to Peter's suspect. Now it was even more important not only to pick up the shoe salesman and question him, but to allow Peter to question him too—perhaps even break him down.

Early next morning Soshnick was at O'Brien's door. He was accompanied by a physician and Detective Davis and Officer Stephen Delaney—the latter recently appointed to Bottomly's task force. Because publicity would certainly attend picking up O'Brien, Peter was told to remain in his motel in Lexington, and out of sight.

O'Brien was not home. Soshnick had no doubt what to do. He telephoned Peter in Lexington. "He's not in his room," he said. "Where's he gone, Peter?"

"He go to church," Peter answered promptly. "He a religious nut. I see him walk into church now." He described the church, the kind of steeple, the neighborhood. "That can only be Our Lady of Victories," said Detective Davis. "It's about ten blocks from here."

Leaving Delaney on the scene in case O'Brien returned, they drove to the church. Services were ending: they made a careful search, but their man was not there. Again Julian telephoned Peter. "God damn, you just miss him," said Peter, in Lexington. "Go back—you find him in room."

When they arrived Delaney reported that O'Brien had walked in a few minutes before. "Did he say where he'd been?" Soshnick asked. Delaney nodded. "At church—Our Lady of Victories," he said, "I told him you were looking for him, and he said, 'I guess I'm in trouble now.' "

A moment later in response to their knock O'Brien opened the door. Soshnick formally introduced himself. "I'm from the Attorney General's office, these gentlemen are police officers, and this gentleman is a doctor. May we come in?"

"Yes, of course," said O'Brien. Then, in his high-pitched voice, "I'm so glad you came, finally."

Soshnick's mind flashed back to the notorious lipstick murders in Chicago in the 1940's, the scrawled message on the walls of the victim's apartment, "For heavens sake catch me before I kill more, I cannot control myself." When he realized that the single cot in the room had no mattress—only bedsprings—he felt a complete sense of unreality.

Was this the Strangler before them?

They saw a small, emaciated man who could not have weighed more than 130 pounds, about five feet seven—exactly the height Peter had marked off in his room in Lexington; he was in his mid-fifties, effeminate in manner, standing almost apologetically to one side, nervously rubbing his hands together. His nose was thin and sharp—"spitzy"—as Peter had said. On his left arm was a scar—as Peter had said. The thumb on his right hand was deformed—as Peter had said. Peter had been right in every detail.

The room was tiny, perhaps eight by ten, in considerable disorder, with books, pamphlets, artists' sketch pads piled everywhere. On a table were health foods—molasses, wheat germ, and the like.

The physician questioned O'Brien at some length. Yes, he had once tried to get himself committed: he had told his brother that he might have blacked out several times. The physician signed the commitment papers on the spot. Minutes later he and O'Brien were on their way to Massachusetts Mental Health Center, and the others were eagerly going through the shoe salesman's possessions.

It was, at first sight, a pathetic haul. Here was a penciled diary, the writing going off in all directions but recognizably the same as in O'Brien's letter, with dates indicating he had been keeping it almost from his college days. On one page, printed in huge capital letters, doubly underlined, were the words: ALWAYS RUN FROM TEMPTATION INSTANTLY! The entries told how O'Brien had sought to become a Trappist monk nearly twenty years before, but had failed. Through the years he tried one job after another, but was able to get mainly dishwashing and laundry jobs; sometimes he sold shoes. "I can't hold a job," he had written. "Total—sixty low-paying jobs, never more than a few weeks each. I have made a shambles of my life."

Then, a heading "Remarks Made To Me By Others." Soshnick read it, moved despite himself. "You're a menace. You're no good. You're a GD liar. You're a disgrace to Boston College. You're a womanish man. I'd rather see you dead drunk in the streets than see you as you are. (Spoken to me by my brother.) When are you going to get married, eh? So you like that boy? Ha, ha! People like you are hit from pillar to post. You're in mortal sin—filthy, rotten, dirty . . ."

This was followed by confession. "Once, while near Harvard, I looked at a girl, perhaps at her legs . . . At frequent occasions while walking in the street I struggle against the impulse to collide with a woman . . . I must stop beating my seed, and during sleep. I have tried various ways to stop this. I have been sleeping on the floor to control my improper acts in my sleep, but surely these I can't be responsible for." Then, later: "I am doing all that is humanly possible to master human nature and I know I am chaste at last. I am going on forty-four years, almost."

Soshnick turned another page. Peter, already telephoned that the coast was clear, would arrive any moment now to join the search. Soshnick could not put down the diary. "I get angry, so angry. Women sitting in doctor's offices exposing their legs. Men walking with their hands behind their backs, strolling before me. Women wearing tight-fitting dresses and highly scented with erotic perfumes . . . I felt I was under investigation, people watching me in the library. I went to see Dr. Flannigan. The advice I got was that I was imagining it. So I was advised to go to St. Elizabeth's Hospital for nerve treatments which turned out to be shock therapy."

On the last page there was a single entry, dated 1953. "Called Archbishop Cushing's home. Was told to snap out of it, that I was O.K. and given the Archbishop's blessing."

Soshnick looked up as Peter stormed in, more excited than anyone had seen him before. He dropped to his knees and began scuttling about the room, crawling under the cot, into the cramped closet, muttering under his breath, "This fellow, he put on paper all killings, we find it—" He snatched a pamphlet from the center of a pile, pressed it to his forehead. "This it!" he cried. He opened it. "Look!"

It was a text on Yoga with black-and-white drawings depicting the various positions. The first half was devoted to male figures, the second, to female. But in the second half, page after page of figures was completely blotted out with India ink. Peter jumped to his feet and held the pages against the light so that everyone could see visible, under the ink, the outlines of female figures, now seated cross-legged in the traditional lotus position, now with legs spread apart. Peter counted aloud. "One . . . two . . . three—" until he reached a triumphant "—eleven!" There must have been a dozen more pages with female illustrations, but only eleven had been blotted out.

One for each strangling.

In a bureau drawer Delaney found half a dozen men's scarves and ties tightly knotted together. In another they came upon a note pad with penciled sketches of apartment buildings, and on other pages, drawings of apartment interiors. One was a bathroom. An X had been drawn over the tub. Victim Jane Sullivan had been found in a tub. Another showed a living room and hall—the X was in the hall. Anna Slesers had been found in the hall of her apartment. Another scene showed a bedroom, an X on the bed, near the headboard. Mary Sullivan had been found propped against the headboard.

When Soshnick first set eyes on O'Brien he thought, Oh, Peter, you're way off here! What has this poor trembling little shoe salesman got to do with the stranglings? O'Brien's diary had made him even more doubtful. But—the eleven figures; and now all this . . .

The landlady appeared as they were leaving. Yes, this roomer was an odd one. She had taken the house over some months before and the previous owner, a woman, had warned her about O'Brien: "Never let yourself be alone with him." She herself knew little about him except that he never used the mattress—"I guess he sleeps on the floor, he must have a bad back"—and that he took showers with his shoes on. "Did you ever hear the like?" she demanded. "Wearing your shoes?" She had complained repeatedly that the metal cleats in his heels scratched the bathtub enamel, but Mr. O'Brien did not change his habits.

Peter, the man who had said, "He love shoes! He love shoes!" looked sharply at the others. "He the one," he said.

O'Brien's questioning at the Mental Health Center occupied the next two afternoons. First Soshnick alone questioned him, then Bottomly, Soshnick, and Peter, who was introduced as "Dr. Spitz," a Dutch psychologist. (The name was chosen in recognition of Peter's insistence on the Strangler's sharp, "spitzy" nose.)

It was a sad experience for everyone concerned.

O'Brien, with a hospital psychiatrist on hand, sat down on the edge of his bed, trembling most of the time, turning earnestly first to one and then the other as they interrogated him. He did not have to answer questions if he did not wish to, he was told. He could have a lawyer if he wanted one. No, he said, why should he need a lawyer? He was ready to tell them what they wished to know.

Why had he written the letter to the Nursing School, Bottomly asked.

O'Brien explained that it was the last of many attempts he had made to meet a Catholic girl. Ten years before he had joined the Correy Club in Cincinnati, conducted by the

Franciscan Fathers. It was a social correspondence club. Later, he joined the Scientific Marriage Foundation Club in Indiana, headed by Dr. Frank Crane; then the Boston College Catholic Marriage Club. None worked out for him. One club last August sent him the name of a nurse in Connecticut. He took a bus there, lunched once with her, and never saw her again. Once a woman came to Boston and telephoned him to meet her in her hotel room at eight o'clock in the evening. "I didn't like that, so I didn't keep the appointment." He finally wrote the Nursing Home, giving as a reference Dr. Wright, Cardinal Cushing's physician, because Dr. Wright once treated him for an ear ailment. He had had many operations for mastoid.

Yes, he had sold shoes, off and on for years. Nurses' shoes, women's orthopedic shoes. Only last January 7 he took a job in a shoe store but they dismissed him after half a day's work.

Peter interrupted. "You was fired because you have trouble with lady. When you fitted lady's shoe, she crossed legs—like this—and you get excited. You could not control yourself. That's why you fired."

"Well, I wasn't very comfortable, I guess," O'Brien said. He stopped. "Please, may I have a glass of water. My mouth is dry." He was given the water. "It wasn't that I wanted to do anything wrong, it's just that it was a new experience for me."

"You never get blackout when you see women with legs crossed?" Peter demanded.

"I don't recall anything like that, no."

Peter asked, "Tom, that fat monk with glasses, why he not like you, so you quit?"

Both Bottomly and Soshnick glanced at "Dr. Spitz." There had been no mention anywhere of a "fat monk with glasses."

"Oh, you mean the Trappist monk?" said Tom. "Well, the life there was very difficult, my ear hurt—"

Peter took another tack. "Do you know you have lost a button when you go into apartment to sell shoes to lady?"

"Lost a button?" O'Brien seemed completely puzzled.

"Yes, she invite you in for coffee, you go in, you lost button from jacket of suit. Right?"

No, no, said O'Brien. He had never been invited into a lady's apartment. He had never sold apartment to apartment—only store to store. When he lost his job January 7, he tried selling a line of shoes to hospitals and stores, but failed to make a single sale in the entire month.

He thought maybe "somebody was following me and stealing my customers." That might be because the police continually watched him. He wanted to turn to someone for help, and he went to Father Kenneth Murphy, of Rescue, Incorporated, who received telephone calls from people thinking of suicide. "I never wanted to harm myself," O'Brien said, "but ten years ago when things were kind of blue I prayed and asked God to take me out of this life, if it was His will. The good Lord decided I live a little longer."

Why should the police watch him?

"I don't know. Maybe because once in Providence I saw a very attractive girl walking and I thought I'd like to talk to her. I began walking toward her, then I realized it wasn't right to talk to a strange girl, so I turned and walked away before I reached her." Perhaps they watched him because on another occasion, when he was sitting on a bench in Providence State House, waiting to apply for unemployment insurance—he had attemped selling oranges from a cart, but that venture failed, too—a strange man sat down beside him, introduced himself as a physician, and "began pressing hard on the idea that I was a homosexual. I had all the signs of such a person, he said—those were his very words."

Julian said earnestly, "Tom, we've looked through your room, we know everything about you. God wants you to tell the truth. God knows you have been hurt, but you don't have to worry any more. Just tell the truth." With this Julian unexpectedly pushed a police photograph of Mary Sullivan's nude body, as she was found, in front of O'Brien. "Look, Tom, you know what I'm talking about. Don't be afraid, Tom—"

O'Brien was looking away, refusing to look at the photograph.

"No, no, Tom, you must look. Here—" He showed him a second, then a third.

Tom's face was gray. "I don't quite understand what you're talking about," he said, agitated. "You show me pictures, pictures of dead women, terrible, terrible, what do you mean?"

"How do you know they're dead women?" Julian demanded.

"I don't know but they look dead, so I guessed they were dead. Oh, they're terrible, terrible." He was trembling violently.

"Don't you remember this girl, Tom," Julian said, holding up Mary Sullivan's photograph. "Tom, don't you remember taking off her shoes, and then spreading her legs—"

"No, no, never, never. This is all new to me."

"But when a woman sits on a sofa and crosses her legs, doesn't that upset you—"

He denied it. "No, no, not upset. Any normal man would be a little excited—"

"People saw you standing in front of this girl's house," said Peter with authority. Witnesses had seen Mary Sullivan—or someone resembling her—before her apartment house on Charles Street taking record albums out of her blue Vauxhall, assisted by an unidentified man, on January 4, the day of her murder.

"Not me," said Tom. "It's all new to me."

He denied every suggestion that put him on the scene of any strangling, or in Filene's, where Mary Sullivan worked during Christmas, or in any hospital when any victim had been there.

Bottomly produced the apartment sketches found in his room. What did the X's mean?

"Oh, gee, those were art exercises," he said. "I was studying to be a commercial artist. You make the overall sketch first, putting the X's as you go along to indicate what you must ink in, then you go over it later and ink them in."

Why had he drawn the exteriors of apartment houses?

That was a game he played with his brother, who used to drop in of an evening. They would sit on Tom's cot and his brother would say, "Do you remember the building we lived in on Leyland Street?" Then each would draw it as they remembered it, then compare drawings and argue who was right. "It was just something to do," said Tom.

Why had he blotted out eleven female figures in the Yoga book?

Was that the number? He didn't know why eleven. But he always covered female figures; when he copied from ancient statues in his art work, he liked to draw in dresses and skirts.

Why were the knotted scarves and ties in his drawer?

"I was saving those to give to St. Vincent de Paul."

Why had he written ALWAYS RUN FROM TEMPTATION INSTANTLY!

"Well, if you leave temptation instantly, you conquer the temptation," he said. "That's very important. That's why we are not all saints. But when temptation comes and we try to fool with it, then we get hurt."

The questioners were silent. O'Brien was obviously tired. What had they achieved? Here was Peter's man. They had questioned him, they had confronted him with the photographs of the victims, Peter had borne down on him—and O'Brien had admitted nothing.

Bottomly asked, not unkindly, "Have you had enough of us now? You look rather tired."

"I guess maybe I have," said Tom. He tried to muster a smile. "I guess you probably have had enough of me."

Late that night Peter left Boston. "My work finished," he said. The next day the Boston newspapers would have a field day with the news of Hurkos' secret visit, the dispute over the Attorney General's use of a psychic, the Back Bay shoe salesman he had picked, but Peter would be away from it all, in New York, resting. He shook hands warmly with Soshnick who took him to the airport. "Julian, you my good friend," he said. "You treat me fine. Be careful. I see broken bicycle—dangerous. Take care." They walked to the gate. Peter patted Julian's shoulder. "That O'Brien—you see, Julian, he the man, he the Strangler."

Driving home, Soshnick wondered, *was* it O'Brien? Could Peter have been thrown off the trail by O'Brien's letter, brought to him that day by Sergeant Leo Martin of the Boston police? Perhaps it was a man like O'Brien, and if Peter had been left to his own devices, he might have zeroed in on him. O'Brien was psychotic, a chronic paranoid. "A classical picture of paranoid ideation" he had been described by a psychiatric social worker back in October 1963, when he panicked on a dishwashing job because fellow workers "were thrusting themselves" against him, forcing him to "think lascivious thoughts." He definitely needed commitment. Had O'Brien told the truth? A psychotic can appear to be in touch with reality when in fact he is not, Soshnick knew. Had their questioning really gotten through to O'Brien? The man himself might not know what he had done. Additional psychiatric tests must be made. It could only be hoped that he would remain committed, either by a probate judge or by his family, who had long urged him to seek hospital care; and perhaps someday the truth about him might be known. Further investigations must be made into the backgrounds of each of the eleven victims to see if their lives had ever crossed the sorry one of Thomas O'Brien.

Julian Soshnick drove his car into his garage. As he was about to pull shut the doors, he thought of Peter's warning. Feeling a little foolish, he unlocked the padlock on the storeroom in which his wife and little daughter kept their bicycles, took each one out, and carefully examined it. His wife's bicycle was fine. But when he turned the front wheel of his daughter's bicycle, a cotter pin fell out and the wheel whirled off.

He stood there, utterly baffled.

Peter had left, but within seventy-two hours of his departure, while the Boston papers were full of his exploits, the FBI roused him from sleep at 3:30 A.M. February 8, in his New York hotel room and arrested him on a charge of impersonating an FBI agent. On December 10, 1963, nearly two months before, while buying gasoline in a Milwaukee suburb, he had allegedly posed as an FBI agent and showed a display of cards. He was then driving to Las Vegas to investigate the kidnapping of Frank Sinatra, Jr. Peter indignantly denied that he masqueraded as anyone: it was a misunderstanding caused by his bad English; anyway, he, Peter Hurkos, was much more than an FBI agent could hope to be.

Bottomly and Soshnick seethed with anger. It was hitting below the belt. While the Boston police had not prevented Peter's visit to Boston, they made no secret of what they thought of him. Peter's arrest, made on the very heels of his Boston appearance, was seen as a move to discredit Peter and the Attorney General as well. No one forgot that Commissioner McNamara was a former FBI agent. Some held, however, that politics, rather than police resentment over the Hurkos publicity, inspired the arrest; that local Democrats had engineered it to embarrass Attorney General Brooke, a Republican, on the eve of his campaign for reelection. Others found an even more Machiavellian plot. The Kennedy family, they suggested, might like to see one of their own candidates as Governor of Massachusetts in the near future, but would be reluctant to have this come about at the cost of defeating so popular a Negro as Edward Brooke, Jr., if, as appeared possible, Brooke were to be the Republican candidate. Far better to trip up Brooke in the Attorney General contest now, thus eliminating him as a gubernatorial candidate later.

Charge and countercharge filled the press. One newspaper headlined its story *Hurkos Framed*. Bottomly demanded to know why the FBI hadn't told him they planned to arrest Hurkos: it was a courtesy due the Attorney General's office. And why had the arrest taken place when it had—so long after the alleged offense? "It took us two hours to find Hurkos in an actor's home in California, yet it took the FBI nearly two months to get their man," Bottomly declared angrily. At the State House rumors flew that the FBI had originally planned an even more spectacular denouement to the Hurkos chapter—to arrest him in the Attorney General's office itself—but finally decided this was going too far.

The brickbats came from all sides. The Civil Liberties Union questioned whether Tom O'Brien's civil rights had not been ridden over roughshod. The Boston *Herald* accused Assistant Attorney General Soshnick and Detective Davis of using an "instrument of tyranny" when they obtained a general search warrant to search O'Brien's room.*

Actually Bottomly had little time to devote to these internecine battles. He had been put in authority, he knew, because he had a reputation for getting things done, for cutting through red tape, for taking aid and information where he needed it and when he needed it.

He urged that the reward for the Strangler be increased from $5,000 to $10,000 a strangling. A bill to that effect went to the House of Representatives and was promptly passed with Governor Peabody's approval. Bottomly recruited additional members to his Medical-Psychiatric Committee. They included Dr. James A. Brussel, of New York, whom Bottomly reached in Uganda—the psychiatrist was on a month-long African safari—and Dr. Carola Blume, chief psychologist of the Massachusetts Department of Mental Health. Since her early days in Berlin, Dr. Blume had made a hobby of graphology, or the analysis of character through handwriting, and she now began to study letters sent in by the public.

Bottomly received the latest report on the computer program. Clerks had nearly finished reading some ten thousand source documents, underlining key data as they did so. This would be encoded on punch cards so it could be fed to the computer. Each card could handle one thousand items. Key numbers would be given to each breakdown: associations, occupations, locations, objects, actions, motivations, and the like, so that all information would be translated into computer data.

* Interestingly enough—and taking some of the sting out of those complaints—on February 13 when O'Brien's ten-day commitment expired, the staff of the Mental Health Department recommended thirty-five days' additional observation. In the end, O'Brien voluntarily recommitted himself to the institution.

10

A few days before, in the maximum security ward of Bridgewater State Hospital—a section that with its heavy bars, massive locked doors, cement blocks, and innumerable keepers is far better described as a prison—Dr. Ames Robey sat with David Parker.

They were seated in the ward outside Parker's cell, with half a dozen guards conveniently near.

David was high, and talking, his eyes shining. "Do you know what I'd do with women?" he demanded. "If I had my way I'd torture them . . ." He hated them, they were not to be trusted. At this very moment they were the "recipients of the justice of my anger," because "they wear the pants and they shouldn't wear them."

From the beginning of David's commitment on January 22, he had been extremely psychotic. He had attempted suicide, ripping his left arm open with his nails, banging his head against the walls of his cell, rubbing the yellow naphtha institutional soap into his eyes. This last gave him severe conjunctivitis but otherwise did not harm him. However the attempt warranted placing him in isolation, and on suicide precaution—which meant a cell in maximum security without clothes or shoes lest he injure himself or even attempt to hang himself. Light came through a small square barred window: food was pushed to him through a narrow opening some six inches across in the heavy metal door through which one could peep at him. In the more violent cases these peepholes were always covered. One slipped the cover aside with great care lest the sick creature inside fling the contents of his toilet pail through it at the observer. Tall, handsome, naked as a child, David had thrown himself about wildly. Now,

133

however, psychotic but at the moment not violent, he was able to talk with Dr. Robey. He was dressed in a faded open shirt, beltless slacks, and was barefoot. Dr. Robey, knowing David was an expert in judo and karate, took no chances, which explained why he spoke with David outside his cell rather than venturing inside it.

"A world without women?" Dr. Robey was saying.

David smiled. "Oh, wonderful, absolutely wonderful!" Some day he would carry out a private plan. "I want to buy an island off the coast of Australia and prohibit any female from setting foot in it. A world without women! A man's kingdom—and to make doubly sure, I'd set machine guns around the perimeter as well as barbed wire, just in case, to keep them out."

He went on. He knew one girl, in Cambridge, whom he did not hate too bitterly. Since he had been kicked out of Harvard he had been living in New York City, working in an office, but he came up to Boston to see her every time he could.

Dr. Robey moved carefully as he led the conversation around to David's sexual habits. Under his questioning David admitted he had had homosexual experiences. "I didn't play any active part, I didn't like it, but I did it," he said.

"Tell me, David, before you were married, how did you get along with that girl friend in Cambridge?"

David pursed his lips. "Pretty well," he said. Sometimes, for no reason at all, however, she "would have nothing to do with me." How did he feel when she acted like this? "Feel?" David flashed a glance at his questioner filled with such hostility that even its glimpse shook Dr. Robey.

"I'd get so angry I just wanted to destroy," he said. He would leave her apartment and walk the streets of Cambridge and Boston, "looking for a woman."

Dr. Robey digested this information. He ventured:

"When would you come up to visit her?"

"Usually on weekends," David replied. "That's the only time I could get away from my job."

Dr. Robey tamped his pipe with a trembling finger. As he knew from the information given him so far, nine of the eleven stranglings took place on weekends, the exceptions being Anna Slesers' on a Thursday, June 14, and Sophie Clark's on Wednesday, December 5. Forgetting those, however, was it only by chance that David's visits from New York coincided with the others? Then Dr. Robey realized: June 14 was Flag Day—a legal holiday in New York State, where David worked.

He asked, "Did your employer let you off on holidays, too?"

David nodded. "Yes, usually the afternoon before."

So he could have been in Boston that day, too.

That left only December 5 to be accounted for. Perhaps further questioning would fit that date into the pattern, too. But Dr. Robey did not pursue this line too far. He wanted to learn as much about David as possible without giving himself away. The boy had no idea that he was under suspicion for the stranglings: all he knew about his internment in Bridgewater was that he had been sent there for possession of a dangerous weapon. He considered it a trumped-up charge—arresting a man for carrying a stage prop!—and had said as much. It did not occur to him that one is hardly committed to a mental institution for such a reason. But one of the marks of a psychotic condition is the inability to recognize the incongruous. Nonetheless, Dr. Robey had great respect for David's intelligence. The boy had admitted he manufactured the drugs he sold. His skill with explosives had already been remarked upon.

Dr. Robey had listened to David, in his extremely psychotic stage, hallucinating wildly in his cell, screaming that he was all-powerful, shouting contempt at all of stupid mankind, marching in circles like some naked, deranged young god hour after hour proclaiming that he possessed a magic to neutralize those who schemed to destroy the universe, that he had gone beyond the Einstein theory, that he had designed rockets and built atomic bombs, that voices implored him to save the world. "I'm going to find the formula that will save mankind!" he cried.

Calmed down but still psychotic, he wept. "The only way I can get the world's attention is to destroy part of it—and especially the women."

"Why the women?" Dr. Robey asked.

"They have only one function. They have to be shown that function." But he refused to explain further and grew agitated when pressed. What was clear was that he rebelled violently at women in positions of dominance.

Dr. Robey changed the subject. "David, do you drink?"

"Only beer."

"Do you have a favorite beer?"

"Well, what I really like best I can't get around here. It's called Lucky Lager."

Dr. Robey almost jumped in his seat. Lucky Lager was sold only in California. What startled him was the fact, among those given him by Bottomly, that tavern keepers in the neighborhoods of two stranglings—Joann Graff in Lawrence, and Mary Sullivan in Boston—had reported that on the day of the strangling a customer asked for "Lucky Lager beer" in one instance, and "Lucky beer" in the other. The request was so unusual that the bartenders remembered it.*

"O.K.," said Dr. Robey. "We'll talk again, David." And he returned to his office and his records to mull over these coincidences.

The last strangling, Mary Sullivan's, was on Saturday, January 4. That was also David's wedding day in New York City. When had Mary been strangled? Her body had been found Saturday at 6:20 P.M. by her two roommates, Pat and Pam, on their return from their jobs at Filene's. Medical Examiner Luongo then estimated that she had been dead "several hours." That might well mean Saturday morning. When had David been married? In the late afternoon. Dr. Robey checked a map. It was only 220 miles from Boston to New York. David could have been in Boston in the morning and in New York in the afternoon.

Dr. Robey thought furiously. When not completely psychotic, David was a likeable youth with considerable charm who made friends easily. He looked like a thousand other personable young men. If you saw him walk by you'd think, There's a college kid—and forget his face. And he had superb physical coordination, the grace of a dancer; he could move like a wisp of fog, slip in and out of places without being seen.

On his next visit to David, Dr. Robey found him much improved. Dr. Robey, accompanied this time by a fellow psychiatrist, had an idea in mind. "David, you're doing fine," he said, after a few minutes of amiable conversation. He turned to a keeper. "Will you get David his shoes? I think he can have them now and his feet must be cold."

He watched as the boy slipped on his shoes and tied the laces—tied them with the extra half hitch, and then the bow—the Strangler's knot.

Dr. Robey's associate, trying to conceal his excitement, handed David a piece of string. "David," he said recklessly, "if you were going to kill somebody, what kind of knot would you tie?"

* The bartender in Mary Sullivan's neighborhood—his bar was on Charles Street, a few doors away—recalled the customer as a young man, light-complexioned, with blond hair, in his twenties, who laughed immoderately. In Lawrence the incident also took place in a bar a few doors from the murder building, but the description of the customer was vague.

It was a grievous tactical error. David drew back. "Hey, what's going on here?" He looked suspiciously from one man to the other. "Do you think I'm the Boston Strangler, or something?" He turned and sat in a corner of the cell, arms hugging his knees. "I want my lawyer," he said. The questioning was over. He knew he was a suspect.

That night David wrote to his lawyer asking him to "close down and destroy my laboratory." The letter was intercepted: the Secret Service, which had kept an eye on David because of his narcotics involvement, investigated. The boy did have a laboratory in New York State, not far from his office.

Later, Dr. Robey tried to summarize what he had learned about David Parker. The high intelligence; the Lucky Lager beer; the medical-hospital background—father a chemist, mother a social worker; the hatred of women and the fantasies of torturing and destroying them; the near-strangling of his wife; the strong possibility that he was in Boston each time, or virtually each time a strangling occurred; the knot he tied—everything fitted. As the murder of Joann Graff the day after Kennedy's assassination fitted, and as the Mary Sullivan murder fitted. For the first might have been an extraordinary act of paranoid egomania—to strike with such God-like power at so awful a moment; the second was sheer omnipotence—to murder in the morning and marry in the afternoon!

If one studied the eleven murders, one saw how they grew more bizarre until in Mary Sullivan's case all the stops were out, almost as though: This is my grand triumph, the most elaborate creation of them all . . . Behold, World!

How like a David!

The question then rose, how did he choose his victims?

Dr. Robey speculated. All of us, he believed, are able to recognize a "kindred soul." Often we can sense almost at a glance if a stranger is someone with whom we can get along, who is *simpatico*. Dr. Robey once had a woman patient who possessed this intuitive ability to an astonishing degree. She could enter a roomful of people and spot the one man there whose company she thought she would enjoy. Seven times she had done it—and seven times the man she chose turned out to be an alcoholic. Even more incredibly, in two instances the man had not yet become an alcoholic; his drinking problem had not yet shown itself.

Now, consider the eleven victims. Similarities in the personalities of the older women had been remarked upon: orderly, reserved, rigidly respectable, compulsively neat, and, in most cases, having had nothing to do with men for years.

Joann Graff, though only twenty-three, bespectacled and retiring, could have been a younger version of the older victims and belonged in their category. Sophie Clark, also reserved, methodical, modest, might be included too. Of the remainder, almost the opposite was true: Beverly Samans, Patricia Bissette, Evelyn Corbin and Mary Sullivan were all outgoing and interested in men.

Dr. Robey thought, Was it possible that these women, whatever their symptoms—overt sexual concern, fear of men, compulsive neatness—was it possible that through nonverbal communcation, through their manner of walk, dress, appearance, glances at strangers—they conveyed a pathology, a sexual personality, unconsciously perceived by the Strangler? Perhaps wandering through the city, not knowing what he sought yet able to spot it, whatever it was, the Strangler saw it in them and responded to it.

Why the ransacking of the apartments? Here Dr. Robey reached far out. Whatever the man sought, he failed to find. If he were a fetishist, he might look for a certain type of shoe, or wig, or article of woman's clothing. But nothing of this sort appeared to have been taken. Dr. Robey could only assume that he searched for something with sexual connotation—some sort of phallic instrument. Dr. Robey recalled a male patient who in his fantasies believed that women had penises. On a conscious level he knew this was nonsense, but when psychotic he believed it. Now, artificial penises did exist. In brothels one could be entertained by prostitutes, one girl strapping such a device upon her to play the male and going through the act of love with the other girl. David had spent some time in Paris where exhibitions of this sort were almost routine. The device was also used at homosexual parties. David had admitted homosexual experiences. If David were the Strangler he might in his madness look for this device in his victims' belongings, because he was a homosexual and yet at the same time feared his homosexual desires. Thus, he was seeking out women, thereby removing the onus of homosexuality, but women with penises, thereby making them less threatening to him. That would explain the molestation—the use of a foreign object, a bottle, a broom—as though the Strangler, enraged because he did not find penises on his victims, were to proclaim, "You don't have it here, but I have this one!"

Was all that too fanciful? Dr. Robey wondered. Yet he had seen such pathology; and after all, one was dealing with twisted minds and twisted hungers.

Whatever the case, these were matters to be discussed with

Bottomly and the Medical-Psychiatric Committee. He called Bottomly. As a result, a day after Peter Hurkos left Boston, Bottomly met at Bridgewater with Dr. Robey and Acting Captain Cullinane to discuss David Parker. Since David was scheduled to be returned the next day to Cambridge for trial, Dr. Robey had to make his recommendation at once.

The coincidences, they agreed, were startling. To be sure, David had told Dr. Robey he had never visited Lynn, Salem, or Lawrence, the scenes of the Helen Blake, Evelyn Corbin, and Joann Graff stranglings, but he could be lying. Obviously he had to be checked out most carefully; his parents had to be interviewed, his employers questioned about when he was actually off the job, his Cambridge girl friend asked if he was in Boston on those fatal weekends, his former classmates interviewed in detail.

Meanwhile, Dr. Robey and his associates expressed their opinion that David Parker was an "extremely good suspect" in the strangulation murders.

On February 7, at Dr. Robey's recommendation and at the request of John Bottomly, and after consultation with David's attorney, the boy was committed to Bridgewater for a further period of observation. He was—no question of it—a dangerous person.

Neither Dr. Robey nor Bottomly at that moment recalled, out of the thousands of words Peter Hurkos had uttered while in Boston, the ten words he spoke when, at one of his early sessions with the detectives, he had been asked the complexion of the Strangler. "Not a colored man. White," Peter had said. "But . . . he make it colored."

David Parker? Othello?

11

In mid-March Leo Alexander, M.D., professor of psychiatry at Tufts Medical College, received an unusual telephone call just as he was finishing his usual lunch of Metrecal and black coffee at his desk.

It came from Assistant Attorney General John S. Bottomly. Mr. Bottomly was in need at once of a private psychiatrist skilled in the use of the so-called truth serums to examine a Mr. Paul Gordon, who claimed to possess extrasensory perception and had a surprisingly detailed knowledge of the crimes.

Dr. Alexander, his caller said, had been recommended to him by Dr. Donald Kenefick, who headed the Attorney General's Medical-Psychiatric Committee, as one of the world's leading experts in the field. Bottomly had also read of Dr. Alexander's work as Consultant to the United States Secretary of War at the Nuremberg Trials after World War II, and of how his skill helped elicit valuable information from high Nazi war criminals. This Paul Gordon, Bottomly went on, had been insisting for months that a mental patient named Arnold Wallace was the Strangler, and had been revealed to him as such through ESP. He felt the police did not believe him. He had therefore offered himself for examination. That would not only prove he was telling the truth, Mr. Gordon suggested, but since hypnotic drugs were said to stimulate ESP, he might be able to reveal even more about Arnold Wallace. Whatever the case, "Gordon just seems to know too much," and Mr. Bottomly felt it his duty once and for all to get to the root of it.

Bottomly was considerably perturbed. Suspects came and went but Arnold Wallace was a prime suspect in more ways than one. Even if David Parker made one's flesh crawl by the neatness with which he appeared to fit the Strangler, the

140

material collected on Arnold by Detective DiNatale and Mellon since their transfer to the Attorney General's office added up to a powerful—but exasperating—indictment. How would one conceive that Arnold Wallace, with his I.Q. of seventy or less, possessed the skill, intelligence, and silent swiftness to carry off so many crimes without making a single misstep?

Item: The two coeds who narrowly escaped being raped in the dark streets near Anna Slesers' apartment by a tall, dirty man with a missing tooth, had all but identified Arnold as their assailant. (So Gordon, despite his melodramatic enactment when he raced up and down the alley that May evening, could be right.)

Item: Five of Arnold's absences without leave from Boston State Hospital coincided with stranglings. Captain Cullinane had determined that Arnold was missing from the hospital on the days Anna Slesers, Nina Nichols, and Helen Blake met their deaths in June 1962. He was returned on August 13, 1962. Two days later, on August 15, he was missing again. Ida Irga was murdered on Sunday, August 19, and possibly on the same day, Jane Sullivan. Arnold was returned to the hospital the next day—August 20—after Phil DiNatale had seized him breaking into a teashop.

Item: In his absences he often broke into the House of the Good Shepherd to see his sister, a retarded delinquent. Once he told Sister Alfreda, the Mother Superior, "You don't have to worry about the Strangler. I'm the Strangler." But later he insisted he had only been joking.*

Item: At a church not far away from Anna Slesers' a priest reported that Arnold often came there for meal tickets.

Item: A boy saw Arnold, or someone resembling him, slipping into the Nina Nichols apartment house on the June thirtieth weekend of her death. In Cambridge, a priest in a church off Harvard Square said he gave him $1.50 for food—that was Monday, May 6; Beverly Samans had been murdered in Cambridge a block from the square sometime after 11 P.M. Sunday, May 5. Another clergyman not far from where Ida Irga lived saw Arnold wandering about the neighborhood the weekend of August 19, when Mrs. Irga was strangled. And still a fourth clergyman whose church was

---

* Here occurs another of the many extraordinary coincidences that were to plague police. Once when Arnold on a daylight visit rang the bell of the convent, the door was opened by Mrs. Margaret Davis, the woman derelict later strangled in a hotel room in downtown Boston on July 11, 1962. She was living there, trying to make herself useful, while fighting to overcome her alcoholic problem.

near Jane Sullivan's apartment came forward to say Arnold had frequently asked him for food money.

Item: Dr. Frank Parodi, a psychiatrist at Boston State Hospital, reported that Arnold once approached him saying, "I want to talk to you about the stranglings." But Dr. Parodi was on an urgent medical call, and later attempts to persuade Arnold to talk about the subject were unsuccessful. Dr. Parodi believed that Arnold, despite his low I.Q., was capable of the stranglings; and so did Captain Cullinane, a man of enormous experience.

Finally, the strong but unprovable suspicion that Arnold was involved in his mother's death, supported by one additional fact, recently learned. Arnold Wallace had been the only one of her children to oppose an autopsy on his mother.

All this Paul Gordon had been saying—or implying.

Three weeks before, Bottomly had transferred Arnold from Boston State Hospital to Bridgewater, where escape was impossible. His mental condition was rapidly deteriorating. Months earlier DiNatale and Mellon could scarcely communicate with him. If he spoke, it was to deny everything: most of the time he simply dropped a curtain between himself and his questioner as if the latter did not exist. Now, at Bridgewater, Arnold was reported completely withdrawn. He spent most of his day sitting on a bench along the wall of his ward, speaking to no one, wanting nothing, interested in nothing—an acute paranoid schizophrenic. Dr. Robey and his staff could do little. It seemed highly unlikely that rational communication would ever again be achieved with him.

What complicated matters now was Paul Gordon's involvement—and Paul Gordon's knowledge.

Why was the man so deep in it all? There was always, of course, the reward. But more important, why was he so uncannily familiar with the murder apartments, and with details known presumably only to police and murderer? Bottomly had assigned a detective to read every newspaper and magazine story on the stranglings from the day Anna Slesers' body was found. Gordon knew details that had not appeared in the press: actually, he knew some that had deliberately been kept out of police reports themselves. Which brought one back to the baffling and ever-present possibility that this man could himself be the Strangler.

Would Dr. Alexander be prepared, Bottomly wanted to know, to administer the necessary drugs to Paul Gordon in his private consultation rooms in cooperation with Dr. Ralph Brancale? Dr. Brancale was the Director of the State Diagnostic Center of New Jersey; he had had long experience with psychopathic criminals. By giving their time to this project, the doctors would render a genuine service to the Commonwealth.

Dr. Alexander was a precise, Viennese-born physician in his early sixties, with many titles, among them Consultant and Director of the Neurobiological Unit, Division of Psychiatric Research, at Boston State Hospital. He had read about the stranglings as they occurred. He was familiar with cruel, gruesome acts. In his practice he dealt with them constantly, acts imagined or actually carried out by patients. He liked to point out to his students that a mark of mental health was the ability to repress our knowledge of the world's cruelty, to be able to live in peace though surrounded on all sides by horror, cruelty, and violent death.

For example, he would say, take a meadow on a perfect summer's day. You lie on the grass, the sun shines warmly, all is serenity and beauty. Yet under every blade of grass a battle rages as fierce, as bloody, as a world war—creatures busily ambushing each other, killing and tearing each other apart, devouring each other alive. We screen all this from our minds. We can do it as long as we are well. He often thought it ironic that if a depressed patient walked into his office and said the world was so grim that he could not face it, he had to treat him as a sick man. Actually, the patient was right. He saw the truth only too clearly. But he was sick, because he had lost certain basic defenses—or, if you will, he no longer had the normal illusions that keep us sane.

A man who claimed to possess ESP powers might have illusions of another kind. If, however, he knew a great deal about unsolved crimes and volunteered to be drugged and in this condition permit his mind and emotions to be probed—that was most interesting. Mr. Gordon, so eager to help, intrigued him. How often the culprit had turned out to be the fellow so ready to help the police, the arsonist who first sounded the fire alarm.

Since 1940 Dr. Alexander had used sodium amytal in the treatment of disturbed patients, finding it helpful in the diagnosis of schizophrenia. Under it the subject reached a zone between conscious and subconscious, a state comparable to deep hypnosis. It had been discovered that in this condition, mute schizophrenics were enabled to express their feelings quite openly. Dr. William Sargant of St. Thomas Hospital, London, considered England's leading psychiatrist, had used the hypnotic drugs with remarkable effect on British casualties after Dunkirk, during the Second World War. Many of these survivors were suffering shell shock—more accurately, a severe inhibitory neurosis. The horror, grief, and terror they had lived through had been too much for them to accept; they had lost the power to speak or to remember, and had become detached from reality. Under sodium pentothal and Dr. Sargant's skillful ministrations, they could recall their experiences consciously, relate to them, and thus once more to reality.

To call such drugs "truth serums," however, Dr. Alexander would point out, was incorrect. Sodium pentothal—and sodium amytal, similar in effect—worked by suppressing the higher critical faculties of the brain so that one more easily revealed his feelings. Under it a man was less inhibited, more gross, more blunt, more tactless. Learned behavior went by the board; natural behavior came out. Natural behavior was not necessarily true or honest behavior. One could lie in a most fanciful manner, because the drug also released the imagination. Yet it did loosen one's tongue, and an experienced practitioner could often catch a subject off guard. Though Dr. Alexander in principle did not approve of using the drug to elicit secrets, Mr. Gordon was clearly a special case. The problem here was to put him under chemical hypnosis and by skillful questioning lead him to reveal whatever there was to reveal.

Dr. Alexander was ready to contribute his services. Mr. Bottomly had called Thursday, March 19; the psychiatrist could take Gordon on Saturday, when he had no patients scheduled. Dr. Brancale, too, agreed to cooperate although he was hesitant about accepting the invitation. Not long before he had been asked to come to Cleveland to administer a truth-serum test to Dr. Sam Sheppard, the Cleveland osteopath fighting his conviction for the murder of his wife. The invitation had been extended by F. Lee Bailey, a Boston lawyer who was handling Sheppard's appeal. Dr. Brancale had refused. This, however, was an invitation by the state, and he wanted to do his part. Like Dr. Alexander he had used the drugs for years and agreed they did not necessarily produce the truth. Sometimes the subject verbalized fantasies, fantasies so real to the patient that he would swear upon his life they actually occurred. Dr. Brancale had not used the drugs to determine guilt or innocence of offenders in New Jersey, but mainly to uncover motivations for behavior.

Since inquisitorial use of a hypnotic drug raised delicate legal-medical issues, both physicians asked that a legal agreement be drawn up, stating clearly what was being done and why.

When Gordon, accompanied by his lawyer, arrived Saturday morning, March 21, 1964, at Dr. Alexander's office, the document was ready. Dated that day, signed in quadruplicate by Gordon, his attorney, Bottomly, and Doctors Alexander and Brancale a few minutes before Gordon took his journey into the depths of his own psyche, it must stand as something unique in the history of crime detection.

It read:

Whereas the parties hereto are desirous of developing further information from the said Paul Gordon relating to the so-called "Strangulation Murders" which have occurred within the Commonwealth of Massachusetts from June 14, 1962 to the present time, and it is proposed by the parties hereto that in order to obtain such information the said Paul Gordon be interviewed while under the influence of hypnosis and/or hypnotic drugs.

Now therefore in consideration of the mutual promises herein the parties agree:

1. That the purpose of the interview is to develop information concerning the above-described crimes.

2. That the interview is to be conducted under the medical supervision and direction of Ralph Brancale, M.D., and Leo Alexander, M.D.

3. That the said Paul Gordon does hereby release and discharge the said Ralph Brancale, M.D., and Leo Alexander, M.D., or any medical personnel acting under the direction of either of them, from any and all claims or causes of action arising from the application of hypnosis and hypnotic drugs to the person of the said Paul Gordon during the course of the said interview.

4. That the said Paul Gordon's attorney shall be present at all times during said interview in his capacity as his legal representative.

5. That any party hereto may employ the use of recording devices during said interview, and that such recordings shall be the sole property of those parties who employ the use of same.

6. That by cooperating in this manner the said Paul Gordon does not waive any rights, past, present, or future, that he may have in regard to his qualification for any rewards that have been, or may be, offered for information leading to the arrest of the person or persons who have committed said homicides.

7. That the said Paul Gordon acknowledges without reservation that no influence, coercion, or duress has been exercised upon him directly or indirectly by any

law enforcement official or agency or by any other person to submit to this or to any other interview.

8. That Paul Gordon may discontinue at any time his cooperation with any law enforcement official or agency. No inferences may be drawn from the withdrawal of such cooperation.

9. That at no time during his contact with law enforcement authorities has Paul Gordon been deprived of his right to counsel, and that this interview has been arranged through his said attorney and that Paul Gordon signifies by signing his name in the left margin of this paragraph that he has read this agreement in its entirety, and that he has adequate time to consult with his said attorney regarding this agreement prior to signing it.

Gordon lay on a couch, in a room made dark by drawn blinds in the rear of Dr. Alexander's office. The group, which now included Detective DiNatale, Mellon, and Steve Delaney, watched silently as the anesthetist inserted a needle into Gordon's vein at the crook of his left arm—the procedure reminded Jim Mellon of a blood transfusion—and the drug, a mixture of Methedrine and sodium pentothal, began to flow. Dr. Alexander stood at the head of the couch, watching Gordon's eyes closely. A subtle change in expression would indicate when the subject was under. "We shall keep the needle in the vein throughout the interview so we can regulate the state of emotional expressiveness as we see fit," he told the others, in a low voice. Drop by drop the drug entered Gordon's bloodstream; two tape recorders were slowly turning, one attended by his attorney, the other by Delaney.

Suddenly Gordon laughed. "I see two Phils, two Jims . . . I guess I better be quick because this stuff is beginning to work . . . I hear my speech thicken . . ."

"Are you comfortable, Mr. Gordon?" Dr. Alexander asked. "Fine, fine," came the answer, "except that I see everything in duplicate and triplicate."

"Good." Then, almost formally, "Now tell us about Mary Sullivan," Dr. Alexander began; and for the course of the next six hours, save for a half-hour rest for coffee and sandwiches that were brought in, Gordon was interrogated as he lay on the couch, mainly by Dr. Alexander, sometimes by Dr. Brancale, and on occasion by DiNatale and Mellon.

The latter two, as well as Dr. Brancale, were all but exhausted. Dr. Brancale had been able to get to Boston only late the night before, and Phil and Jim had stayed up with him in his Parker House suite, briefing him on Paul Gordon, playing tapes of their interviews with him until past 3 A.M.

Tired as he was, he found the officers' summary fascinating. They had reviewed Arnold Wallace's case for him and explained why attention was now focused on Gordon, either as a key to Arnold, or as a suspect himself. Phil and Jim had checked exhaustively on the ESP man. They had visited his apartment, inspected his tropical fish, viewed his impressive collection of weights and lifting apparatus. Gordon had once casually remarked that his hands were weak—he had injured them years ago. (An alibi? The Strangler must have strong hands.) "But," said Phil, "when he left the room for a moment I tried lifting one of the weights and it took all the strength in my arms and wrists to do it." They noted that Mrs. Gordon was older than her husband, twelve to fifteen years older. They had also been struck by her resemblance to the older victims: the same round face, full jaw, even metal-rimmed spectacles.

From other sources they had heard that for a time before his marriage, Gordon had shared an apartment with his mother, who was said to be very affectionate to him; sometimes she gave him his haircuts, she called him endearing names and fussed over him as though he were a small boy.

Dr. Brancale said nothing. Many men who marry women considerably older than themselves are choosing as much a mother as a mate.

Finally the two officers had found Gordon's mother. They discovered her to be a woman of seventy, living alone. She greeted them in excellent humor, at one point patting Phil on the cheek, with, "Oh, you're a good-looking policeman!"

While that was going on, both men were trying to keep their wits. This old woman might have been an older version of Gordon's wife. The round face, the generous jaw, the metal-rimmed spectacles. So now Gordon's wife and his mother resembled most of the Strangler's victims.

Were they mad? Had they lost their perspective completely? Perhaps all elderly women looked alike if one searched for similarities. They had to give up trying to make sense of it.

But Gordon's mother told them little about her son. Instead, she phoned him. He asked to speak to Phil and then furiously ordered them both to leave his mother's apartment at once. There was no reason for her to be harassed by police questioning, he said angrily. They left.

Now for Dr. Brancale the two officers played the tapes of their interviews with Gordon: Gordon expanding on the stranglings, explaining how Arnold got into the apartments, what went through his mind, what drove him . . .

Dr. Brancale was interested in observing this puzzling man on the couch who so blithely, so confidently, offered to undergo this ordeal. If he was the Strangler, what egomania to assume that he could fence with the psychiatrists and detectives examining him—and even under drugs, outwit them!

"Tell us about Mary Sullivan," Dr. Alexander had ordered, and now Gordon, sounding a little drunken, responded. "Well," he was saying, "I came up with a mental image of a guy and you could talk me out of it if you come up with a better suspect."

"What did he do to Mary Sullivan?"

"Now, now," said Gordon. He sounded annoyed. "Strangling to me is repulsive. I don't like it. I don't know what happened there, I don't want to know."

"You say Arnold did this. Whatever he did, how did he feel about it? What was he going through at the time?"

"Oh, the poor guy suffers! How he suffers!" The drug had taken hold. Gordon spoke with surprising emotion. "I feel so sorry for that guy, nobody understands him . . ."

"Can you visualize Arnold in the Nina Nichols case? What is he going through at that point?"

"His crazy urge, this desire . . . He's killed his mother; sometimes he's aware of this."

"What is he doing to her?"

"He hates her! If she'd only say to him, 'Arnold come to me,' put her arms around him, say, 'I recognize that you have problems, I'd like to help you, you poor thing . . . you poor soul . . . You need a mother that loves you, someone to help you over the rough spots' . . . He didn't think, 'This woman resembles my mother and therefore I'm going to strangle her.' No, he saw her as a source of love."

"What did he actually do to that woman?" his questioner persisted.

(Softly.) "Why, he *killed* her. He didn't mean to kill her. He meant to get them into a condition where they had to listen to him. He'd have used this method, this pentothal method, if he thought he could. He wanted to get them into a passive state and his only method of getting them into a passive state was to choke them until they were unconscious."

"Would that satisfy him? Just to kill them?"

"No, because he wants to go back, to start everything all over again. Everything is wrong."

"Was there some sexual element in that?"

"Yes, but not in the way you'd look at it," Gordon retorted. "You see, you want everything cut and dried: he-did-it-for-sex. Well, he didn't do it for sex. He has a sexual frustation, but he didn't do it for sex. He didn't think, 'Well, now she's dead, I can rape her whether she'll like it or not.' He did it to get them into a passive state, and then they were too passive, and he resented it. He would like them to be alive. Remember"—here Gordon's voice died away, then grew strong again—"when he sees them he thinks, You're not my mother but you look like a mother; when you come to, if you understood me, even though you're not my mother you would treat me as a son because you'd understand me. You see, nobody understands me. This is the way he looks at it."

"What's his reaction when he sees this woman, who is the representation of his mother, strangled?"

Gordon's voice burst forth with deep emotion. "Oh God, it was terrible!" He moaned. "He broke down. Oh, the poor guy. He cried, oh, he cried! It was so final . . . He didn't mean it this way—"

"Did he try to cover his tracks? He sees his mother strangled, is he trying to—"

Gordon broke in, sounding annoyed. "She wasn't strangled. She died in the hospital."

"I'm talking of this Nichols woman who symbolizes his mother to Arnold."

"Well, she's not his mother. He knows that. But psychologically she fits the pattern."

"All right. She's strangled now. He didn't cover his tracks in any way?"

"You mean as far as somebody coming in looking for clues, and so forth? No. It never entered his head. He may have, unconsciously, without realizing it, but, it's a situation. It was the same with the others. On his mother's death bed if she looked up at him and said, 'Arnold, I forgive you, I know I was wrong, I've made mistakes . . .' He knows it's not his mother, but God damn her, she shouldn't be so much like her, she shouldn't resemble her so much . . ."

"What was he trying to do to her after she was strangled?"

"He didn't know what to do. He took her into the living room onto the blue chair. It's not all blue, a decorator's chair. He was going to sit her in the chair and talk to her. But then he knew she'd be like the others. Dammit, she died."

"How did he stop her from talking?"

"He put a gag in her mouth, maybe like a stocking . . ."

"What were his sex feelings at that moment?"

"Well, of course you psychiatrists relate everything to sex—"

"Did he try anything sexual?" Dr. Alexander asked imperturbably.

"Not the way you think," Gordon replied.

"Well, what way?"

"Oh, the poor guy . . ." Gordon moaned.

"Why do you feel so sorry for him, Mr. Gordon?"

"Because he does things but they're not backed by reason, they're backed by ideas instilled in his mind by his mother—"

"How did he get into the Nina Nichols apartment?"

"It was a very nice apartment, a very neat woman, too neat. I'd be uncomfortable there."

Dr. Brancale noted how difficult it was to get direct answers from Gordon. In the brief opportunity he'd had to talk with him before he was put under drugs, Gordon had been condescending. "You fellows can't expect me to conjure up psychic images in response to your questions," he had said impatiently. "I get these flashes, but I can't push a button and make them pop up: they have to come by themselves."

Now, the man on the couch was saying: "At one point in the apartment he took off his clothes. . . . He wants to be a little boy." His voice became the singsong voice of a boy of five or six, crooning to himself, "To be a lit-tel boy again, to start all-ll-lll over again, a lit-tel boy . . ."

"You can't but that was his hope." The singsong came back. "To be a lit-tel boy, and free, so free-eee . . ."

Dr. Alexander was speaking almost into Gordon's ear. "Did he have an impulse to do something to the lower part of a woman's body? What was his interest there?"

"Well, this is where things start. He didn't try to do anything. He reads books and he knows—we're all married men here—this is the way he's born. He knows it. Nothing's come out right for him in his life, he wants to be reborn again, to start all over . . ."

"Did he try to manipulate that part in any way?"

Gordon's words came very slowly. "Yes. He played and experimented. But he knew it wouldn't work. He was thinking, How could I be born from such a thing? It just doesn't seem reasonable because it's close . . . tight . . . narrow . . . confined. To-be-reborn-I-must-enlarge-this-thing. He'd do it with whatever was necessary, whatever was handy, broomstick, whatever . . ."

Was that the rationale for the molestation? The Strangler, in his strange sickness, became as a small boy, thus, being innocent, having no guilt in his experimentation, and hoping, as a small child, to reenter the womb and be reborn? Among Dr. Alexander's colleagues there were those who thought it possible.

"What color was the bottle?" one of the detectives suddenly asked. A bottle, as the newspaper had reported, had been found on the floor next to Nina Nichols' body.

"You ask the Goddamnedest questions!" Gordon was indignant. "Who cares what color. Green. I see green." He was right. "A liquor bottle? I don't know."

"Was there any ransacking of Miss Nichols' apartment?"

"Yes . . . I see a bureau. He's looking for something in it. It's a doll. And he thinks, If I can find the doll, I'll find the checks."

What checks? he was asked. Was Gordon saying that Arnold, identifying his victim as his own mother, was hunting in her bureau drawers for the welfare checks he used to steal from her?

Gordon made no answer.

"Where was Mary Sullivan killed?" a detective asked without preface.

"In the bedroom," said Gordon.

"Was anything left on her bed?" his questioner asked. Would Gordon say, Yes, a knife, a New Year's greeting card—facts he should not know?

He was silent.

"Are we coming through to you, Paul?" Mellon asked. "Do you hear us?"

"I'm thinking," came Paul's voice, annoyed. "No, nothing on the bed."

So it went, hour after hour. Among those who came to observe, and sometimes to question, were Bottomly, Donovan, and associates of Dr. Alexander. At one point, Gordon spoke of a framed photograph of a small girl in a ballerina costume, hanging on the wall of Ida Irga's apartment. No one in the room could recall any reference to a ballerina photograph in the press. The little girl, said Gordon, reminded Arnold, when he saw it, of a doll his sister once had, years ago, and he took the photograph off the wall fondly. "Oh, he loved that doll," said Gordon. "Arnold should have been a woman." In those early years he mothered the doll, fed it, gave it a spanking, put it to bed—he'd cradle it in his arms, Gordon went on dreamily. But his mother always snatched it away, scolding him. "That's not yours, Arnold, it doesn't belong to you; it belongs to your sister." Now, in Ida Irga's apartment, Gordon said, Arnold danced about the room with the photograph, hugged it to him, crying, "Oh, I love you, I love you"—then, remembering it was his sister's, not his, cast it on the floor, shouting, "I hate you, you're not mine!"

"Why was Arnold so angry at the ballerina?" Dr. Alexander asked.

"Because she wasn't real. He wanted to dance with it, wanted to make it do what he tried to make the women do—but pictures can't come to life."

"Was that the doll he was looking for?"

"Yes."

"What did he want to do with the doll? Put it in her vagina? So it could be born again?"

"You don't understand," said Gordon with some agitation.

Dr. Alexander's experience with so-called ESP was that such phenomena were comparable to intuitive dreams in which nonessential details are never clear. Gordon's anger because the ballerina was not real—that was not the material dreams are made of, it was the material recollection was made of. Was Gordon, then, not acting as a medium but as himself; not tuning in, as it were, on Arnold's mind but simply remembering what he saw, and what he felt?

Dr. Alexander played a hunch. "Mr. Gordon, don't you think the man who has done all this wants to be caught, so he can be relieved of this terrible burden he carries—"

"No," said Gordon.

"—and show how wonderful he is, and be relieved of this terrible burden he carries?" Dr. Alexander repeated.

"I want to throw up," Gordon said.

"Think how wonderful it would be, Mr. Gordon, he'd be relieved of everything, he could be cured—" Dr. Alexander went on relentlessly.

Gordon began to choke. "Now hold on," he said thickly. Then: "Can I throw up?"

"There's a bucket over there, Paul," said Mellon. Dr. Alexander led the others out of the room so Gordon could be sick in privacy. To whom had his question struck home so sharply that it produced nausea? To Paul Gordon reliving the role of Arnold or to Paul Gordon as Paul Gordon? There was a real Arnold, but was the Strangler that Arnold—or was he "Arnold," the other personality of this strange man now retching in the other room?

Later, they had coffee and sandwiches, all save Gordon, who slept. Then he was roused by an injection of Methedrine, which acted as a stimulant, and the questioning resumed. Now Gordon appeared to go into a mild automatic state in which he became the strangler of Sophie Clark, and actually carried on a soliloquy with his terrified victim before him; then he became the victim herself, all but paralyzed before her murderer, trying to speak in a gasping whisper . . .

That was set off when DiNatale asked how the killer got into Sophie's apartment.

"He was there all day, Phil," said Gordon. "He had a fight with another girl the night before . . . This stuff is beginning to wear off. I want to reach another level, Dr. Alexander. We're really getting somewhere!"

The dose was adjusted; Gordon smiled, and lying on his back, waved his hands gently to and fro as one dreamily conducting a symphony.

"How did you know about the Chesterfield butts behind the door in the cellar?" Phil asked.

"I saw them in my mind."

"What made Sophie come to the door and open it?"

"Ohhh . . . He's knocking on the wrong door. It doesn't open. She goes back into the living room, tense, nervous. She says to herself, 'I wonder if I should have answered it.' *Bang, bang, bang! God damn it, open the door!*" Gordon writhed on the couch, he spoke sharply, dramatically. "He didn't say this but this is what went through her mind and this was the way she felt. Pom! Pom! Boom! Boom! Boom! He rapped, she opened the door, she can't close it because he has his foot in the doorway. As soon as she let him in she knew it was wrong . . . He's moving from one chair to another." Now, in a girl's terrified whisper: "Oh, they won't be home for a while yet, what'll I do, where'll I go, I'm scared . . . What'll I make for him? . . . Well, anyway, she thinks, I haven't eaten yet, I got to eat. She starts to fiddle around in the kitchen, mainly banging dishes to make him think she's busy. Meanwhile he's sitting out there, not planning, just thinking, God damn it, she's a nice girl. Her hips impressed him—"

Phil realized that Gordon was now telling in dramatic detail what he had told him when they first met, months before.

"Then what happened?"

"The phone rang. She couldn't answer it—he grabbed her . . ." Gordon's voice became Sophie's anguished voice again: "I want to jab him but I don't dare, elbow him out of the way so I can get to the phone . . . Oh, if I could only get to it, tell them to come home early because I'm scared . . . If he'd only relax. He's not unattractive . . . But all he thinks about is himself, about sex . . ." Barnett, thought Phil, Lew Barnett, the Negro Don Juan . . . Gordon's voice was strong: now he was relating the story again. "He hit her on the jaw under the ear, the broad part of the jaw, a sharp, quick jab, a lot of weight behind it."

"How did he stop her from screaming?"

"He had something in his hand, a rolled-up cloth, it's dirty, he put it into her mouth . . ."

Sophie Clark had been gagged, but this fact had appeared in the papers. Now Gordon, as the murderer, was whispering to Sophie: "I don't want any noise to come out of this, understand? I've got you right now and you can do any God damn thing you want to but I don't have to listen to it. You're captured. I've captured you." He giggled. "I fixed you. See what it's like to be imprisoned? You're like me. You can't get out. Hahahahaha! Like to suffer? See, I'll come back. You just go ahead and sit there. Think it over for a while. Go through what I went through for a while."

During these surrealistic hour, Gordon appeared to undergo another metamorphosis: he was Arnold Wallace's mother, crooning endearments to her son; then, as Gordon himself, he engaged in a sharp dialogue with Arnold; then he became Arnold following his mother secretly one day to see where she went, only to discover to his horror that she was a prostitute, and in his fury, seek to kill her . . .

His voice came, a woman's voice, warm, caressing, motherly: "No, you don't want a girl like that, Arnold, you want a girl like old Mama, someone that really understands you. Mother knows. Sure, she knows . . ." Suddenly, sternly, in his own voice: "You shouldn't say that! You shouldn't say such things about your mother! No, that's not right, Arnold, you can't talk that way about your mother . . . Oh . . ." —sigh—"What will I do with that boy?" Now he had become Arnold's mother again. "They just don't understand that boy at all. You see how beautifully he does things . . . look at his beautiful hands. Ohhh, and he can be sweet. Arnold is *such* a good boy . . ." Suddenly: "Oh, Arnold, don't tell me that. Oh, don't tell me that, I'll cry, Arnold, don't do that"; Sharply, angrily: "Don't you do that, Arnold, don't do that!" He groaned. "Ahhhh . . . Ahhhh, no . . ."

"What's Arnold doing, Paul?" Jim Mellon asked.

"Oh, why did he do that to me! He shouldn't have! Oh, no!"—groan—"No, well they should have kept him there. Oh, poor boy—"

"What did he do, Paul? Did he do something bad?"

"Oh, God!" Still in a woman's voice, Gordon began to cry, chokingly, with tremendous emotion, almost seeming to break apart. Then unexpectedly, a piercing cry of anguish that almost brought everyone in the room to his feet. "It hurts!" He groaned, as one suffering excruciating pain.

Dr. Alexander asked gently, "What hurts, Paul?"

Had Arnold at this moment flung the word "Whore!" at his mother? Did this explain the Strangler's violent hatred of women, his desire to punish them—this awful vengeance he took against women brought on by this dreadful early experience in observing his mother as a prostitute?

But who was actually speaking? Arnold? Gordon interpreting Arnold? Gordon fantasizing how the Strangler might feel, and creating in his fantasy the scene between the mother and the son?

Again Dr. Alexander asked, "Paul, what hurts?"

Gordon's answer, out of nowhere, only added confusion to confusion. "You people are so mixed up . . . Take it easy. Don't get carried away. Did you ever die?" Then, "Wherever I was, she died . . . Arnold, that poor kid . . ."

"She died . . ." Did this mean that Arnold was killing his mother? Had the piercing cry of anguish been the cry Arnold's mother gave before she expired on the floor of her hospital room where the nurses found her? Or was this the cry out of Gordon's fantasies, stimulated by the drug?

One's mind swam.

At this point Gordon, who was woozy now, was helped to the bathroom, leaving the others pondering.

Dr. Alexander rose and went to the telephone. He had suddenly thought of someone who might be able to help them. He had himself been treating a girl believed to have been the only victim to have been attacked by the Strangler and escaped with her life. This was a twenty-nine-year-old German-born waitress who worked nights, and who will be called Gertrude Gruen. Shortly after noon on February 18, 1963, during a long period when the Strangler had not struck, a man knocked on the door of her apartment on Melrose Street. Gertrude, who had been ill with a virus, was in bed; she had taken a sleeping pill, and she rose, still not quite fully awake, threw a coat over her nightgown, and opened the door. The man, wearing a waist-length dark jacket and green slacks, said he had to fix a bathroom leak. She let him in: he would have to wait a few minutes, he said, until fellow workmen on the roof signaled him to turn off the water. Gertrude paid little attention to him, listening and answering him almost automatically; she turned her back, he suddenly leaped on her, caught her throat in the crook of his arm, and tripped her to the floor. A strong, husky girl, she fought wildly for her life, kicking, biting, trying to disable him. She sank her teeth so deeply into his finger that he loosened his hold for a moment. She screamed, the workmen appeared at the edge of the roof, looking about, and he fled. She was too distraught to recall his appearance except vaguely: a dark face, black hair, about thirty to thirty-five, five feet nine or ten, weighing about 175 pounds. The experience had been so harrowing that Dr. Alexander had been seeing her. On the telephone he asked her to come down immediately and see if she could identify Gordon as her assailant.

Gordon had been back on the couch fifteen minutes when Miss Gruen arrived. She shook her head; she could not make a positive identification. She remained in the room with the others, listening.

Finally, it was over. The needle was removed from Gordon's arm. He slowly awoke. The group proceeded into Dr. Alexander's consultation room, where Gordon sat, yawning, until the influence of the drug wore off completely. Yes, he had had an interesting experience. How long had he been asleep? Six hours? "I'd never have thought it," he said. What had he dreamed about during that time? he was asked. "I didn't dream anything," he said. "They asked me questions and I told them what I thought." He looked around. His eyes met those of Miss Gruen. For all he knew, she was another psychiatrist, for persons had been coming and going through the long day. Others thought Gordon's face went pale when he saw Miss Gruen; but Dr. Brancale, watching him closely, saw nothing like that.

Someone said, "You know, Paul, the Strangler almost got one girl last February. How'd he attack her and how did she get away?"

"I'll show you," said Gordon. He was himself again. He walked up to Phil, suddenly circled behind him, whipped his arm around his neck, and struggled to trip him. "He grabs her this way, then she kicks him—he beats it because she screams and he's afraid of the people on the roof—he sees them through the window—"

Gordon should not have known that.

"What did she look like?" Jim Mellon asked.

Gordon, walking back to his chair, passed Gertrude Gruen. He pointed a finger at her. "Well—she looked a lot like this lady here," he said.

Later, when they were alone, Bottomly spoke with the two psychiatrists. Dr. Brancale did not think Gordon was the Strangler, nor did he think Gordon possessed ESP. How to explain how Gordon knew details not publicly known? Presumably, said Dr. Brancale, Gordon, because of his compelling interest in the crimes, had unconsciously incorporated into his thinking every detail, every experience, he had heard and read about that broadened his knowledge of the cases.

It had been going on for months. Gordon's attorney had had long discussions with the police, and then with Gordon about the crimes. This had undoubtedly helped Gordon to shape and correct his concepts of the stranglings as he went on. At the same time detectives and newspaper reporters, who knew far more than they could print, had also been questioning Gordon. In their very queries they might have dropped hints he seized upon without realizing it. Dr. Brancale did not doubt that Gordon genuinely believed he possessed unusual powers. Hence his readiness to be examined, his impatience and annoyance with anyone who doubted him. As to the question, Was he involved in the stranglings? Dr. Brancale believed he was not. This, however, the physician explained, was a "psychological impression," and it might be well to keep an eye on Mr. Gordon.

Dr. Alexander also spoke cautiously.

"I am not a criminologist and this is speculation," he prefaced his observation. But if no reference to a photograph of a little girl in a ballerina costume had appeared in the press, Gordon must be considered with care. No one could be so clairvoyant as to see a photograph on the floor and also know why it had been thrown there. To be sure, Gordon might have learned about the photograph from friends of Mrs. Irga or from the caretaker who had been in the apartment a few moments after his son discovered the body. On the other hand, attendants at Boston State Hospital had seen Paul Gordon talking to Arnold Wallace, persuasively, suggestively. Dr. Alexander recalled the famous John Christie case in London in the early 1950's. Christie strangled and raped seven women, hiding their dismembered bodies in the walls, flooring, and garden of his home. He managed to find a scapegoat for his crimes—Timothy Evans, the husband of one of his victims. Christie had so influenced the poor man, who was mentally retarded, that Evans finally confessed to murder. He was tried, found guilty, and hanged—Christie appearing as chief witness for the prosecution! Then, four years later, the bodies were found, Christie confessed, and ended on the gallows, too. But for a long time he had hoodwinked Scotland Yard, and some inspectors, to the end, doubted Evans' innocence.

There were precedents, then—

One more possibility complicated matters. Suppose Gordon were the Strangler but did not know it? There were precedents for that, too. In France, a fascinating case was on record in which a detective, after working for months on an extremely baffling murder, discovered to his horror that all

the evidence his skill could uncover led directly to himself as
the murderer! He was, in fact, the killer, but because he
suffered from a dissociative personality, had no conscious
knowledge of his crime.

Was that the case with Paul Gordon?

Considerable public pressure now bore upon the Attorney
General's office. It would not have been too difficult for John
Bottomly to seize upon Gordon. But though he had wanted
to get at the heart of this puzzling episode, he knew he had
not yet done so.

One other factor influenced him. He was aware how powerfully certain drugs could stimulate the imagination: how
much was Gordon fantasying? Once Bottomly had suffered
an illness which required morphine to kill the pain. He discovered that under morphine, half awake, half asleep, he
dreamed the most marvelous dreams, marvelous in their con-
tent but marvelous, too, in their reality. In one he found himself in Versailles, standing at the side of Louis XIV of France
reviewing the entire French army in technicolor. It was extraordinary, he had told a friend, "as though I were really on
the spot, not dreaming and knowing it was a dream, but expe-
riencing it as absolute reality."

Bottomly moved very circumspectly.

Three weeks later, Gordon was asked if he would allow
himself to be interviewed again, this time by Dr. Max Rinkel,
a German-born psychiatrist noted for his work in helping
elicit confessions from Peter Kurtin, the notorious hatchet
murderer of Düsseldorf.* Dr. Rinkel had been present during
part of Gordon's interrogation in Dr. Alexander's office.

Gordon agreed, but at the last moment refused to be put
under the influence of drugs. He was belligerent. Why, he demanded, were the police questioning and requestioning him?
"God damn it, I resent it!" he explained. "I explained my
position. I've got nothing to do with it and I don't care about
it. They've got their murder victims, they've got their pictures, they've got everything they could possibly want—and
what the hell they want me to keep going over and over
again explaining something to them they already know, I
don't know." The only possible reason he could think of, he

* For sixteen years, from 1913 to 1929, Kurtin murdered, committed
sadistic acts, and dismembered women victims in the most perverted
fashion in the Düsseldorf area of Germany. A married man, mild and
courteous in manner, he seemed the least likely of all to have been the
Monster of Düsseldorf. He confessed only when a victim whose life he
had spared finally led police to him.

said angrily, "they must think maybe I was there, I must have done it, I killed those women, they're going to get me to tell how I did it and all that sort of thing—well, for Christ's sake they're all crazy.

"If you want me to confess being the Strangler, to say I did it—" He grew angrier by the moment. "If this makes anybody happy, if this is what they have to have, then I'm going to tell you there's going to be a lot of unhappy people in this world because you're not going to prove something that doesn't exist." They would get nowhere if they approached him with the idea of "settling a problem for Mr. Bottomly or the Police Commissioner."

Dr. Rinkel interrupted him. "Mr. Gordon, I am a doctor, a scientist, I am not a police officer." His task was to help determine if Paul Gordon possessed extrasensory perception, as he claimed. Now, would he explain how he knew about the photograph of the ballerina in the apartment of Ida Irga?

"I don't know how I knew it," said Gordon, "I don't know if there was such a picture at all. All I know is that when I was under sodium pentothal in Dr. Alexander's office, somebody asked me about such a picture and that's what I saw and how I felt. Maybe it's all imagination. I don't know—"

A detective spoke up. "There was a picture, Paul."

"Then I feel better," he said. He came back to the ballerina. "When Arnold saw it, the way it was dressed, it reminded him of the day he saw the little girl attacked in the backyard." He explained that when Arnold was a boy he looked through a knothole in a wooden fence near his home one day and saw a man rape a small girl. "He was at an age when he'd heard about such things but he'd never experienced them," Gordon intoned. "It was so fascinating to him that he just became immobile: everything stopped, but inside of his emotions—why, rapes all over the place. He didn't know what was happening to him. I think he experienced some sort of a sexual climax then . . . I think this is the underlying cause of Arnold's sexual impulses today."

What did he mean?

"Well, you see, he'd like to approach a girl, to go to bed with her, but he can go just so far and then everything happens to him. His unconscious memory is triggered to produce the same sensations he went through while watching this little girl in the backyard." For Arnold, then, the photograph of the ballerina reminded him of the doll, and the doll reminded him of the event in his boyhood.

"You see this in the Ida Irga apartment," said Dr. Rinkel. "What else do you see, Mr. Gordon?"

"After he killed her, somewhere near the kitchen there's a chair and he sat in it looking out the window, so peaceful, so quiet, daydreaming . . ."

"Paul, that bothers me," a detective said. "Have you any idea how he could be so relaxed, not worrying about someone coming in? Doesn't that indicate that he must have known these people well?"

"No, that's the way he was," said Paul with spirit. "All I can say is, if I'd killed someone, I'd be out of there so fast . . . I can't help it, I'm telling it as I see it. He just doesn't care. He has no idea of escaping; no idea of covering his tracks. It's all peaceful, calm, relaxed. He's just drained of feeling and emotion. Now I can relax, he thinks, just go some place, curl up, and sleep."

In the course of the long afternoon Gordon went over his story repeatedly. Finally, Dr. Rinkel asked two questions.

"Mr. Gordon, first, let me ask you: does he kill because he hates or because he likes? And two, a question which has never been answered. Did he rape this victim while she was alive or after she was dead?"

Gordon replied carefully. "Arnold," he said, "feels responsible for his mother's death, because he killed her. Now, he's trying to re-create a feeling of communication between his mother and himself. He looked upon these women as mothers—but they do the same thing his mother did. They get away from him. They're nervous, afraid of him. He tends to get a bit madder: 'You're just like my mother, you're acting like my mother!' He's looking for a little bit of attention, and finally he says, 'You're just like my mother, I'm going to do to you what I did to her—kill her, shut her up!' He wants to put them in a position where they've got to listen to him, to what he has to say. I don't think he meant to kill them. He meant to shut them up, to make them sit still, to make them immobile so he could sit down and talk to them and they'd have to listen to him." It was a reprise of what he had said before.

Then there was a silence for a moment as Gordon reached for what he saw, or knew, or fantasied. "Rape them while alive or dead? Neither. I don't think he raped them. I think he'd like to have tried it but I don't think he can. He's incapable of it."

Nothing was settled.

There was nothing to do but to probe even more deeply into the stranglings, to examine even more exhaustively every possible suspect, meanwhile keeping an eye—and an ear—on four men:

On Thomas O'Brien, at this moment behind the walls of the Massachusetts Mental Health Center, who protested that he had nothing to tell anyone about anything;

On Arnold Wallace, at this moment behind the walls of the State Hospital at Bridgewater, who could not tell anyone anything;

On David Parker, at this moment behind the same walls, who would not tell anyone anything;

On Paul Gordon, free to go about Boston holding to himself whatever secrets he possessed beyond the reach of hypnotic drugs, yet ready to tell everyone everything.

PART THREE

12

Months before, John Bottomly had turned to Boston's leading psychiatrists to ask if they could produce a psychiatric profile of the Strangler. Could they re-create the criminal from the crime? Give police an idea of the sort of man to look for? His age, appearance, personality, type of work? What drove him to his deeds? Where might he be found? And—if every man had the latent capability within himself—how pinpoint the target of the search?

Dr. Donald P. Kenefick and his Medical-Psychiatric Committee* had been working on the problem. At intervals through the spring and summer of 1964 they had met at Boston University's School of Legal Medicine, studying details of the stranglings. Other meetings had been held with police.

Now one of these was in progress. Seated about a rectangular table with Dr. Kenefick in the chair were the distinguished psychiatrists, psychoanalysts, psychologists, and pathologists. Elsewhere in the room were Lieutenants Donovan and Sherry, Bottomly and his staff, and chiefs of homicides in the suburbs where stranglings had occurred.

Covering most of one wall were photographs of the scenes of the stranglings—from the apartment house exteriors to the victims' bodies. On a projection stand stood a case with hundreds of color slides made on the scene by the medical examiners. On another wall hung charts, prepared under Dr. Ke-

---

* The Committee's official membership, as announced by Brooke: Donald P. Kenefick, M.D., of the Law-Medicine Research Institute, Boston University; Michael A. Luongo, M.D., Medical Examiner, Suffolk County; James A. Brussel, M.D., Assistant Commissioner, Department of Mental Health, New York State; Arthur J. McBay, Ph.D., Massachusetts Department of Mental Health; Leo Alexander, M.D., Max Rinkel, M.D., psychiatrists in private practice; and several other physicians among them one whose specialty included clinical anthropology and who preferred to remain anonymous.

nefick's direction: location of crime, type of building, date, time of day, weather, age and background of victim, nature of sexual injury, type of ligature, details of the autopsy.

As of that moment, committee opinion ranged from the belief of Dr. James A. Brussel, of New York's "Mad Bomber" fame, that one man might have committed all eleven stranglings, to the belief that there might be any number of murderers.

A major question the committee had wrestled with was this:

Would the Strangler, driven to kill five elderly women because each represented in his madness the mother he hated-/loved, also be driven to kill Sophie Clark, aged twenty, and a Negro; Patricia Bissette, twenty-three; Beverly Samans, also twenty-three; Evelyn Corbin, fifty-eight (but appearing far younger); Joann Graff, twenty-three, and Mary Sullivan, nineteen?

Or might these younger women have been killed by someone else, and for other reasons? Might not one man have strangled the five older women and others have been responsible for the six murders that followed—murders in which scarflike decorations and bizarre stage effects had been deliberately added to make them appear the Strangler's work?

The committee was increasingly coming to this conclusion. It would appear far more logical to separate the victims into two groups—in Dr. Kenefick's words, the Old Women, and the Girls.

As Dr. Kenefick put it in a report issued later, the majority of the committee agreed that one man probably had killed the Old Women. He would be "Mr. S."—the Strangler. As to the others—the Girls—they probably were not slain by Mr. S. but by one or more men, likely to be found in the circle of the Girls' acquaintances, most probably "unstable members of the homosexual community" who had tried to make their acts resemble the stranglings of the Old Women as reported in the newspapers. The more one considered this theory, the more persuasive it seemed.

The Back Bay in which Sophie Clark and Patricia Bissette lived, and Beacon Hill where Mary Sullivan lived, were neighborhoods frequented by homosexuals. Charles Street —Mary's street—was the most Bohemian of all Boston's Bohemian West End. Every night was a Mardi Gras. With each change of semester new friends descended. It was colorful, bizarre, offbeat. "If a two-headed man walked down Charles Street nobody'd turn to look at him," one of the detectives liked to say.

For whatever it meant, before Mary Sullivan moved to Boston, she had roomed in a Hyannis motel; among her neighbors were the owners of one of Boston's most popular homosexual gathering places. Sophie Clark lived on Huntington Avenue, a seedy area marked by a weird mixture of artistic, Bohemian, and academic people because of its proximity to art schools, colleges, and music conservatories. A short distance away was Boston's notorious "Hot Corner"—the intersection of Massachusetts and Columbus Avenues—an area spotted with barber shops catering to homosexuals and at night the hunting ground of fifteen-dollar prostitutes.

Evelyn Corbin's apartment house in Salem was in a quiet residential section, but not far away were slums. Beverly Samans lived in Cambridge, a block from Harvard Square, which had more than its proportion of avant-garde coffee shops, sexual deviates, beatniks, and oddball characters. Beverly, moreover, was writing a thesis on homosexuality, one of her friends had escorted her to one of the better-known homosexual clubs, and many of her callers were, as Dr. Kenefick put it in his summarizing report to Bottomly, "uncertainly sexed young men." Even Joann Graff, murdered in Lawrence, an almost pathetically inhibited farm girl from Illinois, who with her frugality* was the most spinsterlike of the Girls, had such associates. Many of the men she met in the course of her work were homosexuals.

As to the character of the man or men capable of the stranglings, Dr. Kenefick pointed out that he and his colleagues at most could only hazard a few guesses toward a "common profile." Generally, he explained, the sex murderer contains within himself "an encapsulated core of rage" directed at an important figure in his early life—usually a dominant, overwhelming female. To cope with his rage he engages in powerful, sadistic fantasies in which he kills this figure. The sex murderer differs from other psychotic killers in his ability to keep his terrible daydreams to himself. He keeps quiet about them: he exhibits no odd behavior. Thus he is able to move among friends and fellow workers without calling attention to himself. Chances were that he might appear bland, pleasant, gentle, ingratiating—even compassionate. Because of the training given him by the hated female

---

* In many ways Joann resembled the Old Women. She kept a record of every penny she spent, tried to live on six dollars a week for food, and when she exceeded her budget, ate doughnuts and coffee. Even five cents spent for a chocolate bar was jotted down in her cashbook, and one came upon such notes to herself as: "For the rest of the week NO chocolate, NO dinners, NO movies."

figure he would most likely be neat, punctual, polite—in brief, the personality often seen in confidence men, homosexuals "and in many normal lower middle class men." No one would think of him as "crazy."

What, then, would trigger his crime—cause him to kill?

Certain stresses that would bring about sadistic impulses too great for him to cope with. The loss of his mother, either by death or because she turned him out of the house; anything that contributed to a loss of self-esteem, such as being fired from a job; or anything that made him feel a loss of masculinity. That could result from a late marriage to a woman who expected him to function as an adult, although such a man would most likely find himself marrying a second mother.

Whatever the case, he would find himself in a deepening depression from which he was able to emerge only by a sudden explosion, a violent venting of his hate, frustration, impotence: in short, murder, the destruction of the terrifying female image, but murder in the special ritualistic, fetishist manner of his illness, both sadistic and loving. Because each murder solved nothing—the specter was not eliminated, it would rise again—he was doomed to repeat the crime again and again.

What kind of mother would he have? "A sweet, orderly, neat, compulsive, seductive, punitive, overwhelming woman. She might go about half-exposed in their apartment, but punish him severely for any sexual curiosity." Chances were that he once lived with a woman possessing characteristics similar to those of his victims, and in a similar environment. His father had died or perhaps deserted the family before his son's puberty. In any case, he was not close to him.

"The boy grew up to feel that women were a fearful mystery. He was inhibited heterosexually but the overwhelming respectability of his background probably kept him from much overt homosexuality," Dr. Kenefick speculated. He might have attempted sexual relations with women but was successful only if he could imagine himself humiliating, beating, and torturing them.

Each time he murdered, the physician suggested, he was attempting to "reestablish a seductive scene, to carry out buried incestuous fantasies, and to exorcise certain fears by acting out a fantasy of degrading and controlling an overwhelming and fearsome mother."

"Mr. S." was probably not an exceptional man in appearance—not too tall, not too short, not too deformed—or someone would have noticed. He probably was admitted on some pretext, or entered by slipping the lock.

"It is an easy matter to strangle someone from behind, enough to induce unconsciousness, with a forearm grip." Or he could clout them on the side of the neck with the edge of his hand. He would be at least thirty—perhaps older; strong enough to carry or pull heavy women (Blake, Jane Sullivan, Irga) about the room; neat and orderly (he left no fingerprints, probably wearing gloves at all times); probably single, separated, or divorced; a man "who knew how to kill efficiently, who was attracted by neat, pleasant old women with fair complexions and firm flesh . . . who felt a certain savage titillation in partially exposing women, who left them with a grotesque imitation of scarves, often elaborately tied around the necks; who contemptuously injured their sexual parts with a fantasy-phallus of glass or wood (whose firmness and bigness revealed his own wishes and fears), who looked for some small object—money? photographs?—in desks, closets, and bureau drawers." He left his victims in such shocking positions not only to degrade and debase them, but also to make it appear that they tried to entice him—a tribute to the masculinity he desperately wished he possessed.

The police might do well to search for a man who had periods of idleness in summer, Christmas, and the holiday seasons, since most of the stranglings occurred then. At such times, Dr. Kenefick speculated, Mr. S. was left "face to face with his thoughts," depression seized him, and he was driven to kill. He would probably be too busy at other times to be depressed. "What manner of man is relatively unoccupied during summer and holiday seasons?" One might think first of a school teacher or a college student; perhaps a charities collector. But it was difficult to think of other occupations which would be apt to be slack in the summer and winter holiday seasons.

Here Dr. Kenefick interposed an interesting observation. All this elaborate speculation would be eliminated "if it turned out that Mr. S. was a sneak thief who struck at someone who surprised him, thereby discovering, like an aged tiger who accidentally pounces on a villager, how easy humans are to kill." The multiple dwellings in which virtually every victim lived were the haunt of sneak thieves, and perfectly suited for burglaries because of the thick walls and adjoining roofs—the latter allowing both a way of approach and retreat.

Observing that the murders took place in "mixed lace-curtain Irish, lower-drawer Yankee, student-type neighborhoods," Dr. Kenefick noted that although one of the largest ethnic groups in Boston was the Italian, "no Italian name occurs among the victims."

Why had the killer not struck since Mary Sullivan, January 4, 1964?

Some committee members believed he might have committed suicide. He might have been driven by a compulsion so overwhelming that in the end only his own destruction satisfied him. Or he might have been arrested for another crime, and might now be in prison, or in a mental institution. Perhaps he was one of those safe behind the walls of Bridgewater. Or, frightened off by the Attorney General's manhunt launched immediately after Mary's death, he might have taken cover and might be waiting for the search to subside before killing again.

One other possibility was presented—and that turned out to be the most alarming speculation of all. It came from Dr. Brussel, the New York psychiatrist who had already suggested that one man might be responsible. Now he advanced another theory to explain the halt in murders. Although virtually every member had his own conception of the Strangler, Dr. Brussel's success in the Mad Bomber case led one to pay attention.

The Mad Bomber might have come from the pages of Sherlock Holmes. For nearly fourteen years New York had been terrorized by homemade bombs found in subways, bus terminals, and theaters, followed by taunting letters to the police. The bomber was obviously demented but also cunning enough to leave no clues. In 1956, Dr. Brussel, Assistant Commissioner of Mental Hygiene of New York State, who had assisted the police in many cases dealing with psychopathic criminals, suggested that they should look for a man between forty and fifty, probably unmarried, sexually abnormal, a Roman Catholic of Central European stock, probably living with a sister or brother in Westchester County of New York or in southern Connecticut. As if this detailed description were not enough, he added that when police seized the man he most likely would be wearing a double-breasted suit. *With all the buttons buttoned.*

How did he arrive at these conclusions?

Dr. Brussel explained. The man was between forty and fifty because paranoia reaches its peak then and the crime was obviously that of a paranoiac. He was sexually abnormal, and so probably unmarried, because each bomb was shaped like a penis, and the *W* in his notes looked like a woman's breasts, although he printed all the other letters in block type.

Roman Catholic of Central European descent living in Westchester or southern Connecticut because bombs are a traditional method of protest in Central Europe, most Central Europeans are Roman Catholics, and the largest concentrations of this ethnic group near New York City are in Westchester and southern Connecticut. Living with his family because close knit family life marks the people of Central Europe. Finally, the double-breasted suit: because the Bomber, as proved by the fact he left no clues, was extremely neat; his femininity, added to his neatness, would lead him to wear what is perhaps the neatest (especially when primly buttoned) and most protective of suits (if he knew the police were searching for him).

With Dr. Brussel's help, an open letter to the Mad Bomber was drafted and published in the New York *Journal-American*. The idea was to tempt him into an overt act that might bring about his arrest. The strategy worked. The Mad Bomber replied, writing vaguely of a grudge against a utility company. A search of Consolidated Edison records led police to a former employee—fifty-three-year-old George Metesky, unmarried, a Roman Catholic of Central European stock living with two sisters in southern Connecticut, wearing a double-breasted suit with all the buttons buttoned. He had been setting bombs, he explained, "to get even" with the company.

Now in the case of the Boston Strangler, Dr. Brussel thought he would be in his early thirties or forties, perhaps of Southern European or Spanish stock because garroting was associated with such backgrounds.

Then he advanced his theory: that each killing was a psychotic act committed by a man searching for his potency. As he put it, here was the ancient story of the Oedipus complex, a man's unconscious sexual desire for his mother, an impulse he dares not yield to. Yet each time he approached another woman he found himself impotent, because his sex drive was fixed upon his mother. Since the man was demented he coped with his problem in a demented fashion: if he could destroy his mother's image, he would be free to direct his libido elsewhere—to be as other men.

First, then, he stalked and killed Anna Slesers. She must have resembled his mother: elderly, gray-haired, wearing metal-rimmed glasses. After killing her, however, he discovered to his surprise and rage that he was still impotent. At this, furious, like the character Popeye in Faulkner's novel *Sanctuary,* he assaulted her sexually with a substitute—a bottle, broom, anything that was on hand.

Then he strangled his second mother-image, Helen Blake,

who looked much like the first. Again, he discovered no change in himself; again, enraged at his helplessness, he assaulted his victim. So with Nina Nichols, Ida Irga, and Jane Sullivan.*

Then, for whatever reason, he attacked twenty-year-old Sophie Clark. Here, for the first time, he found a change in himself. He was potent. Witness the seminal stain on the rug next to Sophie's body. Thereafter, he attacked only younger women—the Girls. In each instance, unmistakable signs of a man's virility were found by police, and in the most recent strangling, that of nineteen-year-old Mary Sullivan, spectacularly so.

Why had there been no strangling since?

Because, suggested Dr. Brussel, the Strangler had achieved his goal: he had found his potency. He was "cured." The use of the word was grotesque, to be sure, but so far as it reflected the fact that he was psychosexually maturing, that he was progressing to more heterosexual activity—however sadistic—it was relevant.

And "cured"—so the psychiatrist suggested with chilling calmness—he might be found in everyday society going about his business, mingling with the crowds in the streets, in the trolley cars, in the movies, at parties at people's homes—with no one the wiser.

"I know I'm sticking my neck out," said Dr. Brussel. His theory, though medically possible, was put down as a minority report.

In late 1964, had one stood in busy Park Square of an evening, not far from the Statler-Hilton Hotel, one might have observed men strolling by, jotting down the license numbers of automobiles parked in front of a number of cafés, bars, and nightclubs. To the police the Square was known as Homosexual Row. Boston was dotted with small communities of sexual deviates, but this area was the largest.

The search had entered another phase.

It had been suggested by Detective Lieutenant Andrew Tuney of the Massachusetts State Police, a smiling, unassuming, forty-year-old ex-Marine whose reputation had led Bot-

---

* The physical resemblance among the Old Women had been remarked upon often. (It will be recalled that Ida Irga's son Joseph almost mistook Jane Sullivan, another victim, for his mother.) If the Strangler was killing a mother-image and if most men, as is contended, resemble their mothers, would the murderer be found to resemble his victims? This was one of the avenues explored by the medical anthropologist on the committee.

tomly to appoint him to direct his investigative squad and to act, as well, as liaison with all police authorities. There were a number of reasons for Bottomly's choice. As a member of the State Police, Lieutenant Tuney had authority to move into any area in Massachusetts. Because he was a trained police officer, his presence in the Attorney General's office would help assuage the resentment still felt by Boston police at Brooke's entry into the investigations. At the same time the manhunt had become so massive and demanding that Bottomly, still saddled with the Eminent Domain Division, could make good use of a skilled deputy, and one on good terms with all parties.

Lieutenant Tuney took on his new assignment grimly. Like Donovan and DiNatale, Tuney was the son of a police officer: his interest in the legal aspects of crime detection had led him to take three years of criminal law courses at Suffolk Law School, but he had been too busy to complete his studies. He had been involved in many of the strangling investigations, often on his own time. He had taken the murders in his stride until Mary Sullivan. He had been outraged by the others, but when he saw what had been done to nineteen-year-old Mary—a year older than his own daughter—"I wanted to smash him. I wanted to hit him." In the beginning he had been inclined to write off the murderer as one more psychopath who would be quickly captured, but as the search continued and no lead came to fruition, he confided to a fellow officer, "My biggest fear is that he'll turn out to be someone we could have picked up long ago—but we haven't been adding the right facts together."

Tuney moved into action on three fronts. When he was appointed on July 20, he at once held a full-scale review of everything done so far—a meeting lasting long after midnight, attended by all high police officials from Boston and the suburbs in which the stranglings had occurred, as well as by detectives from the Cape Cod area where Mary Sullivan had grown up. Also present were technicians—police photographers, stenographers, fingerprint experts, artists, chemists—who had been on the murders or worked on the evidence. Perhaps one of these men might have observed a clue, however insignificant; perhaps he nurtured an idea, a way to proceed, that he had hesitated to suggest because protocol restricted these matters to the detectives themselves. Here was his opportunity to unburden himself, to bring out the notes and memos he might have made.

Secondly Lieutenant Tuney brought about a closer relationship with the Dan Sullivan Agency, a private Boston detective organization that had been quietly assisting in the search. Such an agency had the capacity and the sources to move in fields in which Bottomly and his investigative squad were limited. Its operatives could use highly sophisticated electronic devices to tap wires, "bug" rooms, tape-record conversations in offices or even in the street without the participants' knowledge, take infrared photographs in darkness; they could intercept mail, rent apartments adjacent to suspects, pose as physicians, census-takers, house-movers, make use of stool pigeons, informers, and hundreds of underworld contacts they had developed through the years—in short, could avail themselves of numerous methods of detection that the Attorney General's office, as the chief law enforcement agency of the Commonwealth could not employ.

Although laymen are generally unaware of it, federal, state, and local law enforcement agencies constantly work closely with private investigative agencies, thus doubling and tripling their effectiveness. Most ironic is the fact that crime, by virtue of illicit money, often has far greater financial resources than police or sheriff's offices, limited as they are by city and county budgets. The underworld, with these funds at their disposal, were constantly ferreting out and thwarting traditional detection methods.

A private detective agency had every right to carry on its own search for the Strangler, in its own fashion, at its own expense. If successful, it would not only render a valuable service to a harassed community, but stood to be well paid for its pains. It would be eligible for rewards ranging from $10,000 to a possible total of $110,000 for all eleven. The agency's only obligation was to turn over important evidence to the proper police authorities. Meanwhile, additional skilled investigators had been brought into the search.

Finally, Tuney considered the emphasis put upon the homosexual community by the psychiatrists. (Dr. Kenefick had discussed their deliberations in his report, cautiously entitled "Preliminary Notes for the Project to Establish a 'Psychiatric Profile' of the Boston Strangler.") Although the homosexual aspect had come up repeatedly it now deserved more attention, particularly since links seemed to exist not only in the case of the Girls but also with respect to some of the Old Women. Sometimes these were as tenuous as the report that Helen Blake in Lynn had to pass a notorious café to and from work each day. She might have dropped in there for a beer without knowing its clientele. Who was to say that her killer had not followed her home and learned her routine well enough to know when he could attack? That might be true of others, too. Dr. Ames Robey's speculation that the Strangler's victims might have aroused him by some nonverbal sign was recalled. There had also been vague rumors that certain of the Old Women, some of whom had had nothing to do with men for decades, were associated with Lesbians. How much of that was true, and how much pure nonsense, no one knew.

Even more important was the growing discovery that the homosexual community in and about Boston appeared to be linked together, might even have an overall directorate—a syndicate—similar to organized crime. Although little written about, sexual deviation and the money derived from it, the growing numbers of homosexuals of both sexes gathering openly in luxurious clubs and resorts—all that, not excepting such collateral enterprises as blackmail—was becoming Big Business. Big Business hand in hand with crime could mean severe punishment for those who wittingly or unwittingly caused trouble . . . If some of the Strangler's victims were enmeshed in this community, who knew that error might have been committed by one of them that led to murder? Perhaps some had not met their death at the hands of a madman, but only appeared to have done so.

It was all bafflingly vague but there was something there worth searching for.

Until now no important lead had been produced by Bottomly's computer program. The machines had been working week in, week out, on victims, friends, and suspects. Lieutenant Tuney thought, Let's try a new run on the computers, this time concentrating on homosexual data. On the assumption that the floater or derelict homosexual was not likely to be involved in murder for cause, this meant checking out patrons of the better homosexual haunts. Granted, not everyone whose car was parked in the vicinity of homosexual clubs and bars belonged to this society, but certainly the owner's identity should be learned, his name checked against those in the victims' address books, shown to friends and family to see if it was familiar. His telephone number, social security number, place of employment, restaurants in which he ate, resorts in which he vacationed—all would be fed into the computer to be matched with data from the victims. If he turned out to be a member of the homosexual hierarchy, his telephone calls should be monitored day and night. Some day he might utter a name associated, however vaguely, with one of the victims.

July moved into August. At the State Identification Bureau Bob Roth's machines hummed. By September 1964, more than thirty-five thousand items had been run through the computers in this new attack on the mystery of the strangulation murders.

And still no key card dropped out.

13

All that could honestly be said at this point was that no one was sure of anything. There was no orderly progression of events. Everything happened simultaneously. Donovan's men continued to work on the Boston cases even as they coped with other homicides, a new one almost every week. Bottomly's investigators checked out suspects—men suspected in a specific strangling, and general suspects, men who might have been involved in any or all. Lynn, Cambridge, Salem, and Lawrence detectives pushed deeper into their cases, filing report upon report that found their way to Bottomly's office to join those from other sources to be copied in quintuplet, collated, indexed, and added to the eleven casebooks by twenty-seven-year-old Sandra Irizarry, research assistant in charge of the files. Dr. Carola Blume, the graphologist, studied letters sent in by the public, seeking to separate those written by reasonably balanced citizens from those written by the emotionally disturbed.* The Medical-Psychiatric Committee studied the casebooks, the computers labored to match victim and victim, victim and suspect, suspect and suspect, and to provide, in seconds, information on any one of twenty-three hundred persons whose names had come up, even remotely, in the investigation to date.

No one knew when a man might be seized for another crime, a tip phoned in, an admission made, that would send

* Dr. Blume discovered that most of the letters—fully half of them were anonymous—came from women, many of whom had a homosexual turn of mind and were given to elaborate sexual fantasies. Often a sentence read, "I'm sure I know who the Strangler is. He came to my apartment, he looked strangely at me. . ." As Dr. Blume interpreted it, these writers nourished a subconscious wish that the Strangler *would* call on them. What Dr. Blume hoped for, above all, was that the Strangler himself might be compelled to write—and give himself away by his calligraphy.

everyone off in a new direction. Virtually every person in the huge Attorney General's office on the second floor of the State House—Bottomly, his aide Bill Manning, Detective Lieutenant Tuney, and the investigators DiNatale, Mellon, Delaney; Sandra Irizarry and Bottomly's "Strangler Bureau" secretary, twenty-one-year-old Jane Downey, at one time or another had a favorite suspect. When a new fact emerged, or another letter arrived, or a jagged piece of a subsidiary jigsaw puzzle fell into place, one heard, "Do you like him better now?" Or "Oh, I *like* him!"—almost gleefully—"like" meaning to consider him a more plausible suspect. The horror had become secondary, eclipsed by the excitement of the chase.

For Sandra Irizarry and Jane Downey, the only women in the inner sanctum of the search, it was an extraordinary and moving experience. As one development succeeded another, the detectives used them as a touchstone to feminine reaction in Boston.

The younger victims of the Strangler—the Girls—were their contemporaries. Sandra had lived on Beacon Hill herself; often she had visited "The Sevens," a crowded, steaming young people's hangout across the street from 44A Charles Street, Mary Sullivan's apartment house. She had more than once gone into the same beauty parlor and used the same pay telephone from which Mary's roommates, Pat and Pam, had called the police that dreadful dusk. Sandra and Jane knew the narrow streets, the drugstores and cafeterias of the Back Bay and Beacon Hill so familiar to the Strangler and his victims.

Now, as they read the pages of the eleven casebooks they collated and cross-indexed in the office, as they read the Girls' confidences to friends and schoolmates, as they read the reports of psychologists to whom some of the Girls had turned for help with their emotional problems, as they read the letters the Girls had written and received, as they read of their private possessions, including the contents of their purses the day of the deaths, the Strangler's young victims were all but alive to them. Sandra and Jane spoke of them familiarly and with the assurance—and understanding—of intimate friends. "Oh, Sophie would never do that!" or "Joann's mother was very possessive," or "This problem came up and Pat just didn't know how to handle it."

Of no one in their own circle of the living did Sandra and Jane know as much as they knew about the dead girls. They defended them in spirited discussions with detectives (who were inclined to agree with the psychiatrists that the younger victims might have brought their fate on themselves): Don't be too hard on Mary, she was turning over a new leaf; yes, Beverly was forever involved with offbeat characters but all she wanted was to help—she just had too big a heart; Sophie was integrity itself and if she'd been ready to cheat on her boyfriend, she might be alive today; Evelyn hoped to marry Bob but there was this cozy threesome with Bob and his mother . . .

Against one wall of the vault room leaned an enormous bulletin board ten feet long, six feet high. Tacked on it were the glossy police photographs of the stranglings—exteriors of each apartment house, interiors of each apartment, photographs of front and back staircases, halls, roofs, service entrances. Missing only were photographs of the victims' bodies as they were found. In deference to Sandra and Jane (as well as to secretaries going in and out of the offices), these had been tacked on the reverse side of the board so they faced the wall. By tacit agreement only detectives and visiting out-of-town police were permitted to move the board aside and slip behind it to look upon the Strangler's work.

Few emerged unmoved. It was a shattering experience to look at the photographs.

The excitement in the office was constant. For one tense twenty-four-hour period Bottomly had a confession to Beverly Samans' murder, dictated and signed by twenty-eight-year-old Daniel J. Pennacchio, a busboy in a Cambridge cafeteria. Pennacchio had been arrested in Mount Auburn Hospital in Cambridge after nurses saw him lying on the floor outside the ladies' rest room, peeping under the door. A quick check disclosed that he had been a student for eleven years at Fernald School for Retarded Children, where Beverly Samans had taught. He had been discharged in June 1963. When his photograph appeared in the press, letters poured in from women in the Belmont area where he lived. They knew him well. They had seen him standing for hours beside his car, watching girls pass by, every now and then opening the door of the car and smilingly inviting one girl or another to enter it. One letter, summing up most of the others, warned, "Don't let this man get away. He's the man you're looking for. If he gets off free, you will have a lot of people storming the State House. Get going on him and he will confess, and don't let him off on a lie detector test. That is a lot of hooey. He could control his emotions while under the machine." It was signed "A Woman Who Lives Alone."

As it turned out, no lie detector was needed. In the interrogation room, surrounded by detectives, Pennacchio suddenly blurted, "All right, I'll tell you everything. I did it." While a police stenographer took down his words, he described the murder, step by step: how he had knocked on Beverly's door just before midnight of May 5 (she had returned home around eleven o'clock, police knew), how she had let him in, how he had talked with her while she typed her thesis . . .

Detective Paul Cloran of Cambridge police questioned him:

"Did you stab Beverly Samans?"

"Yes."

"How?"

"With a knife."

"Where did you get the knife?"

"In the kitchen."

"How many times did you stab her?"

"About fifteen—I'm not sure."

"With which hand?"

"My right."

"Where was the body facing?"

"Toward the window."

"What did you put in her mouth?"

"A rag."

"Anything else?"

"I put a cloth over her mouth."

"Did you get blood on you?"

"Yes, my pants and shirt."

"What did you do with them?"

"I threw them into an ash barrel behind the building."

He described the apartment, and what she wore, and how he let himself out, and where he went.

Then Pennacchio, small, dark, intense, signed his confession and sat back, exhausted.

None of it was true. He had imagined it all.

Because he had confessed, he was booked for murder but certain details he told police made it clear that he was lying, and Cambridge Judge A. Edward Viola refused to issue a murder complaint. He was held instead on the original charge of lewd and lascivious behavior. Pennacchio was mentally retarded, with the intelligence of a fifteen-year-old boy, said his lawyer. The sheer suggestibility in the situation—that detectives *could* think he had done it—might have led him to place himself in the Samans apartment and even to see himself going through the act of murder.

Not long after, Pennacchio eliminated himself forever as a suspect. While swimming with two teen-age girls at Pleasure Bay in South Boston, he attempted a high dive from a bridge. He struck his head and drowned.

A few days after Pennacchio's arrest, police seized a twenty-nine-year-old man who wore horn-rimmed spectacles, a carefully trimmed moustache, and a three-quarter length jacket. His black hair was shiny with pomade. He lived in a shanty on Brownsville Street four blocks from Helen Blake, the nurse who had been strangled in Lynn on June 30, 1962. A patrolman, looking for stolen bicycles, had come upon two suitcases hidden behind the shanty. They were stuffed with newspaper clippings of the eleven stranglings. In one a diary was found, a clipping pasted on each page. Under one clipping reporting Anna Slesers' murder on June 14, 1962, was written in ink, "I took a long walk today with my beloved Anna." Under Helen Blake's, "Lunched with dear Helen today." Under Evelyn Corbin's, "Goodbye, I'm a gone goose."

The news flashed through Boston that a prime suspect had been caught. Reporters crowded into Lynn Police Headquarters to question Bottomly, hurriedly called to the scene. Not only was there the damning evidence of clippings and diary; the man's history was almost too "good" to be true. He lived in Lynn (Helen Blake); had recently roomed in the Beacon Hill area (Ida, Irga, Mary Sullivan), as well as in the Back Bay area (Anna Slesers, Sophie Clark, Patricia Bissette); he had lived briefly near Nina Nichols, and again near Jane Sullivan. He had worked in a bookstore in Cambridge (Beverly Samans), and—this really interested the investigators—held a job as a counterman in a doughnut shop in Salem. No one had forgotten that the day Evelyn Corbin was strangled in her Salem apartment, a fresh doughnut had been found on the fire escape outside her kitchen window. To top this formidable array of facts—only lacking was a tie-in to Joann Graff's murder in nearby Lawrence—the man had worked as an orderly in Lynn Hospital, where Helen Blake was then associated as a practical nurse.

It meant another twenty-four hours of intense excitement—then deflation.

It was nothing, nothing at all, Bottomly and Police Chief John Donnelly of Lynn had to announce at a press conference. The man was a "writer of sorts"; his diary was fiction, an attempt to work out his own sexual fantasies; he claimed to belong to the American Nazi Party, which had some membership in that area; but so far as could be determined, he was harmless. The reporters were free to hasten back to cover the major story of the hour—the arrival in Boston from Toronto of the newly married Richard Burton and Elizabeth Taylor, an event that had caused a near-riot at Logan

International Airport. The writer from Lynn became merely one more page, checked in and checked out, in the growing Suspect file on the second floor of the State House.

When Bottomly left Lynn to return to his office that day he did not know that one of his most indefatigable volunteers had just returned from an out-of-town mission also dealing with the Strangler. That was Mrs. Margaret Callahan, who was just then marching furiously into her apartment after a frustrating trip to Manchester, New Hampshire, to alert police that her neighbor, Dr. Lawrence Shaw, was there on a "skiing vacation."

In these past months Mrs. Callahan had been more diligent than ever, as entries in her journal revealed:

In November 1963, she had made a quick trip to New York to see Dr. Brussel after reading his analysis of the Strangler that appeared in the October 1963 issue of *Pageant* magazine. Dr. Brussel, she told friends later, suggested she take her material to the Boston authorities, but she knew how far that would get her. Nevertheless, she had been able to persuade Sergeant Leo Davenport of the Cambridge police to call on her on December 16 to discuss Beverly Samans' murder. Beverly's apartment in Cambridge was only a block from Harvard Square; and had she herself not followed Dr. Shaw to his favorite bookstore in Harvard Square and watched him purchase volumes on crime, sex, perversion, and bloody acts of murder, including even cannibalism? Not long before he boastfully showed her a Christmas card he received in December 1962 from a girl living on East Eighty-ninth Street in New York City—an address, Mrs. Callahan emphasized, that was practically around the corner from 57 East Eighty-eighth Street, where Janice Wylie and Emily Hoffert, two New York career girls, had been so depravedly stabbed to death on August 28, 1963. As Beverly Samans had been stabbed to death only three months before.

When Sergeant Davenport called on her, Mrs. Callahan made it a social rather than a professional occasion. She greeted him barefoot, in a colorful muumuu, her hair piled, queenly fashion, atop her head. She served him coffee, and only after he was comfortable in a deep easy chair did she seat herself cross-legged on the floor, arrange her voluminous costume about her, and began to read from her material on Dr. Shaw, now almost as thick as a book. "Don't you dare ask me any questions," she warned. "I've spent too much time collecting this material to be interrupted. You just be quiet and listen." But Sergeant Davenport was impatient, and as she complained to friends later, "oversecure and arrogant," and finally she showed him out with a sharp warning that if the police were not interested she would sell her material on Dr. Shaw to the Birch Society.

On January 3, 1964, she telephoned Lieutenant Sherry to predict, on the basis of Dr. Shaw's strange behavior the last few days, that another strangling was imminent. It was small comfort for her to say, "I told you so," when Mary Sullivan's body was found twenty-four hours later. On February 8 she reached Assistant Attorney General Bottomly, who invited her to bring her data to his office. She preferred instead, she told him, that he send his detectives to her home where they could look it over carefully. Two days later, on February 10, Sergeant Leo Martin and another detective visited her. They wanted to take her material to be copied and that she would not permit: they left, obviously annoyed. Then Dr. Shaw went off to New Hampshire and she dropped everything to trail him there and back.

Now, with still more evidence, Mrs. Callahan sat down at her telephone and methodically called *Life* magazine; then *Time* magazine; then *Newsweek;* then *Look.*

Then she put in another call for Mr. Bottomly, but found herself repeatedly shunted to lesser persons in his office. She hung up in disgust.

Was there nothing a conscientious citizen could do?

She began telephoning neighbors.

In the Attorney General's office Bill Manning typed a brief memo. It was about Mrs. Ann Johnson (which is not her real name).

A Mrs. Ann Johnson called. She lives in the same apt. bldg. as Dr. Lawrence Shaw. She reports that most of the people in and around the building believe him insane. He, according to her, has an amazingly high interest in cannibalism. He taught at Carnegie Institute when Sophie Clark went there, and Mrs. J. believes he taught Sophie. He is reported to be associated with the Golden Age Society and would therefore "get to know these older ladies that way."

This communication, Manning added with some perplexity, was only the most recent of several—both telephone calls and anonymous letters—received from persons who named the same Dr. Lawrence Shaw as the Strangler.

For Dr. Shaw, the moment of truth came soon after. When

Mrs. Callahan had first sent in his name the police made a discreet inquiry. Her description of Dr. Shaw as a man of odd habits, with few friends, was not borne out by his hospital colleagues and Mrs. Callahan's accusations were filed away. Now, however, her material had become so formidable, her dossier so carefully documented, her complaints so clearly confirmed from other sources, that a full-scale investigation began, in the course of which Dr. Shaw was asked if he would take a lie-detector test. It was purely voluntary, the police said. He was free to refuse.

Dr. Shaw, obviously a very harassed man, was only too willing. He opened his life to the police. He told questioners that he had been having an affair for some months with Mrs. Callahan, which he ended in the summer of 1962. That was just before the Anna Slesers strangling. Rejected, humiliated, vengeful—who knew how such a woman's mind worked?—Mrs. Callahan had managed, apparently, to convince not only her niece, but virtually every other tenant in the building that he was the Strangler. He had been living an absolute nightmare: neighbors spying on him, making notes on his visitors—he was a bachelor, and enjoyed feminine companionship—following him when he left the building, telephoning each other when they saw him stop in the street to chat with a friend, keeping vigil in their cars outside his office, even trailing him on his skiing trips—and Mrs. Callahan masterminding it all!

There was little to be done with Mrs. Margaret Callahan,* Bottomly knew. Her lawyer had advised him that "Nothing you could say could satisfy my client in her present mental condition." But a careful letter was sent to Mrs. Ann Johnson:

. . . As a result of our investigation you may be assured that Dr. Lawrence Shaw has never been connected with the Carnegie Institute in any way. He was never a member of its faculty. He was never a teacher of Sophie Clark. You may be assured that the Director of the Golden Age Society advises that Dr. Lawrence Shaw is not connected with that group in any official capacity and his name does not appear in any of the groups' rosters or other listings of individuals informally connected with the group. Further inquiries have been made with the active groups of the Golden Age Society and none

---

* Mrs. Callahan emphatically denied she had had any intimate relationship with Dr. Shaw.

of the members interviewed have any knowledge of Dr. Shaw.

It was not possible to develop any evidence which supported your allegation that Dr. Shaw has an amazing interest in cannibalism . . .

And, because he was dealing with the public and no lead from whatever source dared be overlooked, Bottomly added the paragraph with which he signed every letter of this nature—by now he must have dictated nearly five hundred of them:

Please be assured that either this Department or any appropriate local police department will give immediate reply on any information you may be able to provide in connection with the investigation of criminal activities.

The door had to remain open. Yet only two days before, a former attorney had submitted the name of a man he considered a suspect. The address on the letterhead was one of distinction, the letter couched in such precise language, the arguments advanced such as to merit immediate attention. Bottomly's letter inviting the writer to call at once crossed a second note from him:

"Dear Mr. Bottomly," he wrote. "In my previous letter I fear I was derelict in failing to mention that I was recently assaulted by a company of Boston firemen and suffered a badly injured right ankle. I regret, however, that I found it necessary to kill each and every one of them with my Berretta automatic. I sued for damages but I have not received the court award of some one hundred eighty million dollars as yet. Respectfully yours . . ."

Bottomly looked at it ruefully, and passed it on.

There was no investigator who was not involved in similar episodes. One dared not separate the plausible from the implausible, for often what was dismissed as absolute nonsense—wild suspicions, elaborate hypotheses created out of hysteria and sexual fears—turned out to confound them by their relevancy.

The letter from the owner of the Berretta automatic still waited to be filed when attention suddenly centered on an Italian music teacher who might have played Mephistopheles in Gounod's *Faust*. Slender, dapper, faultlessly tailored, with compelling black eyes, he will be called Pietro Achilles. Two elderly sisters (who will be known here as Mrs. Mary Baker and Mrs. Alice Miller) had worn out their welcome not only with the police but the newspapers by their repeated calls about him. According to Mrs. Baker, in 1962, Mr. Achilles, who was about fifty, had been hired to give piano lessons to her two nieces, daughters of her sister Alice. Achilles had all but cast a spell on her when he met her; he told her that if he had not been a pianist, he would have loved being a doctor. He could hypnotize people (she could well believe this); he enjoyed doing harmful things to his mother, he told her; he saw great beauty in a broom, and, sooner or later, was going to write a book about a broom.

On one occasion, on Thursday, August 10, 1961, at 12:45 P.M., when Achilles thought himself alone with Mrs. Miller in her house, Mrs. Baker, from another room, saw him come up behind her sister. Mrs. Baker put it graphically in a letter: "He had on red plastic gloves with an archery of black seams through them, he was grinning, and he stretched out his hands clawing at the air as though he was about to strangle her. When she turned he immediately dropped his hands to his side. I walked into the room and said to Mr. Achilles, because I felt I had to talk to break the tension and fear, 'Why don't we get a recording of your voice? We understand you sing so well.'

"He said nothing but relaxed and began removing his red gloves. He pulled off the glove on his right hand and it had two snaps on the wrist. He put it into his jacket pocket and in that instant out popped the fingers of a surgical glove and part of the wrist. It was beige-shade rubber and somewhat transparent. Mrs. Miller and I both saw it, it was powdered inside with a pinkish powder. With a smile he pushed it back . . . He is a consummate actor. He once said, 'Put a wig on me and I'm my mother.' He has dressed as a woman and fooled everyone . . ."

The sisters had been telephoning police about Achilles and the murders for some time, but a quick check of him had disclosed nothing incriminating. They had since written the Boston *Record American*, and repeatedly telephoned every law enforcement official they could reach. One of the first notes on John Bottomly's desk when he took over as coordinator months before was a memo reporting an urgent call from the sisters at 2 A.M. that morning. Now Stephen Delaney, to stop the avalanche of calls and letters, was assigned to placate them. He had twenty other names to check out that day but something had to be done about the two ladies.

Delaney, thirty-two, and appearing at least ten years younger, was a man of great tenacity. He had set his heart on becoming a criminologist. On evenings and days off he attended Boston University under the G.I. Bill of Rights, majoring in Sociology. Although he was married and had eight children, with a ninth on the way, he took every available moment away from his family for the search.

Now, when he got on the telephone to Mrs. Miller, his ears rang. "I don't think much of the Boston police," she began angrily. "I've been calling and calling. Now you'd better listen to me. Have you checked Rockport where Mr. Achilles has a summer cottage?"

"No, we haven't," said Steve, "Why?"

"Why? Because Joann Graff spent her last night in Rockport!"

Steve knew nothing about that. He made a note to look into it. Mrs. Miller went on sharply, "And you should have checked the conservatory, because I saw Beverly Samans there when Pietro Achilles was there. Those two knew each other."

The name of Pietro Achilles had never appeared in the Beverly Samans file. Steve asked, "What makes you so suspicious about this man Achilles?"

Mrs. Miller could hardly control herself. "Doesn't it mean anything to you that he sees great beauty in a broom, that he wants to write a book about a broom?"

"Why should that be important?"

"You fool, you fool, you know why a broom is important! Because the Strangler used it—"

Steve was surprised. The details on the assault on Mary Sullivan had never appeared in the newspapers, although it was common knowledge in the street. He heard Mrs. Miller's voice, "And he's just as the psychiatrists say the Strangler would be—a loner who hates women, who came from a South European background . . . Oh!" She literally stamped her foot at the other end. "I tell you, young man, I've been making novenas and praying to the Blessed Virgin Mary—" She stopped. "Are you a Catholic?"

"Yes, I am, ma'am," said Steve.

"I made a special novena. I prayed for a sign to tell me who the Strangler is, and the other night I woke up and a ball of fire was flying through my room writing out the name Achilles on the ceiling."

Steve asked, "Well, what did your priest have to say about it?"

"You damn fool, what's the priest have to do with this?" she demanded. "He's not looking for the Strangler!"

"But, lady," Steve protested weakly, "if it's a miracle don't you think you ought to have it verified by the priest?"

"Oh!" said Mrs. Miller, and hung up.

Steve checked. How had Beverly Samans obtained her position singing in the choir of the Second Unitarian Church? In the autumn of 1962 Mary Vivien, the organist and musical director, asked the conservatory to recommend candidates. One of the names sent to her was Beverly Samans. Another was Pietro Achilles.

The two sisters had been right. Beverly and Pietro Achilles knew each other. They had auditioned together on October 4, 1962, at the church. Beverly had obviously known Achilles before: when he entered she walked up to him—they had angry words—"They were both tense," Miss Vivien reported to Steve—and when Beverly walked away she was noticeably upset.

Miss Vivien had decided immediately to hire Beverly, who had a lovely voice. Although she had been ready to hire Achilles to sing with her, in view of Beverly's obvious dislike of the man she chose another candidate.

Further investigation by Steve disclosed that Achilles, a bachelor, had once told a friend how he hated his "terribly overbearing" mother.

Stephen Delaney returned to his office and wrote his notes carefully. Achilles had a cottage just outside Rockport, in Gloucester. Although Joann Graff did not spend Friday night, November 22, the night before her murder, in Rockport, she *had* visited Rockport that evening with a fellow worker. Achilles knew Beverly Samans and had reason to bear her a personal grudge. In casual dress Achilles invariably affected ascots; and for whatever significance it had, an ascot bought by Pat Delmore, Mary Sullivan's roommate, as a gift for a boyfriend, had been slashed into three parts and flushed down the toilet in her apartment the day of the murder. On that day, too, cigarette butts—Salems—had been found crushed out on an ash tray near her body. Neither Mary nor her roommates smoked Salems. Pietro Achilles did.

Delaney asked himself, Could these two excitable sisters have stumbled upon an important lead? But a ball of fire writing across the ceiling . . . a grinning man clawing at the air with red gloves . . . pink-powdered surgeon's gloves popping out of a pocket . . . ?

He turned to Phil DiNatale, busy writing at the adjoining desk, and spoke his thoughts aloud: "Boy, we must be running scared—" Yet he marked Achilles for additional investigation and filled out a request, to be sent to the proper authorities, for Achilles' immigration record.

As for Phil, he only shook his head at Delaney and continued working on his own report. A month before he had gone to investigate a tip turned in by Mrs. Marjorie L. Spearing, a housewife, of 28 Webster Place. An attractive woman in her thirties, Mrs. Spearing appeared quite nervous when Phil arrived. She apologized for telephoning the Attorney General's office, but citizens *had* been asked to cooperate. For some time, she had been hearing disturbing noises outside her apartment. She thought nothing of them until her attention was attracted by one of her neighbors, an athletic young salesman. "He really acts quite odd at times," she told Phil. "He always smells of shaving lotion—not that that's anything to hold against a man," she hastened to add, "but so many times when my husband and I go out, we see him standing at his window behind a curtain, peering out at people." One afternoon when she was doing laundry in the basement, her neighbor entered so silently—"on tiptoes"—that she almost screamed when she looked up to discover him watching her. But he spoke quite normally, they exchanged a few pleasantries, and he walked to the door. He could not open it, whereupon he turned to her and said sharply, "You've locked me in!" She was a little upset, hurried to the door herself—and had no trouble opening it. It hadn't been locked at all.

Then about nine o'clock the night of January 4—she knew the hour because she and her husband were returning from the wake of a relative—as they were about to enter their building, the front door burst open and her neighbor, his eyes wild, carrying a brown briefcase, rushed out, jumped into his car and roared away.

"I just shivered," she told Phil. "I turned to my husband and I remember my exact words: 'If there was a strangling today, I'll bet he's the man the police should look for.'"

Next morning she opened her newspaper—and there were the headlines—Mary Sullivan, a nineteen-year-old girl, strangled! She did not know what to think. One day recently when she went out to shop, the salesman's car was parked at the curb. On impulse she peeked in. On the dashboard where a small religious statue of the Virgin usually stood, there was now a small bear, standing on his hind legs, its arms up in a strangling position. She finally decided she would have no peace until she reported him. "I don't know whether it means anything," she said, "but I read that some people believe the Strangler was not after Mary but one of her roommates—and one of her roommates came from Malden. So does this man. And his actions that day . . . !"

Phil asked, "What else can you tell me about him?"

Mrs. Spearing rubbed her fingers agitatedly. "He's quite charming when he smiles. But at other times his eyes seem to glare and when he's angry they're like an insane person's." She was also troubled because he told her he attended night school in order to become a state trooper, and everyone knew, she said, that there are no state trooper night schools.

Phil had dutifully taken down her information—she was certainly in a state, he thought, or she wouldn't be so upset over what was probably a miniature Smokey the Bear on the man's dashboard—but he wrote his report and turned it in to Bottomly. A check on the salesman produced nothing suspicious. Now, a month later, Phil was adding a final paragraph:

Mrs. Emily Powers of 27 Maplewood Street reported she was cleaning the Venetian blinds in her kitchen about 9 o'clock this A.M. when she looked out to see a woman opening a third floor window across the street in the building at No. 28 Webster Street. Mrs. Powers reports she saw the woman open the window about a foot high, stick her head through, wiggle her body forward until she pushed herself all the way through the opening, and then drop head first to the ground. Woman identified as Mrs. Marjorie Spearing, 34, dead on arrival. Husband says wife has been suffering nervous breakdown for the past two months over the stranglings. Husband said her doctor has been trying to convince Mrs. Spearing to go to a hospital. She was supposed to have an appointment with the doctor this afternoon.

Before the Strangler was finished, Phil thought, how many victims would there be whom he had never even touched?

14

For nearly a year, even before he had been transferred to Bottomly's investigating squad, Stephen Delaney had been quietly following a middle-aged Finnish dishwasher with the growing conviction that this strange, taciturn man, ignored by everyone, could be the Strangler. With every murder the man, who will be known here as Carl Virtanen, looked more and more the part.

Virtanen had interested Delaney since a late October afternoon in 1962, when five stranglings had been recorded. Delaney was about to leave the Lower Basin Police Station when he glanced out the window to see an arresting sight: a well-dressed, middle-aged man, complete to soft hat, white shirt and neatly tied tie, business suit and gray topcoat, racing at top speed, his coattails flying behind him, along the grassy Esplanade that borders the Charles River. As Delaney watched, the man suddenly veered off and ran up a catwalk. He stood there for a minute, looking down, both hands clutching his head, as if in absolute despair. Was the man about to jump and try to kill himself? Then he wheeled, ran down the catwalk, and began racing as swiftly in the direction from which he came, which would bring him near the station house. Delaney, then a patrolman in uniform, dashed out and headed him off. "What's the matter, fellow?" he asked seizing his arm.

"Nothing, nothing, let me go!" He spoke in a foreign accent.

Delaney kept his grip. Though the man was tall, broad-shouldered, with a fine physique, he must have been at least in his forties, and was now pale and gasping for breath. To let him rush on might mean a heart attack. "Why don't you come in and sit down for a minute?" Delaney suggested,

191

leading him, still protesting, to a bench inside the station house.

The other finally caught his breath. "I was running for exercise, that's all," he said. Then he burst out, "I have to run. I have terrible things on my mind. If you only knew what I have on my mind! If I run, I forget them." He jumped to his feet, impatient to leave.

Delaney had no right to hold him but before he left he learned his name, his address—a rooming house—and that he was a Finn. Delaney watched him hurry out into the street, then dart into the North Station. Was he going to jump in front of a train? But a moment later Virtanen reappeared and began to lope, like a long-distance runner, down Canal Street.

Something ticked in Delaney's memory. Anna Slesers, he had read, had worked as a seamstress in a shop in Canal Street. What "terrible things" had this man on his mind? Anna Slesers had come from Latvia; Virtanen from Finland. Vaguely, Delaney recalled from his high school geography that the two countries were near each other. Might not Latvians and Finns seek out each other in this country? Might Virtanen have known Anna? Although Delaney was eager to get home—today was his twin daughters' birthday and a party was waiting for him—he decided he must follow Virtanen.

It was an arduous task. The man ran here, there, stopped; once, after nearly half an hour of steady trotting, he sprang into a cafeteria, had a cup of coffee, talked vigorously to himself, pounding on the table several times, then leaped to his feet and shot out into the street again. Once he turned, caught a glimpse of Delaney, and began darting into side alleys, ducking into one entrance of a department store and out the other, redoubling on his tracks, until Delaney lost him altogether. What's this man afraid of? Delaney thought all the way home, meanwhile wondering how he could explain to his family why he was two hours late.

Between work and classes Delaney checked on Virtanen and the death of Anna Slesers. The dishwasher was a bachelor who lived alone. He moved frequently from one rooming house to another. At work, in a popular Cambridge restaurant, he was known as quiet and industrious, having nothing to do with anyone else. But early in June 1962 he had been ordered to leave the men's hotel in which he was living because of his odd behavior. He had refused to allow the maid to clean his room; wherever she looked, she reported, were newspapers, piled in closets, piled under the bed, in the bathroom; even his clothes, instead of hanging in the closet, were tightly rolled up in newspapers.

After he left, the maid found that Virtanen had spent hours deliberately tearing hundreds of pages of newspapers into shreds—small quarter-inch strips, no more than an inch long—and piling them several feet high in the bathroom. He had taken every bar of soap and as painstakingly shredded it.

When he left the hotel Virtanen chose a rooming house four blocks from Anna Slesers and three blocks from Sophie Clark.

On June 14 Anna Slesers was strangled.

Virtanen worked nights, which meant he was free to move about the city during most of the day. At what time of day had Anna Slesers actually been strangled? The original investigation had placed it in the afternoon, as late as 6:10 P.M., when the interior decorator who lived directly below her apartment had been awakened by loud bumping noises upstairs.

The more Delaney checked on the Slesers case, however, the more convinced he became that she had been murdered early in the day. Studying her casebook, he found that the autopsy report showed little food in her stomach (could she have gone nearly a whole day without eating?); she was known as an immaculate housekeeper, yet her kitchen wastebasket was full and her daughter, coming for her burial clothes, had found the bed unmade (would Mrs. Slesers not have emptied her wastebasket and made her bed before going out for the day?); her dentures had been found soaking in a glass of water, as if left there over night, and the mail, delivered at 10:30 A.M. that Thursday, was still in her mailbox when Juris Slesers had called for his mother just before 7 P.M.

If Anna Slesers had died in the morning, Delaney concluded, Virtanen could have been her murderer.

It was during the period of Anna Slesers' strangling that Virtanen began to act unpredictably at work. He threw trays about, and accused fellow workers of insulting him, of telling him "filthy stories." Time and time again he had to be calmed down. Generally, Delaney knew from experience, dishwashers could not be depended upon; they were lonely men, usually unmarried, often mentally ill, frequently alcoholic, tending to drift from one job to another. But for a year and a half Virtanen had been a quiet, steady employee. Now he was a different man. At one time he turned and without explanation dumped a bucket of swill on a worker next to him. Because of the ease and swiftness with which he moved—because of his tremendous chest and arm development—others thought he might have been a professional boxer at one time, and they hesitated to antagonize him.

On June 20, he failed to show up for work. Usually he would telephone when he was ill; now nothing was heard from him until July 5, when he arrived at his usual time, donned his apron, and without a word began washing dishes as though he had never been gone.

In that interim Nina Nichols and Helen Blake had been strangled.

Then, in August, came Ida Irga and Jane Sullivan, on December 5, Sophie Clark, and on the last day of 1962, the discovery of Patricia Bissette's body in her apartment not far away. Letting his school-work slide, through January, February, and March of 1963, Delaney spent every day off following and checking on this strange troubled man whose absences were timed so suspiciously, and who lived so near the victims. He discovered that Virtanen maintained a daily routine. Since he worked nights, he rose late, around 10 A.M., walked briskly on the Esplanade, went to the Boston Public Library in Copley Square, read newspapers until 3 P.M., walked briskly back along the Esplanade, returned to his room, ate, napped until 7 P.M., and then in the early darkness walked along the Esplanade again, until it was time for work.

With warmer weather Delaney, who had been on guard duty at the Bunker Hill monument (a job which allowed him to study), was transferred to the police boat patrolling the Charles River. Repeatedly, as it cruised along the river banks, he saw the familiar figure of Virtanen, so easily recognizable—the man wore his hat on the back of his head—striding on the Esplanade.

On May 8 Beverly Samans was found murdered in Cambridge.

Delaney began to theorize. Beverly had attended Boston University. A natural route for her to take to and from classes would be along the Esplanade where Virtanen walked several times a day. She sang in the choir of the Second Unitarian Church of Boston. The church was in Copley Square, near the library—the very library Virtanen visited each day. Could not Virtanen on his daily walks have seen Beverly on her way to school on weekdays or on her way to church on Sundays?

This is too big for me, thought Delaney. He was a policeman and homicides were the province of detectives. He gave Carl Virtanen's name to Boston Homicide to be checked.

They reported that Virtanen had no police record, but had been a mental patient some years before in Medfield State Hospital. "He's a harmless kook," a detective said. "Mind if I check a little more on him?" Delaney asked. "Go ahead," said the other. "It's one less headache for us."

Medfield State Hospital.

Beverly Samans had done rehabilitation work at Medfield State Hospital.

Delaney dug doggedly though the records.

Yes, Carl Virtanen had been a mental patient at Medfield in 1955 and 1956. Diagnosed as a paranoid schizophrenic. He had been committed because he threatened to kill his mother.

And more—

In 1957, Virtanen's mother had been taken to Massachusetts General Hospital for gall bladder surgery. She spoke only Finnish and her physician had to interpret for her. She was returned from surgery to her own room at 8 P.M. After visiting hours that night she was found half out of bed, in convulsions. "She was trying to tell us something," a nurse told Delaney. "But we couldn't understand her language and she went into a coma and never regained consciousness."

Delaney, in the course of days, finally found a sister of Virtanen's living in Boston. There was no charge against her brother, he assured her, but since Carl lived in the Beacon Hill area and had been a mental patient and since the police were checking such persons, "We just want to know something about him."

"I can't tell you much," she said. "Carl never got along well with me—or with Mother. But don't take that wrong," she hastened to add, and her next words set the little hairs on the back of Steve Delaney's neck bristling. "He loved Mother. He was with her when she died." *

Now Delaney was all but obsessed. He gave up his studies altogether. Because of Virtanen he had already dropped behind in his education: he might as well forget it. He could always work out a college degree but he could not always catch the Strangler.

After Evelyn Corbin's murder in Salem on September 8, Delaney spent his days off trying to determine if Virtanen had been in Salem. He had little success. In the midst of his search came new stimulation—a widely-quoted article in the October 1963 issue of *Pageant* magazine in which Dr. Brussel

* Whatever parallels existed here with Arnold Wallace and his mother, Delaney was unaware of. The detailed biographical data of suspects was known only to a few at the very heart of the search.

predicted the type of man the Strangler would turn out to be: "I would say he has an athletic, symmetrical build and a burning desire to get rid of energy . . . He is between thirty and forty, the time of age when a paranoid reaches the peak of his mental disorder. He has never been married, and never will be, because he is sexually abnormal. He is a lone wolf. . . . He could never work with anyone standing over him. . . . The killings have something to do with his mother. The hospital angle is too strong to ignore and the chances are excellent that the trouble surrounding his relationship with his mother has something to do with a hospital. . . . He definitely lives alone, probably near the center of the city . . ."

Delaney read this with mounting excitement. "Athletic . . . build . . . burning desire to get rid of energy . . . between thirty and forty . . . paranoid . . . never married . . . lone wolf . . . trouble . . . with his mother . . . something to do with a hospital . . . lives alone . . ."

Dr. Brussel, the man who had described the Mad Bomber down to his buttoned double-breasted suit, might have had Carl Virtanen in front of him as he wrote this description.

Then, on Saturday, November 23, the day after President Kennedy was assassinated, Joann Graff was strangled in Lawrence. Delaney thought, Joann was a Lutheran. Virtanen, he had learned, was also a Lutheran. That was one bond between the two. Joann had asked a Latvian minister to help her meet people when she first came to Lawrence. A glance at the map showed that Latvia was, indeed, just across a fjord from Finland. Virtanen might have known Anna Slesers. By the same token, he might also have come to know Joann—this shy girl, who would permit no one she did not know to enter her apartment. Had Carl Virtanen been in Lawrence when Joann Graff was murdered?

Now every moment that he had off Delaney spent in Lawrence making the rounds of places where Virtanen might have been seen, especially hotels, restaurants, and diners. At one restaurant the short-order cook said, "I've seen that man."

It was a Saturday, the day after President Kennedy had been assassinated. He had been walking sadly to work when he saw his friend Luigi just ahead of him. He needed someone to share his deep emotion over the terrible thing that had happened, so he had quickened his step and with a subdued "Hi, Luigi," put his hand on the other's shoulder.

Luigi turned. It was not Luigi. It was the man whose photograph Stephen Delaney held before him.

On Saturday, January 4, 1964, Mary Sullivan was murdered in her apartment at 44A Charles Street. Delaney checked on Virtanen's whereabouts that day. Carl Virtanen had been washing dishes in a restaurant—one block away from 44A Charles Street. Delaney went over his information again and again. There was no doubt of it. Virtanen had gotten into a violent argument with the assistant manager on Thursday, January second, called in sick on Friday, the third, but reported for work early Saturday, the fourth. He was free to leave when he washed the batch of dishes awaiting him. At any time he could go out for a smoke, and remain out for a considerable length of time until another batch of soiled dishes accumulated. Number 44A Charles Street was four minutes—Delaney paced it off—from the kitchen entrance of the restaurant.

Twice Delaney called on Virtanen in his rooming house and tried to question him. Virtanen said he knew nothing, and would say nothing. The second time he ordered Delaney out of his room, and Delaney had to leave.

He decided to check again with the manager of the men's hotel from which Virtanen had been forced to move. The manager said, "That man has more hatred for people stored up in him than anyone I ever met." He told of watching Virtanen's glances at others, his demeanor, the silent fury in his eyes. "I don't know if he's the Strangler or not," he said, "but by God sooner or later he will be."

Steve Delaney, walking away, felt absolutely frustrated. How perfectly Virtanen fitted the Strangler! Sooner or later, Steve was convinced, the murderer would be found in some desolate, depressing area of the city—a loner with a grudge against the world, enduring a lonely existence in a rooming house with strangers, sharing a bathroom with the others yet having nothing in common, seeing in his fellow roomers mirrors of his own empty, meaningless days. Delaney thought, How such a man must feel when vacation and holiday time comes around—students packing, happy, expectant, everyone having somewhere to go, and he remaining where he is, going nowhere. How he must resent it, and how he must want to lash out against the world . . . And at just such times, many of the stranglings did take place.

Delaney had two solaces. One was the opinion of psychiatrists, after reading Virtanen's medical record, that the man was probably too disturbed to have been able to carry out the stranglings without calling attention to himself. They emphasized that this was an opinion only. The man could not be eliminated. The other was promotion to Bottomly's special investigative staff in recognition of his zeal and devotion to duty.

But as for Virtanen himself—Delaney had no proof. No physical evidence to warrant an arrest, none to link Virtanen with any of the stranglings, as there was none to link anyone else. Who was to say that these suspicious crossings of Carl Virtanen's path with those of the Strangler's victims were not coincidence? Chance? Chance beyond the roll of the dice, but chance just the same?

15

Jim Mellon, hand to forehead, sat reading the Mary Sullivan casebook. Across the table from him, in the large offices of Eminent Domain given over to the investigations, sat Phil DiNatale, as deeply immersed in the Sophie Clark book; to one side, Steve Delaney, lost in the reports, interviews, statements of friends, schoolmates, neighbors, that added up to the tragic story of Beverly Samans.

Each morning when the three men came to work to follow new leads in the ceaseless probing into the life and death of the Strangler's victims, they pored over the casebooks in an effort to absorb new material, to spot discrepancies in testimony missed at a first, second, or tenth reading, to analyze facts thought unimportant originally but meaningful now in view of succeeding murders.

Jim Mellon devoted himself at this stage to Mary Sullivan, because she had been the most recent, the last of the series of stranglings so far. All that Donovan's men had learned in the preceding ten investigations stood them in stead here, and they had gone about the business of collecting information as swiftly as possible. Mary Sullivan's casebook was almost twice as thick as any of the others. Each morning when Jim took it out of the vault, he opened it with a silent plea, "Come on, Mary, let's go! Tell me more!"

Somewhere within these nearly two thousand pages must lie the answer. Somewhere in these photographs of the apartment at 44A Charles Street, of the building itself, of Mary in life and in death, of her roommates Pat and Pam, in her autopsy report, her employment record, the interviews with everyone who knew her back to her Sunday School classmates in Hyannis (it was incredible how many people one person in one short lifetime could meet, talk with, and confide in!), in the statements by teachers, parents, family physician, and priest, in the letters she wrote and those written to her, in the names in her address book, the telephone numbers jotted down on scraps of paper in her purse, the three sticks of Beechnut spearmint chewing gum, the matchbook from Whitman's Savings Bank, the parking ticket, the gasoline coupons, the department store receipts—somewhere here must lie the clue to Mary Sullivan's death. And perhaps to the others.

Was Mary's death, as Dr. Brussel theorized, the Strangler's climactic deed? As Dr. Robey put it, the icing on the cake, the most elaborate creation of all?

Four clues had been found. The first was the red ascot Pam Parker had bought as a Christmas present for a friend and hadn't yet given him that had been found slashed into three parts and flushed down the toilet. It had caught in a bend of the drainpipe, and some days later, been pulled out.

The second was the three Salem cigarette butts found in an ash tray not far from Mary's body. The three girls smoked only Marlboros.

The third was a small metal-alloy washer, found on the bed under Mary's body. No appliance in the apartment had a washer missing. Jim Mellon had had it examined chemically and microscopically. It was the kind stamped out by the millions in Japan. It might not be a washer at all but the backing of a button. He now carried it around with him in a small test tube and brought it out half a dozen times a day to study it. "People think I'm becoming a nut," he told friends.

The fourth clue—the most important and most frustrating—was a tiny charred piece of paper, the size of one's thumbnail, with a few lines of print barely legible, found on the bathroom floor behind the toilet. The police laboratory identified this as the top inner corner of pages 307—308—Treg to Tucker, Tucker to Tuiler—of the 1963 Boston Suburban Telephone Directory. The girls had no telephone. Someone had brought the page there. Had it been Mary—or her murderer—who went to such pains to destroy it? Her roommates knew nothing about it.

The slashing of the ascot—the act of a jealous homosexual?—was puzzling enough, but Jim believed he could explain the telephone page. Mary, at sometime in some telephone booth, must have looked up a number, could not reach it, wanted to jot it down and try later, found herself without a pencil—she was not too well organized—and simply ripped out the page, folded it, and tucked it into her purse. There the Strangler found it. Because it bore his name or a number that might betray him he had taken it to the bathroom, lit a match to it, held it until it burned down almost to his fingers, then dropped the charred fragment into the bowl to be flushed away. Unaccountably, he failed to see it flutter to one side and fall behind the toilet.

For weeks Jim had been checking the listings in the inside column on either side of the page, as the result of an experiment he conducted with thirty persons. Because it had been an inside top corner, he assumed a full page had been torn out. His experiments had proved to him that most persons tear out a full page if the number they want appears in the inner column. Otherwise they rip out only the portion containing the number. Even limiting his investigation to one column on either side meant an endless task. Each commercial listing could represent hundreds of employees, any one of whom might be Mary Sullivan's mysterious friend—and murderer.

Doggedly, Jim went ahead with it.

What complicated matters was Mary's enormous acquaintanceship. She had only to meet someone in a bar or drugstore to jot down his name in her address book. She constantly sent off postcards and letters. When, a year before, she worked as a long-distance operator in the Hyannis telephone exchange, she was in her element, calling friends all over the country. If she accepted strangers so readily, she might have placed herself in many dangerous situations. The question rose, what kind of a girl was she?

Here no two agreed. Some knew her as gregarious, yet quiet, unassuming, and behind the facade of her informality, extremely circumspect as far as boys were concerned. But others saw her going from one crush to another, driven to melt before any offer of friendship. The most troubling evidence came from nearly a dozen youths who had rented a cottage in Dennisport during the summer of 1962. Mary had been a guest there. They painted the picture of a promiscuous girl—one, however, who admitted, "I'm ashamed of the way I've been behaving," and later would allow them no liberties of any kind. The detectives listened stolidly to this testimony. Many had daughters, some Mary's age; they found the subject unpleasant, but, true or not, they had to pursue it because, if true, Mary's murderer might have been someone she entertained so casually. What was done to her was conceived by a crazed mind, but it might also have represented—as with Jack the Ripper in London—a moral judgment passed by a madman.*

---

* That possibility opened many doors. The detectives were now examining the lives of the Girls. What of the Old Women? Not their later years, but their youth. What secrets lay there? Who, out of their

Whatever Mary's problems, she was obviously looking for something. Her restlessness could be read in her letters. Repeatedly, she made plans with other girls to go to California, to Florida, to Europe. These never materialized. She wanted to be a woman of the world, but she also wanted to marry and rear a large family. Sometimes, when baby-sitting for a friend, she would hug the infant, and exclaim, "Oh, gee, I'll just die if I don't have a boy first thing I'm married."

She had lived away from home during the two years following her graduation from Barnstable High School in Hyannis. She moved 150 yards down the street from her house to a motel, where she shared a room with another girl. In those two years she held four jobs: in Hyannis, then in suburban Whitman, then as temporary holiday help at Filene's. She had begun her fifth job, at the bank, the day before her death.

Perhaps a clue to her murder could be found in her movements during her three days at 44A Charles Street, or in what happened there during that time.

1. She had moved in at noon New Year's Day, Wednesday, January 1. She was discovered dead at 6:10 P.M. Saturday, January 4. Could she have met her murderer in that interval? Or had he known her in Hyannis and followed her to Boston to kill her there? She must have let him into the apartment herself, that fatal Saturday. There were no signs of forcible entry. Of course, there were ways to trick even the most cautious woman into opening her door. No need to knock. For example, one had only to meow like a kitten. (One Boston girl had been so terrified when her boy friend told her this astonishingly simple ruse that she immediately reported him to the police.)

2. At 5:30 Friday, January 3, the day before her death, having finished her first day's work at the Boston Safe Deposit Company, Mary drove her blue Vauxhall, which she had bought five weeks earlier, to a Gulf station around the corner where an attendant replaced her 1963 license plate with a 1964 one.

3. About 7:30 P.M. Friday, nineteen-year-old Christopher Reid (which is not his real name), a Boston University student who dated Pat Delmore, one of Mary's roommates, climbed the stairs of 44A to call on Pat. He had been there the night before with another friend of the girls, and met Mary then for the first time. Now, three or four steps below

past, might have emerged now, years later, to render his insane judgment? It was discovered that one of the older victims at sixteen had won a beauty contest, at seventeen had borne an illegitimate child. But this line of investigation seemed going desperately—and cruelly—far afield. The fact was noted, but not pursued.

the third floor landing, he heard voices coming from the apartment—a man's voice, then Mary's. The man was chuckling, then Christopher made out one word "Yes." At first he thought the voice came from the radio, but it stopped the moment he knocked. He heard footsteps coming toward him, and from the other side of the door Mary called out, "Who's there?"

"Christopher Reid," he replied. He wanted to see Pat.

Pat had gone to visit her parents in Lowell, said Mary, through the door.

Wondering who the man might be, Christopher left. Voices interested him—he himself stuttered sometimes—and this voice was fairly low, and he got the mental image, as he told police later, of "someone tall and thin, about six feet tall, with a voice of such a frequency as caused by the Adam's apple—a nasal type." He knew that was a surprisingly detailed description to be built up from a voice heard through a closed door, but that was his impression. His curiosity led him to check WMEX and WBZ, both broadcasting then. No voice resembling that he heard was to be found on either station.

4. At 7:45 P.M. Friday—ten minutes after Christopher left, his friend, Bob Auld, a nineteen-year-old Emerson College student, knocked on the door of No. 2.

"Yes," came Mary's voice.

"Is Pat home? This is Bob Auld."

"No," Mary replied, through the door.

"Is Chris there?"

"He was, but just left. Pat should be back around eleven o'clock."

"O.K.," said Bob. He heard no man's voice.

5. At 9:10 P.M., two other boys, friends of Pat's, walked into the vestibule of 44A and buzzed Apartment 2. After a moment, they heard Mary's voice shouting down the stairwell to them. She was leaning over the bannister, in her bathrobe. "Pat's gone home to Lowell," she called down. They left.

6. About 11 P.M. Pat and Pam, who had been visiting their parents—Pam's lived in suburban Malden—returned. They had met at the train terminal so they could come home together. Mary told them about the four boys but made no mention of the man whose voice Christopher Reid said he heard.

7. About midnight, Barbara Carbelle, twenty-one, and Gail Watson, nineteen, who had been having a late snack at a nearby rathskeller, dropped in "just to talk." They found Pam and Pat in nightgowns, doing their hair, Mary asleep on

her day couch in the living room. The two left forty-five minutes later. As they were about to get into Barbara's car, they saw a curtain pushed aside in a second-floor window in the building opposite 44A. A man stood silhouetted there, his features indistinct, staring into the Sullivan apartment. Then the curtain was drawn.

8. At 7:30 A.M. Saturday, January 4, the day of her murder, Pam and Pat prepared breakfast before leaving for Filene's, where Pam sold men's ties and Pat worked in the cashier's office. Mary appeared, sleepy-eyed, in her nightgown to join them for coffee. "Why are you up so early?" Pat asked. Now that Mary had a job at a bank she didn't work Saturdays. "Why don't you sleep today?"

"I've got a lot to do," Mary said. She had to telephone about night school courses she planned to take. She wanted to clean the kitchen shelves, too; everything had become pretty untidy over the holidays, what with so many friends dropping over at all hours.

9. At 11 A.M. Saturday, a clerk in a bookshop across the street from 44A Charles Street looked out the door of his shop to see a blue Vauxhall sedan with its hood up. Peering into the engine was a girl in a long blue coat and a man—"one of those Charles Street fellows, dark raincoat, no hat."

10. About noon Richard Chicofsky, manager of a grocery store at 48 Charles Street, a few doors from Mary's building, saw a girl taking things out of a small blue car. She appeared to be having trouble with the car; the hood was up.

11. Just before 1 P.M., Sims Murray, a neighbor, out walking his Afghan dog, saw a blue car parked on Charles Street. A girl carrying a bundle of record albums tied with a string was about to enter 44A Charles Street, and a man, whom he could not remember distinctly, was opening the door for her. The difficulty was that Murray, who had glimpsed them for only half a minute as he turned the corner, could not remember whether this was Wednesday, January 1, the day Mary moved into her apartment, or Saturday, January 4, the day she was strangled.

12. At 2:50, a schoolteacher living on the second floor of 2 Pruner Street, which faces the rear of 44A Charles Street, was standing at her bay window looking down into the street, waiting for her escort to pick her up at three o'clock. It was too cold to wait outside. She happened to lift her head and saw the left profile of a man framed in a third-floor window of 44A. She saw him quite clearly; the street was about fifty feet wide, the sun was shining into the window, he stood mo-

tionless, a tall man with reddish-brown hair, looking straight ahead of him. She guessed he must be standing in the hall waiting for an apartment door to open. She thought to herself, "What am I doing, staring like this at a strange man!" looked down into the street, saw her friend's car arrive, and hurried downstairs.

It was not a hallway window. It was the bathroom window of Mary Sullivan's apartment. The man she saw was staring at himself in the mirror.

At 6:10 Pam and Pat returned from work. They had stopped to shop and their arms were full of packages. Mary's car was parked in the street; she must be home. But there was no answering buzz when they pressed the bell downstairs. Pam managed to fish out her keys and open the downstairs door. The two girls trudged upstairs. The apartment door was locked. Pam knocked and shouted without avail.

"She must be sleeping," she said, and unlocked the door. The lights in the hall and bathroom were both on. Mary was not on the day couch. Pam glanced into the bedroom. In the gloom she made out Mary, sitting up in Pat's bed as though she had fallen asleep against the headboard. "She must be sleeping," she said again, when she came back to the kitchen, "but it's a funny way to be sleeping." And why had Mary taken Pat's bed? She removed her coat and hat, vaguely troubled. "Come here, Pat." Both girls tiptoed to the bedroom and peeped in. They could make out very little. They returned to the kitchen. They looked at each other, suddenly frightened.

"Call her," Pam suggested. "No, you call her," the other said. Pam called Mary's name loudly, three or four times. Only silence. "Oh, really!" she exclaimed, angry at herself and Pat. She strode into the bedroom and switched on the light.

It was then they stumbled into the dusk of busy Charles Street and called the police.

Aside from the fact that 44A Charles Street and particularly Apartment 2 must have been busy as a bus station, what was one to make of all this? There were two additional, completely inexplicable facts. At 6:30 P.M. Friday, January 3, the day before Mary's death, the telephone rang in the home of Mary's parents in Hyannis.

"Long distance calling for Mrs. John T. Sullivan," said the operator. "This is Mrs. Sullivan," said Mary's mother, who had answered the phone. She heard the operator's voice: "Sir, there's your party." Then silence. "Hello, hello," said Mrs. Sullivan. She heard—it was unmistakably clear—

someone breathing heavily into the telephone. But he uttered no word.

"Hello! Can you hear me?" she shouted into the mouthpiece.

Only heavy breathing for what seemed an interminable time, though Mrs. Sullivan repeated again and again, "Can you hear me? Hello! Hello! This is Mrs. Sullivan—"

Then came a click. He had hung up.

Mrs. Sullivan replaced the receiver. Bad connection? But the breathing was so distinct he might have been in the room with her. Would he not have called back immediately? A prank?

Little more than twenty-four hours later, on Saturday night, only a few moments after the police had called to notify them of their daughter's death, the telephone rang again in the Sullivan home. Again it was long distance, a person-to-person call, for Mrs. John T. Sullivan.

The family was in a state of shock. Mary's sixteen-year-old brother David answered the phone. "No," he said to the operator, "Mrs. Sullivan can't come to the telephone. Will he talk to anyone else?" He heard the operator say, "All right, sir, go ahead." He listened, as had his mother the night before. There were no words spoken at the other end. He heard only a heavy breathing—and after several seconds, the click as the caller hung up.

Wherever Mary had applied for a job, she had left her parents' name, address, and telephone number in Hyannis. Was her murderer to be found among those who employed her, in the many places where she had sought jobs?

The clues in hand were the telephone page, and for whatever value they had, the slashed ascot, the Salem cigarette butts, the metal washer.

Who was the stranger whose voice Christopher Reid said he heard as he climbed the stairs to the apartment Friday, the stranger he imagined to be tall, with a protruding Adam's apple, who was alone in the apartment with Mary the day before her death?

Who was the man seen through the window of her bathroom on the day of her death at the hour that might well have been the very hour of her death?

None of these had come forward to identify—and clear—themselves. If they were innocent, why should they not have done so?

In an all-night cafeteria on Homosexual Row, Jim Mellon

sat at a table along the wall, slowly disposing of a plate of ham and eggs.

It was 10 P.M. The man for whom he waited each night had arrived only minutes before.

He was short, thin, about forty-six, trying desperately to hold on to his youth, Mellon thought: the inch-and-a-half crepe rubber soles to make him appear taller, the iron-gray hair carefully pomaded, the face shaved to the quick, the clothes a little too sharp. Mellon had heard others call him "Jack." Mellon, in his own mind, had dubbed him "The King of the Fags." Years of patrolling the Public Gardens before teaming up with Phil DiNatale in a cruising car had given Mellon an almost unerring eye in picking out homosexuals.

Now the detective was convinced that this powdered, elaborate man who sat at the same table in this cafeteria from ten to midnight dawdling over a tray of coffee and toast, and smoking innumerable cigarettes, played an important role in the homosexual community. Jack, Mellon had concluded—and he had discussed it with Lieutenant Tuney—was a traffic supervisor handling the busy flow of nightly homosexual activities in Boston. He served a purpose. Youths under eighteen could not be served at bars and had to turn to private parties if they wished to drink with friends. Mellon had seen boys, obviously homosexuals by their manner, enter the cafeteria, order a snack which they took to a table, then, before leaving, drop over to Jack's table, chat a few minutes, sometimes jot down a note or two, and hurry off. Jack knew all that was going on each night in the city's busy netherworld—its society of sexual deviates of both sexes, homosexuals, Lesbians, transvestites. Jack was a communications center. He told the boys and girls where the action was.

Mellon had checked on him. Jack worked as a restorer of antique furniture. The first time Mellon had seen him, weeks before, had not been in the cafeteria, however. It had been, interestingly enough, in an antique shop whose name and number were listed in the first column of the telephone page resurrected from the thumbnail-size piece of charred paper found in Mary Sullivan's bathroom.

Were two separate lines of investigation beginning to converge, at last?

Jim Mellon sat, and watched.

16

If the Mary Sullivan case was baffling, that of Beverly Samans, stabbed to death in Cambridge, was equally so because of the puzzling bypaths into which it led investigators. Not only had she been writing a thesis on homosexuality, but one of her best friends was a homosexual youth whom she had recently helped break off a relationship with another boy. Beverly's own emotional problems had caused her to seek help from a therapist.

Because her murder had the earmarks of a classical homosexual stabbing—wounds in throat and breast—Sergeant Davenport wondered whether she might have been killed by someone in her circle of friends who became enraged when he discovered she was using his private life as material for her thesis. Or it might have been another, a sexually abnormal, emotionally disturbed boy who thought himself in love with her, who wanted to prevent her from leaving Boston—and so centered his attack on her throat, because it was her voice that was taking her away. He might have stabbed her in that almost mathematically precise bull's-eye pattern in her breast because her breast held a fetish significance for him. Sergeant Davenport spent hours talking with psychiatrists. Could Beverly have teased her killer—not necessarily on the night of her murder—by offering her breasts as a token, allowing him to fondle them, yet holding back the ultimate reward?

One thing seemed certain. In no other case—not even Mary Sullivan's—had a victim been surrounded by so many bizarre persons; some played a role in her life, others were simply part of the world in which she lived.

Aside from the Indian student with his whips and quotations from Shakespeare, there were many others. One was a nineteen-year-old hospital orderly whose specialty it was to

208

"cut open heads and bellies" for autopsies. The job description was his own. He had visited friends in Beverly's building, 4 University Road. His friends reported that he spoke constantly about the stranglings. He denied killing Beverly. He had never known her, he said. As police questioned him, he toyed with a small silver pocket knife. Another was a husky, one-time Harvard student who made a practice, when a girl companion glanced away, of placing the tip of his lighted cigarette next to her ankle. She would jerk her foot away in pain and look down to discover a hole burned in her stocking and a blister forming on her leg. "Of course I'm not the Strangler," he told police disdainfully. "But I am sadistic and girls from coast to coast bear my trademark." The professor with whom Beverly was briefly involved—married, with a family—once suggested to her they commit hara-kiri together, because he saw no future for their love. "He's out of his mind to suggest such a thing," Beverly said to a friend. "I have a lot of things I want to live for. I'm not ready to die." The professor was an odd man indeed: reports came to police that he would describe to listeners in detail the finer techniques of strangling, topping that off with a dissertation on the art of seduction.

It was true that Beverly, as she complained, seemed to draw kooks to her. Sunday, May 5, only a few hours before her death, she told her friend Edith Scarcello, twenty-five, that she had received an invitation from a man to spend the next weekend as his house guest in the New Jersey nudist colony to which he belonged. "It's crazy, isn't it?" Beverly exclaimed. She thought it hilarious.

If there were strange friends, there were also strange premonitions. On her twice-weekly visits—each Tuesday and Friday—to Medfield State Hospital to carry out field work with disturbed persons, she would be driven by Nicholas Thiesse, twenty-five, a married graduate student taking the same course. One morning, two months before her death, when he picked her up, she greeted him with, "Nick, I'm scared."

"What about?"

"I've been receiving crank calls." Someone had telephoned her two nights before explaining that he was a singer "and would like to get together to sing with me and when could he come over. I said, 'Who are you?' and he said, 'Oh, that doesn't matter,' and hung up. He called me the next night, too, and I hung up on him this time because only a week before that some fellow called and said, 'Bev, I want to talk to you about the Kinsey report.' I didn't know him and that frightened me."

Apparently, some kind of campaign was under way to annoy Beverly, and two other girls who often sang with her. All three had had their photographs in a newspaper advertisement announcing their appearance at a Palm Sunday service.

First, one of the girls had received an obscene telephone call. A day later, the other girl's phone rang. "Phyllis," said an unfamiliar voice, "I want you to accommodate me. Ruth told me to call you because she said she couldn't accommodate me, but that you could." Phyllis, who knew nothing of Ruth's call, assumed this might be someone wanting to take voice lessons.

"Who is this?" she asked.

"Oh, you know who it is," the voice said teasingly. But Phyllis could not place it. Was it one of the boys in the orchestra? "Well, what is it you want?" she asked.

As Phyllis told the story later, "He seemed hesitant. Then he finally told me what he wanted. I said, 'Oh,' and hung up."

In the following week the three girls were called again. They compared notes. Sometimes the voice was that of a young man, sometimes an older man. Was it a group, two or three fellows, setting up this inexplicable, frightening siege?

Beverly was upset when she talked about it to Nick. At other times, in other ways, she seemed fatalistic. Once, discussing the stranglings on their drive to Medfield, Nick asked, "What would you do if the Strangler came knocking at your door?"

"Nothing, I guess," she said. "He won't have a hard time getting in—my door lock isn't good and I can't lock my windows."

"Why don't you get them fixed?"

She shrugged her shoulders. "Oh, if he really wants to get in, locks won't keep him out."

Death had struck her at a crossroads in her life. She was trying to decide whether to continue rehabilitation counseling or "chuck it all" and devote herself to a singing career. Beverly had a promising mezzo-soprano voice; she was soloist every Sunday morning at the Second Unitarian Church, took weekly voice lessons, and participated in many operettas and concerts. A future seemed assured. But she was almost irresistibly drawn to emotionally troubled people. That had led her after graduation in 1959 from a music conservatory to take a job as a music therapist at Fernald School for Retarded Children. She left there in August 1962 to study for a master's degree in rehabilitation counseling at Boston University. This was the course that required field work with disturbed patients at Medfield, so that she found herself drawn in even deeper.

Nor did Beverly make matters easy for herself. She continued her friendship with her former students at Fernald, in violation of institution rules, allowing them to drop in on weekends at her apartment to play the piano and talk over their problems. Friends warned her against this open house. These boys—some were over twenty—were disturbed,* and at least one was so infatuated with her that he had been taken out of Fernald and given a job as a hospital orderly in another town. "But these kids have no parents," she would say. "Somebody's got to help them."

Beverly told herself she was really giving therapy to her homosexual friends, and in any event, gaining data for her thesis. She realized it was not a healthy situation. "I've got to stop this," she would say. "I'm fed up with mothering mentally crippled men. It drains me. . . ." And then she would lament, "Where can I find a man who knows how to treat a woman as a woman?" Yet one of her closest friends was a twenty-three-year-old student who, after dating her several times, said suddenly, "I've got to tell you something you'll hate me for—you'll never go out with me again—I'm homosexual."

"I know," she said. "I've known it almost from the first time we went out."

"And you don't mind?" he asked anxiously. "You'll still go out with me, you don't hate me?"

"No," she said. "Why should I hate you? It's just a thing, a thing, that's all." †

She told her friend Phyllis, "That's the kind of a person I am. Therefore I could go out with him, although I felt as if I were mothering him. Still, he could enjoy my company, and I could enjoy his . . ."

Beverly had problems with men generally. Scarcely anyone

* Daniel Pennacchio, the twenty-eight-year-old cafeteria worker who falsely confessed to Beverly's murder, was, the reader will remember, a former Fernald student.

† She had taken the same cool, clinical attitude in her thesis. Pointing out that the subject was considered "taboo" in the study of man, she wrote: "This paper attempts to examine some of the causative factors contributing to homosexuality in males . . . It will be obvious that, whatever the causation, this writer feels that the practice of homosexuality is a matter of personal choice and that part of the difficulties connected with it stem from the attitude which society maintains toward it."

knew—not even her parents, she said—that she had once been secretly married. It was during her first year in Boston, just after she came from her home town, Beckley, West Virginia, and enrolled in Boston University. She was only seventeen, he was eighteen, she was Jewish, he was Catholic. It lasted scarcely two weekends, and was annulled. Even then, "the more we were together, the more it seemed I was a leaning post, a sister, a mother—but not a wife," she told one friend. And with insight into her own problems, Beverly added, "I guess my going out with homosexuals, my interest in rehabilitation and sick people, all ties in with my marriage that never worked out."

But now, when she did seek out other, stronger men, it seemed that most of them bristled in her presence, that they would "go on the defensive." In recent months she had been depressed, although she tried not to show it, and that, together with her inability to "meet the right man" was part of the entire complex of difficulties that led her to seek psychiatric help not long before death came to her.

There was little to be learned from her last days.

On Friday before the Sunday of her murder Beverly called Nick Thiesse to say he could go on to Medfield without her that morning. She felt unwell. Saturday he saw her in class: she still felt unwell. Nick's wife was expecting a baby at any moment and Beverly's last words to him as they parted in class were, "Be sure to call me as soon as the baby arrives."

Sunday morning, May 5, Beverly sang in the church choir as usual. On the way home, about 12:30 P.M., she stopped at her friend Edith's, to leave a medical book she had borrowed for research on her thesis. About 8:30 that night she telephoned Edith; she had just returned from rehearsing *Cosî fan tutti* with the full cast of six at the Brookline home of John Ring, the producer. Would Edith join her for a late snack? The two girls met about nine o'clock in the Beacon Restaurant around the corner from Edith's apartment at 90 St. Mary's Street. Beverly was full of enthusiasm; the rehearsal had gone splendidly. First she had rehearsed individually with her singing coach who came up from New York to teach in Brookline. He felt certain she had a good chance to get a job with the Met, once she came to New York after receiving her degree. Then the entire cast had rehearsed. Everything had gone off fine, just fine.

After a while, Edith looked at her watch. "Oh, my, it's nearly eleven o'clock," she said. The two left the restuarant a few minutes later. Beverly's car was parked in front of Edith's apartment. The two strolled there and talked for about ten minutes. Beverly was in high spirits, thinking of New York and the future. Then she got into her car and drove away.

Beverly Samans drove home to her death.

And what was one to say about her fellow-victim, Evelyn Corbin, in Salem? Evelyn's death seemed even more puzzling because of the precision with which her killer had to carry out his murder, assault, and search. He had to get to her between the time she returned from brunch with her neighbor, Mrs. Manchester, and the time she left for church—at most, a half hour—in a busy apartment house on a Sunday morning, with tenants going in and out, a newsboy making repeated visits to collect money, and neighbors at the window watching the church-day traffic outside.

Consider the timetable of Evelyn Corbin's last hours at 224 Lafayette Street, in Salem, that Sunday, September 8, 1963.

At 9:15 A.M., someone tampered with her door. A few minutes later she answered Mrs. Manchester's telephone call—someone had been at *her* door. At nine-thirty, Evelyn dropped into Mrs. Manchester's apartment for breakfast. Less than an hour later she returned to her own apartment to dress in order to go to Mass, to leave at eleven-ten for the eleven-thirty services. She never got out of her apartment.

At ten-thirty, a tenant on the floor above came down the stairs on his way to Eaton's Drug Store to pick up his Sunday paper. He noticed a man standing in front of Evelyn's door. He was unable to describe him later because—as luck would have it—he was without his glasses, which had been broken the night before. He returned and made breakfast. Suddenly he heard a long scream, followed by a short one—"as though someone had been startled." It was about eleven o'clock. He dismissed it as noise from the children playing outside.

About 10:15, in her ground-floor apartment across the street, a woman saw a strange man walk by looking up intently at the windows of 224. She was tempted to open her window and call out, "Can I help you? Who are you looking for?" but thought better of it. The stranger was heavyset, about thirty-five or forty, with brown wavy hair. He walked with a distinct limp.

About 10:25, Richard and Susan Bernard awoke in their third-floor apartment at 224. Susan was making toast when the fuse blew out. It was eleven o'clock—the electric clock had stopped. Richard went to the basement, fixed the fuse, and returned. He heard and saw nothing.

At 10:30, Mrs. Alice Finch left her apartment in 224 to go

across the street for her paper. When she came back, noting and hearing nothing, she prepared for a visit to her sister in Marblehead. Just before she left she heard a door slam somewhere in the building. She looked up and down the hall. Nothing was to be seen. Later that afternoon, over her sister's radio, she heard the news of Evelyn Corbin's strangling. It took hours for her to muster enough courage to return home. She left finally at six o'clock saying, "I have to go back sometime—"

At 10:30, Victoria Deutch and her sister Charlotte were sitting reading—as was their Sunday morning habit—in their front parlor in 231 Lafayette Street, across the street from the Corbin building. Charlotte happened to look up from her paper to see, through the window, a man with a briefcase emerge from the entrance of 224.

"Isn't that odd," she remarked to her sister, "a salesman soliciting on a Sunday."

He stood on the sidewalk, looking intently up and down the street. Then he turned and walked quickly away.

At ten o'clock or so Denis Angelopoulis, the fifteen-year-old newsboy who delivered papers in the neighborhood, left his apartment at 32 Hazel Street, around the corner from Evelyn Corbin, to begin his Sunday morning collections. He had four customers in the Corbin building. First he decided to call on his girl friend Donna, fourteen, who lived across the street at 233, before she went to church. He walked with her out of the building: she went on to church, he returned home for a bite and then, at eleven o'clock, began his collections in the Corbin building. Two of his customers were in; a third, in Apartment 13, had left the money under her mat; the fourth was out. Going through the halls and up and down the stairs of 224, Denis saw nothing, heard nothing.

In the apartment next door to Evelyn's, Mrs. Carl Lesche was not feeling well and stayed in bed all morning. Her bed backed against the wall of Evelyn's bedroom. Mrs. Lesche heard nothing—"not a sound"—and she would have heard, she said, as much as a cough.

From 9:45 until 10:45, James Halpin was sitting in front of his building at No. 232 waiting for Denis to show up with his paper. During that time he saw nothing out of the ordinary. About ten-thirty, he recalled later, he saw Denis and his girl friend Donna walk out of No. 233, across the street. They held hands a moment then parted, she going in one direction, he in the other.

It was all peaceful, with only the sound of people going and coming from church: a quiet Sunday morning in a green and peaceful suburb, similar to a thousand quiet Sunday mornings in a thousand green and peaceful suburbs.

Who was the man standing in front of Evelyn Corbin's door? The man with the briefcase? The man limping by, looking so searchingly into the windows of her building?

Curious, too, were the events of the night before her murder.

About 9 P.M. that Saturday night, Alan Spanks, whose wife Betty, like Evelyn Corbin, worked at Sylvania, heard a knock on his kitchen door at 233 Lafayette Street. A man over six feet tall, between thirty-five and forty, with iron-gray hair, wearing a gray sweater and dark gray pants, stood there. "May I see Betty, please?"

"She's not home," said Spanks. His wife worked the 3 to 11 P.M. shift. "I'm her husband. Is there any message?"

"My girl friend said your wife is looking for another job and I thought I might have something for her," said the stranger. "I'll come back." He left. He did not return.

When Betty came home that night her husband told her about the visitor. She did not know the man he described. She was not looking for another job. She had never, never said anything like that to anyone.

Not until they heard of Evelyn Corbin's murder did they tell the police of the incident.

That Saturday night—at almost the same time the stranger knocked on the Spanks' door—Evelyn herself came out on the back porch of her apartment to take the air. She had a date later with Bob Manchester. George Tremblay, the janitor, walked through the backyard on an errand. "Isn't it a beautiful night!" she exclaimed, and stood there for a moment, breathing deeply. Then she went in. Although she was known for her good spirits, she had recently felt depressed. A week before her doctor had prescribed a tranquilizer for her. He remarked upon her youthfulness. On Friday, September 6—two days before her death—she would be fifty-eight, and she had not yet reached the menopause.

That Friday began auspiciously. Fellow workers serenaded her—one brought her a vial of perfume—but she became upset just before leaving when she learned she was to be shifted from a sitting to a standing-up job, paying less money. She spoke then of quitting, perhaps, and marrying Bob Manchester very soon. No one at Sylvania, where she'd worked for the last twenty years, had known her to go out with anyone but Bob.

The two had first met in January 1959 in Mrs. Manchester's apartment. Evelyn had moved into the building two years earlier, after her mother's death. As she lived alone—she had been divorced for many years and was childless—she began joining the Manchesters for an occasional meal. Soon she was taking at least one dinner a week with them, and all her meals on Sunday. She had few other friends—less than half a dozen names were found in her address book—and she and the older woman became close, spending time together, going shopping together. Lately, she and Bob had begun to discuss marriage. Neither mother nor son had any idea of Evelyn's true age. They assumed, as did nearly everyone else, that she was perhaps a few years older than Bob, who had just turned forty-one.

About nine-thirty Saturday night, she and Bob went on their date to Revere Beach, a strip of Ferris wheels and amusement centers on the outskirts of Boston. They returned about midnight and he said good night to her at her door. When he walked into his apartment his mother was waiting up, having a snack. "You'd better phone Evelyn about the chicken," he said. The three were to have broiled chicken for Sunday dinner, and Evelyn, who had the fowl in her freezer, was to be reminded to take it out so it could defrost overnight. Then Mrs. Manchester got on the phone for a cozy midnight chat.

At nine o'clock Sunday morning, Bob breakfasted in Eaton's Drug Store and drove to his office in Newton Highlands, twenty-five miles away, to catch up on work. He came home about 1:15 P.M.—a few moments after his mother had telephoned the police. As he walked in she said in great agitation, "I think something's happened to Evelyn." He ran down the hall into her apartment, pulled the gag from her mouth, and tried mouth-to-mouth resuscitation—but in vain. He covered her with a blanket and waited for the police. On the table was a letter she had written to his sister, telling her they hoped to marry, perhaps as early as June.

Bob was interrogated by the police. He rarely went to his office on Sunday—why this Sunday? Could he produce anyone to prove he had been there all morning? He could not.

Then, unexpectedly, came the discovery of a far more likely suspect as the result of a series of events which at first glance had nothing to do with Evelyn Corbin.

It began Monday, September 9, the day after her murder, when an irate father strode into the office of Police Inspector J. W. Moran of Salem to announce that his sixteen-year-old daughter Sue was missing, and he was sure she had run off with a twenty-five-year-old wife-beater and ne'er-do-well who will be known here as George McCarthy. Only a month before he had complained to the police about the man: Moran had called McCarthy in and given him a stern warning.

Now, however, Sue had vanished—she had walked out of the house just after their Sunday dinner yesterday, about one-thirty—and hadn't been seen since.

Little was known about McCarthy except that he was separated from his wife and child, was frequently in trouble with women, and numbered among his friends one Gilbert Johnson, which is not his name, who lived at 233 Lafayette Street—across the street from Evelyn Corbin's building. If McCarthy had left town with the girl, was there any meaning to the sudden departure at almost the very hour Evelyn Corbin's body was found?

Inspector Moran sent a teletype alarm. Eight days later, on September 17, a teletype message alerted him that McCarthy had been picked up in upper New York State on a stolen car charge. Yes, he admitted to police there, he had gone off with Sue, they'd had a fight, she'd left him. A week later, the girl was picked up with another man in a neighboring town. Inspector Moran went to New York, brought Sue back, and questioned the two separately.

McCarthy knew nothing about Evelyn Corbin's murder, he insisted. Saturday night, the night before her death, he was out drinking with his friend Gilbert Johnson. He had been locked out of his rooming house in Lynn for nonpayment of rent, McCarthy said, so he slept Saturday night in Johnson's apartment on Lafayette Street. Next morning, Sunday, about 11 A.M., he left the apartment, he said, drove to a diner, had a cup of coffee, drove to his rooming house in Lynn, climbed in a window to pick up some clothes, and drove back to Salem where he telephoned Sue to meet him just after one o'clock. On the way, he passed a friendly little dog, wagging its tail; he backed up, picked up the pup, and put it in his car.

In Salem he parked down the street from Sue's house. She came out about one-thirty. "We're driving to New York," he told her. "How much money have you got?" She had seven dollars. All he had, he said, was five or six.

As they drove she reached out to switch on the car radio. To her surprise he knocked her hand away roughly. "Leave it alone," he growled. "It's not working." They got as far as Claverack, New York, when the car broke down. They walked until they reached an apartment house. McCarthy talked the woman owner into allowing them to occupy an empty furnished apartment. She felt sorry for them, she said later—such a bedraggled young couple, with their hungry little dog.

Sue found it impossible to live with McCarthy, she told Inspector Moran. He was cruel, unpredictable, given to sudden rages. He got a job picking apples but lasted only a few hours, earning sixty cents. He began kicking the dog, for no reason, so viciously that another tenant had to take it to a veterinarian. McCarthy went into frightening tantrums, jumping up and down, shouting at the top of his voice, bursting into tears. Sue left McCarthy, met a boy, and went to live on a small farm in nearby Hudson. McCarthy, now alone, followed her to Hudson, got a job as a dishwasher, but was fired after five days when his employers found money missing. He bought a car for forty-five dollars; it broke down after a few miles. He stole another car, which brought about his arrest.

That was his story.

But when Inspector Moran checked with McCarthy's friend Johnson, important differences appeared. McCarthy had said he left Johnson's apartment, across the street from Evelyn's building, at 11 A.M. Sunday morning. But Johnson distinctly recalled that his alarm clock awakened them both at 9 A.M.; that they had a breakfast of doughnuts and coffee in his kitchen; that McCarthy left the apartment a few minutes later, about nine-thirty. "I remember waiting for him to get out so I could lock the door and go back to bed." He made sure to lock it, he explained, because he suspected McCarthy was a thief. "I slept all night with my wallet under my pillow."

What, now, did Inspector Moran have?

Doughnuts for breakfast . . . and a doughnut was found on the fire escape outside Evelyn Corbin's kitchen window.

McCarthy leaving Johnson's apartment at about 9:30 A.M.—and Evelyn Corbin strangled in her apartment across the street between 10:35 A.M., when she left Mrs. Manchester, and 11:15 A.M., when she did not answer Mrs. Manchester's telephone call.

McCarthy leaving town at 1:30 P.M. with Sue and violently preventing her from turning on the radio—which would have carried news of Evelyn Corbin's murder.

McCarthy telling Sue he had "five or six dollars." Evelyn's purse had been emptied by her killer. She rarely had much cash in it—usually, said Mrs. Manchester, five or six dollars.

Like all police involved in the search for the Strangler, Inspector Moran knew through what heartbreaking detours one could be led by coincidence. Yet . . .

He spoke to McCarthy's wife. They had been separated for

two years. Her description of the man echoed sixteen-year-old Sue's. Not only had he beaten her and thrown her about—he was tremendously strong, said Mrs. Mc-Carthy—but once, when their eighteen-month-old daughter annoyed him, he turned on the baby like a madman, kicking her in the face, and blacking both her eyes. His own background was vague, and always upset him; he was illegitimate, his wife said, and had learned his mother's identity only a few years before. When he was sixteen he had "some kind of mental trouble." In bed he was a brutal, selfish man and often forced her to commit unnatural acts with him.

Inspector Moran left, pondering this last of coincidences. Evelyn Corbin's autopsy showed that she had been forced to engage in such an act—whether while living, or dying, or dead, no one knew.

After serving a brief sentence for abducting Sue, Mc-Carthy was released from the House of Correction in late November 1963. He lived with a woman he had picked up until the early evening of Friday, December 12, when they fought over his sexual demands. He stormed out of her apartment and paced back and forth on Roslyn Street, which runs into Lafayette Street at a point less than fifty yards from the Corbin apartment. A fifty-two-year-old woman walked by: McCarthy turned, jumped her from behind, put his hand up under her dress, punched her, gouged at her eyes, tried to rape her, stifling her screams by stuffing his fingers down her throat, and left her bleeding and semiconscious on the street, in such a state that police could not question her for fifteen hours. She remained three weeks in Salem Hospital. The night before a woman had been similarly assaulted in Peabody, three miles away. Both women identified McCarthy as their assailant. He denied the assaults, though he admitted that he had passed the fifty-two-year-old woman on the street in Salem, turned, and come up behind her—but then he had simply walked away, he said.

This man, thought Moran. He claims he was in Johnson's apartment until eleven o'clock Sunday morning. Johnson swears he left at nine-thirty. If he left at nine-thirty, he could easily have walked into the Corbin building, slipped the lock on Evelyn's door with a celluloid strip, waited for her to return from the Manchester apartment, and jumped her from behind the moment she turned her back to lock the door. She had not even had time to remove her robe and slippers . . .

Moran questioned McCarthy about Evelyn Corbin. The man laughed. He laughed through most of the interrogation. It was not a rational reaction. Moran accused him bluntly of Evelyn Corbin's death. "We've got enough to convict you," he said, bluffing.

"Oh," said McCarthy airily, "you'll find I'm not guilty."

"Suppose you're not guilty but you're convicted anyway and sent to prison for life. Doesn't that worry you?" Moran demanded.

"Nope," said McCarthy. Though he hired an attorney, he still appeared to treat it all as a joke.

Would he take a lie-detector test? No, said his attorney.

Nor would his client answer any further questions about the murder of Evelyn Corbin.

There was no way to compel him, as there had been no way to compel Carl Virtanen. Though Salem police strongly suspected that McCarthy had killed Evelyn Corbin, there was no legally acceptable evidence against him. As there was none, so far, against any other suspect, whether believed to be the multiple or individual murderer in the strangulations.

That was the immovable barrier against which, time and again, the search had to crash. Rarely are there witnesses to murder. There were none to the stranglings.

While Moran made his reports to the Attorney General's office, the team of Mellon and DiNatale were wrestling with a parallel problem—a suspect who could not be pinned against the wall. He was the six-foot-four, twenty-three-year-old Negro Casanova, Lew Barnett, believed involved in the strangling of Sophie Clark. Barnett was wily and cunning. He admitted nothing save that he knew Sophie, and had been in her apartment once or twice.

Sophie's friends had always been suspicious of Barnett. In school in his early years he was known as a troublemaker; later many girls shunned him because of his belligerence and his habit of bragging about his conquests, true or fancied. Yet there had been nothing to hold him for; after questioning, he had been told he was free, but to notify police if he left the city. Some weeks later he was discovered gone; he had simply vanished from his job as a porter at Filene's, and given no one a forwarding address. He was traced through several states as far as Florida, finally back to New York, and there, in May 1964, Phil DiNatale and Jim Mellon called on him. They had traced him by his social security number. With the exception of one's fingerprints, this apparently is the one unchangeable fact about all of us.

When the two detectives walked in on him in a Harlem hotel room, the pressure had been off Barnett for some months; they felt it the psychological moment to approach him.

Barnett was astonished to see them. Yes, he was still broken up about Sophie's death. As her friend it had been a terrible blow to him.

"If you're her friend, you won't mind taking a lie-detector test, will you?" he was asked. All Sophie's friends had done so as a routine procedure to eliminate them so police could move on in their search for the killer.

Thus challenged, Barnett said, sure, he would take the test.

He had maintained he had been alone with Sophie only once: the night of November 11, 1962, when he took her to see the film *The Longest Day*. Her roommates, however, had told the two detectives they were sure Lew had spent at least two afternoons with her. Barnett was asked if this was true.

"I don't know, man," said Barnett. "I think I remember one other time when I brought records to her apartment—" But that was it, he insisted. He had not seen her alone again; he had seen her Saturday, December 1, four days before her death on Wednesday, December 5.

On the dresser in Sophie's apartment had been a book of short stories. "Lew," Mellon asked, "did you ever read that book?"

No, Barnett replied. But he recalled reading a letter she was writing to a "Dearest Chuck"—something about her having liver and onions—

Mellon stiffened. Lew Barnett must have been in the apartment the very hour of her murder. How else could he have known about the letter?

"Where'd you see it?" Mellon demanded.

Barnett thought. "On Lieutenant Donovan's desk at police headquarters," he said. "Could of been the letter or a copy of it—"

Was he telling the truth? A quick check only ascertained that Barnett had been questioned in Lieutenant Donovan's office, that a photostat of Sophie's letter might have been on the desk—no one was sure.

Barnett refused to budge. He insisted that on the day of Sophie's murder, he had not gone out until evening; it was wet, slushy, a miserable day, and after he came home from work at Filene's about 3:30 P.M., it was too nasty to go out; he took a nap, woke about two hours later, had a sandwich, and dated a girl that evening. That was his story. Once, Lew admitted, he had hurt his head playing football and since had suffered dizzy spells and blinding headaches, but he had never blacked out, he said. He knew exactly what he had done that December 5.

Barnett underwent the polygraph test in New York. To put him in a proper frame of mind, the examiner said, "Lew, I'll show you how this thing works." He placed a dollar bill, a five-dollar bill, and a ten-dollar bill in three unmarked envelopes, moved them about behind his back, then brought them in front of him, and asked Barnett to take one. "Don't show it to me," he said. "Just look at it." Then the examiner attached the various wires from the little black box to Barnett's arm.

"I want you to answer no to all my questions," he said. "Do you have the dollar bill?" "No," said Barnett, grinning. "Do you have the five-dollar bill?" Again Barnett replied No. "Do you have the ten-dollar bill?" A third time Barnett said No.

The other looked up from his dials with a little smile. "Lew, you have the five-dollar bill."

Barnett looked shocked. "Hey, that's not bad!" he said. Then: "Oh, all right, man, go on, shoot any questions you want."

The examiner asked ten questions, carefully worded so that each one played on the following one. Some dealt with Sophie's murder; others were completely extraneous. One question was, "Were you in the apartment at the time that death came to Sophie Clark?" In his negative reply to this question, according to the polygraph, Barnett lied.

"Lew," said the operator. "We have some discrepancies here. I'm going to ask the same questions over again, possibly not in the same sequence."

Then, after the second series, "Lew, you are lying."

Barnett jumped to his feet, furious. "Take this God damned thing off me! No box is telling me I'm lying!"

Denial or no, Barnett could not be eliminated. Phil Di-Natale and Detective John Flynn of New York, who was working with Phil and Jim Mellon on the case, drove Barnett back to his apartment. The two Boston detectives had insufficient evidence to arrest Barnett; they would have to return without him. But Phil decided, as they drove, to bluff him. He said: "Lew, we're driving you home and when you get there I want you to get some clothes that'll last you a long time because the place we're going to take you now, the clothes have to last you a long time."

Barnett, sitting in the back of the car, kept silent. Then, casually, he asked, "What kind of clothes you think I ought to be taking?"

"You just take what you think will last a long time," Phil

repeated. After a moment, he added, "On the other hand, come to think of it, you don't have to take anything but a toothbrush. Because the place you're going to they'll give you what you need."

Silence again from Barnett. Detective Flynn, driving, said nothing.

"If I was the guy who did it, would I get the electric chair?"

Barnett asked the question almost conversationally. Phil had to control his voice when he answered, "No, of course not."

"Why not?"

"Because you're sick," Phil said gently. "They don't do that, if you're sick. They take you and put you in a hospital and give you the best of care until you're cured and then they let you go."

"Don't they try you for murder?"

"No, because you're sick and now you're cured," Phil said. "You were sick when you did it; now you're cured."

Barnett thought that over. The two detectives scarcely allowed themselves to breathe. Flynn was ready at any moment to jam on the brake, halt the car, and take down Barnett's confession.

"Well . . ." came from the back seat. Then, in a rush of words, "I'll tell you, Phil—" But whatever he was prepared to tell, he changed his mind in midstream. "Aw, the hell with it." And he said nothing more. The detectives waited. Nothing.

I've lost him, thought Phil, despairingly. There was nothing to do now. The psychological moment had passed. I've bluffed him, thought Phil, and I couldn't hold him. Now the son of a bitch is just sitting back there waiting to hear what we have to say.

They rode in silence until they were in front of Barnett's apartment house. Phil turned to him. "I'll tell you what, Lew. We've going to give you another chance. We're not going to take you anywhere. We're going to cool you off a bit—just let you alone."

Barnett exclaimed, almost in shock, "You mean you're not going to arrest me? You're not going to take me in?"

"Nope," said Phil.

He and Flynn watched Barnett scramble out of the back seat as though the car were about to explode.

Phil let Barnett cool for a week, then they approached him again. They found him in a bar. He looked startled to see them. Phil, acting as though he carried a warrant, said, "Look, Lew, you left Boston without telling us. That means anytime you go back, you're going to be picked up and held for questioning. That's always going to hang over your head. You say you're innocent; why don't you help us wrap this up and help us get off your back? Come back to Boston with us now and on your own accord to take a second lie-detector test. If you're innocent, what have you got to be afraid of?"

Barnett agreed. He returned to Boston with them.

Zimmerman, the polygraph examiner, chatted with Barnett before the test. Barnett was on his mettle. "You tell me how I got into her apartment and we'll talk turkey," Barnett challenged him. Zimmerman interpreted this to mean that he knew something he had not yet told, and was fencing to learn just how much the police knew.

The polygraph, when Barnett took it, indicated that he was hiding something. Zimmerman reported to Jim Mellon, waiting in an adjoining room, that Barnett was involved "by personal or remote contact with a person who died by other than natural causes."

Mellon decided to bluff, as Phil had done in New York. He strode into the test room to confront Barnett, still attached to the machine. "Kid, this is it, you flunked it. You couldn't make time with Sophie, so you knocked her off. Now, why don't you come clean? You go along with us and we'll go along with you. You're lying—you can't fool the machine."

Barnett shook his head doggedly. "Oh, no, man, oh, no," he said. "These boxes are for the birds. This thing isn't going to make me a killer. I need more than that."

What now?

"Okay, Lew," said Mellon. "But in fairness to you, we think you should be interviewed by some psychiatrists at Boston University School of Medicine. You game?"

"Sure, sure," said Barnett expansively. To Mellon it appeared as though the youth, in his enormous conceit, was playing a game with them—a kind of Russian roulette in which he was prepared to admit everything but only if they trapped him.

The session that same afternoon at Boston University was equally inconclusive, save that the psychiatrists had no doubt that Barnett was emotionally ill and in need of psychiatric help. For his part, Barnett only grew more incensed. "Man, you think I could have killed Sophie and not known about it?" Yes, of course he had had dizzy spells, but he had never blacked out . . .

Such things were possible, he was told. Would he be willing to find out—to be placed under a hypnotic drug? Again, challenged in this fashion, he agreed.

May 14, 1964. Even as Lewis Barnett lay down on Dr. Leo Alexander's couch, a sample of his handwriting was analyzed by Dr. Carola Blume. She found him cruel, violent, impulsive; able to control himself; probably psychotic; intelligent and vain. "He looks like a person who should not be left on his own in the community." He could not be excluded from the investigation, she felt.

Under Methedrine Barnett emerged, surprisingly enough, as a bisexual, kept by both men and women, and a man who enjoyed sadistic lovemaking—he called it "constructive lovemaking"—with women. At that time he was supported by a homosexual hairdresser with whom he lived. The hairdresser had been a guest at Sophie Clark's twentieth birthday party, two days before her death. As Barnett went into a deeper hypnotic state, he began to weep. He was conscience-stricken, he said, but not because he had killed Sophie Clark. He had never touched her. He was overcome by guilt because he had not dropped in on her the afternoon of her death—that December 5, 1962. He'd been thinking of telephoning her, he'd been thinking of dropping over to see her, but hadn't wanted to leave the house because the weather was so bad . . . "If only I'd been there," he cried emotionally. "I'd have saved her, I'd have protected her . . ." Later, moaning and twisting, he whispered, "I know confession is good for the soul, Doctor. I want to confess my failure to save Sophie's life. I'm ready to serve time until they find the real killer . . ."

To Dr. Alexander, this seemed out of character with Barnett's personality, which he described as "not that of an over-conscientious person but rather that of a totally amoral psychopath." Dr. Alexander felt that Barnett protested far too much: that he spoke of his guilt to cover his positive reaction to many damaging questions in his polygraph. He shared Dr. Blume's view that Lewis Barnett could not be altogether eliminated from the investigation into Sophie Clark's death.

It meant one more man to be kept under surveillance. Barnett's great weakness was his braggadocio. He might yet boast to friends, to girls, to fellow employees, how he had taken in the police and all their experts in two cities. He was given a bus ticket back to New York where Homicide detectives were asked to watch him indefinitely.

17

It was November 1964, a full ten months since Mary Sullivan's murder, and Jim Mellon in his frustration was like a man possessed. Although he had been involved in so many sorties—Arnold Wallace and Paul Gordon and Lew Barnett and many less important suspects—he had been unable to get Mary's strangling out of his mind, and had made it his special assignment.

He had begun to be convinced there were four possibilities. Mary had been killed (1) by someone out of her old background, the Cape Cod area in which she had been born, grown up, and worked before coming to Boston; (2) by someone out of her new background, the Charles Street circle, which included Christopher Reid and the other youths who were in and out of her apartment; (3) by a total stranger, that is, the Strangler. The fourth possibility he considered was that she had been killed in error, by someone who meant to kill either Pat or Pam, her roommates, or perhaps even the girl—a nurse—who had been the two girls' roommate before Mary.

Jim, with Steve Delaney, had spent weeks in and about Hyannis, questioning all who had known Mary. They had interrogated and cross-checked the boys whose cottage in Dennisport she had visited the summer of 1962; they had interviewed all her fellow employees at each place she had worked since leaving high school; they had questioned and requestioned Pat and Pam. Jim had all but worn a hole in his pocket carrying about the test tube containing the washer he found on her bed; he had exhausted himself running down names and firms listed on the mysterious telephone page; and now he had come back once more to Christopher Reid, and to the old police proverb, "Investigate your informant."

He could not get Christopher out of his thoughts. The boy's high-strung character; his story about the male voice he heard through the door, his elaboration of that voice into a tall, thin man with a protruding Adam's apple, his zeal in checking radio stations to prove that the voice did not come from the radio . . . why this need to provide a lover for Mary Sullivan?

Was it an alibi for himself?

There was also the question of a missing key.

On January 2, two evenings before Mary's death, Christopher and a friend had dropped into the apartment at 44A Charles Street. Pam and Mary were there. Christopher had met Mary for the first time then; he had been there from 7:30 P.M. until 11 o'clock, long enough to familiarize himself with the layout of the rooms. The next day, January 3, the day before the murder, Pam Parker noticed that one of the three keys in her keycase—the middle one, that to the apartment—was missing. She remembered having left the case on the table for a day or so.

Someone had extracted the key. Could it have been Christopher? It would have taken several minutes because a small removable metal tab linked the key tightly to the ring. It was a nuisance, one had to struggle to detach it; could Christopher have managed to do it without being observed?

In the months since Mary's murder Mellon had made it a point to keep in touch with him. Christopher had said he wanted to help, and often chatted over the telephone with Mellon on one phase or another of the investigation. Only a few days before, after returning from the Cape, Jim telephoned Christopher to say he was back and to ask if anything new had come up. Just before ending the conversation, Jim asked, "By the way, Chris, when you were in the apartment on January second, did you have occasion to go to the bathroom?"

"Yes," Christopher said. "Why?"

"Oh, I don't know. It just seemed a natural question to ask." But Mellon had learned what he wanted to know. If the boy had taken the keycase into the bathroom with him he'd have had time to detach the key. Interestingly enough, the metal tab had been replaced, the act of a compulsively neat person—such as Christopher Reid.

Repeatedly in the course of the search a suspect became almost an obsession with one detective or another. That was the situation now. Mellon could think only of Christopher Reid. One night, about ten o'clock, while watching TV with his wife—his six youngsters were in bed—Mellon stood up. "I'm going to drop in on Chris."

His wife reacted as most wives would. "Jim, at this hour? You're crazy."

Mellon had come to the conclusion that Christopher Reid must take a lie-detector test. He had a number of reasons for this decision. One involved Christopher's small stutter which, his mother had said, was the result of a hearing defect; he had had several operations on his ears. Jim had checked clinics to learn the degree of hearing loss, for the hearing loss cast doubt on Christopher's story that he had heard, two nights before Mary's death, a man's voice through a closed door just before he reached the third-floor landing. Mellon suspected that Christopher might have visited the apartment Friday afternoon, January 3—the day before the murder, when the three girls were at work—looked through Mary's personal effects, and made his plans then. There had been discrepancies in the stories Christopher told. Each time he was asked about the man's voice, he added more details. Mellon had suggested to Bottomly that Christopher be asked to take a lie-detector test, and Bottomly agreed it should prove useful.

Mellon wanted to call on Christopher now, late at night, hoping he would be out and only his mother would be at home. Then he would ask her if he might use the phone, allowing him to examine the Reid telephone directory. Suppose Christopher had torn out the page, brought it to the Sullivan apartment that Friday, and deliberately planted the charred fragment behind the toilet to throw police off his trail? If Mellon found pages 307–308 missing, he would be entitled to ask for a search warrant. Somewhere in Christopher's house, then, he might find something taken from Mary Sullivan's apartment.

The Reids lived only a few streets away from Mellon. When Mellon knocked, Christopher himself came to the door. Regrettably, the telephone directory would have to wait. "Hi, Chris," said Mellon. "I just wanted to go over some of the information you gave us." Christopher had made his request possible by volunteering the statement that he had heard the mysterious voice. At that point he became a witness.

After a few words, the detective dropped his bomb. "Chris, we're not getting very far, as you know, but we're trying our best. I think we'd like to question you a little bit more. Would you take a lie-detector test?"

The boy's face turned ashen. "What if I don't?"

"Well, that's up to you," said Mellon. "Of all the people who have given us information on the stranglings so far, I should tell you that only one has refused, and he was an extortionist who didn't want that to come up."

Mrs. Reid, listening to this exchange, said, "Christopher, of course you'll take the test. What have you to hide?"

"Oh, well, okay, then," said Christopher.

A few days later, on Friday, November 27, at 2 P.M. he was given his polygraph examination in the office of Charles Zimmerman. Jim Mellon and Steve Delaney waited in the anteroom.

Presently the door opened and Zimmerman and a harassed Christopher came out. "Jim, I'm stopping the test," Zimmerman announced. "Chris is having a hard time remembering about the key." He turned to the boy. "I want you to go home for a week and just think about it, Chris. I'm convinced you know whether you had the key or not. You come back next Friday, December fourth, same time, and pass that test, or tell me why not."

The two detectives took Christopher home. "Damn it, did I have the key in my hands or didn't I?" Christopher wondered aloud.

The detectives watched him closely. Was he pretending?

At 11:40 A.M., Friday, December 4, the day Christopher was to take his second test, Pamela Parker, who now lived with her parents in Malden, received a telephone call. She found herself engaged in a nightmare conversation.

"Who is this? Pamela?" a man's voice asked.

She wasn't sure if she recognized it. "Who is this calling?"

The voice grew intense. "I'm going to do the same thing to you that I did to Mary. I'm going to take that broom and shove it right up . . ."

"Who is this? Who is this?" Pamela cried, aghast.

"I'm even going to take your underwear off, even your underpants! How would you like that? How would you like that?" He spoke jerkily, staccato, under such emotion that he began to stutter. "I'll get you like I got Mary, sooner or later! Would you like that? Would you really like that? Well, you won't have to wait."

Then the caller slammed down the receiver.

Pamela was too distraught to call the police, but her mother did so, and Detective Tuney and Jim Mellon were at the house soon after. No, she could not recognize the voice. She knew only two boys who stuttered. One was stationed with the Army in South Carolina. The other was Christopher Reid.

Stephen Delaney checked at once. Christopher Reid had missed his first morning class at Boston University but had arrived in time for his second. At 11:40 A.M. he was en route from home to the University. He could have gotten off the trolley and made the call. Delaney hurried to Zimmerman's office, to meet Mellon there. They brought the examiner up to date on this new development.

The three men speculated. Would the boy show up for his repeat test? Had he cracked under the strain and made the threatening telephone call to Pamela, blaming her because her keys were involved, blaming her for what was now happening to him?

But at two o'clock Christopher Reid walked in, schoolbooks in hand. He seemed depressed.

Was anything the matter?

No, just one of those days when everything went wrong, he said. Like a man going to his execution, he followed Zimmerman into the test room. The two detectives waited outside. Both were tense.

Twenty minutes later Zimmerman emerged, shaking his head.

"He's lying! I asked him if he made any phone calls to a girl this morning and the needle went way over! I think we've got him on the ropes." He went back.

Now excitement ran high. Mellon telephoned Bottomly. Stand by, anything might happen . . .

Moments later the door burst open and Christopher ran out. "Jim! Help me!" Tears streamed down his face. He had failed the test: Zimmerman had told him so. "I didn't do it, I didn't do it! God, you've got to believe me! Oh, God, how did I get into this?"

Mellon put his arm around his shoulders. "Of course, I'll help you." He held the boy comfortingly for a moment. "But I have to warn you, Chris, as of this moment you are a suspect in the Mary Sullivan homicide and anything you say can be used against you." He added, "I don't want you to think I'm cold-blooded but I have to make this statement to you for your own protection."

"I know you're only doing your duty," Christopher managed to say. Detective and suspect slowly walked across the street to a cafeteria and sat over coffee and talked. "This is the toughest part for me," Jim said. "You're a minor and so I've got to go home to your mother and tell her you're a suspect."

Christopher tried to gulp his coffee. "Maybe it's just as

well," he said miserably. "You can explain it better than I can."

Mellon had a single thought. How could he push this boy toward self-revelation, perhaps even confession? Aloud he said, "You know, Chris, who among us is to know what is right and what is wrong? The things people can do in the heat of passion . . . At such moments we're not really ourselves."

But Christopher only sipped his coffee in anguished silence.

In midafternoon Mellon called on Mrs. Reid. He was circumspect. Christopher's mother was a lonely, high-strung woman in her early forties who had been divorced four years ago after a long, unhappy marriage. Mother and son were known to have bitter emotional scenes. "Mrs. Reid," Mellon began carefully, "I feel like a thief because I'm going to rob you of something that's very dear to you." As she looked uncertainly at him, he went on. "If you're angry, I'll understand. In fact, if you react in any other way I'd be shocked. But I have to tell you that Christopher is a suspect. We consider him as such."

Mrs. Reid jumped to her feet, and screamed, "Oh no, he couldn't have done it, he couldn't have done it!"

"I think you better get yourself a lawyer, Mrs. Reid," Mellon said as gently as he could, and left.

An hour later Christopher was on the phone. "Jim, that lie-detector test mixed me all up. I want to have a sodium pentothal and convince you people I had nothing to do with it. I want it. Now. Today. As soon as possible."

It was done. At eight o'clock that evening Christopher Reid was on Dr. Alexander's couch. He had come with his mother and his lawyer. Christopher suffered through his ordeal. During the time he was under sodium pentothal, Bottomly, members of his investigative staff, Lieutenants Donovan and Sherry, and other police officials entered, left, entered again. Sometimes the boy wept, as when he spoke of his parents' immaturity, their violent quarrels, their divorce—"the saddest experience of my life." He denied that he had taken the key. He denied that he had telephoned Pamela. "I didn't use the phone all day."

Was he telling the truth?

If he did not call, who did call Pamela on *this* day? The only other supposition was difficult to accept—that someone who knew Christopher was to take the test today had telephoned and threatened Pamela in an attempt to incriminate Christopher.

"Did you kill Mary Sullivan?" he was asked.

"No."

"Do you know who did?"

"Not the remotest idea."

A few questions later: "Are you close to tears? Your voice suddenly changed. What thought occurred to you?"

"I'm scared," said Christopher. "I'm scared the Mary Sullivan case will be pinned on me."

"How can it be pinned on you?" Dr. Alexander asked.

"By a process of my not answering the lie-detector test correctly in relation to the results they wanted. They seem to think I had a key to the apartment for a period of time, which I didn't. They seem to think I was in the apartment on Friday, the day before it happened. I wasn't."

He had heard a man's voice when he climbed the stairs Thursday evening, two days before the murder? Yes, yes. Why hadn't he gone into the apartment? Mary wouldn't let him in. Why? "I don't know—maybe she was taking a shower, or in her lingerie."

"Why should she do that with another man in the apartment?"

Christopher lay silent for a moment. "For sexual reasons," he said. He had been told that Mary had been "a naughty girl," but "I never tried to provoke sex on her. She wasn't that appealing to me."

He had never had a homosexual experience, he said, though he had been approached. Nor had he ever had sexual intercourse with a girl.

"Who was the killer after?"

Christopher answered surprisingly: "He was after Pat."

"Who was the killer?" Everyone in the room was on edge. But he replied, "I don't know."

"How do you know the killer was after Pat, then?"

"She's very beautiful, a very sexy girl."

He had no other explanation, he said.

Why had he done so badly on both polygraph tests?

"The examiner scared hell out of me. I admit I'm, shall we say, brilliant . . . You might not think so . . . I knew I was nervous and every time I'd hear the word Sullivan I'd jump."

In the end, the interrogators concluded that Christopher Reid could control himself under drugs. Nothing conclusive had been determined. The situation stood where it had stood before.

There was one more test. It was to place Christopher in Mary Sullivan's bathroom, standing before the mirror, and ask the schoolteacher, who on the day of Mary's murder had seen a man's face framed in that bathroom window, to stand again at her own window—and see if Christopher Reid resembled him.

That was done. On a sunny day, at the same hour—2:50 P.M.—Christopher stood in Mary Sullivan's bathroom, facing the mirror, his left profile to the window. Phil DiNatale, Jim Mellon, and Steve Delaney took turns standing there, too, to give the schoolteacher a multiple choice.

She could not say that it was Christopher. She felt the man she saw January 4 was taller than any of them. But she could not be sure.

The next morning Jim Mellon, determined to come to a conclusion, began a campaign.

He telephoned half a dozen of Christopher's fellow students, introducing himself: Jim Mellon, Attorney General's office. What could they tell him about Christopher Reid? Was he subject to fits of temper? Capable of great violence? Had they noticed any change in behavior recently? Each friend, he knew, would immediately telephone Christopher to warn him that an Officer Mellon had been making inquiries about him. That would exert one pressure on the boy.

To build up a second Mellon stationed himself in front of Boston University each morning and afternoon where Christopher could not fail to see him when he came and left classes. To know he was under such surveillance would certainly wear him down.

If Christopher had an accomplice, Mellon reasoned, sooner or later the pressure would lead one to telephone the other. Accordingly, he obtained court permission to place a twenty-four-hour tap on the Reid telephone.

Finally, he left orders with a tailor who serviced the Reid household that any clothes sent out to be cleaned or repaired should be delivered immediately—before anything was done to them—to the police for overnight chemical examination. One could not know what might be found, even at this date, on one of Christopher's suits—perhaps a thread from the red ascot, or lint from the blanket on Mary's bed, or a torn button with its washerlike backing missing.

Three days later on Monday, December 7, Christopher Reid dropped out of Boston University. He was giving up school for a while; he could no longer concentrate on his studies. The campaign, thought Mellon hopefully, was beginning to pay off. But again—as with so many other suspects—one could only wait.

On Christmas Eve 1964, Mrs. Frances Sullivan, Mary's mother, made a sad journey to St. Francis Cemetery in Centerville, where Mary was buried. She told no one. She wanted to kneel there and weep, alone.

As she came near, she stopped. Someone had been there before her—perhaps only a few minutes before. One single long-stemmed red rose, still fresh and budlike, had been laid on the earth of her daughter's grave.

Mrs. Sullivan became hysterical.

Eleven days later, January 4, 1965, would mark the first anniversary of Mary's death.

Lieutenant Tuney mused. In analyzing the complex character of a sex murderer, the Medical-Psychiatric Committee had pointed out that such a man might be sentimental, might even reveal a sense of compassion. Had Mary's strangler placed the rose on her grave? If so, might not the anniversary of her death draw him to the scene of the crime? Perhaps only to stand at a safe distance and look again at the place?

January 4 would fall on a Monday. Lieutenant Tuney decided to set up surveillance of 44A Charles Street over the entire weekend—Friday, the first, through Monday, the fourth. It was done quietly. No one could have known that the white-aproned clerk in the Italian sandwich shop two doors from No. 44A Charles Street was Jim Mellon. From the interior he had an unobstructed view across the street so that he could observe anyone (Christopher Reid, perhaps) who stopped on the opposite side and gazed at the building, particularly the third floor where Mary had lived and died. Directly opposite No. 44A, on the other side of the street, was a laundromat, from whose large plate-glass window one could see the front and entrance of Mary's building. One man, reading a newspaper, sat among customers awaiting the completion of their wash. He was Steve Delaney.

At intervals, Lieutenant Tuney and Bottomly's secretary, Jane Downey, strolled by, their eyes alert for any lingering spectator.

Friday, Saturday, Sunday, Monday, they kept vigil.

Nothing untoward occurred.

They were still—as Lieutenant Tuney had put it often before—sitting in the middle of nowhere. They did not know that the end of the search was almost in sight.

PART FOUR

18

It began slowly enough in 1960, nearly two years before Anna Slesers, the first of the victims, was murdered on June 14, 1962. There was nothing to indicate at the time that one of the most extraordinary chapters in the extraordinary story of the Boston Strangler was now opening. A dark-haired man in his late twenties would knock on the doors of apartments in the Harvard Square area about 9 or 9:30 A.M. If a young woman came to the door he would say, quite courteously, something like this: "My name is Johnson, I'm from a model agency. Your name was given me as someone who might make a good model." The job could pay as much as forty dollars an hour. She needn't worry about posing in the nude or anything like that—the jobs involved modeling evening gowns and sometimes swimsuits. He had been sent to take her measurements and other data—with that he produced a tape measure from his pocket—and if she proved suitable, a "Mrs. Lewis from the agency" would drop by in a few days to conclude the business arrangements. He was boyish, articulate, if not too grammatical, and as he deftly measured her waist, her hips, her breasts, her legs from hip to knee and knee to ankle, he said with a surprisingly winning smile, "I hope you don't mind this, I do it all the time."

These calls went on for some months. Mr. Johnson never returned. Nor did a Mrs. Lewis ever drop by later. There were variations to his approach. On October 26, 1960, about six in the evening, Nancy Davis opened her door at 30 Boylston Street in response to a knock. Her roommate, Mary Wood, was in the shower. They had reported a gas leak and Nancy expected to see the handyman standing at the door. But it was a soft-spoken stranger in his late twenties wearing a jacket and dark green work pants, who said he was looking for an apartment to rent. "You must have the wrong place,"

237

Nancy told him, but he was already in their foyer. "I just want to get an idea how the rooms run," he said. He glanced about, then turned to her. "I'm a photographer," he said, and added admiringly, "You have a fine figure. You could probably earn forty dollars an hour as a model. Do you know your measurements?" With that he dropped to his hands and knees in front of her and felt each ankle. "I ought to measure you," he said. "I got my tape with me—"

He put his hand in his pocket but Nancy had already drawn back. Everything had happened so quickly she had hardly had time to react sensibly. "No, thank you," she said. "I'm not at all interested."

She showed him out.

On February 17, 1961, a Boston housewife opened her door to a man who said he came from a talent agency. He named the friend who had recommended her, brought out a tape measure such as tailors use, and began, as she said, "to measure me all over."

"I didn't stop him at first, I don't know why," she said later. "He actually lifted my skirt and touched the skin of my thigh—I jumped away then." When he had finished jotting down her measurements, he said, "You're good for at least forty dollars an hour—why don't you talk to your husband about it tonight?" gave her a handshake, and left.

Three weeks later the story began to take on darker overtones. Sarah Craig and her roommate, Sylvia McNamara, were at breakfast in the kitchen of Apartment 3 at 268 Harvard Street about 11 A.M. Saturday, March 11, 1961, when they heard a soft tapping. Was it at their door, or someone knocking at the apartment across the hall? Sarah unlocked the door and swung it open to disclose a young man standing there, dark-eyed, with dark hair, and obviously nervous.

"Can I come in and talk to you, please?" he asked. She led him into the living room. The reader must remember that this incident took place before the Strangler appeared on the Boston scene. Standing in the room, the young man said, "I was sent to Apartment Number Three. I'm an artist's agent. Are you a model?" When Sarah said no, he began to speak so rapidly that she couldn't make out what he said, though she asked him twice to repeat his words. Apparently it was about photography, modeling, sculpture, Harvard University, and a fee of forty dollars an hour. She finally broke in, "You really must have the wrong party—"

"I don't know," he said. "Could it be your roommate?"

When she shook her head, he said, "Well, in case you're interested, Mrs.——" —she could not make out the name—

"from the agency will be in the building later and she'll have papers you can fill out." He was gone, out the door, as nervous as when he entered.

The two women decided the whole thing was a fraternity stunt—probably a student carrying out a silly assignment for his initiation. But next day their janitor showed them metal shavings outside their door. Around the lock were marks of a screwdriver used in an attempt to jimmy it.

That, then, must have been the tapping they heard. Had their caller of the day before been trying to force his way in? Why did he not simply knock?

The following Friday, March 17, just before dusk, the elusive dark-haired man was seized. There had been a series of housebreakings in Cambridge and six police cruisers were on the alert for the burglar. Sergeant Leo Davenport, cruising in one car, heard a call over his radio: "We're chasing a man who just ran into the yard at Ellery and Harvard." Sergeant Davenport, finding himself at that very intersection, jumped out and was about to vault a fence when he heard a gunshot. Someone shouted, "Colleran shot!" Colleran was a fellow policeman. Davenport leaped the fence, gun in hand, just as a dark-haired man of medium height raced across the yard thirty feet in front of him. Davenport shouted, "Stop, or you're dead!" just as someone else boomed out, "Halt, or I'll shoot!" It was Colleran, unhurt, his gun also trained on the fleeing man. The latter stopped in his tracks. Half a dozen detectives surrounded him. Behind him he had dropped a two-foot-long screwdriver with a bright yellow handle. Skeleton keys and a jackknife were in his pocket. In his car parked nearby were four more screwdrivers. He had just tried to break into an apartment, he admitted to Lieutenant Chester E. Hollice, who was leading the search. Earlier in the week he had measured two nurses who lived there—"I just wanted to get into the apartment and wait for them to come home."

Why? He could not think of an answer.

His name was Albert H. DeSalvo, and he was twenty-nine years old. A check showed that he had a juvenile record and had once been committed to Lyman School, an institution for delinquent boys. In 1958 and 1959 he had been arrested for numerous breakings into apartments and houses, stealing small amounts of money he found. Now, he admitted, he was engaged in a different type of activity. In the past weeks he had measured more than a dozen women, promising them modeling jobs with nonexistent agencies. He lived in suburban Malden, and he was married—his wife was a German girl he had met while serving abroad in the Army of Occupation. He had two small children, a six-year-old daughter being treated for a congenital pelvic dislocation, and an eight-month-old son, and he worked as a press operator for a rubber factory.

Why had he done these things? What was the purpose of measuring women and promising them jobs?

He just liked to talk to women, he said. But later, the day before his court appearance, he poured out a story of a wretched upbringing, a childhood of deprivation in a large family frequently on relief, tyrannized and later deserted by a father who abused his wife and six children and went openly with prostitutes.

"Can you accept a man after what he's done to his family?" DeSalvo demanded. "What kind of a man is that?" He spoke almost in tears. "I have three brothers and two sisters. All of us brothers graduated from jail. To show you how bad it was, my own brother and father were in jail at the same time."

Visiting the girls about Harvard, measuring them, gave him "a big kick. I'm not good-looking, I'm not educated, but I was able to put something over on high-class people," he told probation officers. "They were all college kids and I never had anything in my life and I outsmarted them. I felt they were better than me because they were college people. Telling those girls they could be models built up their egos, so they let me do it. Anybody with any sense would have found me out, because, gee!"—he flashed his dark-eyed, boyish grin—"they never even asked me for proof and I never had a camera. It was a real crazy idea."

Police officials looked at him. So this was the Measuring Man. A harmless figure who derived some kind of pathetic sexual satisfaction from touching strange women? Or just another small-time burglar who posed as a model's agent in order to have an excuse for loitering about hallways?

After psychiatric examination at Westborough State Hospital, he was diagnosed as a sociopathic personality—a man whose behavior and emotional reactions deviate from the normal—and on May 4, 1961, sentenced on charges of Assault and Battery, brought by some of the women he had measured, and attempted Breaking and Entering, to a two-year term in the Middlesex County House of Correction. He was found not guilty of two counts of lewdness. Later the judge, sympathetic to DeSalvo's tearful promise that he would turn over a new leaf and his attorney's plea that his family needed him, reduced the sentence to eighteen months. Shortly after, the Parole Board took a similarly sympathetic view. The result was that with good behavior this dwindled to eleven months and DeSalvo was released in April 1962.

Nearly three years elapsed—years in which a DeSalvo and his petty sickness were eclipsed by the overwhelming presence of the Strangler.

In early November 1964, while Jim Mellon was beginning his reinvestigation of Christopher Reid as a suspect in the Mary Sullivan case, and Phil DiNatale was checking the death of Daniel Pennacchio who had falsely confessed to killing Beverly Samans, and Steve Delaney was trying to determine if Pietro Achilles had been in Rockport when Joann Graff visited there the night before her death, Albert DeSalvo was seized again by Cambridge police.

This time the accusation was far uglier.

A week before, on Tuesday morning, October 27, a twenty-year-old coed, a bride of a few months, was in bed in her Cambridge apartment. It was a few minutes after 9:30 A.M.; her husband had just left for his teaching job. She dozed off for a moment. When she opened her eyes, a man stood in the bedroom doorway, staring at her. He was of medium height, his eyes hidden behind huge green aviator's sunglasses, his dark hair combed back, wearing a dark waist-length jacket and green slacks. "Don't worry," he said quickly, "I'm a detective—" But as he spoke he was approaching her bed.

She managed to find voice enough to say, "You leave this room at once!" She struggled to sit up in bed.

He pushed her down, hard, and she screamed. She felt the blade of a knife against her throat. "Not a sound, or I'll kill you," he warned. As she lay there all but paralyzed, he stuffed her underwear into her mouth, and using her husband's pajamas and her own clothes, tied her in a spread-eagle position on the bed, each ankle tied to a bedpost at the foot of the bed, her wrists to those at the head. Then he kissed her about the body and otherwise sexually abused her. "Don't look at me," he said again and again. Then, after a long while, she heard him say, "How do I leave this place?" She could only think, *Oh, God, get him out—* She told him how to find the front door. He bent over her, his face averted, and loosened her hands and feet so she would be able to free herself. "You be quiet for ten minutes"—he warned, then added apologetically, "I'm sorry," and slipped away.

But she *had* looked at him. She would never forget his face, she told detectives. An artist's sketch was made from her description: Detective Paul Cloran, studying it, said,

"This looks like the Measuring Man." He had operated in the same area, and knew how to enter locked apartments. Police telephoned DeSalvo at his home. Would he come down to answer a few questions about an assault on a woman? On Wednesday, November 3, DeSalvo came to Cambridge Police Headquarters. Sitting in the interrogation room he denied any knowledge of the attack, but even as he spoke the girl herself stood in an adjoining room, studying him through a one-way mirror; and after making doubly sure by hearing his voice through a partly opened door, she identified him. Still denying it, he pleaded innocent to charges of Breaking and Entering, Assault and Battery, Confining and Putting in Fear, and Engaging in an Unnatural and Lascivious Act. He was released on $8,000 bail for hearing two weeks later.

As a matter of routine, his photograph went over a six-state teletype network. Within thirty-six hours it brought detectives from Connecticut where similar sexual assaults had taken place through the summer and autumn—in every instance, a man tying up women on their beds. He had become known as the "Green Man" because he wore green work pants. Sometimes he was in the uniform of a building maintenance worker. His energy was extraordinary. If the records were correct, on one day—May 6, 1964—between 9 A.M. and midday, he had bound and assaulted four women in four towns—Hamden, Meriden, New Haven, and Hartford.

Acting on this new information, police on November 5 suddenly descended on DeSalvo's home, a modest, neatly kept one-family house at the end of a dead-end street in Malden. He was away. They waited. DeSalvo drove up, saw the police cars, attempted to reverse his car and drive off, but was trapped and seized. He was brought again to Cambridge Police Headquarters. This time several women victims from Connecticut were on hand to identify him.

He would not talk to anyone, he said, until he spoke to his wife, but he begged police not to let her see him in handcuffs. That was agreed to. Mrs. Irmgard DeSalvo, a tall, dark-haired woman of thirty, and Albert's sister Irene came to the station. For nearly an hour he talked to them in the presence of three detectives.

Toward the end, he broke down in tears. "Please," he pleaded with his wife, "please, Irm, let me be a man just this once. I've done some very bad things with women—I've broken into houses, I've used a gun but it was a toy gun, I used a knife but I never killed anybody—I'm tired of running, I want to get it off my chest, I need help, I want help. When they had me before I didn't know how to ask for it."

His wife, who suspected he had been "doing something," was not surprised at his sexual assaults on women. She could not bring herself to tell police now, but the man was insatiable—no one would believe how oversexed Al was. It was a shameful thing. He wanted her in the morning; he wanted her again when he came home for lunch; then in the early evening after supper, and again before they fell asleep at night. On weekends, when he was home from the job he now had as an outside maintenance man for a construction company, he needed her five and six times each day. Nor was that enough. When they went out he made suggestive remarks, even in her presence, to attractive women. It was impossible to satisfy him; she had given up trying to do so. He had complained she was frigid to him, and they had argued bitterly about it.

Aloud, she said in her heavy German accent, "Al, tell them everything, don't hold anything back," and the two women left the room.

DeSalvo turned to the detectives. "I've committed more than four hundred breaks, all in this area, and there's a couple of rapes you don't know about," he said. They drove him about Cambridge and he pointed out fifteen apartments he had broken into. He never had difficulty getting into them. At first he slipped the locks by using the cardboard corner of a stenographer's pad. Later, he perfected his technique, using 2½-by-6-inch strips of polyethylene foam which he cut from bottles containing household detergent. These were stronger than cardboard, left no mark, and made no sound.

Other women came forward. In one instance he had blindfolded his victim, held a knife to her throat, and had his way with her for nearly an hour. As the investigation widened, it became clear that DeSalvo had been sexually assaulting women not only in Massachusetts and Connecticut, but in New Hampshire and Rhode Island as well. Police estimated that his victims numbered more than three hundred women.

Repeatedly Cambridge detectives questioned him. DeSalvo was by turns truculent and agreeable. But he was especially grateful to Sergeant Davenport, who had him in his gunsights but did not fire, and spoke more easily and familiarly with him. Sergeant Davenport's general air of breeziness helped matters considerably.

"Leo," DeSalvo said at one point during an interrogation, "if you knew the whole story you wouldn't believe it."

"Al, what are you doing—bragging or telling the truth or lying? What the hell you doing?" the detective demanded.

DeSalvo took a long breath. "It'll all come out, Leo," he said. "You'll find out."

Sergeant Davenport considered the man before him. What DeSalvo had said about breaking into apartments had turned out to be true. Sometimes the women he said he had measured—and often been intimate with—denied having ever seen him. That was understandable. In the instances where DeSalvo had tied up his victims, none had given all the details to police. But the horror in their eyes indicated that DeSalvo had told the truth as far as he wanted to tell it. The lengths to which he had gone—the actual indignities he had committed upon them or forced them to commit—most likely would never be completely revealed by his victims. Davenport followed a train of thought. At the time DeSalvo broke down before his wife, detectives had asked him about the strangulation murders. "No, no," he had said. It was as he told his wife Irmgard. Terrible things with women—but he had never killed anyone. But, thought Sergeant Davenport, he was a powerful man—swift, agile, athletic. He knew how to slip in and out of buildings, how to enter apartments silently. And he had a gift of gab, too, so he was able to talk his way into apartments. Sergeant Davenport suddenly said, "Al, what do you know about the Beverly Samans killing on University Road?"

DeSalvo shot a hurt glance at him. "You can't put that one on me, Leo. I don't go that one at all." Then: "Where is that street? Is that the one down near the post office?"

So DeSalvo knew Beverly Samans' street and did not mind revealing that he knew it. But DeSalvo, begging that his wife be spared the sight of him in handcuffs, apologizing profusely to his victims for attacking them, certainly seemed to lack the murderous hatred for women exhibited by the Strangler. Nothing here seemed to fit the Medical-Psychiatric Committee's psychiatric profile—no consuming rage toward his mother, no Oedipus complex, surely no problems of potency—rather, fear and contempt for his father, and shame for the way his father had treated his mother.

"Okay, Al," said Sergeant Davenport. Next day DeSalvo appeared in court again, this time with the out-of-state warrants against him. He was held in $100,000 bail and sent to Bridgewater for the customary thirty-five-day pretrial observation. When the reports on DeSalvo reached the Attorney General's office, Lieutenant Tuney asked Jane Downey to telephone Dr. Robey to say that a man named Albert H. DeSalvo had been sent to Bridgewater pending trial for sexual assaults; he had denied knowing anything about the stranglings and Cambridge police thought he was telling the truth. Nevertheless, would Dr. Robey look him over as he had the others?

Dr. Robey and his staff concluded that DeSalvo suffered from "a sociopathic personality disorder marked by sexual deviation, with prominent schizoid features and depressive trends." In short, a borderline psychotic, but competent to stand trial. On December 10 he was returned to Cambridge jail. But he began to behave strangely. One night he claimed to hear voices. He insisted to a guard that his wife was in his cell, denouncing him; he begged her not to be indifferent to him. A moment later he turned on her furiously, ordering her out of his cell. Then he became despondent and threatened to kill himself. On January 14, the court ordered him to be returned to Bridgewater for a second evaluation. This time Dr. Robey and his colleague, Dr. Samuel Allen, concluded that the stress of waiting for trial—in Massachusetts rape is punishable by life imprisonment—had pushed DeSalvo over the brink. Sometimes he appeared sane, in touch with reality; at other times he heard voices, was "potentially suicidal and quite clearly overly schizophrenic." If brought to trial he would most likely be unable to advise his counsel: he was judged not competent to stand trial.

On January 27, Dr. Robey sent the necessary papers to Middlesex Superior Court in Cambridge and at a hearing on February 4, 1965, Judge Edward A. Pecce ordered Albert DeSalvo recommitted as mentally ill "until further order of the court."

He became one more inmate at Bridgewater.

Four days after DeSalvo had been returned to Bridgewater, a new prisoner arrived for observation pending trial for murder. One might not have given him a second glance at this institution, where almost every other inmate might be a murderer, had it not been for his appearance. He could have been typecast as a gang leader out of the bloody 1920's. He was nearly six feet, broad-shouldered, lean, with black hair and somber black eyes, a dark-complexioned face with furrowed cheeks; a man acutely aware of everything going on—in the psychiatrists' words, "very paranoid, very bright, very angry."

He had been charged with a particularly brutal killing. At 3:50 P.M. September 29, 1964, Mrs. Rita Buote, forty, and her fourteen-year-old daughter Diana drove into a Texaco station in Andover, Massachusetts, to come upon a horrifying tableau: the attendant on his knees, pleading for his life, a lean, black-haired man with a tan trench coat standing over him, gun in hand, and as they watched, firing bullet after bullet—they heard four loud reports—into the kneeling man. As Mrs. Buote stared, unbelieving—was a movie being made here?—the man turned, saw her car, and gun in hand, walked swiftly toward her. She had sufficient presence of mind to snap the inside door catch. The killer was on her side, the driver's side; she saw his face clearly on the other side of the glass, the gleaming black eyes, the furrowed cheeks. He raised his hand, he pointed his gun at her through the glass—she heard two clicks. The gun was empty. He pounded on the door. "Open up! Open up!"

Mrs. Buote seized her daughter and slid down with her onto the floor, huddling under the dashboard. "Pray, Diana! That man has a gun! He's going to kill us—"

At almost the moment that Mrs. Buote drove into the station, William King and Reginald Mortimer of Andover in their truck pulled in from the opposite side. They saw the same terrible scene from another vantage point, and as of seconds earlier: the attendant suddenly crumpling before the man, the other standing over him. And they heard what sounded like firecrackers. The man wheeled—a gun glinted in his right hand—he walked to Mrs. Buote's car. They saw him aim, squeeze the trigger soundlessly, saw him pound on the side, tug wildly at the door, then turn, run to a dark sedan parked near a gas pump, and drive off.

A dead man lay sprawled before them, his blood staining the gray pavement of the station. He was Irvin Hilton, forty-four. His death actually resulted from a single stab wound in the center of the spine. It was not difficult to reconstruct what had happened. Hilton's assailant had come up behind him and plunged a knife into his back. Hilton, dying, fell to his knees, turned to plead with his killer—and received six bullets at point-blank range. It seemed a cruelly senseless crime, for though robbery was assumed the motive, the cash register appeared untouched and Hilton's wallet was intact in his trouser pocket.

The dark sedan, found abandoned a few miles away, had been stolen from the parking lot at the Massachusetts Institute of Technology, in Cambridge. Its owner, a twenty-eight-year-old graduate student, told police two guns were missing—a black .22 pistol and a .32 revolver, with ammunition for both, which he kept under the driver's seat. A .32-caliber slug was discovered in one of the gas station's drains not far from Hilton's body.

Given an artist's sketch based on Mrs. Buote's description, it took police twenty-four hours to find the man they charged was Hilton's murderer. His name was George Nassar, and he lived in surburban Mattapan; he was thirty-three, unmarried, a parolee who had killed a man in a grocery stickup in 1948, when he was only sixteen. He had been paroled in 1961, after serving eleven years of a second-degree murder sentence. In prison his intelligence, his willingness to rehabilitate himself, and his general ability had impressed several ministers, as well as the parole board. Indeed, since his release he had taught Sunday School classes, and on some occasions actually substituted for a minister in his pulpit. There was no question that he was an unusual man; he had been studying Russian, and planning to enter Northeastern University, and he had been working at various jobs from hospital attendant to newspaper reporter.

He vehemently denied Hilton's murder. "If I had done it, I would have killed myself," he exclaimed. One only had to look at his record since he had been paroled. It was all a case of mistaken identity. But both Mrs. Buote and her daughter identified him in a police lineup. They were positive he was the man.

At Bridgewater, Dr. Robey and his staff found Nassar a man of extremely high intelligence—his I.Q. was above 150—but now showing paranoid and schizophrenic symptoms. After thirty-five days' observation Dr. Robey recommended that he be kept for further study.

Usually Bridgewater State Hospital has about seven hundred inmates. In January, when Nassar arrived, he found himself in the same ward as Albert DeSalvo. They struck up a friendship.

To other inmates DeSalvo had always spoken freely of his sexual escapades. During group therapy he eagerly stood up and talked about his experiences. Once, he boasted, he had assaulted six—not four women—in one morning. Everyone knew of his sexual prowess. When he was on his measuring kick, how easy those girls were! Some stripped down right away. One girl was so excited at the idea of becoming a model she ran into her bedroom, changed to a tight-fitting jersey and leotards, then exclaimed, "Oh, these are too bulky—you'll get the wrong measurements," and slipped everything off. He couldn't count how many times he had ended in bed with them. When he began tying them up, he learned still more about women. One actually paid him a hundred dollars and "begged me to come back again."

To his wardmate George Nassar, however, DeSalvo began to confide other matters. What he said so impressed Nassar that he sent for his attorney.

Sunday afternoon, March 7, in her sister's home in the Denver suburb of Northglen to which Irmgard DeSalvo had fled secretly several weeks before with her two children to escape the shame of her husband's exposure as a rapist, she received a long-distance telephone call.

"I'm Lee Bailey, an attorney," said the voice at the other end. It sounded crisp and authoritative. "I'm calling from Boston. I am your husband's lawyer, Mrs. DeSalvo. Now, please listen carefully to what I say—"

Mrs. DeSalvo had never heard of Lee Bailey. She did not know that there was in Boston a youthful, driving attorney named F. Lee Bailey who had become nationally known when he had obtained the release from prison of Dr. Sam Sheppard, the Cleveland osteopath convicted of killing his wife ten years before. She knew only that her husband Al had a lawyer, Jon A. Asgiersson, who had been handling his case. But she listened to the voice on the telephone.

What the man who called himself Lee Bailey was saying, in effect, was, as she recalled later: In the best interests of your children and yourself, you must take a different name and move away—go into hiding at once, because reporters and photographers from the national magazines will be searching for you day and night. "Something big is going to blow up about Albert—it will be on the front pages of every newspaper in twenty-four hours. I'm flying out to see you tomorrow so I can help you myself—now, work fast!"

Mrs. DeSalvo, dazed, replaced the receiver. She thought she had left all this behind her. On her flight west she had already taken an assumed name for herself and her children. She planned to divorce Al anyway—she could never go back to him—and to change her name legally, but she hadn't quite known how to go about it.

What could the man who said he was Mr. Bailey be talking about?

The next afternoon she received another call from Boston. This time a man on the wire spoke in German. He was speaking, he said, for Mr. Bailey, who did not want to get on the phone himself and use English because he believed his telephone had been tapped. Mr. Bailey, he continued, wanted her to know that a representative from his office was en route by plane from Boston that very moment and would call on her in a few hours. Mr. Bailey, he said, was too tied up in the case to come himself. The representative was named Daniel Bloomfeld. She was to follow implicitly whatever instructions Mr. Bloomfeld gave her.

"But—" began Mrs. DeSalvo. Another voice came on the

phone. She recognized it as Frank DeSalvo, Al's brother. "Irmgard, do just what you're told because Al has confessed he is the Boston Strangler." A moment later Al's brother Joe got on the line. Yes, Al had confessed he was the Strangler. He'd given all sorts of details no one else could have known. She must follow instructions.

Mrs. DeSalvo hung up in a state of near shock. Al—the Boston Strangler? Impossible!

At 7 P.M., a third telephone call. Mr. Daniel Bloomfeld had arrived in town. Twenty minutes later Mr. Bloomfeld walked into the house. She must move at once. Here was two hundred dollars to pay the cost. Mr. Bloomfeld wrote down the name of a local lawyer. Arrangements had already been made with him to start proceedings immediately to change her name legally and obtain her divorce at no cost to her.

"Where's the money coming from for all this?" Mrs. De-Salvo asked, bewildered.

"Sufficient funds will soon be made available," her visitor said cryptically. Any time she needed more money, she needed only telephone Mr. Bailey in Boston. He gave her the number.

What had happened to Mr. Asgiersson, Al's lawyer? (the last she had heard from Mr. Asgiersson was a phone call during which he strongly suggested that Albert was insane and had been for some time.)

Mrs. DeSalvo understood Mr. Bloomfeld to say that Mr. Asgiersson was representing Albert as the Green Man, but her husband's wardmate "recommended Mr. Bailey to Al for this case two days ago."

Her caller left.

All but distraught, Mrs. DeSalvo carried out her instructions. She moved from her sister's home to a trailer court. Al could not be the Strangler, she thought miserably, confession or no confession. She knew her husband. But why would he confess to such a thing? Unless he really *was* insane. She could not believe that. A number of other reasons came to her. Perhaps he was revenging himself on her because she had fled from him with the children; because she would not answer the letters he constantly wrote her from Bridgewater. He always wanted to be important; that was why he bragged, lied, made up big stories. And Al was always chasing an easy buck. She gathered that there was a tremendous amount of money involved—a huge reward, and magazines and newspapers ready to pay a great deal for the story—the lawyer calling from Boston the day before had said she must hide from reporters from *Time* and *Look*. But if Al only knew what such a thing would do to his family, the damage especially to Judy, making her think she was the daughter of a murderer—a monster . . . She wept. It was too much, too much. Her mother used to send her clippings from the German newspapers about the Boston Strangler, warning her to be careful and keep her doors locked. Al had seen those clippings.

When could he have had time to commit all these crimes? He had gotten out of jail on April 9, 1962. The stranglings, she remembered vaguely, began that summer, and continued for some time. But those were Al's first months out of jail and when he was not at work he was with her almost every moment. He hadn't even owned a driver's license his first few weeks of freedom and she herself had had to drive him to and from work. Later he obtained a license, good only from 7 A.M. to 7 P.M., and in any event, he never got home from work later than 4 or 4:30 in the afternoon. When would he have had time to plan and carry out the murders? Besides, he had been renovating their house in Malden beginning early in 1963—he worked at that every weekend. And even if he *had* done those terrible things, he could not have kept it from her—not a husband from a wife who knew him like a book. She always knew when he was breaking into apartments and stealing small sums—guilt would be written all over his face when he walked into the house. And though he was a man sick with his need for women, he could never kill. He was so soft-hearted, so considerate—he could not torture, mutilate, strangle.

Yet Mr. Bailey, she gathered, was a very important attorney. Would he be taken in by Al? Would Al's own brothers be taken in by him?

What was happening here?

What had happened was that Albert DeSalvo had dropped a tantalizing hint to George Nassar that he was the Strangler. One afternoon he interrupted his tiresome boasting with an unexpected query: "George, what would happen if a guy was sent up for robbing one bank when there were really thirteen banks robbed?"

It was an odd question and Nassar, who in his brief time at Bridgewater had already assumed a kind of authority because of his superior intelligence, looked at DeSalvo. "You must be a nut like the others around here," he said to him. "Get away from me. I don't want to have anything to do with you."

DeSalvo had walked away, but after a few days, accosted Nassar again. "You thought that was a nutty question," he said. "Well—." Then he confided in Nassar, Nassar got in touch with his attorney, F. Lee Bailey—and Bailey moved with characteristic swiftness.

Indeed, it became evident as one pulled together information from various sources that for some weeks DeSalvo had been trying to claim—now explicitly, now by intimation—that he was the Strangler. In January, while in Cambridge jail awaiting recommitment to Bridgewater, he had suddenly asked his attorney, Jon Asgiersson, "What would you do if someone gave you the biggest story of the century?"

Asgiersson, a bright, personable lawyer in his middle thirties who knew little about DeSalvo—he had been brought into the case by DeSalvo's brother Joe, whom he had once represented in a civil action—said, "Albert, what are you talking about?"

DeSalvo went on, "Bigger than the Brink's robbery." On January 17, 1950, masked bandits robbed the Boston offices of Brink's, Incorporated, of securities valued at more than a quarter of a million dollars.

Asgiersson searched his memory. "You mean the Plymouth mail robbery?" Little more than two years before, a gang of half a dozen men and women had waylaid a U.S. Mail truck near Plymouth, escaping with more than a million and a half dollars in cash—the largest cash robbery in the country's history.

"No, not like that," said DeSalvo, whereupon the lawyer, annoyed, said, "Stop playing games with me, Albert. Come out with it. What is it?"

Albert rubbed an ear. "It only happens once in maybe two million times," he said slowly. "Like Jack the Ripper."

Asgiersson stared at him. Albert went on, "I've been known as the Cat Man—the Green Man—the Phantom Burglar—and now the Boston 'S' Man."

Did he mean the Boston Strangler? Asgiersson asked. Yes, said Albert. "Are you mixed up in all of them, Albert?" the lawyer asked again, as calmly as he could. "Did you do them all? Did you do some of them?"

All, said Albert. He added in a troubled voice that he thought his story might bring some money to support his wife and children, but "I don't want to die for it."

Asgiersson was in a dilemma. If the man was mentally ill, could one accept this self-incrimination? If one could accept it, was it a lawyer's duty to protect his client from himself, or protect society from one who might be a mortal enemy if he was ever freed? Assuming that the man, incredibly enough, *was* telling the truth. Even as he pondered the question, Asgiersson began a discreet investigation.

A few days later, on January 13, one of DeSalvo's Army friends, Edward M. Keaney, visited him. Al and Ed had served together in Germany. They had double-dated, Al with Irmgard, Ed with her girl friend Hilda. In fact, the two girls had introduced the two Americans to each other. After both couples married and came to the States, they saw each other three or four times a year. Now Al was in trouble and Ed paid him a call.

DeSalvo looked strange, he remembered later. His eyes would fix and stare as they talked. Ed pretended to observe nothing. He understood Al was wanted in four or five states for rape. "Al," he said, "you know you're going to get life imprisonment for this."

Al looked at him with his queer, unblinking gaze. "Eddie, I could get life fifty times and they couldn't pay me back for what I've done. My family would have to change their name."

Ed was not too impressed. Al was always topping everyone. Whatever you had, he had three of. The man never stopped talking about his power over women. "Oh, I think I know what you've done," he said.

Al wasn't satisfied. "Yeah, Eddie, you know but you don't know." And he stared at him as if he were not there.

Ed Keaney drove home, thinking, He's really gone off his rocker. Then it struck him. Could Albert mean that *he* was the Strangler? For all his boasting, Al was quite a fellow. Keaney had seen him box in the service, and he could surprise you with his power, ferocity, endurance—Al could do almost anything, if he put his mind to it. But this—this was ridiculous. When Ed arrived home he said to his wife, "I think Al has flipped." He did not tell her more.

It was the next day, January 14, that DeSalvo was sent back to Bridgewater. For some time then he tried to see Superintendent Charles Gaughan. Inmates constantly demanded to see administration officials, and DeSalvo had to wait his turn. He fidgeted under the strain. On February 2, while being interviewed by a social worker, he said, unexpectedly, "I'm known as the Green Man now but soon I'll be known by another name." That cryptic notation was put down in his file for whatever significance it might have.

DeSalvo tried to talk to his fellow inmates, but most of them avoided him. Rapists are cordially disliked in prisons because their victims might be anyone's mother, wife, or sister. Al was so eager to talk he followed his wardmates about.

Finally he cornered twenty-five-year-old William Lewis (which is not his real name), who was under observation pending trial for murder. Lewis had killed his young wife because he thought she had been unfaithful, then tried to kill himself.

"Hell, what you did was nothing," Al said disdainfully to Lewis. "When you find out what I did—I've killed a couple of girls."

Lewis walked away thinking, *Brag, brag, brag.* He had his own problems at the moment. He was planning suicide again (he attempted it, unsuccessfully, a few days later), and Al's stories of his Casanova role, now embroidered with murder, were the last things Lewis was interested in.

George Nassar, too, was not eager to be DeSalvo's confidant. But in the end he did listen. Whether it was Nassar or DeSalvo who first thought about it, the impression was that $110,000 in rewards—$10,000 for each strangling—awaited whoever gave police information leading to the arrest and conviction of the Boston Strangler.* One can only speculate as to whether an agreement was made in the hope that De-Salvo would be accepted as the man. Nassar could claim the reward, keep a percentage, and turn the rest over to Mrs. DeSalvo and the children. DeSalvo himself had little further to lose. Although nine men were in Death Row, no one had been electrocuted in Massachusetts in the past seventeen years. As things now stood, if the psychiatrists continued to judge DeSalvo insane, he would remain indefinitely at Bridgewater. If he ever stood trial for rape, the numerous charges against him would mean certain conviction, so that he would also find himself spending the rest of his days in prison. In any event, then, it was unlikely that he would ever be free again.

Meanwhile, Bailey, having learned about DeSalvo from Nassar, talked to DeSalvo himself on Thursday, March 4. On Saturday, March 6, armed with a Dictaphone, he questioned DeSalvo in detail. The man, Bailey said later, confessed not only to murdering the eleven women attributed to the Strangler, but to killing two more: Mary Brown, sixty-nine, brutally beaten and stabbed in her Lawrence apartment at 319

---

* Actually, the text of the reward offer stated that a ten-thousand dollar reward would be paid "for information leading to the apprehension and conviction of the person or persons responsible for the murder of any one or all of the following persons," and then were listed the names of the eleven victims. The reward would reach $110,000 only if each woman was found to have been murdered by a different man.

Park Avenue on Saturday, March 9, 1963; and a Boston woman, about eighty, whose name DeSalvo could not remember. Nor could he recall the date. He thought it was in 1962. She had died, he said, of a heart attack in his arms.

Had the police said he sexually assaulted three hundred women? They underestimated him, declared DeSalvo. The figure was closer to eight hundred or a thousand, in recent years. His lifetime total, including those in Germany, he said, might well reach two thousand.

And no one could charge that he was imagining all this and cite, as proof, the hallucinations which had sent him to Bridgewater the second time. He had faked them, he declared, in order to fool Dr. Robey and the other doctors, because he had been told that by so doing he'd escape trial, be sent to Bridgewater, and after a few years, released. When he learned that wasn't so, he determined to tell the truth.

Lee Bailey, despite his youth—he had yet to celebrate his thirty-second birthday—was an attorney who had already made a considerable mark in Boston. A stocky, handsome man constantly in movement, he was born in Waltham, attended Harvard (entering at sixteen) and Boston University Law School, then served several years as a Marine fighter pilot. Enormously resourceful, charming or belligerent as the need might be, he was a dramatic performer in court, and nearly always the subject of controversy. Because of his love of electronic gadgets and his courtroom technique, one admiring Boston writer described him as "The Perry Mason of New England." He lived with his wife and small son in Marshfield, thirty-five miles from Boston, in a fourteen-room ranch house which contained eleven telephones and an elaborate intercom system, and to which he commuted by car or private plane, depending on his mood. The legend on one door of his offices in downtown Boston read INVESTIGATIVE ASSOCIATES. He maintained his own staff of private detectives—each of whom was a lawyer—and communicated with them (and his plane, cars, and home) by two-way telephone and a shortwave radio system operated from his office.* The Dr. Sheppard case in Cleveland had challenged

---

* Prominent on one wall of his waiting room was a framed diploma certifying that F. Lee Bailey had "completed with honors" the "Comprehensive Fall Seminar," held in Los Angeles in November 1961, "devoted to the Study of Hypnosis, Hypnoanalysis, Hypnoanesthesia, Hypnotherapy, Interrogation, Use of Polygraph, Memory Recall, Fact Retention, the Art of Persuasion, the General Study of Psychiatry, all these subjects employed to educate the trial lawyer in the accepted medical uses and practices relating to these subjects and to aid him in his never-ending search for truth, making him a

him and he had thrown himself into it, reportedly without a fee. Against all expectations he won Dr. Sheppard's release from the Ohio Penitentiary in July 1964 on an appeal claiming that he had not had a fair trial because of adverse newspaper publicity. Now, nearly a year later, pending final disposition of the appeal, Dr. Sheppard was still out of jail, living the life of a free citizen, married to a German-born divorcée who had been his pen pal while he was in prison. Bailey had taken George Nassar's case, too, because it challenged him. Funds for Nassar's defense had been raised by Boston's "Committee for Reasonable Justice," a group of citizens interested in rehabilitating criminals. Some of its members had originally helped Nassar win his parole. In defending Nassar, Bailey was once more fighting what seemed a hopeless case—an admitted killer charged with a second murder, before eyewitnesses. Now, through Nassar, Bailey found himself involved in perhaps the most sensational multiple murder case of the century.

Three weeks earlier, Bailey had told Detective Lieutenant Donovan that he had an informant who knew the identity of the Strangler. He would not reveal his informant, but asked Donovan to give him questions to ask the man so he could determine if it was a hoax. Donovan did so; Bailey returned a day or so later with what Donovan felt were "good answers"—answers suggesting that the man knew far more than he should. Donovan felt disturbed. He thought that even a man who had studied the stranglings could not so readily have answers to these questions.

Bailey revealed nothing. But Lieutenant Donovan learned that during this period, Bailey had visited his client George Nassar, at Bridgewater. When he returned he had the answers to Donovan's questions. Could Nassar be his informant? Was the Strangler, then, someone Nassar knew? Perhaps even a fellow mental patient?

As coincidence would have it, on Friday, March 5—the day after Bailey first spoke to DeSalvo—Detective Phil DiNatale, doggedly pursuing one lead after another, found himself checking one Albert DeSalvo, the Green Man. Tips had come to him from two sources. A neighbor of Patricia Bissette had reported a man in a green uniform prowling about the building the day Pat was murdered. Earlier, Andrew Palermo, Security Officer at Massachusetts General Hospital, told Phil of an anonymous telephone call from a girl com-

more proficient advocate." The seminar was given by William J. Bryan, Jr., M.D., a Los Angeles hypnoanalyst of whom more shall be heard later.

plaining that she had been tied and sexually abused by an Albert DeSalvo, who lived in Malden. Phil talked to Cambridge police; he had read their inch-thick dossier on an Albert De-Salvo of Malden, ranging from a January 1955, New Jersey indictment accusing him of carnal abuse of a nine-year-old girl (which had been nol-prossed when the mother refused to press charges) through his metamorphoses as the Measuring Man and the Green Man. What struck Phil, in addition to the M.O.—sexual assault plus use of nylon stockings as ligatures—was the discovery that DeSalvo's jobs were such that he was either off from work, or on a shift that put him on the street and so free to commit the murders at the day and on the hour *that every one of the eleven deaths occurred*. Why had DeSalvo escaped Commissioner McNamara's round-up of sex offenders in the early months of the search, and why had his name not been produced by Bottomly's computers? Because the official records identified Albert DeSalvo as a B and E man—not as a sex offender. Phil learned that an Albert DeSalvo of Malden was now at Bridgewater. Bottomly, interested in DeSalvo's dossier, sent Phil to Bridgewater with it Friday afternoon, March 5, to brief authorities there on the Attorney General's latest suspect. Phil wanted to ask DeSalvo where he had been the day of Patricia's murder, and also wanted to check the man's palm print against one found above the doorway in Ida Irga's apartment. Not much had been done with this because, unlike fingerprints, palm prints are not unique.

At Bridgewater Phil received a copy of DeSalvo's print. Did he wish to speak to the man? "Does he have a lawyer?" Phil asked. Yes, as of yesterday, his lawyer was F. Lee Bailey. Phil, knowing that as a result of a recent Supreme Court ruling, he should not question a suspect without his lawyer present, refused to talk to him. Even were the man to confess, the confession could be thrown out of court later. Instead he reported back to Bottomly.

It was the next day that Bailey recorded his interrogation of DeSalvo at Bridgewater. That night Bailey telephoned Lieutenant Donovan. "This is it!" the lawyer exclaimed. Could Donovan come down to his office and hear the story from the mouth of the Strangler himself?

Late that night Lieutenant Donovan, with Commissioner McNamara and Lieutenant Sherry, sat in Bailey's office until long after midnight, listening to the voice of a man whom Bailey identified as the Strangler. So that the police officials would not be able to identify the voice, and so be unable to testify against the man, Bailey varied the speed of the playback. But the voice was calm, authoritative, matter-of-fact, punctuated by the snap of fingers as the man would correct himself: "Now, wait a minute, no—I'm wrong. I took the pillow from the left side of Nina Nichols' bed, not the right . . . Yeah, there was a picture of Helen Blake's niece, I guess, on top of her radio. When you stand in her hallway, the bedroom's on your right, you look straight into the bathroom. . . ."

Not only this, said Bailey, but the man drew sketches in detail of each of the thirteen apartments!

What else did DeSalvo say?

He said the door leading into Patricia Bissette's apartment opened outward. That was true. He said she had a black jewelry box on the bureau, and Christmas packages on the bed. True.

He said he had a cup of instant coffee with her. A cup half full of coffee had been found in her living room—a fact that had not been published anywhere.

He said he killed Sophie Clark just after 2:30 P.M. He remembered the day—December 5, 1962—because it was his wedding anniversary, and he had taken the afternoon off. A check showed he had reported working three hours that day—8 A.M. to 11 A.M.

He said he had gagged Mary Sullivan, placed a sweater over her face, and raped her. He said that as an afterthought he inserted the end of a broom two or three inches into her vagina "to make it look different." He had left a knife on the bed—he drew a sketch of it. The handle was accurately drawn but not the blade. He remembered the design of the headboard against which he propped her body, he said, and sketched it. It was accurate.

He said Anna Slesers lived on the top floor. Here he was wrong. Her apartment was one floor below. He got in, he said, by telling her he had been sent by the superintendent to repair a leak, and when she led the way into the bathroom, he struck her on the head from behind with a piece of lead pipe he had brought with him. He recalled a highly polished floor, either wood or linoleum, and a painters' scaffolding outside the window. When he entered, a portable record player was playing "long hair" music. He turned the knobs in front and the music stopped, but he did not think he'd turned it off completely. He got blood on his clothes so he grabbed a raincoat he found in the apartment and wore that when he left. Later he bought another shirt in an Army and Navy store. He also said he raped her. Anna Slesers' autopsy, however, was negative as to rape.

He said he first tried to strangle Nina Nichols with a belt, but it ripped in his hands near the buckle. A ripped belt *had* been found near Nina Nichols' body, but that fact had appeared in the newspapers. He said he pushed the neck of a wine bottle into her vagina. The color of the bottle, as he described it, was incorrect. The papers had printed that a bottle had been found next to her body.

He said he strangled both Jane Sullivan and Ida Irga but could not remember which he had done first. Jane Sullivan, he said, was a big, strong woman—"She almost got away from me"—who talked with a "from Ireland" accent. He described the position he said he left her in, in the tub, but tub and sink were incorrectly described.

Ida Irga, he said, was afraid to let him into her apartment because of the publicity about the Strangler. He said he told her, "All right, it doesn't matter to me—I'll come back tomorrow," and began to go down the stairs, when she said, "Well, never mind, come in." Actually, detectives pointed out, there was comparatively little publicity about the Strangler until *after* Ida Irga's body had been found. Then the panic really set in.

He said he had not planned any of his attacks. He had no idea who the victims were. He had usually pressed buzzers downstairs—whichever woman opened her door first, that was the one he chose.

As to the knot, the Strangler's knot—he had not attempted to "decorate" anyone. It was the kind of knot he always tied. He had used it when he tied the removable casts on Judy's crippled hip. He tied them with a big bow because she was a little girl and a big bow somehow made it more gay, more playful.

In all his years on the force, nothing in his experience had caused Lieutenant Donovan as much anguish and frustration as the stranglings. In May 1962, when Edmund McNamara had been appointed Police Commissioner, Donovan could say to his new superior, "We've had twenty-five homicides since the first of the year, and twenty-five homicides have been solved." Then came June 14, 1962—and Anna Slesers. To Lieutenant Donovan, Chief of Homicide, each of the stranglings since had been like a personal assault upon him and his men, and he had lost nearly forty pounds since that date, literally spending his days and nights on the cases. Until this moment the most likely police suspect—however doubtful, however unsatisfying—had been Arnold Wallace, and Donovan took little solace from the knowledge.

Now, however . . . He and Sherry had heard the Dictaphone recording Saturday night. Next morning they hurried with Bailey to Bridgewater to see DeSalvo in person. The two detectives were impressed when they saw him. Since they were police officials and anything the man might say could be used against him, they exchanged no more than a hello with him. Albert's eyes were sharp; he shook hands with a firm handclasp. To meet Albert even for a moment was to realize how impossible it was to consider Arnold Wallace with any seriousness. Donovan, particularly, felt a surge of hope. "This man is the best so far," he said to Sherry as they left. At home, he telephoned Bottomly and related what had happened.

Bottomly phoned Bridgewater and gave two orders: that DeSalvo and Nassar be placed in separate wards immediately and that DeSalvo have no visitors without the Attorney General's permission. Bottomly was upset. Donovan's phone call came just as he was about to call Donovan to tell him about their latest suspect, DeSalvo, and what DiNatale had learned. Now, Lee Bailey, who was not DeSalvo's attorney of record, who had not had anything to do with the strangling investigations, had gone to Bridgewater and without authorization recorded a "confession." Bottomly was particularly vexed because his office had had an eye on DeSalvo months before, when he was first committed, and had asked Bridgewater then to give him special attention as a possible strangling suspect, as the hospital authorities had done with David Parker, and others.

Next morning Bailey learned of the order forbidding visitors to DeSalvo, and of an order from Attorney General Brooke that he—Bailey—was not to see Nassar.

Bailey, angered at being denied access to his client Nassar, who was soon to go on trial for murder, and to DeSalvo, who had asked him to be his counsel, moved into action on several fronts. He telephoned Irmgard for the second time, enlisting Charles Zimmerman, the polygraph expert, to speak to her in German, and then sent the following telegram to DeSalvo in Bridgewater:

Since I saw you last the thing that I warned you about has happened. Because I have chosen to deal for your protection with people I could trust in Boston Homicide, the Attorney General of this Commonwealth has seen fit to attempt to take over this case and announce to the public that he and his men have "solved" it. You are to be placed under tremendous persuasion to deal with the office of the Attorney General with his political ambitions. The reach of their power extends to the very institution in which you are confined. I suggest that you evaluate this matter on your own. Call for the help of your brothers if you wish to, and do not be bulldozed into doing anything which I have already told you might be to your own harm. Meanwhile please be assured that all you have asked me to do about the person for whom you personally care is being done, and at this moment a representative of my office is providing her with an opportunity to escape the deluge of publicity which could chase her if no move was made. . . . If you wish to see me of your own volition, and demand to see me, I will produce you in court forthwith through a writ of habeas corpus. This telegram is dictated in presence of your two brothers Joe and Frank, who are duly concerned for your welfare.

F. Lee Bailey

Then, after several vain attempts to meet with Brooke, Bailey fired off a telegram to him accusing him of planning to exploit the case and the resulting publicity for his own ends.

Behind the scenes were questions that puzzled observers. Apart from the breach between Police Commissioner McNamara and Attorney General Brooke which began when Brooke entered the investigations and had widened with Peter Hurkos's arrest in New York, how much was politics involved? If the Boston Police Department—and not the Attorney General's office—solved the stranglings, would this not constitute a tremendous boost for Democratic Mayor Collins, who had appointed McNamara and who was himself a possible candidate for Senator and perhaps Governor? By the same token, might a police triumph be a blow to Republican Brooke's political aspirations? Brooke had his eye on the United States Senate if Republican Senator Saltonstall, now seventy-two, retired.

If anything was clear, it was that a struggle was going on for possession of Albert DeSalvo and the story he seemed so willing to tell.

These maneuvers aside, it was striking that although Albert DeSalvo had spoken freely about his sexual escapades, his tying up of women, his numerous rapes, he had steadfastly denied until now that he was the Strangler. He had denied it vehemently to Cambridge detectives. He had denied it to Sergeant Davenport. He had denied it in the presence of his wife and sister. Once a Malden detective had asked him slyly, "Kid, are you the Strangler?" Albert had retorted angrily, scornfully, "Cut it out!"

And no one had pursued it.

19

Damn it, thought Dr. Robey in his office at Bridgewater, DeSalvo doesn't fit. He can't be the Strangler. Because, in his opinion, DeSalvo did not fit, Dr. Robey had not reported back to John Bottomly as he had done, months before, in the case of David Parker. No, said Dr. Robey to himself, reason as one likes, let DeSalvo say what he wants, he still doesn't fit in my book. Which poses a fascinating question: if he does know more than he should about these crimes, from whom could he be learning what he knows?

Why, thought Dr. Robey, marveling at the simplicity of it, he could be learning it from his wardmate—from George Nassar.

Could Nassar be the Strangler?

The man fitted like a glove, thought Dr. Robey with mounting excitement. He possessed the required psychopathology to carry out such crimes. He was paranoid, schizophrenic, highly intelligent, and cunning. As he and the medical staff had noted from the day he arrived, George Nassar was an angry man, carrying a tremendous rage. And he was a killer.

Was it conceivable that Nassar had engineered a gigantic hoax? He might have sold the idea of confessing to DeSalvo, fed DeSalvo facts about the murders, announced to Bailey that he had discovered the Strangler, and then allowed matters to take their own course, depending upon Bailey's energy and resourcefulness to force the issue.

Why should DeSalvo buy the idea of confessing? For the money, of course. He knew he would never be free again. How far that money would go to help his wife and children . . .

Dr. Robey turned it over in his mind. Now, he thought, the gaps were filled. He had always considered David Parker a prime suspect, but he questioned whether David could also have strangled the women outside Boston—specifically, Evelyn Corbin in Salem and Joann Graff in Lawrence. These towns, however, were Nassar's home stamping ground: he had grown up in that area, and his mother still lived in Lawrence.

What, then, did this add up to? There must be *two* stranglers, as the Medical-Psychiatric Committee had speculated months ago: David Parker for the Old Women, because of his psychotic hostility toward the domineering mother-image; and Nassar for the Girls, the more psychosexually mature, the more heterosexual criminal.

Dr. Robey notified John Bottomly that he and his colleagues now were inclined to consider Nassar a more likely suspect than DeSalvo.

Nassar had never been questioned about the stranglings. Dr. Robey now proceeded to do so. Nassar appeared before him, quiet, poised, a man on guard. He said nothing, admitted nothing. To such questions as *Where were you on January 4, 1964? What beer do you drink?* Nassar replied with a stock sentence: "I will not answer any questions on advice of counsel."

Was this really the situation? That the man who refused to admit he was the Strangler was the Strangler and the man who confessed he was the Strangler was not the Strangler? Dr. Robey thought, With every step I take it gets a little deeper, a little crazier, a little wilder. Where will it stop?

In his State House office, John Bottomly studied the information before him. He echoed Dr. Robey without knowing it: This, he thought, is the most fantastic caper of all. Was it DeSalvo? Was it Nassar? And what was Bailey's role? The Boston *Record-American* had already carried a copyrighted story asserting that a "mental patient" in a Massachusetts institution, a married man who was the father of two, had "allegedly confessed" that he was the Boston Strangler. Why was Bailey releasing such information?

Even as Bottomly pondered this, word came from Bridgewater that a TV camera crew was in the act of photographing the building in which DeSalvo was held. Superintendent Gaughan had succeeded in ordering them off the grounds, but this was obviously only the beginning. There were reports that other network reporters and cameramen had moved into the Hotel Lorraine and were waiting only for the moment when the entire case would explode. Bottomly consulted with Brooke, who went into Massachusetts Supreme Judicial Court with a petition to prevent Bailey, Asgiersson, and others from releasing any details of the alleged confession, including the name of DeSalvo. Such publication might be detrimental to the prisoner and to "the due course of justice and the general interest of the Commonwealth." It was interesting to remember that Bailey had won Dr. Sheppard's release in Ohio on the ground that publicity had prejudiced his case.

Associate Justice Arthur E. Wittemore dismissed the petition after Bailey and Asgiersson assured him they would not release the information, but the jurist asked for a report on DeSalvo's mental condition from "disinterested psychiatrists."

On Wednesday, March 10, Lieutenant Tuney and Jim Mellon, armed with front and profile photographs of DeSalvo, showed them to Kenneth Rowe, the twenty-two-year-old engineering student who lived a floor above Joann Graff in Lawrence. Was this the man who rapped on his door the day Joann was murdered and wanted to know which was her apartment?

Rowe did not recognize DeSalvo as the man.

Lieutenant Tuney and Mellon showed the photographs next to Jules Vens, the bartender into whose tavern in Lawrence, down the street from Joann's building, a man had walked that afternoon and asked for "Lucky Beer."

Vens failed to identify DeSalvo as his customer.

Next day they showed the photographs to Sims Murray, who saw a man help a girl carry record albums into 44A Charles Street either on January 1 or January 4, 1964, the day of Mary Sullivan's murder. Was this the man he saw?

Sims Murray did not identify DeSalvo as the man.

One of Albert DeSalvo's most recognizable features was his prominent beaklike nose, particularly in profile. The witnesses said, in effect: 'f this had been the man, we would have recognized him at once.

On Wednesday, March 17, in her hideout in suburban Denver, Mrs. Irmgard DeSalvo spoke on the telephone to her husband in Bridgewater. She was hysterical. If he did not stop claiming to be the Strangler, she would kill herself—she would turn the gas on herself and the two children. She was still weeping when she hung up.

The next day, at Bridgewater, a woman psychologist on the staff was preparing a routine test for DeSalvo. He was already seated at her table, when he suddenly refused to go through with it.

"I don't want to make you do anything you feel you

shouldn't," she said finally. "So if you want to go back to your ward now, you may." But DeSalvo seemed in no hurry. What did everyone think "about all the excitement" that had been going on at Bridgewater, he asked her?

She told him she had no wish to discuss the stranglings or anything in which he might be involved with the courts or his attorney.

"I understand that," said DeSalvo. "Besides, I never confessed to being the Strangler. My name's never been in the papers in connection with those things." He looked at her calmly. He'd heard some patient had confessed, but he, Albert DeSalvo, knew nothing about it. He thought for a moment. But if the patient's story was true, he said, then all the people connected with the case—the doctors, the police, the district attorneys, the Attorney General—they'd all be ruined. That's why, he said, they were trying to disprove the patient's story and "bury the whole case." Anyway, this patient who said he was the Strangler—"He should be studied, not buried," DeSalvo said. He sighed. The poor always got punished, he said. That's the way the world was. Rich people could do all kinds of sex things and get away with it. They just bought their way out.

He rose and, brooding, left the room.

In an attempt to prove or disprove that DeSalvo was the Strangler, John Bottomly arranged to confront him with two more witnesses.

On Saturday morning, March 20, at 10 A.M., Detective DiNatale drove to Bridgewater accompanied by a woman. A few minutes later another car driven by one of Phil's colleagues, also with one woman passenger, followed.

One woman was Gertrude Gruen, the twenty-nine-year-old German waitress who on February 18, 1963, fought off an assailant who tried to strangle her after gaining entrance into her apartment on the pretext that he had to turn off the water in the bathroom. Months before, she had failed to identify Paul Gordon as he underwent a sodium pentothal interrogation in Dr. Alexander's office. She had since changed her name—her terror had never left her—and moved to another city. Now she had agreed to come to Bridgewater to see if she could identify DeSalvo.

The other was Mrs. Marcella Lulka, the housewife who lived in the building adjoining Sophie Clark's and who on the day of Sophie's murder was visited by a stranger with "honey-colored hair," who had checked the painting in her apartment and then talked about hiring her as a model.

Was it DeSalvo? He had used this technique before.

Or was it Nassar?

Both women were to have a chance that morning to see DeSalvo. They did not know that George Nassar would also be on display. The idea was that DeSalvo would be brought down to the visitors' room to speak to Dr. Samuel Allen, Dr. Robey's associate. This chamber was a large room divided down the center by a wide table with benches on either side. Inmates sat on the inner side, their visitors opposite them on the other. The two women were to pose as relatives waiting for other inmates.

Neither DeSalvo nor Nassar would know the true reason for their appearance. While Dr. Allen spoke to DeSalvo, a social worker would talk with Nassar as if checking details of his history.

George Nassar was the first to enter the visitors' room, wearing a slight, sardonic smile on his face. Gertrude Gruen, waiting for the patient she was told would sit opposite Dr. Allen glanced idly at Nassar as he walked in. The latter darted a sharp glance at her, and then a second. She thought, There's something upsetting, something frighteningly familiar about that man. Could he know her?

At that moment, DeSalvo entered and took his place across the table from Dr. Allen. Miss Gruen looked at him. No, he was not the man who talked with her, attempted to strangle her, the man with whom she fought, the man who fled when her screams brought workers on the roof peering into her windows.

But the man now talking to the social worker, the man who had turned his dark eyes on her so sharply—

Moments later, in Dr. Robey's office, surrounded by police and staff members, she said agitatedly, "I don't know what to say . . . I'm so upset—" She appeared on the verge of a breakdown. She was taken to another room and left alone to compose herself, but when Dr. Allen entered a few minutes later he found her sobbing. Finally, she was able to talk.

It was not Albert DeSalvo, she said. When she had been shown his photographs a week earlier, she'd thought she saw certain similarities. "Now, I know he is not the man," she said. But the first man who entered—George Nassar—"I realize how shocked I was when I saw him. To see this man, his eyes, his hair, his hands, the whole expression of him . . ." He looked like the man who attacked her, walked, carried himself like him, his posture . . . from where she sat in the visitors' room she had been unable to hear Nassar's voice. His prison clothing and prison haircut had also thrown her off. She could only say, "My deep feelings are that he has very great similarities to the man who was in my apartment."

But—she was not sure. She wept with frustration. She wanted so badly to identify this man.

And Marcella Lulka, who had also been brought to identify DeSalvo.

She had not been sure when shown his photographs a few days before. Now, she said, seeing him in person, she must definitely eliminate him. But the patient who preceded him—Nassar—when she saw him enter, her heart jumped. In every way but one—his eyes, his walk, his furrowed face, his dark, speculative gaze—he was her mysterious caller of that dreadful afternoon. Only his hair was different. "Mr. Thompson" had honey-colored hair, as she had told detectives. This man's hair was black.

Might it not have been dyed the day she saw him, the day of Sophie Clark's murder?

Confusion was added to confusion. After leaving the visitors' room, Albert DeSalvo walked up to William Lewis in their ward. He nudged him. "They had a couple of women here just now looking me over," he said, Lewis reported later. "I know both of them." One, he said, was "the colored girl in the Sophie Clark building—I was in her apartment." The other "is a German girl—I was in her apartment, too."

Bailey labored to prove that DeSalvo's story was true. That afternoon, Saturday, March 20, he arranged for Albert to be hypnotized by Dr. William J. Bryan, Jr., the Los Angeles hypnoanalyst* with whom Bailey himself had studied. Dr. Bryan was a huge man, weighing nearly three hundred pounds; blond-haired, blue-eyed, and bespectacled, a man capable of great enthusiasm. Not only did he conduct seminars in hypnosis and allied subjects for lawyers, but he was Executive Director of the American Institute of Hypnosis, whose address was the same as his offices on Sunset Boulevard, in Los Angeles. He was also author of a book, *Legal Aspects of Hypnosis,* † in which he described at length his hypnoanalysis

* Hypnoanalysis is a combination of hypnosis and psychoanalysis in which the patient, while in a hypnotic state, is encouraged to free-associate and recall memories that he has long since blocked out. The physician makes use of suggestion and interpretation to help the patient talk freely about his concealed fears, guilts, and experiences. Although all psychoanalysts may use hypnosis now and then in their treatment, Dr. Bryan had been described as the only M.D. in the United States who limited his practice to hypnosis.

† Charles C Thomas, Springfield, Illinois, 1962.

of a twenty-nine-year-old man who had strangled three elderly women on the West Coast a few years before. Bailey had remembered the case and was excited by the apparent parallel.

DeSalvo's hypnoanalysis was held in a room off the dispensary at Bridgewater. The witnesses included Dr. Robert Ross Mezer, Dr. Samuel Allen, and other psychiatrists. Dr. Bryan, who had a habit of calming his patient by placing both hands heavily on his shoulders, used no drugs. DeSalvo sat at his ease in a chair while the hypnotist sat facing him, so close they were almost knee to knee. Speaking gently and persuasively, Dr. Bryan began slowly moving his right forefinger back and forth before DeSalvo's eyes, assuring him that he would not become unconscious but would at all times know everything that went on. It was not sleep, but a state more relaxing than sleep. In sleep one tossed and turned, but in hypnosis one was utterly at peace. As Dr. Bryan spoke, his finger slowly moving from one side to another like a pendulum, DeSalvo's eyes grew heavy. They closed.

Dr. Bryan's voice went on gently, smoothly, with relentless, insistent repetition: "I am going to raise your right arm and as I raise your right arm it becomes stiff and rigid as a steel bar, all the way to the fingertips, stiff and rigid, stiff and rigid as a steel bar, stiff and rigid as a steel bar, stiff and rigid as a steel bar all the way to the fingertips. As it becomes stiff and rigid as a steel bar, in your mind's eye, in your mind's eye, it becomes cold and numb. Cold and numb from the shoulder to the fingertips. Cold and numb. And you imagine in your mind's eye that a cake of ice is surrounding the arm. It is frozen in a cake of ice. Frozen, cold and numb, cold and numb." His voice never ceased. "And you feel pressure, lots of pressure, but no pain. Pressure, lots of pressure, but no pain. Pressure, lots of pressure, but no pain. Pressure—"

Without changing the hypnotic rhythm of his words he slowly pushed a two-inch darning needle through the fleshy part of DeSalvo's upraised right arm. "Cold, cold and numb, cold and numb, and you sink deeper and deeper, way down, and you feel pressure, lots of pressure, but no pain. I'm going to count to two, and you'll remain deeply hypnotized." The needle was all the way through now. "You remain deeply hypnotized, your arm will remain very stiff and rigid, but you'll open your eyes, your eyes will be wide open. Deeply hypnotized when I count to two."

He stepped back. "One. Two. Open your eyes."

DeSalvo's eyes opened.

"Look at your right arm." DeSalvo did so. "There's a needle clear through it," said the hypnotist. "That's all right, close your eyes. Sleep, sleep, deep, deep, relax. Deeper and deeper and deeper . . ."

In the same fashion, never ceasing his words, he told DeSalvo he would remove the needle, he would feel no pain, and "at the count of five your right arm will be normal and completely relaxed." He counted one, two; DeSalvo opened his eyes; he saw Dr. Bryan slowly pull out the needle. At five, DeSalvo's right arm dropped to his side, as before.

DeSalvo's eyes closed again. "You see a calendar, a desk calendar, the top page shows the date March twentieth, 1965, today." The hypnotist paused. "Now you tear off that sheet, and you see March nineteenth; you tear that off and you do it with each sheet, back, back farther and farther, back farther and farther, right back, deeper and deeper, all the way back." He took him through the months, through the years, "to a page reading Sunday, September eighth, 1963"—the day Evelyn Corbin was strangled in Salem.

"Now, Al, you're right back there now. You see everything that's happening. You feel every feeling you felt then. You're right there, and right there will be Evelyn Corbin. Sunday, September eighth, 1963, and you're approaching her apartment door. Now tell me what's happening. You can talk, tell me what's happening—"

DeSalvo spoke slowly, his eyes closed. ". . . I walk into the apartment house through the front door . . . The buzzer rang and I opened the door and I walked down the corridor, all the way down to the left. I moved open the door. I talked to her . . ."

Dr. Bryan: "Now you're talking to her. You hear her voice. You hear your own voice. Right now, what are you saying?"

DeSalvo: "'I came here to fix the bathroom connection that you were complaining about.' And then she said, 'Who sent you?' I told her the superintendent sent me. There was something wrong with the bathroom. There was a leak in it and I walked in and she walked in with me . . ."

Dr. Bryan: "Relax. Relax, deep, deep, relax. I don't want you to *remember*, Albert. *I want you to be right there. Right there.* Who sent you?" (A pause.) "Who sent you?"

DeSalvo: "The superintendent."

Dr. Bryan: "For what? For what?"

DeSalvo: "To fix the bathroom." He stopped. Then, in a woman's voice: "What's wrong with it?" Then, his own again: "She walked in and when she went in she turned her back to me and I put a knife to her throat."

Dr. Bryan: "Relax, now, one moment, relax. You're right back before then. You're right back before then." He repeated the sentence many times. "I'm going to count to two and at the count of two I'm going to stand you up; you remain deeply hypnotized in every way." He counted: "One, two—stand right up."

DeSalvo rose, his eyes closed.

"You've got a knife in your hand. Is that the hand it's in?"

DeSalvo: "No."

Dr. Bryan: "Which one? All right, all right, you're coming in the door—"

DeSalvo: "She says—" His voice became falsetto again, " 'Who sent you? Who sent you?' 'The superintendent. There's something wrong with your bathroom. I've got to check it out.' 'Oh, just a second now,' she said. 'I'm going to church.' She took me into the bathroom to the right."

Dr. Bryan: "All right, you're in the bathroom now, you're in the bathroom. She turns her back on you, she turns her back on you. Now what, now what?"

DeSalvo: "I took her over to the bed and I—"

Dr. Bryan: "All right, you take her over to the bed, now what, now what?"

DeSalvo: "She says she can't do nothing, the doctor told her no . . . She said, 'Don't hurt me, please.' I told her I won't hurt her."

Dr. Bryan: "All right, sit down." DeSalvo sat in the chair again. "Now, deep, deeper, relax, relax. You don't want to hurt her. Why do you want her on the bed? In your mind's eye you see somebody on the bed. What do you want to do? Talk, talk, come on, talk." DeSalvo had opened his mouth, but no words came. "Talk. What do you want to do? With her thighs, with her thighs, with her thighs, with her thighs. Get the feeling—" Dr. Bryan's voice rose. "Get it, come on, *get it!* With her thighs, come on, it's a good feeling. Go ahead, go ahead, what do you want to do? It's okay to have it. Go ahead, go ahead, what do you want to do?"

DeSalvo screamed—a piercing scream that shocked the spectators in the room.

Dr. Bryan worked swiftly: "Deep relax, deeper, deeper and deeper and deeper. Now you had that feeling for a moment, didn't you? You were doing something good. What was it? You won't hurt anybody, you were doing something good. Come on, what was it?"

DeSalvo spoke: "Judy!" It was like a groan.

Dr. Bryan: "Judy, yes. That's right, Judy. You were working on Judy with those thumbs, weren't you? That's what made her well, wasn't it? With your hands you made her well. Isn't that so? . . . Now, what about those people? What did you want to do with them? Did you want to hurt them? Well, what did you want to do?"

DeSalvo began to cry. The tears squeezed from under his closed lids. "I don't know."

Dr. Bryan: "Yes, you do. Come on. What is it? What did you do with Judy?"

DeSalvo: "I massaged her."

Dr. Bryan: "You massaged her, that's right, with your thumbs, and what happened?"

DeSalvo: "She got well."

Dr. Bryan: "She got well, that's right." He paused, and said slowly, "You had her legs up there, you massaged her right on the thighs. Now, isn't that what you did with every other victim, too? Yes, and you hadn't told anybody that, not a soul, but that's what you did, wasn't it? You wanted to make them well. All right, now why was it necessary to keep repeating that? Why? Tell me why? Why was it necessary to make them well? *She wasn't Judy enough,* eh?"

DeSalvo: "I don't know."

Slowly, but with mounting excitement in his voice, the hypnotist led DeSalvo through it again: the massaging of his child's crippled limbs to restore them to use, the sound of Judy crying—"I think I'm hurting her, I don't mean to hurt her, I'm going to help her, she doesn't understand, she's a child, I'm trying to help her and I must hurt her to help her—"

Dr. Bryan (triumphantly): *"You want to help her and you've got to hurt her.* Isn't that the idea? All right, now, sleep . . . I am going to wake you in a minute or so, but I will give you one suggestion before you wake. Tonight while you are asleep, you will have a dream so vivid that it's going to wake you up in the middle of the night. And you're going to write down everything about this dream because it's going to tie this in together. And why these women represented beauty, how you helped them and how you hurt them—"

At this, DeSalvo uttered a loud, uncontrolled scream. For a moment, he seemed to be fighting to leap from his chair.

Dr. Bryan, bringing both hands down heavily on DeSalvo's shoulders, said authoritatively: "Sleep, sleep!" He put him in a deeper trance. "At the count of three, now, you'll be wide awake, clear-headed and refreshed. One, coming up now; two, almost awake; three—awaken!"

DeSalvo's eyes opened.

"How are you, Al? Okay? You okay, Al?" Dr. Bryan asked.

"Yeah, I'm okay," he said. He yawned and was led back to his cell.

The next day, Sunday, March 21, sitting in the chair before the hypnoanalyst again, DeSalvo told about the dream he had.

"I went to bed about eight-thirty and fell asleep. About three o'clock I woke up in a sweat, my pillow was wet, and I was crying. I had a horrible dream with a person I had done something with. I got out of bed and walked back and forth. The guard walked by, shone a light in my cell, then kept going. I sat down on the edge of the bed where the light was and started writing. This morning I thought nothing about it—just a dream—and that was it until I got up out of bed and there was the pad on the floor with the piece of paper I dreamed I was writing on."

Dr. Bryan took the pad and read aloud:

"Now, the dream you wrote is this, Al. You wrote: 'I went in the apartment, rang a bell. It buzzed. I opened the door and walked down the hallway. E. C. was at the door. I said, "Hi." She said, "Yes, can I help you?" I said, "The superintendent sent me to check the leak in the bathroom." She and I went into the bathroom and then she said, "I don't see any leak." Her back was turned to me. I put a knife to her neck and told her, "Don't scream, I won't hurt you." She said, "Okay—" then she said, "You're not the Strangler, are you?" I said, "No, I just want to make love to you." I took her into the bedroom. She said, "I can't have intercourse, I am not well." I said, "Okay, will you blow me?" She said, "Yes, but please don't hurt me." I said, "Okay." I took a pillow from the bed, put her on her knees at the foot of the bed, I sat on the edge while she blew me. Before coming she reached over and got a white Kleenex tissue and finished it with her hand. After that she got up and I told her to lie on the bed and she did so I could tie her hands up in front of her. When I got on top of her and put my hands on her neck and pressed very firm and then I spread her legs apart and pre—' "

Dr. Bryan stopped reading and looked at DeSalvo. "That's where it stops. P-r-e— that word stops in the middle." He put DeSalvo into a hypnotic state again, and again he ordered him to visualize himself tearing off the pages of the calendar from March 21, 1965, back to that Sunday, September 8, 1963, the day Evelyn Corbin was strangled.

"You went into the apartment. You rang a bell. The door

buzzed—" The hypnotist reconstructed the account in De-Salvo's dream, sentence by sentence. "You tell her, 'Don't scream, I won't hurt you.' But the way you say it is the way you said it yesterday. The way you say it on September eighth, 1963, and the way you say it in the dream are all the same. You say it real lightly: 'Don't scream. I won't hurt you.' Yes. Yes. That's what you said to Judy. She said, 'Okay, Daddy.' Isn't that what she said? You're not really in September of 1963. You're all the way back with Judy. This dream isn't about Evelyn Corbin. *This dream is about Judy.* Every bit of it. Isn't it? Isn't it? Isn't it? Isn't that true? *And all the other women are identified with Judy.* Every time you're doing it over and over again. Isn't that so? Isn't that so?"

DeSalvo wept.

Dr. Bryan: "Why are you crying? Please stop. Quickly!"

DeSalvo breathed the word. "Judy."

Dr. Bryan: "Judy is going to be all right. *But you have to hurt her before you can help her.* 'Don't scream. I won't hurt you,' and she said, 'Okay.' "

DeSalvo: "No."

Dr. Bryan: "What did she say?"

DeSalvo: "She can't talk. She's only a baby."

Dr. Bryan: "She can't talk, she's only a baby. In other words, if these women were really going to be identified with Judy, the way they should be, they couldn't talk. Is that it?"

He paused. "How could you keep them from talking? Come on, how could you stop them from talking." A pause. *"Strangle them!* That's true, isn't it? Isn't it? That's why the stranglings." He emphasized each word. "It was after that that you used the thumbs to press the thighs. Isn't that so? Now of course she couldn't talk." His voice dropped almost to a whisper. "She says, 'I'm not well. Please don't hurt me.' You say, 'Okay,' and you take a pillow on the bed and put her knees at the foot of the bed, all right, tie her hands up. You tied Judy's hands up." His voice burst out, he shouted, "DeSalvo, come on! Have you ever tied Judy's hands up so she wouldn't bother you while you were working on her?"

DeSalvo said no. Judy's hands scratched him, but he did not tie her hands.

The hypnotist sent DeSalvo into a deeper state. "Al, the reason why you didn't finish that dream when you said 'and pressed'—that's p-r-e, that stands for *pressed*, doesn't it? Isn't there an s-s-e-d on the end of that? *Pressed* your thumbs against their thighs? Isn't that true? That's the rest of the dream, isn't it?"

Was it not the truth that DeSalvo identified each of his victims with his crippled daughter, and each strangling was a reenactment of his attempt to cure his daughter? Step by step the hypnotist led DeSalvo on. Wasn't the real truth that De-Salvo secretly wished to strangle Judy, to eliminate her because she came between Irmgard and himself, because she took away Irmgard's love and attention from him? Sitting knee to knee with DeSalvo, Dr. Bryan, leaning forward, cupped one enormous hand about the back of Albert's head, drawing him to him until their faces were a few inches apart, and then brought his mouth to Albert's ear, whispering, "Each time you strangled, it was because you were killing Judy, wasn't it? Wasn't it? You were killing Judy . . ."

DeSalvo cried out passionately, "You're a liar!" and unexpectedly, his eyes still closed, his two hands, fingers outstretched as if to throttle, shot out directly at the hypnotist's throat. Dr. Bryan, with astonishing speed, ducked back and his hands came down hard on Albert's shoulders. "Sleep!" he commanded. "Sleep!"

Albert's arms fell to his sides and he sat in his chair, chin on chest, eyes still closed, limp.

The others in the room began to breathe again.

Dr. Bryan tried a different tack. "Now, Al, I'm going to ask you a question and I want you to give me the very first answer that pops into your head. The first answer. You don't think of it, you just give the answer immediately. Can you give us any more important information today? Quickly. *Quickly!* Come on, come on!"

DeSalvo: "Yes."

Dr. Bryan: "What is it then? What is it?"

DeSalvo: "Irmgard."

Dr. Bryan: "What about Irmgard? Tell me about her?" He paused. "What about Irmgard's neck? Is that important?"

DeSalvo: "She don't like nobody touching or going near her neck at all. Not even to touch it. She'd faint."

Dr. Bryan (with excitement): "She'd faint if you touched her neck, eh? Al, you'd like to have her faint, wouldn't you?"

DeSalvo: "No."

Dr. Bryan: "Isn't that why you touched her neck?"

DeSalvo: "Never."

Dr. Bryan: "You knew that if you touched her neck, she'd faint. That's right. You didn't want her to faint. You wanted to kill her altogether—"

DeSalvo struggled in his chair.

Dr. Bryan: "Sleep! Deep, deep, relax. Deeper and deeper. . . . Was Irmgard in on this? Come on, Al! Did

Irmgard help you strangle these women? In what way is she in on this?"

DeSalvo (weakly): "I don't know."

Again and again the hypnotist hammered on this theme. Did DeSalvo want to strangle his wife? No, he said without emotion now. "I just wanted her to be nice and gentle."

A few minutes later the session was over.

Slowly, the hypnotist brought DeSalvo awake.

That night DeSalvo, given pen and paper, laboriously wrote to his wife. He did not know that his letters to her would pile up, unopened and unread. They had had the one hysterical telephone conversation a few days before and now he tried to express how he felt.

Hi, Irm,

I hope this letter finds you and the children well. As for myself, I'm okay and even though I have a lot of trouble I am still concerned mostly about you and how you feel about me. I don't blame you for my troubles or blame anyone else. But you will admit that if you treated me different like you told me all those years we lost, the love I had been searching for, that we first had when we were married. Yes, Irm I stole them. *But why*. Think Irm. What happened when Judy was born and we found out she may never walk. How you cried Al please no more babies. Irm from that day on you changed. All your love went to Judy. You were frigid and cold to me, and you can't deny this. That's why we were always fighting about sex, because you was afraid to have a baby. Because you thought it would be born abnormal. Irm I even asked doctors what was wrong with our sex life and they all said—until you have another baby, and it is born normal will you then be free to love again. Irm they were right, the doctors. Remember how much you were worried after Michael was born, how many times you went to doctor Karp and when Michael was born the first thing you asked doctor Karp was is he normal, and you went every week to his office til you were sure he was okay. Irm then you came to me and gave me love I had been starving for—it was to late. More than four years you made me suffer, from the time Judy was born til Michael was born.

I went to jail. Why Irm. Even Hilda knew. She told you. But you didn't believe or want to. I didnt no how to make you love me. I found out to late why you were to frigid. Because you were afraid to have a baby, but I was in jail and this is what hurts me now. When I came out I believed in you and thought you kind and good. But later I found out different. Instead of you saying Al lets start out clean now, forget the past no matter what and think of the future,—no not you Irm. My suffering a whole year in jail was not enough for you. All alone in one room while you were free outside doing what you wanted.

You knew how much I loved you. But when I came out the first thing you said was you waisted one year. And if I hurt you again you would leave me with the children. And you said I would have to prove myself to you. But you forget about the four years witch put me in jail because of you—in witch you made me suffer. Yet because I loved you I didn't leave you. You gave me no love. To prove I'm right, when we went to Germany, two months, look how cold you were. Love is a two-way affair not one Irm, not just when you want it.

Irm I'm not saying this is all your fault. Because I am the one who did wrong. But I had reason I loved you. After I came out of jail—despite everything I tried to do—you denied me my rights as a husband you constantly told me I had to prove myself and in short you tried to make my life a hell wether you knew it or not. I am really and sincerely sorry for what I have done and I will have to pay for it with years of my life. But apparently that is still not enough for you. You tell me not to write or if I write not to express in any way my love for you. So that even in this critical time when I need you most of all you are still making me feel hopeless and if I cant turn to you, I have no hope, no ambition. . . . You can't no how awful it is to wait for letters that do not come, or to love someone and be laugh at for that love. As for myself I will all ways feel the same in regards to my love for you and I can only hope that some day, you may realize, the extent of my love and feelings for you . . . I will close for now wishing the best for you and the children.

P.S. Give my love to my Judy and Michael—there Daddy always.

I will love you forever always
Love,

Al

He turned the letter upside down and filled the space that

remained on the last page with another postscript, a bitter postscript:

> Only untill things started changing, us going out weekends, having everything you wanted, house fixed up, all the money coming in, did you change and start showing a little love for me. Our last two months together you made me feel for the first time like a man. You gave me love I never dreamed you had to give. But why—only because you had just about everything you dreamed of. If you really loved me as you said you did, you would love me now. But you closed the house and everything in it. you lost that and everything you dreamed of. all your love was in the house and now you hate me again. When you really love someone, no matter what they do if you really love them you stay by them.

Those who witnessed the hypnoanalysis wondered how much DeSalvo had been led or influenced by Dr. Bryan, so forceful and domineering. If they were to consider this man at all seriously, how significant was his sense of sexual rejection by his wife and how significant was her apparent fear of being touched about the neck? Again, DeSalvo's references to Evelyn Corbin made it clear that he spoke with knowledge of the apartment, and what might well have taken place there. Semen had been found in her mouth; on the floor next to the bed a tissue had also been found with semen. Had DeSalvo learned that (after all, the newspapers had all but spelled out everything) or had he known it? Or had his suggestibility been so great that—like Daniel Pennacchio—he saw himself enacting what he read, or had been told by Nassar, or perhaps unwittingly, by Bailey's questions?

Yet DeSalvo had given Bailey details about the other murders that had not appeared anywhere, so far as could be determined by members of Bottomly's staff, reading and rereading the published accounts.

At that moment DeSalvo appeared to the police and the Attorney General's office the most likely suspect so far unearthed in the search, although some pointed out that Paul Gordon's knowledge was as baffling as DeSalvo's. In addition, one fact continued to work powerfully against DeSalvo: he exhibited none of the classical traits of the Strangler as analyzed by psychiatrists—the sadistic, impotent male bearing an unendurable rage toward his mother and all women like her.

And one other fact: no witness had been able to identify him.

And hovering over all, a huge question mark: George Nassar.

If only, thought Bottomly, trying to make sense out of this jumble, if only Gertrude Gruen, the one victim believed to have looked upon the Strangler's face and lived to tell the story, could remember her assailant. She had almost made a positive identification of Nassar, but she could not be sure . . .

Two weeks later, in early April 1965, the Boston Society of Psychiatry and Neurology played host to an international psychiatric convention. Among the distinguished psychiatrists who came from abroad to address the meeting was Dr. William Sargant of St. Thomas Hospital, London—the man who had had such a success with the shell-shocked survivors of Dunkirk nearly a quarter of a century before. Dr. Alexander asked him if he would volunteer to help Gertrude Gruen attempt to recall her assailant's face. The British psychiatrist was challenged by the proposal, but reluctant to accept it. He had not attempted anything of the sort since the war, and the experience would bring back distressing memories. But he went ahead. Bottomly arranged for him to use the facilities of Bournemouth Hospital in Brookline. There, for three successive days, the third, fourth, and fifth of April, 1965, Dr. Sargant worked with Miss Gruen.

To the spectator, these attempts to break through to the memory she had erased so completely were like visits to one of the lesser hells of Dante's *Inferno*.

In a hospital room whose walls were lined with tanks of oxygen and carbon dioxide, Miss Gruen lay in bed. The sickly sweet smell of ether—used by Dr. Sargant—hung over everything. Other physicians—anesthetists, psychiatrists, staff doctors—as well as Bottomly, Lieutenant Tuney, and other detectives, remained behind a screen as witnesses.

Repeatedly, Dr. Sargant dripped ether upon cloths applied to Miss Gruen's face. The tanks whistled and hissed as he adjusted the oxygen and carbon dioxide. During these long sessions, Dr. Sargant used all his skill to make her relive her attack, and in the vividness and terror of that recollection see again the face of her assailant. She lay gasping, struggling for breath, now moaning, now uttering panic-stricken . . . "He is standing there, he is coming nearer, nearer, oh, my God, ohhhhhhhhhhhh!" Through her words the crisp, British accents of the psychiatrist: "There's a knock on the door. A knock on the door. He's coming in . . . he's coming in . . . He wants to—what? . . . He wants to—what? . . . Hold my hand, take a deep breath, hold my hand . . . You hear the knock. You open the door. You see his face, his face . . ."

"No! No!" screamed Gertrude. "I see him walking around the room, but I cannot see him—"

Dr. Sargant's voice was smooth, persuasive. "Take a deep breath. Again. Again. Can you see the man? Can you see the man? He's coming into the room—that chap's coming into the room . . . Can you see him now? Can you see him now?" Gertrude shrieked, the sound of it filling the room and seeming to echo down the corridors outside. "Can you see him now?" Relentlessly. "Can you see him now? Can you see the man?"

Gertrude struggled, half-asleep, tearful. "I was sleeping . . . He was standing in the corner . . . There was a little wooden table . . ." Carefully she described everything in her apartment, always avoiding the description of the face of the man who sought to strangle her. Then, at one point, "Oh, I am so sorry. I cannot see the man. It will take a long time until I see the man again. It might not be possible if I am like I am now—if every move, every whisper, every thought, is in my stomach, like now . . ."

She turned and tossed.

Dr. Sargant tried again. "You're opening the door, aren't you? He's in that room . . ." She began to tremble. "He's in that room . . . Putting his hand around your neck . . . Putting his hand around your neck . . . You're fighting for your life, aren't you? Look at him! Look at him! Call for help! Call for help! Call—for—help!" His voice was firm, insistent. "Call—for—help!" Gertrude sobbed hysterically. "I can't . . . I can't . . ."

He revived her. Had she been back in the room? "Yes," she said. "But I couldn't scream until he left. I screamed and I was frightened and I ran out—I heard him running away—I screamed like I never screamed in my life. Then I closed all the doors. I ran to the window first and I screamed to the two people who were on the roof, 'Where is the other man you're working with?' and one said, 'There's only the two of us . . .' At this moment I saw him running around the corner. I closed everything and I was sweating, I was so panicked I was afraid even to be in the room . . ."

Then she was under again, and Dr. Sargant approached her and put his hands around her throat.

She jerked convulsively. "What happened?" she cried in panic.

"I'm touching your neck like that man did," Dr. Sargant said quietly. "Do you see him? Bring that man in! Bring that man in!" His hands touched her neck again, the sound of hissing gas grew louder. She began to choke. It was a reenactment of her terrible experience. Over her gasps for breath, the psychiatrist's voice: "See his face. See his face. Close your eyes . . . Is he coming back? Is he coming back?"

"No, no," cried Gertrude, "I try—"

"Take some deep breaths. Again. Again. Now, you're opening the door, aren't you? What do you see? You're opening the door—is that right?"

Her voice, like an automaton: "I open the door—"

"What do you see?"

"I see there was this man standing there. In this moment I am thinking that . . . I looked at him . . . It wasn't a man I knew, it was *no* man I knew! . . . I know it—"

"You're looking at his face now, aren't you? Just look at that face—"

"I don't know this man—" Plaintively.

"Just look at that face. He has a sarcastic look on his face, hasn't he?"

"I see him, but I can't . . . describe him."

"That's all right. Just look at him now. Take a good look at him. Are you taking a good look at him?"

"Yes—" A long sigh.

"You're going to let him in now, aren't you? You let him in. He's going into the bathroom to tell you about the leak, isn't he?"

"I let him in . . . In the room there was—" A pause. "I have to explain the bathroom," she began, and again a catalogue description of her apartment—everything, save the face of the murderer.

So it went for the three days, Gertrude laboring to remember yet unable to remember. On the third day, Dr. Sargant suggested that she bring to the hospital the attire she wore the morning of her attack—her nightgown and the coat she wore over it when she answered the door.

She lay in bed in her nightgown, she rose, threw on the coat, and under drugs tried again to relive that moment. She could see him, his hands in his pockets, his white T-shirt. But not his face.

The wall of her memory that had blotted out completely the eyes, face, features of the murderer, held firm. She was beside herself at her failure.

Bottomly, too, was almost ready to explode with frustration. For the school teacher who saw a man in Mary Sullivan's window the afternoon of her murder stated that George Nassar resembled the man she saw. Mr. Bottomly must not eliminate him. In height and profile, the likeness was very strong. Yet she, too, could not be absolutely sure. She had seen Albert DeSalvo. She did not recognize him, she said, as the man in Mary Sullivan's window.

So it stood, still a stalemate. The man who said he was the Strangler and gave details with such uncanny accuracy was not recognized by the few witnesses available. The man who denied he was the Strangler was all but identified by them.

Listening to the tape of DeSalvo's hypnoanalysis by Dr. Bryan, Lieutenant Tuney was impressed particularly by the words the man attributed to Evelyn Corbin. Her doctor had told Tuney that he had cautioned her against sexual relations because of her great discomfort as she approached the menopause. Tuney asked himself how Albert DeSalvo could have known this unless she had, indeed, told him.

DeSalvo said the original attack took place just outside her bathroom. That was true. The buttons from her robe were found there. The type of intimacy he said he had with her also accorded with laboratory and autopsy reports.

DeSalvo's claim that he simply stumbled upon his victim by chance also carried the mark of truth, Tuney thought. For had the Strangler planned his attacks, had he chosen his victims, followed them, bided his time until he found them alone—surely something would have gone wrong.

Again, reasoned Tuney, had he planned them he would not have chosen elderly women—nor girls with roommates. How could he be certain that one of the roommates (Mary Sullivan's or Sophie Clark's) might not return unexpectedly . . . And in the case of Mary, she had been at 44A Charles Street only three days. No routine had yet been established; it would have been impossible to plan an attack there. Even more so, Evelyn Corbin. She lived in a busy building; down the corridor lived her boyfriend and his mother, the three visiting back and forth at all hours—certainly he could not have planned *that*.

How persuasive, too, was the logic of DeSalvo's approach—that of the maintenance man. Many had theorized that the Strangler disguised himself as a mailman, a messenger boy, laundryman, even a priest—allowing him to move about without calling attention to himself, and at the same time, giving him entry into most apartments. But, thought Tuney, even though a cautious woman might allow such a man to come into her apartment, how could he determine that she was alone? How could he justify wandering about so he could check if a husband or son might not be in the rear of the apartment?

A handyman, however . . . Most women living alone are always complaining to their landlord of maintenance work that needs to be done. When a man, therefore, shows up, saying, "The super sent me," a woman would be apt to invite him in gratefully. He could then go from room to room, saying, "Yes, we'll have to fix that pipe," or "We'll have to tile that—" making sure that no one else was in the apartment.

John Bottomly, however, was doubtful about Albert DeSalvo. Dr. Kenefick, Dr. Robey, and Dr. Allen declined to accept him as the Strangler. Dr. Luongo, the medical examiner, had found no spermatozoa in his autopsies of the Old Women. DeSalvo said he caught his victims about the neck in the crook of his arm. Dr. Brussel questioned this; it would mean a struggle, signs of which would have to show in the victims' faces—fear, terror, distortion—and the faces of virtually all the women were peaceful.

In short, on the basis of what was now known, the doctors and psychiatrists would not accept him.

And no witnesses had been able to identify him.

Finally, Bottomly himself faulted the man. To remember every detail, the interior of every apartment, the position of the bodies, every type of ligature, the location of every piece of furniture, and all the rest . . . How could he? Could a man driven by an insane compulsion, caught up by an uncontrollable fury, have his wits sufficiently about him to see all this, register it, remember it?

And to accept the blame for every strangling listed in the newspapers, every one of the eleven, and two more, in addition, that no one had even attributed to the Strangler . . .

The confusion was only underlined by a letter from C. Russell Blomerth, owner of the construction-maintenance firm for which DeSalvo had worked from September 1962 to September 1963. In response to a request by Lieutenant Tuney for DeSalvo's employment record on December 5, 1962—the day of Sophie Clark's murder—and December 30–31, 1962—the period of Patricia Bissette's death, Blomerth wrote:

There was no doubt that Mr. DeSalvo only worked for three hours for me on December 5. During the December 30 period, which was a Sunday, he would have been going to Belmont to check diesel heaters that he had on the job to keep concrete from freezing. This required a couple of visits each day. The exact hours that he did this I have no way of knowing. He would just call and say it had been done. Although my record books show a full day's pay for Christmas Day, and also for the Saturday just prior to New Year's Day, he did not work the full day; he just went out and maintained those heaters.

DeSalvo would have had time to commit those murders. What remained with Lieutenant Tuney—and John Bottomly—however, was the final paragraph in the letter from DeSalvo's employer:

Thinking it over now, I must tell you that Albert was truly a remarkable man. He had unbelievable strength, energy, and endurance way beyond anything that could be expected of the average man. He was completely lovable to every individual while working for me. Never was there any deviation from the highest proper sense of things.

"Completely lovable . . . the highest proper sense of things . . ." Was this the man who murdered thirteen women?

Astonishingly enough, he was.

20

It is hard to know when the conviction first struck home that Albert DeSalvo was indeed the Boston Strangler.

He had said so; he had told his attorney F. Lee Bailey enough to indicate that he had an extraordinary knowledge of the crimes. Yet obviously his guilt had to be proved. Police and doctors assumed that any man qualified to be a suspect must be demented. Therefore, he might well be unable to distinguish between truth and fantasy. DeSalvo might have strangled one victim and imagined that he strangled the others as well. He might have killed one and wanted to pretend that he killed the others. He might have murdered two, three, five, ten. He might have murdered them all, He might have murdered none of them. Any other suspect—Arnold Wallace, Paul Gordon, Thomas O'Brien, David Parker, Lewis Barnett, Carl Virtanen, George McCarthy, Christopher Reid, George Nassar—any of these might have committed one or more of the crimes for which Albert DeSalvo took full responsibility.

It was now spring of 1965; the manhunt, in its third year, had begun to slow down. Bottomly's investigative squad had been reduced by two. Steve Delaney had returned to his original duties as a patrolman; and Jim Mellon, realizing that his obsession now with one suspect, then with another, was actually undermining his health, had at his own request been transferred to another department.

Yet perhaps at no time had those leading the hunt found themselves in so exasperating a position. If DeSalvo was the Strangler, he had been under their noses all the time! More, the police and the courts had actually had their hands on him several times before. And one could only ask—after the ceaseless interrogations and checking out of thousands of leads, after the mystics, the ESP experts, and the computing machines, after the sodium pentothal examinations and the

284

lie-detector tests, after the wild speculation by press and public, after the assumptions of a master criminal of near-genius ability, after the dogged attempts by police to find a common denominator among the victims, after the painstaking psychiatric analyses of the madman who held an entire city at bay, after all that—was he to turn out to be this nondescript house painter and handyman who killed at random, this mild-mannered, tearful husband and father living quietly with his wife and two children in a Boston suburb? A Jekyll and Hyde living in a mortgaged one-family house in Malden? A man treated all but contemptuously by his wife and dismissed as a bore and a braggart by his friends?

And where before in the annals of crime had a man whom no one accused of murder virtually pleaded to be given the opportunity to prove he was not only a murderer, but a multiple murderer? No novelist would have dared create an Albert DeSalvo because no reader would have believed him.

The question rose: Who could authenticate DeSalvo's confession? His victims could not testify against him. There were no eyewitnesses to the crimes. How could he be proved the Strangler so the city of Boston need never fear him again?

After several meetings, John Bottomly, F. Lee Bailey and former Corrections Commissioner George McGrath, DeSalvo's court-appointed guardian, agreed upon the next step. Obviously, psychiatrists had to examine DeSalvo. They would have to base their evaluation on his history, and as things now stood, they did not know whether or not he was telling the truth or fantasizing the murders. Therefore, Bottomly would go to Bridgewater and interrogate DeSalvo first. He would ask, "How do you kill? How can you place yourself, beyond all question, in each apartment at the time of each murder? What can you tell us that will convince us beyond all doubt that you committed these thirteen crimes?"

DeSalvo, a mental patient, had to have his rights scrupulously protected. He would tell all to Bottomly but nothing he told could be used against him in court. Bottomly would interrogate him in the presence of McGrath. Then Detectives Tuney and DiNatale, in consultation with Lieutenants Donovan and Sherry in Boston, and with police officials in Cambridge, Lynn, Salem, and Lawrence, would check every statement by DeSalvo.

The law has its curious features. One might ask why Donovan, Tuney, and DiNatale could not interrogate DeSalvo themselves? The answer is that the district attorney of any of the three counties involved in the stranglings could, if he wished, subpoena them to testify as to what DeSalvo had told them; and if that happened, his account *would* be used against him. The detectives could refuse to testify but this could cost them their jobs as police officers. Bottomly, an independently wealthy man whose career was not at stake, might risk that possibility.

If DeSalvo was found to have been telling the truth and was then ruled competent to stand trial, psychiatrists would examine him to determine if he had been insane or sane when he committed the murders. If their conclusion was that he had been insane, he would make a formal confession to Donovan, Tuney and DiNatale to be used in court: there he would plead not guilty by reason of insanity with expectation of a directed verdict of acquittal and life commitment to a mental institution. The Strangler would have been found and identified. For the city of Boston the long ordeal would have been ended.

If, however, it appeared that their conclusion would be that he had been sane, all proceedings would halt. For a sane man to confess he was the Strangler would put him in the greatest jeopardy and no defense attorney could allow this. DeSalvo, then, would not formally confess, and without his formal confession there would be no trial, for there was no evidence to indict him. He would return to his original status as the Green Man, against him the charges of Breaking and Entering, Assault and Battery, Confining and Putting in Fear, and Engaging in an Unnatural and Lascivious Act—the charges on which he had been arrested so many months before—one more mental patient detained at Bridgewater awaiting trial on those charges. His insistence on being identified as the Strangler would be viewed—medically and legally—as the product of a deranged mind.

The sessions began.

The man whom Bottomly and McGrath saw standing before them in the small room assigned to them at Bridgewater was of medium height, his head small, well shaped, with hazel eyes, crew-cut black hair over a low forehead, a long, beaklike nose, and a sullen mouth that could unexpectedly break into a surprisingly winning smile. He was five feet eight and one half and he stood in his favorite pose, legs slightly apart, hands in pockets. He was solidly built, built like a wedge—broad, powerful shoulders tapering to a narrow torso. While overseas DeSalvo, attached to a tank corps, had been injured when a shell backfired, and had suffered a temporary paralysis of the left arm. He still received a 20 percent disability stipend as a result. But there seemed no evidence of any disability now.

DeSalvo's face intrigued Bottomly. It was at that moment a suffering face; with its close-set eyes above that sharp beak of a nose (Peter Hurkos had said the Strangler would have a sharp, a "spitzy," nose, but Hurkos then was talking about Thomas O'Brien, the shoe salesman—or *was* he?),* it reminded him of an owl, the more so because the eyebrows, growing dark and black and straight above the eye, at their outer corners curved downward, like half-parentheses, as if to outline the intent, dark, watchful eyes. The mouth was thin, a little crooked, slanted down to the left; the chin strong, jutting, with a suspicion of a dimple in the center. His upper lip and jowls were blue; he seemed always to need a shave.

His voice was thin and rather high; hearing it, one might think one was listening to an eighteen- or nineteen-year-old boy, not a man of thirty-three. He spoke in the accents of Boston—"apahtment" and "pahlor"—sometimes his choice of words was surprisingly sophisticated—but his diction was semiliterate: full of "I done" and "Y'unnerstan' me?" punctuated with "So I goes here, right? Right?"—quick, sometimes curt, businesslike. Sometimes he spoke so rapidly that his words ran together and Bottomly realized he was hearing DeSalvo's double-talk—Albert telling and yet not telling, slurring over what he preferred not to talk about. As the interviews went on Bottomly was to become increasingly aware of DeSalvo's persuasiveness. That voice, however youthful, was immensely earnest; it conveyed sincerity, a disarmingly boyish eagerness to please you with its honesty—the mark of the con man, the Measuring Man who found women such easy prey.

At these first sessions, however, DeSalvo seemed almost formal. Later he told Bottomly, "I was sizing you up all the time, testing you out—I was using reverse psychology on you, Mr. Bottomly, to see if I could trust you."

"All right," said Bottomly. He wanted to preface their conversation with a simple statement. "Albert, I don't think you did these things," he said. "I don't believe it. But I'm here to listen—let's talk about them." Would he begin at the beginning, then, and explain how he had gone about these murders he said he had done?

First, DeSalvo explained, he drove a 1954 two-door green Chevrolet coupe, registered in his wife's name. Most of the

---

* Hurkos, it will be remembered, also said the Strangler would have a scar on his left arm from an injury, and would have worked with diesel engines—both true of Albert DeSalvo.

murders occurred on weekends—"I could always get out of the house Saturday by telling my wife I had to work." As a maintenance man he was on the street most of the day, anyway. He would drive about, the urge would come upon him, he never knew where he was going—he had no specific apartment in mind, no specific woman in mind. "You got to realize this, Mr. Bottomly," he said. "I just drove in and out of streets and ended up wherever I ended up."

He began with Anna Slesers. He thought that was "the first one." He placed it sometime in the summer of 1962, in June. He had to work that day. "I said I was going fishing—that was my excuse for getting out of the house," he said. "I had a fishing net, it was weighted down with three lead pipes, and a fishing rod in the back of the car." But instead, he shot out across the Mystic River Bridge into Boston, and found himself driving down St. Stephen's Street. He parked his car in front of St. Anne's Church, walked around the corner into Gainsborough Street, and at random chose one of the identical bay-windowed, four-story red brick houses that lined both sides of Gainsborough. He climbed the six or seven cement steps to the stoop, opened the heavy metal door with its "No. 77" in old-fashioned gold script, and walked up the stairs. He was wearing a raincoat over a charcoal-colored sport jacket, and in his pocket he carried one of the lead weights he'd taken from the fishing net. He knocked on the door of 3F. A slight woman wearing a light blue robe—"I guess it was flannel"—opened the door.

"I was sent to do some work in your apartment," he told her, and she let him in. Carefully he described what he saw as he entered: "To the left would be a kitchen, then the bathroom about ten feet on. The light would be on. I see a sewing machine, brown, a window with drapes, a very pretty bedroom set, light tan, a couch, a tan record player with darker color—you know, dark cocoa-color knobs." As she led the way toward the bathroom telling him what had to be done, he was behind her, and "I hit her on the head with the lead weight." As she fell he put his arms around her neck and they fell together on the floor. For a moment she had put out one hand to support herself on the sewing machine, but then crumpled. "Her blood was all over me . . . I got up, I took her robe, I had the robe belt, and I put it around her neck and left it on her."

To Bailey he had said that "she was still alive and I had intercourse with her." He did not say this to Bottomly.

"Then I washed up in the bathroom and I noticed I was wearing gloves." Time and again DeSalvo was to talk about himself as though he were another person and to speak of things "being done" to the victims as though he had had no part in what took place.

The bathroom was yellow with a white sunken tub, as he remembered it. She must have been preparing to take a bath "because there was maybe four, five inches of water in the tub." When he went into the parlor, music—"symphonies and stuff like that"—still came from the record player, so he turned one of the knobs and the sound vanished, but he wasn't sure if he'd completely switched off the instrument.

"I saw I had blood all over, on my jacket and shirt, so when I left I grabbed a raincoat that was hanging in a cabinet and put it on."

"What kind of cabinet?" Bottomly asked. "Where was it?"

"It was metal, about seven feet high, in the bedroom." When he put his hand in the cabinet, he felt a bill on a shelf and took it. It was twenty dollars—"the only money I took at any place," he said.

The raincoat, a tan one, was short in the sleeves, "but I went out, got into my car, and drove around until I came to an Army and Navy store." When he emerged from No. 77, a policeman happened to be passing. DeSalvo simply walked by him to his car. He had ripped off his shirt and cut up the jacket into small pieces, using his fishing knife, wrapped his own raincoat, which was also bloody, about that, and hid the bundle in the back of his car. Now he walked, bare-chested, into the store and bought a white shirt which he put on there. He drove toward Lynn; he came by the Lynn Marsh, one of the many inlets of the Atlantic to be found there. It was low tide. He parked his car, waded out into the mud, and threw his jacket, piece by piece, into the water, then the raincoat, and watched the heavy current take the stuff away. As he was about to leave he looked up and saw a man, about a hundred yards down the shore, observing him. Calmly, he got back into his car and drove home.

That was Thursday, June 14, 1962. He had been out of jail two months.

Saturday morning—he remembered it was a Saturday, probably the last Saturday in June—he told Irmgard that he was going out on a job. He had a cup of coffee in a little restaurant near his home, got into his car, and "I shot out toward Swampscott to see a fellow I was doing some work for. Instead, I went to Salem, and I rode around for a while and I ended up in Lynn. I was just driving—anywhere—not knowing where I was going. I was coming through back

ways, in and out and around. *That's the idea of the whole
thing. I just go here and there. I don't know why.*

"Okay. So I go through the different streets—right? Right?
I find myself in front of Seventy-three Newhall Street. Now,
I'd been in this same building before."

What had brought him there then?

"Same thing as now," DeSalvo said simply. "But I didn't
do anything. I talked to a dark-haired girl, about thirty-five,
five foot seven and a half, about a hundred and thirty
pounds—not bad-looking. I passed a remark . . ." He
stopped to think.

He and Bottomly sat across a table from each other in a
room whose walls were completely bare and whose only
other furniture was a wooden high-backed bench against one
wall. Between the two men was the microphone of the tape
recorder Bottomly had brought with him. McGrath, a nationally known criminologist, penologist, and attorney of high reputation—all parties involved had agreed upon him as guardian—sat at the head of the table, listening intently. His role
was to advise DeSalvo if any question arose as to his rights.
He had met him some months before and DeSalvo had impressed him with his apparent sincerity and honesty. To keep
an open mind McGrath had avoided learning any details of
the crimes. Only now and then did he ask a question.

On the table was a detailed street and building map of Boston, and a blue-lined school pad. Each time DeSalvo spoke of
a building, at Bottomly's request he sketched it on the
pad—the entrance he used, the stairs he climbed, the layout
of the apartment, the location and kind of furniture, the windows, fire escapes, exits. To refresh his memory as to streets,
he consulted the map. But his memory was extraordinary.
More than once he was to say, "I know you're telling me
what your photographs show, but I'm telling you what I
saw."

"Now, why didn't I do anything?" he asked himself. "Did I
get scared that first time because I saw a woman and that
made me take off? I don't know." On this second visit to 73
Newhall Street he entered, began to mount the back stairs,
but seeing someone, went around to the front, opened a dark
oak glass door, and climbed to the second floor.

"I went to the right and knocked on a door." It was Helen
Blake's apartment. He stopped again. "Was it her front door?
Back door? This hallway's got me bugged," he said, talking as
he sketched it. "There's a curve in the hallway there . . .

"When I knocked she opened the door. She was wearing

cotton-type pajamas, bottoms and top, some kind of pink print, buttoned down the front—"

"What kind of print?" Bottomly asked. DeSalvo dutifully sketched the pattern as he remembered it.

"I told her, 'I'm going to do some work in the apartment,' and she said, 'This is the first I've heard about it,' and I said, 'I'm supposed to check all the windows for leaks and I'm going to do some interior painting.' 'Well, it's about time,' she said." There were two milk bottles in front of her door. "You got milk bottles here," he said politely, and "reached down and got them up in the crook of my thumb and first finger so there's no prints and I talked my way right into her fast and she let me in."

McGrath suggested that Albert draw the shape of the bottles. Were they wet and cold to the touch? Not wet, said De-Salvo; maybe a little cold. Probably just had been delivered, he thought. "I handed her the bottles and she put them on the refrigerator—"

Bottomly caught him. "Wasn't it odd that she didn't put them *in* the refrigerator?"

DeSalvo dismissed the question. "I wasn't paying much attention. She was doing her housecleaning because the bedroom windows were open and she had rugs hanging out over them. There was a white mantelpiece in the parlor, she had pictures on it and an older-type TV with a picture of a girl—say eighteen, twenty on it—her daughter, I think, or her niece. We had some conversation, she was telling me about her, a very nice woman, you know, talking about her niece . . ." DeSalvo's voice took on an indulgent tone. Then he told her, "Your ceilings need only one coat of white paint. I'd like to check the windows in the bedroom, too."

Bending over the note pad, his forehead furrowed, he industriously sketched the apartment, complete to mantelpiece, TV set, sofas, tables. His straight lines were wavering, almost like a James Thurber cartoon. "This door is on the left, it's the bedroom at the end of the hall, right? On the back was some articles of clothing hanging. Over here a closet, then a little table, underneath the bed was a chest or something . . . So I'm in the living room, talking about painting the ceiling, working my way toward the bedroom."

In the bedroom, Helen Blake pointed to one window. He was behind her. "While she was pointing I grabbed my hand right behind her neck; she was a heavyset, big-breasted woman—"

"Did you have to bend over to grab her?" Bottomly asked.

De Salvo shook his head. "No . . . we were standing near the bed. She went down right away—she fainted, passed right out—"

"You hardly touched her, and she fainted?"

Yes, said DeSalvo. "I noticed she was wearing glasses, and plus I grabbed her and I held her very tightly, right?" He spoke animatedly. "I noticed a little trickle of blood come out of her nose, so I took off her glasses with one hand and laid them down, I didn't want to break them, I put them on the floor. Maybe it was on the dresser. She just slumped, went down on her knees, halfway against the bed, and just a trickle of blood coming down her nose . . ."

Was it light or dark in the bedroom, Bottomly asked? When Helen Blake's body was found all the blinds had been drawn.

"It was light because the shades were up," said DeSalvo. "Later they were down, I can't explain it, I guess I done it, I pulled them down . . . So I picked her up—"

Since Miss Blake was a heavy woman, wasn't that difficult?

"Not for me," said DeSalvo promptly, with the same note of braggadocio that must have grated on his fellow inmates. "I picked her up, took off her pajamas—the buttons popped—I took everything clean off. She was unconscious. I got on top, I had intercourse . . ." He paused.

Think carefully, he was told. He was to try to recall everything he did. Bottomly did not tell him that no evidence of sexual intercourse had been found by Dr. Luongo during Helen Blake's autopsy.

"Here's what I'm trying to say to you, sir," DeSalvo said, half-eager, half-annoyed. "I do remember biting on her bust, possibly other parts of her body, too, her stomach, maybe, right? . . . I'm trying to see if I had intercourse with her . . . It's possible. I think I put a bra around her neck, if I'm not mistaken. A nylon stocking, too . . . I got it out of the right dresser drawer, right here." He pointed to his sketch. "I went to the bathroom, wiped the sweat off my face . . ." He paused. "That stocking bothers me. Maybe it came from the bathroom. I'm not sure. But where *did* I get it?" He shook his head. "There's no use guessing here, I just want to tell you the facts."

Then, "I went into the kitchen, got a long carbon steel knife—maybe twelve inches of blade—and tried to pry open the chest under the bed." He stopped. "Wait a minute!" he exclaimed triumphantly. "This is it!" His voice became softer with emphasis. "I tell you, this—is—it!" He rapped on the table. "That bra and that stocking were right there, on top of her dresser. That's where I grabbed them from—" He stopped to sigh. "I've been in so many apartments, and won't lie to you, Mr. Bottomly, I'm having a very difficult time because I've been in over thousands—that's not exaggerating—and I am doing my utmost to give you the clearest picture I can without giving you false details which will hurt me rather than help me."

As he attempted to pry open the chest, the knife broke in it. "I just dropped the handle then and took off," he said. "I left her about ten-twenty A.M. What happened between then and four-thirty that afternoon, when I went to Nina Nichols'—" His voice lowered almost dreamily. "Well, I was just riding around, like in the middle of the world." Somehow, then, he found himself no longer in Lynn, but in Boston, driving down Commonwealth Avenue, turning into the parking lot adjacent to No. 1940. He left his car and walked into the front entrance. "When you open the door there are bells to the right. I pressed two bells. First button was number thirty-something, on the third floor. I rang the bell, right? Nothing happens. I ring another one—I see the name Nina Nichols over it. Then the buzzer sounds. I guess she must have been the one that hit the buzzer. It rang twice."

There was an elevator in the center of a circular staircase. He was going to take it but saw it descending with a woman passenger. He kept out of sight until she left, then he went up the stairs to the fourth floor. "On the way I saw two crazy sisters, two floors below Nichols—I guess on the second floor. I knocked on their door. I remember I'd rung their bell first downstairs. When I hit their floor the door was open—I met the first sister—she was batty as all hell."

What did he mean, batty as all hell?

"Oh, she was talking real ragtime; I could see right away I wasn't making any sense to her. Behind her I saw the other sister—I guess it was her sister—back further in the apartment. So I kept on going up the stairs, and I heard, 'Who is it?' I was high up, I was when I looked out the window. I bore to the right. Nichols' door was to the right. She was standing at the door wearing a housecoat—something pinkish. She was wearing glasses." He remembered "there was something funny about what she had on her feet." Then it came to him. "Something different . . . like tennis shoes."

" 'What do you want?' she asked.

"I explained I come up to check the windows for leaks." The night before it had been raining.

"She said, 'Who sent you here? Did the superintendent, Mr. Burke,* send you?'

"I said yes.

"She said, 'Well, I don't know anything about it.'

"I said, 'Look, you can call him up—'

"She said, 'Oh, all right, go ahead—but make it fast, because I'm leaving—I'm on my way out.'

"I felt funny. I didn't want to go in there in the first place. I just didn't want it to happen. But I went in and I proceeded from one room to another. When we got to the bedroom I looked at the windows. She said, 'What's wrong?' I said, 'I don't want to wrinkle your curtains—will you check that window?' Then I told her, 'Check this one'—and as she checked this one, she was turned away—that's when it happened. Because I grabbed her and she fell back with me on the bed, on top of me. I was in this position, my feet around the bottom of her legs—"

"You really had her pinned, then?" said Bottomly, in an attempt to maintain a man-to-man approach.

DeSalvo said, embarrassed, "I don't like to talk about this."

"You've got to talk about it," said Bottomly.

"I'd almost swear that it was here she took her fingernails and dug into the back of my hand—it didn't bleed, she did pull the skin—and then she stopped. You must have found skin under her fingernails."

How did he know she got skin under her fingernails?

"Because it was off of me," said DeSalvo. "She kept doing it until she . . . went."

The he slid out from under her, picked her up and put her on the floor—

"Was she alive at this point?"

There was a silence. Then DeSalvo replied in a suddenly hushed, suddenly humble voice of a small boy who has been rebuked, "I don't know."

But he had told Bailey that Nina Nichols was still unconscious, that he had placed her on a rug there and had intercourse with her, then he had grabbed a belt, put it around her neck, and tried to strangle her, but the belt broke, near the buckle.

Had he left anything around her neck?

A silk stocking, he said, which he knotted three times.

Would he demonstrate the kinds of knots he tied?

* The superintendent was Mr. Bruce. It was possible, thought Bottomly, that DeSalvo heard it as "Burke."

Obediently DeSalvo bent over, untied his shoelaces, and tied them again. Bottomly noted it for the record: "He just tied his shoe by taking one strand and putting it twice over the second strand before pulling it tight and then tied a second knot on top of that to make it secure." It was the Strangler's knot.

Now DeSalvo described the room, the furniture in it, the camera equipment all about—

"You searched the apartment," Bottomly said. "What were you looking for?"

DeSalvo said hesitantly, "I didn't know at that time—probably anything."

Money? "Possibly," said DeSalvo.

"Checks? Ever pick up checks?" No, he did not, he said. Jewelry?

"To be honest with you, I never took anything from that apartment—from any of the apartments." He corrected himself. He had taken that twenty-dollar bill from Anna Slesers' apartment.

Bottomly asked, "How come you didn't take any of those cameras? They're pretty negotiable."

"I wasn't up there for money, for stealing."

"But you ransacked the place."

"That's right," said DeSalvo.

"Well, what did you do that for?"

DeSalvo gave an embarrassed half-giggle. "That's what I'm trying to find out myself. I done these things, I know, I went through them—"

"Now, Albert," Bottomly said, reasonably. "You're a professional B and E man, you've been in and out of a thousand places, you've got it down to a fine science, a work of art. If you hadn't got mixed up in this sex thing you'd probably still be doing it. Now, you went into Nina Nichols' apartment, you know how to go through a place, you knew what you were looking for, and you knew what you could sell."

DeSalvo nodded.

"All right," went on Bottomly. "You see a lot of valuable cameras—why didn't you take one?"

"Because to be honest with you, I just didn't want to take them."

"Doesn't that sound strange to you?"

"Yes," said DeSalvo. "It also sounds strange to me why I went into the apartment in the first place."

"It doesn't sound strange to me," Bottomly retorted. "This looked like an apartment which might have some valuable property in it—"

"Yes—why didn't I take it?" DeSalvo demanded. "That's what I'd like to know, too. I understand she had a diamond, too. Why didn't I take that?" He thought for a moment. Yes, he always ransacked the apartments after his attack. "I don't think I was actually looking for anything to steal. After this here thing happened, I think in my own mind I might have searched to make it look that way—that something was being taken. But I didn't have in my mind the idea of taking anything."

He sketched the rooms, the position of the body. There were a number of liquor bottles an arm's length away. He picked up one bottle— "For what reason I don't know, I stuck the bottle in her." He thought he left it in her—a wine bottle that might have had wine in it.

Questioned again to go over what he had done, DeSalvo squirmed uncomfortably in his chair. "These things, I'm ashamed of what I done. I know I inserted the bottle, but I don't want to talk about it now."

"Why are you so reluctant about this?" Bottomly asked. "Because you don't understand it?"

That was part of it, DeSalvo admitted. "And because it's so unbelievable to me that it was really done by me. Why I done it I don't really understand, but I know at this moment that to do it—" He ended up lamely. "Well, I wouldn't."

"You do now understand why you searched these places and mixed things up?"

Well, he knew he had said a moment ago it was to create the impression of burglary, but he only assumed this—he did not know the real reason.

"Do you remember ransacking the apartment, as you remember grabbing her?"

"No, I remember going through things but as to how I did it I don't recall. I know I done it."

Bottomly thought for a moment. "Albert, tell me what happened to you when you grabbed Nina Nichols. What was going on in your mind?"

"You mean the feeling I had? Well . . . as her back was turned to me and I saw the back of her head, and—I was all hot, just like you're going to blow your head off—like pressure right on you, right away—I—"

"You just had to do something?" Bottomly prompted him.

DeSalvo all but stuttered. "I—I—to—to explain it or to express it, as soon as I saw the back of her head, right?—not her face, seeing nothing but the back of her head, right?—everything built up inside of me. Before you know it I had put my arm around her and that was it. And from whatever happened through that time, I can remember doing these things. As for the reason why I did them, I at this time can give you no answer." He remembered doing what he did, he remembered biting her breast—

"Did you draw blood?"

"Oh, no—" almost shocked. "Nothing like that."

After everything had been done, the telephone rang. "I was sweating like anything and when it rang I just took off. It was still ringing when I went down the stairs. I stopped on the stairs for a minute when I saw a woman getting into the elevator—"

Once outside the building, he walked to his car. Two elderly women, carrying packages, were coming from the parking lot. He passed them, he looked at them, they looked at him. He got into his car and drove home. "It was coming close to six o'clock then."

That was Saturday, June 30? Yes. In his shamed, small boy's voice: "It was the same day I was in Lynn the morning Mrs. Blake died."

The first session was over.

Bottomly and McGrath, driving back to Boston with Detectives Tuney and DiNatale, who had been forced to remain outside in an anteroom because of the legal technicalities, were impressed. Still, everything Albert had said *could* have been read in the newspapers or learned from some unofficial source.

Details of the murders—some unprintable—were in the very air; over the months they had been told, whispered, confided to friends, family, colleagues by any number of persons: the janitors, the police, the technicians on the scene: photographers, stenographers, chemists, artists. Anna Slesers' bath, her hi-fi partly turned off in the living room; Helen Blake's rugs hanging out her windows, the knife blade broken in her footlocker; Nina Nichols' cameras, her haste to leave that afternoon, the telephone call that had frightened DeSalvo—all. To be sure, his sketches were accurate. By his own admission, however, he knew the apartments in these neighborhoods: he had been breaking into them for the past seven years. Nothing he had said so far proved he had been in each apartment at the time of each murder.

And how explain the lack of evidence, in the autopsies of the Old Women, of sexual intercourse?

"Unless he's lying," suggested Tuney. DeSalvo might use the term "sexual intercourse" to cover other acts which he was too embarrassed—at least, so far—to reveal.

They would check Army and Navy stores. Surely a clerk should recall a bare-chested man buying a shirt. They would seek out the "crazy sisters" in Nina Nichols' building. They should remember DeSalvo, perhaps even establish the exact hour they saw him continue up the stairs. DeSalvo said he had taken Anna Slesers' raincoat. They had an excellent check here. Mrs. Slesers' daughter Maija, two months before the murder, had bought two identical raincoats, one for herself, one for her mother. When her mother's effects were sent to her, the raincoat was missing. They would ask Maija, who lived in Maryland, to send hers to Boston: they would hang it on a rack with a dozen others, and challenge DeSalvo to pick out the one most resembling the one he had taken.

They would check, check, check. And Bottomly would have to hear more—much, much more.

At the next session, a few days later, Bottomly brought with him a folder of sixty photographs of women aged between forty-five and seventy-five. These were the faces of women derelicts, victims of other murders, alcoholics, taken from police files. Among these he had interspersed photographs of the eleven victims. All had appeared in the press with one exception—Nina Nichols. Her family had refused to release any photograph to the newspapers. Now, however, to assist Bottomly, they had given him one that he included in the album.

Would Albert go through these carefully and each time he recognized one of his victims, identify her?

Albert studied them, photograph by photograph. Yes, this was Anna Slesers. This was Sophie Clark. This was Mary Sullivan. This was Evelyn Corbett. (He always called her Corbett instead of Corbin.) He chose ten—correctly. Then he went through the album again.

"This one bothers me," he said, tapping it with his finger. "I'm not sure, but it could be Nina Nichols." Bottomly tensed. It was the Nina Nichols photograph. "She was frail, her hair was a lot grayer than it is here," DeSalvo was saying. "Yeah, sure—this is her, okay, but she's a lot older."

Bottomly placed the album on the floor beside him, saying nothing. The Nina Nichols likeness, her family had told him, had been taken five years before, but it was the most recent they had. *Well*, thought Bottomly, *I'll accept Albert for Nina Nichols.* Else how could he have recognized her? Yet she might have been pointed out to him before—he was forever in and out of those apartment houses. And Bottomly could not forget that Peter Hurkos, handling sealed manila envelopes, had accurately described the photographs inside them, and that Paul Gordon had pinpointed a pile of hidden cigarette butts and a nailed service door . . .

"All right, Albert," he said aloud. "Whom do you want to talk about next?"

After a moment, Albert said, "Ida Irga."

"When was that?" Bottomly asked.

Albert sat lost in thought. He began muttering under his breath. It was an astonishing scene to be repeated more than once: Albert stitting there, thinking half-aloud, running through the chronology of the murders he said he committed: "Slesers was June fourteenth, then Blake, Nichols . . . it had to be Saturday, the last Saturday in June, the thirtieth—that was Blake. July . . . Then two and a half weeks—around the twentieth—no, the twenty-first—it was hot weather, mid-August—no, the nineteenth, it's around the nineteenth." He looked up. "It could possibly be a Monday," he said. He fixed it as Monday, August 20.

He had been driving around aimlessly, he remembered, as always when this mood came upon him, and finding himself in a narrow street—it turned out to be Grove Street—he saw a place to park along the curb, and he did so.

"Did you know Ida Irga?"

"No, no, no. I didn't pick her out in advance. I didn't pick a building. If there was no parking place on Grove Street, if I'd parked on some other street, I'd never even've gotten to her. I just happened to walk into her building. I rang about four different bells—somebody buzzed the door, it opened, and I went up the stairs. Whoever came to the door first, that was it. She was the first to answer. When I get to the top of the stairs, she's on the landing, looking down over the iron railing, waiting for me. I told her I was going to do some work in the apartment but I could see she didn't trust me. So I said, 'If you don't want to be bothered by me going in, I won't bother you.'

" 'But I don't know who you are,' she said. She spoke in a kind of accent—Jewish type. She was heavyset, about a hundred and sixty pounds, white-haired with streaks of black hair in it. She was wearing a black and white checked cotton housedress. We talked, and I said, 'If you don't want it done, forget it. I'll just tell them you told me you don't want it done,' and I started to walk down. She says, 'Well, never mind, come on,' and I walked in on her. We went into the bedroom to check the windows and when she turned around—I did it. My right arm around her neck, she went down—"

He paused. "She passed out fast. I saw purplish-dark blood, it came out of her right ear . . ." He stopped again. ". . . . just enough for me to see." His voice almost died away. "I saw it more clearly when I put the pillowcase around her neck, but I strangled her first with my arm, then the pillowcase." He had intercourse with her—"I think I had intercourse . . ." He was not sure. Bottomly pressed him. Finally, reluctantly, "I would say yes."

"You don't sound very positive to me," Bottomly said.

"It's—to me—" DeSalvo mumbled. "To me it's sickening even to talk about this. It's so damn real—that blood coming out of her ear—"

Yet other details, he admitted, were blurred.

When Bailey had interrogated him, Bailey had remarked that Mrs. Irga, aged seventy-five, could not be thought of as sexually attractive. DeSalvo had bristled. "Attractiveness had nothing to do with it," he had said. "She was a woman. When this certain time comes on me, it's a very immediate thing. When I get this feeling and instead of a going to work I make an excuse to my boss, I start driving and I start in my mind building this image up, and that's why I find myself not knowing where I'm going."

Now he told Bottomly how he looked through Mrs. Irga's apartment. He opened the drawers of a dark walnut dresser, "but there was nothing in them, nothing at all." He recalled "putting her legs in a wide position, one leg in each chair. I got them from the dining room, they were dark straight-backed chairs; I moved them away from the table and put her legs on the chairs between the slats—"

"Were you thinking of anything?"

"No, I just did it." He could give no further explanation.

Next was Jane Sullivan. It was two days later—Wednesday, August 22.

He drew a sketch of her building: "You have to step up, you walk inside, there's a little hallway, black and white tiles, with another step up. There's a buzzer—if they don't buzz the buzzer, I can open the electric lock downstairs—"

Albert stopped, as if waiting to be prompted.

"How?" asked Bottomly.

"All I need is a plastic toothpick. Why, my daughter once took her plastic ruler from school and slipped the lock of the door of our house. 'I put this in and the door opened, Daddy,' she said."

Jane Sullivan was a heavyset woman, about a hundred and fifty pounds, five feet seven, who spoke with a "from Ireland" accent. Her apartment was on the first floor.

"Albert, how did you talk your way in?"

"I did it fast," said Albert. "She was in the midst of moving in. I saw all these cartons—things's weren't set up. Now, she's looking into a closet to show me something—that's where it happened. I'm behind her—"

Bottomly asked, "How did you get her to open the closet and show you something? What were you talking about? What kind of a line were you giving her?"

"As soon as I saw her, I had a quick look at the room"—he snapped his fingers— "I knew what I was there for. Whatever it came to, that was it. I said, 'Have you got straightened out yet? I thought I'd drop in because I've got some other places to do. I'm going upstairs later this afternoon, I want to check a few things out to make sure they're in order.'"

Miss Sullivan wanted to know who sent him, but he talked fast, so she assumed he came from the movers or the landlord to check up on the job.

"I went through the place, seeing how things were. I looked into the parlor. 'Boy, they didn't do a good job here,' I said. 'No, they left a mess,' she said. Then she looked into that closet—and that was it. I was behind her, I put my right arm around her, we both fell back on the floor. She struggled and struggled, she was so big there was nothing to grip hold of—she finally stopped struggling. It took about a minute and a half—I put a scissors grip . . ." He was not sure whether he had intercourse with her. "She was an older woman, about fifty-five to sixty."

Later Bottomly asked, "Why did you pick her up and put her in the tub?"

"The tub was filled with water," Albert said slowly. "Maybe she was getting ready for a bath." He thought for a moment. "There was nothing about Anna Slesers to interest any man—why did I do it? She was getting ready for a bath. Why didn't I put her in a tub when I put Mrs. Sullivan in a tub? Just like why did I leave a broom and a bottle? I don't understand it." He sat, musing.

Wednesday, December 5. Sophie Clark, the Negro girl.

"Yeah, I remember that day. It was supposed to be a workday but December fifth is my wedding anniversary, so I took the day off." He drove about, found himself on Huntington Avenue, parked his car, and walked into No. 315. "I was wearing green pants with a shirt and I talked to a woman in the building first—not Sophie." He had knocked on the door, a woman opened it, he told her his name was Thompson.

"Can you describe the woman?" Bottomly asked, remembering Marcella Lulka's story of the man who entered her apartment that day, spoke about painting it, then frightened her by talking about her "form" and the money she might earn as a model.

"She was a colored woman, she wore glasses—this woman had a piano in the room," said Albert. "I was trying to con her, telling her she was very pretty." He left suddenly, just walked out—

"Why?" asked Bottomly. Albert thought. She had said something about her husband— "Now I know—she had a child, a boy, I think, maybe five or six years old."

After Albert left Mrs. Lulka he walked into the other wing of the building, he said. In the lobby he noticed a bell under which were three names—Audri Todd, Sophie Clark, and a third he could not remember now. He wrote them on the back of his hand with a pencil, then mounted the stairs and sought out the apartment—4C. A tall, pretty, dark-skinned girl opened to his knock.

"She presented herself to me," said DeSalvo. "A Negro girl, really beautiful, with beautiful long hair; her eyes were dark brown; she looked like a Hawaiian girl, she was so tall—" He seemed unable to get over the fact of her height. "About five ten—taller than me—at least a hundred and forty pounds. She was built solid. She had on a sexy whitish-type robe—she had black high heels on, I remember—it was very appealing, the way she was dressed."

He told her that he was to do repair work in the apartment. "She didn't want to let me in because her roommates weren't there, but they would be home shortly. She said they were taking a course across the street in the YWCA and she was waiting for them." He pretended that he knew them. Then, "I gave her fast talk. I told her I'd set her up in modeling"—it was the first time he had reverted to his Measuring Man technique—"I'd give her from twenty to thirty dollars an hour." He talked himself into the apartment, and in the course of their conversation, said, "Turn around, let me see how you're built—" She turned around. "That was it. I grabbed her around the neck with my right arm, she was very tall, because she fell on top of me on the settee, my legs went around her legs—she didn't give me any struggle at all."

She was unconscious. He had intercourse with her, he said, but she was coming to. "To keep her from screaming, I grabbed two nylons out of a drawer." In doing so he knocked several packs of cigarettes to the floor. He was silent, and then, as so many times before, as if ashamed to hear his own words, said under his breath, "She was the one I had to tie really tight. She started to fight. I made it so tight, I couldn't see it . . ." He had put her on her back on the other side of a coffee table in the center of the room. "I ripped her clothes off her, ripped off her slip, and put it around her neck, then the stockings . . . Too deep . . ." He shook his head in dismay. "Whew! . . . So tight—"

Bottomly asked, "When was this?"

"My anniversary, my wedding anniversary," DeSalvo said. "December fifth. I remember it very clearly."

"What time of day was it? Do you remember that?"

"I do—around two thirty-five," said DeSalvo.

"Why do you remember the time so clearly?"

"Because I'm right there now." Then, as if he must explain: "If I sit back calm, and I'm not bothered, I can go way back and remember everything. I'm right there."

"You talked to Sophie about modeling? Was she interested in becoming a model?"

DeSalvo looked into space. "It was too fast, too fast . . ."

"Then you struck her—"

DeSalvo, stung, interrupted him. "When you say 'struck,' I don't like to hear that. She was very upset, number one, letting me in. She didn't let me in on that modeling bit. She wasn't a tramp; she was a good person. She let me in on the pretense of work. You got to look at her side, too. She didn't want to let me in, yet she did. She seemed *scared*. I'm seeing *her* feelings now too, you understand?" DeSalvo's voice sounded aggrieved, as if Bottomly, by his use of the word "struck," impugned his humane sentiments. "We talked, maybe a minute—that's all. Then she turned her back . . ."

"She was a strong girl. How come she went out so fast? Were you surprised? Did you expect it?"

DeSalvo shook his head. "I didn't expect anything," he said dully. Whatever happened, happened.

After a moment he said, "She was doing some writing—studying or writing—on the coffee table. Afterwards I looked through some magazines there."

"Were you taking your time?"

"I don't know how to answer you—" He searched for words. "You might say I seemed calm, but if you were there to see it, when this happened . . . There was no need for it to happen."

"No need to kill her?"

"No," said DeSalvo.

"You could have had her?"

"It wasn't the reason for having her. This is where the whole thing is messed up. There was no reason to be there, period. There was no reason for her to die. Nothing was taken away from her, no money, no nothing. How can I explain it to you? I'd sit there, looking to find something, looking through photographs like I was looking for someone . . . It didn't take no more than five, ten minutes. This is what I feel. It could have been half an hour, but it seemed like five or ten minutes."

"When you left the building did you feel any remorse?"

Again DeSalvo shook his head. "All I can tell you is, it's like *What am I doing here? I got to get away.* I never ran when I left a building. Even when I saw people I nodded to them very politely. I never met anyone when I walked out. I was just plain lucky."

But he took care: "When I came across a person I never let him get to see me and I don't get to look at him too fast. I don't duck, but I put my hand up to my face, I never let them see me directly."

Little more than three weeks later, at 515 Park Drive, on a Sunday morning, Patricia Bissette. It was December 30.

"I knew this apartment," he said. He had been in it "at least four or five times before" when other girls lived there. "I used to work this area regularly," taking advantage of the fact that new girls moved in with each change of semester.

He had parked his car on Beacon Street, across the street from a laundromat, and it was around 8 A.M. that Sunday morning when he found himself in front of Pat's door. He had no idea who lived there now. Expecting no one home on a holiday weekend, he slipped the lock; when he pulled open the door, he said, he heard the jingle of bells. Pat had hung a miniature Christmas log with five tiny sleigh bells on the back of her door. "I was so quiet opening it—but the bells woke her up." She stood in the doorway of her bedroom, a blanket held to her, peering out at him. "Who are you? What do you want?" she demanded. "I gave her fast talk, I said I was one of the fellows living upstairs and where was her girl friend?—there were three names on the door, and I named one of them—

"She said everyone'd gone out of town, but she stayed home because she had to be at work Monday morning. We started talking." She assumed he did live upstairs and knew mutual friends, and said, "Wait a minute—I'll put some coffee on." Albert said, "Okay—want me to go out and get some doughnuts?" Oh, no, she said. He closed the door with its tinkling bells, they went into the kitchen, she brought out "two pear-shaped cups," set a kettle of water on the gas range, and made instant coffee for them both.

"We sat in the kitchen for a few minutes. Then we moved to the living room." He was too nervous to drink his coffee—he had never liked coffee anyway—so he sipped it very slowly. When they left the kitchen he took his cup into the living room, making sure he left no fingerprints on it. Patricia sat on a chair to the left of the Christmas tree; he on a couch on the other side of the room.

"She put a record, I think it was a Christmas song of some kind, on her record player—it was blue and white—and we listened. But I was looking at her and getting worked up. I went over to her, I was on my knees . . ." He stopped, but did not explain further. "She said, 'Take it easy.' I said, 'Nobody's here, nobody can hear you. I can do what I want to you—' "

At this Patricia grew angry. " 'If that's the way you're going to talk, you'd better go right now—' " She rose and turned her back to him. "Next thing, before she knew it, I had my arm around her neck, she fell back on top of me, and she passed out." She had put on a robe; under it she was wearing "very sexy leopardlike pajamas. I ripped them off—I don't know exactly, but I did reveal her busts. I picked her up. I remember seeing her on the floor stripped naked. I took her into the left bed because the other one had Christmas packages on it. I had intercourse with her . . ."

The easy flow of words began to halt. "I don't know," DeSalvo began vaguely, "if I did this—well, for a sex act, or hatred, or for what reason." Obviously he had read various explanations for the Strangler's behavior. "I think I did this not as a sex act," he repeated, "but out of hate for her—not her in particular, but for a woman. After seeing her body, naturally the sex act came in." He sighed. It was hard to explain, but he did not enjoy his "sex relations" with her . . . "There was no thrill at all."

"What did you strangle her with?"

"Some gloves were hanging up there—nylon stockings . . . At the end, I covered her up."

"Why did you cover her up, Albert?" Bottomly asked. He had been reluctant in the earlier sessions to press DeSalvo as to motivation, lest it inhibit him from telling his story. But now, as DeSalvo felt increasingly at ease with him, Bottomly began to venture into areas that he knew must ultimately be probed by the psychiatrists.

DeSalvo searched for words. "She was so different . . . I

didn't want to see her like that, naked and . . ." He was silent. "She talked to me like a man, she treated me like a
man—I remember I covered her up all the way. She was still
breathing, her face was swelling up, I put the blouse and
stocking around her neck, her face still kept getting
bigger. . . . Whew!" After a moment: "That Sunday morning we had coffee. I don't know why I did it. She did me no
harm—and yet I did it. Do you follow me? Why did I do it
to her? Why did I do it?"

Bottomly said softly, "She must have got to you."

DeSalvo continued in the same wondering voice: "We
talked for about an hour. I asked if she was married or going
steady. She said, 'No, I'm not, but I do have friends.' I asked,
'Do you have a car?' and she said, 'No, but somebody picks
me up . . .' " His voice trailed off.

How had he been able to get out of his house so early on a
Sunday morning? What did he tell Irmgard?

"What *did* I tell her?" DeSalvo asked himself, aloud. "Did
I tell her I was going fishing? No . . ." Then: "That's it! I
know." He was employed at the time by Russell Blomerth's
construction firm as a maintenance man, and it was his job to
keep kerosene heaters burning over the weekend at construction sites so that newly poured cement would not freeze and
crack. "I volunteered to go down and keep them lit—this was
in Belmont. I'd go out early Sunday to Belmont, get the burn-
ers going, then shoot into Boston. I came to this building
. . . it all happened before eight A.M. I was home before nine
A.M." Then again, as if to himself: "Why did I do it to her?
She treated me like a man." He looked up, his eyes met Bottomly's; he seemed on the verge of tears, but he controlled
himself and was returned quietly to his cell.

On their way back to Boston Bottomly, Tuney, and Di-
Natale were silent for some time. How relentlessly the conviction was growing that DeSalvo was indeed the Strangler!
Ida Irga, Sophie Clark, Patricia Bissette. Ida Irga's bureau
drawers *had* been empty. Her son had told the police this
fact; it had not been published anywhere. DeSalvo said he
had gagged Sophie Clark with her underpants. Every
published report had stated that a handkerchief had been
used. This had been taken from the original police report, but
the report had been wrong; DeSalvo had not been wrong.

Yet if he had entered Mrs. Lulka's apartment, and had
spoken with her, why had she not identified him? That could
be attributed to human error. Detectives knew by experience
how uncertain identification is: experiments had been carried

out in which one man, brandishing a gun, pursued a second through a huge room while fifty detectives watched. Interrogation of the observers only moments later showed an astonishing variance: the tall pursuer was described as short, the man without a gun was seen to have a gun . . . Through fear, apprehension, whatever, Mrs. Lulka could have carried away from her encounter with Albert DeSalvo the impression of a man who looked nothing like him.

DeSalvo had said he drove to Patricia Bissette's apartment direct from Belmont where he had been tending kerosene heaters. Tuney spoke aloud: "That explains the soot." Traces of soot had been found on Patricia's ligatures by police chemists. At the time this seemed to implicate the janitor of Patricia's building, and the man had gone through a grueling examination, complete to lie-detector tests. Where else, police had thought, could the soot have come from save from the hands or clothes of a janitor busy with a furnace that cold December day?

In Patricia's kitchen a coffee cup in its saucer had been found at one end of the table; opposite it, only a saucer. A man, taking his coffee into another room, is likely to take his cup only. Women, less careless, more conscious of moisture stains on furniture, will take cup and saucer.

And a cup, still with coffee in it, had been found in the living room, its handle facing left. Albert DeSalvo was left-handed.

How could it not have been DeSalvo for these three victims, too?

Phil DiNatale snorted. "I told you!" he exclaimed. "I said he'd be sitting somewhere, laughing at us all the time—"

On June 26, 1965, a jury found George Nassar guilty of murder in the first degree in the shooting of Irvin Hilton, the Texaco station owner, the previous September. There was no recommendation of mercy. Nassar's attorney, F. Lee Bailey, having taken nearly one hundred exceptions to the court's ruling, announced he would appeal the verdict. Nassar was placed in a cell in death row at Walpole State Prison.

But by this time, to those reading the news in the Attorney General's office, Nassar as a suspect in the stranglings had dwindled to a smaller and smaller size.

DeSalvo loomed larger and larger.

21

Slowly through the summer and early autumn of 1965 the sessions between Assistant Attorney General John Bottomly and Albert DeSalvo continued. The two men, although separated from birth by less than ten years and the width of a city, were by nature and backgrounds worlds apart. Bottomly was the result of everything our society has to offer a fortunate and gifted man; DeSalvo, the reject and misfit, the juvenile delinquent, the child molester, the housebreaker, rapist, and possible murderer, was the result of the failure of the same society.

The two men met in secrecy. Once every week or so Tuney and DiNatale drove Bottomly to Bridgewater, where he vanished into a room with his tape recorder and awaited DeSalvo; McGrath would join them; the three sat down; the incredible story unfolded, growing more bizarre as it continued. In an anteroom, waiting restlessly, Tuney and DiNatale sat, talked, smoked, played gin, studied maps of the city, consulted with Bottomly as he emerged to check a fact, to formulate a question. When the sessions were over, transcripts were made and the two detectives studied them in detail with Lieutenants Donovan and Sherry in Boston, and with their colleagues familiar with the stranglings in Cambridge, Lynn, Salem, and Lawrence.

Sometimes Bottomly felt himself a participant in an unbearably tragic drama. Only the man before him knew the last hours of these women; only he knew the last words they uttered, the way their lives ended. And only now were these victims, whom Bottomly had studied and knew so well, really coming alive for him—this, in the final hours of their lives. Sometimes as DeSalvo revealed new facets of himself, Bottomly felt himself a participant in a grotesque masquerade, a mad parody of an inquisition. Surely it could not be real, this

308

conversation, the words he heard, DeSalvo suddenly giggling, conspiratorial—

"This is going to be comical," he was saying. "We're all at a New Year's Eve party, the family, see? Well, I find out one of my sisters is taking judo to protect herself—against the Strangler! She and her friends, they all get together and they're taking lessons at a gym. I says, 'Sure you can handle the Strangler if you get him?' She says, 'Oh, I'm pretty well prepared for him.' I says, 'What would you do if he got you in this hold?' And before she knew it I had her in that hold. She couldn't do nothing. She says, 'Well, I'm learning.'"

He looked up with his boyish grin. "Her husband has eleven sisters, all beautiful—fabulous! I tried to make all eleven of them."

He began to chuckle. "One of them says to me one day, 'You know what I think you are? I wouldn't be surprised if you ain't the Boston Strangler. The way we remember you as the Measuring Man, and how fast and sharp you were with all those women, and now this guy is operating the same way . . . Bah, it can't be you!'" Hugely delighted, he mimicked her.

Or, commiserating with Bottomly because the police had never been able to catch him. "I never knew where I was going, I never knew what I was doing—that's why you never nailed me, because you never knew where I was going to strike and I didn't either. So we were both baffled. You didn't know and how did I know? I didn't know so how could you know?"

Or, in a sudden change of aspect, he spoke as if he were the impersonal tool of fate. He told of Gertrude Gruen, the German waitress who escaped him:

"She was in the position, she was ready to go, she was good as gone." He spoke with finality. "I had both arms around her from behind—but I couldn't do it. I don't know why. She grabbed my finger in her mouth, she was biting it down to the bone—I had a knife, I could have ripped her open . . . and I didn't."

When he knocked on her door the morning of February 18, 1963, she opened it, a tall, sturdy, dark-eyed girl with a red coat thrown over her nightgown. "Go away," she said, "I don't feel well, I've got a virus, come back some other time." But he said, "I got to turn off the water in the bathroom." His fellow workers on the roof (he'd seen men working on the roof just before he entered the building) would give him a signal. She reluctantly let him in. While we waited, he took off his Air Force style jacket and draped it over a chair—a blue chair, he recalled—so that he was in his T-shirt. "You're very pretty," he said to her. "You could be a model." At that she became nervous, and walked to the front window and opened it, saying, "It's hot in here." "No, you better not do that," he said, and walked over and closed the window.

"You didn't stop thinking, did you?" observed Bottomly.

DeSalvo went on as if nothing had been said. Bottomly had observed how earnest the man was; small talk, even the pleasantries Bottomly resorted to in an attempt to establish rapport, were either passed by or obviously resented. "She got a little more upset and opened a back window. I said nothing about it. Then I mentioned, 'There's some dirt on the back of your coat'—she turned and I had her."

She was a strong girl, she fought, kicked, bit, and still—"I couldn't hit her. I could see her brown hair, dark brown hair, and when I turned and saw her face, I couldn't put my hand to hit her. I said, 'I'm going to let you go," and I started to give up, but she still had my finger in her mouth and I was doing everything to get her to open her mouth and she wouldn't. I could of laid her open, I could of hit her with my fist and knocked her out—I don't know what held me back." He broke free. "I ran out of the place, grabbing my jacket from the chair, my hand was all bloody—boy, was she screaming. She was really sounding off.

"When I hit the stairs and came into the street, some guys were there, they'd heard the screams, they saw me. I yelled, 'Quick, he's upstairs, look at my hand, I couldn't hold him,—you got to stop him, he's coming down—' So they shot up.

"I kept running, past my car I'd parked halfway down the block—it was too near for me to get into it—I ran around the corner, pulled off my jacket and threw it in the alley, circled back so when I came back to my car I'm only in my T-shirt; I get in and take off. I picked up my jacket later."

It was the nearest he ever came to capture.

He drove immediately to the office of his attorney, Robert Sheinfeld, in Chelsea. "I wanted to establish an alibi"—at least his attorney could be witness that he *was* in Chelsea—"and he said 'Hi,' and put out his hand to shake hands with me and I wouldn't. It was bleeding so much I had it wrapped in a handkerchief and kept it in my pocket. 'What's wrong with you? What did I do to you?' he asked. He was hurt because I wouldn't shake hands." Albert sighed. "I felt pretty bad. I liked the guy because he was very concerned and kept me out of trouble. He was a very good attorney."

Attorney Sheinfeld was a warm, gregarious man of sixty-two who had practiced for more than forty years in a suite of offices above a drugstore on Chelsea's main street. He had known the DeSalvo family before Albert was born. Time and again through Albert's childhood Sheinfeld, acting for his mother, had haled his father into court for nonsupport and assault and battery. In 1944, when Albert was thirteen, Sheinfeld had finally gotten her a divorce, and a year later she remarried. In the years since, Sheinfeld had watched Albert grow up, had met Irmgard and the children, and had defended Albert on one petty B and E charge after another—charges so minor that Albert's punishment had never been more than a suspended sentence. Sometimes no money was taken; once Albert escaped with nine dollars from a piggy bank he had broken open. In 1961, when he was seized as the Measuring Man, Sheinfeld had defended him again, and it had been his pleas that helped reduce Albert's sentence in the House of Correction. Sheinfeld's mother had died in early 1961 and Albert, behind bars, had written him a touching note of consolation. After his release Albert had faithfully called on the lawyer every three months to pay off, fifty dollars at a time, Sheinfeld's $750 fee. Certainly Sheinfeld had no idea when Albert dropped in on him that February morning in 1963, his hand stuck doggedly in his pocket, that as Albert was to say later, he had just come from attempting to strangle a woman. He would not have believed it then had Albert told him so.

Three weeks after his abortive attack on Gertrude Gruen, Albert found himself in Lawrence, twenty-seven miles from Boston. It was Saturday, March 9, 1963: Mary Brown was found murdered in her apartment that day, her head covered with a sheet and beaten repeatedly with a blunt instrument.

DeSalvo, who was now much more free and animated in his recital, exclaimed, "Oh, that's a terrible one!" when Bottomly wrote Mary Brown's name in his notebook. "Whew! This is like out of this world! This is like something unbelievable!"

Mary Brown was sixty or sixty-five, he said. He walked into her building, his eye caught sight of a nine-inch brass pipe, about an inch and a half thick, lying behind a door. "I picked it up, I don't know why, but I picked it up. I had gloves on." He paused. "Oh, this is terrible—"

"Were you sober?" Bottomly asked.

"I don't drink," DeSalvo replied, almost primly. Then: "I know you had to be drunk to do this one, but I wasn't." Unexpectedly, he said to Bottomly: "You're thinking this is so different from the rest, right? And you're saying to yourself, Well, this guy is trying to get a name for himself, why is he bringing in this one? He's better off to leave her out because she doesn't match—neither does the other one in Cambridge match. Right?" He looked challengingly at the tall man seated opposite him, almost like a child testing a teacher. "I could just as well forget about it—I don't have to explain nothing to you."

"That's right," said Bottomly, imperturbably. "You can do that with all of them, Al."

DeSalvo sighed. "I picked up the pipe, put it in my back pocket; I knock on her door. I tell her we got to paint the kitchen and I got to see it. There's a table there with a little yellow radio, to the right a refrigerator, a sink with brass faucets, a back door in the right back corner of the kitchen, when you look out the kitchen window you see a slate roof—" He rattled off these details as if compelled to prove beyond any doubt that he had been there, that he had committed this untypical Strangler murder—

"As she walked from the kitchen, her back to me, I hit her right on the back of the head with the pipe. She went down. She had on a blue square-print housedress with buttons—she was gray-haired, a big woman. Her things were ripped open, her busts were exposed." Again, the description of events taking place as of their own accord. "I got a sheet from a chair and covered her. I kept hitting her and hitting her . . ." His voice faltered. "This is terrible . . . because her head felt—it felt like it was all gone. Terrible!" He rubbed his hand over his face and began again. He found himself with a fork in his pocket. Perhaps he had picked it up from the kitchen table. He wasn't sure. "I remember stabbing her in the bust, the right one . . . and leaving it in her."

With an effort, Bottomly recalled that Mary Brown had difficulty sleeping in a bed because of asthma. She found it easier to doze off at night seated upright in a living room chair covered with a bed sheet. Could anyone but her murderer know that a sheet was on the chair? Would not anyone else have said he got the sheet from a drawer or a closet?

"That sheet you covered her with must have been bloody," he said aloud.

"Oh, was it, my God!"

"Were you upset? Did you check your clothes for blood?"

"No," muttered DeSalvo, almost as if to himself. Then, again, emotionally: "Oh, it was really bad . . . My God!"

Bottomly did his best to keep the recital flowing in chronological order, although it was difficult because DeSalvo might or might not go into one murder or the other, as the mood was upon him. Many of his replies were as circuitous as those of a patient on a psychoanalyst's couch: one image would lead to another one, having no relationship to the first; and this would often serve to sharpen details that had been blurred earlier.

Each time a session opened, DeSalvo ran through the roll call of his victims under his breath until he reached a woman he had not yet discussed. At one session he suddenly remembered that a week before Anna Slesers he had almost strangled a girl in her Boston apartment. She was Scandinavian, she had long dark hair like Irmgard. "I looked in a mirror in the bedroom and there was me—strangling somebody! I fell on my knees and I crossed myself and I prayed, 'Oh, God, what am I doing? I'm a married man, I'm the father of two children. Oh, God, help me!' " The words came out in a rush. "Oh, I got out of there fast. It wasn't like it was me, Mr. Bottomly—it was like it was someone else I was watching. I just took off."

Now he spoke about Joann Graff, the shy pattern designer in Lawrence.

"I was in Lawrence maybe two months before the Graff thing," he said. "You don't know where you're going, you're just driving around, and I see I'm in Lawrence and I spot this building." It was on Essex Street, across the street from Joann Graff. "I saw a woman's figure, she was about thirty or thirty-five, in a third-floor window. It stuck in my mind. So this time, two months later, when I come back through Lawrence, I go to this building and up to the third floor where this woman lived, but nobody was there."

He came down and wandered across the street into Joann's building, and glanced at the names on the mailboxes. Many were commercial; one was a union headquarters. "I spotted her name. I didn't know who she was, what she looked like, but it was the only single girl's name, all the others were businesses or married couples. It was the only logical name, right? The apartments weren't numbered, so I didn't know which one was hers." He climbed the stairs and rapped at random at one door. "A guy opened it. Naturally I didn't want to talk to a man," DeSalvo said. "I kept my hand over my face. I said, 'Can you tell me where Joann Graff lives?' "

Bottomly remembered the story told by Kenneth Rowe, the twenty-two-year-old engineering student who lived on the floor above Joann Graff, and who was waiting for his wife to return from the Laundromat that Saturday afternoon.

"So this guy points to an apartment across the hall and says, 'You see that apartment there?—it's the same one down one flight.'" DeSalvo went on: "I kept my hand over my face and kept talking and walking away at the same time, I just kept going. I wanted to get away from him, period."

Once he got to the floor below, he knocked on Joann's door. She opened it slightly: "The super sent me to do work in the apartment," he said. Joann was nervous about letting him in, "but I kept talking to her; I said there was repairs to be done in the bathroom, and she said she didn't know about it and who sent me? I said again, the super. So she finally let me in. It was a one-room apartment." He spoke disdainfully. "It was a very cheap apartment with really cheap furniture—even the Salvation Army wouldn't take it. Just like she was living out of a suitcase. The kitchen was terrible, the flooring was very bad—"

Joann wore a leotard with something over it, he said. He walked directly to the bathroom, she following him. "But she wouldn't go into it at first. So I said, 'See, that's bad.'" Joann stood outside the bathroom, looking in. "What is?" she asked. DeSalvo said, rebukingly, "Well, look at it—I mean, this is your place. If you want it fixed, then I'll fix it for you. If you don't want it fixed, I'll leave right now—"

"Well," she said, "I'm expecting some company. Somebody's coming to pick me up for dinner."

Finally, she took two or three reluctant steps into the bathroom, and he cornered her. She tried to fight her way out; he grabbed her; "'Don't scream and I won't hurt you . . . Now, walk over to the bed.' That's when she walked from the bathroom to the bed."

"How'd you keep her from screaming? Or was she too scared?"

"I had a knife," said DeSalvo. "Now, here's what happened. I says, 'I'm going to tie you up.' She didn't want no part of being tied up. She was lying first on the bed, and she refused to allow me to tie her up. I put the knife away—I let her get up—somebody went by the door outside, I told her to be quiet, she was standing up, she turned around, and I put my hand right around her neck and pulled her backwards on the bed, and we fell on the bed, she was on top of me . . . and she passed out. I got from underneath her, I took off her clothes, I ripped off her blouse. Her busts were large, thirty-eight, very smooth—hefty, well-built, beautiful body, but she had no face." He was completely matter-of-fact. "Five feet six and a half . . . I'm sure I stripped her naked. That's how I see her in my mind, her head, the bed not made up, the legs over the edge of the bed toward the door.

"I played with her busts. I know I possibly may have bitten her—not to draw blood," he said hastily. "Possibly on her body. I just had intercourse with her, and that was it." He thought for a moment. "It was very fast—all over within a matter of probably ten minutes, maybe fifteen, from the time I went in. It only took two minutes at most to talk to her, right? It only took about a minute, a minute and a half, to get her to the bed, right?"

Bottomly could not help observing dryly, "And you were ready?"

"Well, when you say you were ready—this word 'ready' —any way you want to use it, it happened," DeSalvo said, with a hint of annoyance in his voice. "No matter how it happened, it happened." Then he paused. When he grabbed her, he said, "at the same time the leotards came off and went tight around her neck."

"This seems a blur in your mind?"

It was, he said. He added, "There is a possibility that a stocking was around her neck." He remembered that when he was about to leave the apartment—it had all been so fast because of the visitor she expected—he opened the door just as a man was coming down the stairs. He closed the door silently, waited, then opened it, left the building, and drove home to Malden—about forty minutes. Then, "I had supper, washed up, played with the kids until about eight o'clock, put them to bed, sat down and watched TV—it came over about her."

"Did you get any kick when news of Graff broke?" Bottomly asked, thinking, *I had supper, washed up, played with the kids, watched TV* . . .

DeSalvo said no. "I knew it was me. I didn't want to believe it. It's so difficult to explain to you. I knew it was me who did it, but why I did it and everything else—I don't know why. I was not excited, I didn't think about it; I sat down to dinner and didn't think about it at all."

He was vague about the date. Bottomly tried to lead him into an association between the date of Joann's death and the assassination of President Kennedy the day before. How had DeSalvo felt when he heard of the President's death?

"I cried," he said. He was then employed by Highland Contractors, and had been sent with another workman to put in a new retaining wall in a factory near Andover. "I went across the street to the Dairy Maid to get two milkshakes" for himself and his companion "when people started talking about how the President was shot—then, that he was dead. I just stood there and cried." He stopped for a moment now, thinking hard. "Could the President be killed that day and I went out and still did something? Could I have shot out that way toward Lawrence that day, that afternoon? I heard someone say later it wasn't bad enough the President died but someone had to strangle somebody . . ." He seemed confused. "To me, I think that day, it could be the Graff girl . . ." But later he realized that he had attacked her the following day, Saturday, November 23.

"That Graff thing—" Albert DeSalvo stared at the wall. "It was so senseless that it makes sense, y'know?" And again, the refrain: "To me it's so unrealistic as to why these things occur."

Outside, in the corridor, one heard the footsteps of the keepers making their rounds—powerful, massive men with jangling keys at their belts—and the indistinct sound of hundreds of men shuffling all through the day in the huge wards. Bottomly had seen them—men vacant-eyed, lost in their own world, insane men, each in his faded gray denim shirt and trousers and slippers.

Who was next? Bottomly had asked, and DeSalvo, going through the list of the murdered, snapped his fingers. "That must be the one in Salem—Evelyn Corbett."

To Bottomly, DeSalvo's repeated failure to get Evelyn Corbin's name right seemed the final indignity. The man had killed her and yet could not fix her name in his mind.

"Yeah," Albert was saying. In essence he told the same story that had been elicited from him under hypnoanalysis, save that he now went into the actual killing. Twenty minutes before he entered Evelyn's apartment house at 224 Lafayette Street, Salem, that busy Sunday morning, he had walked into a nearby building. "I talked to an old lady on the second floor over a store but I didn't go in—I heard voices from inside, so I took off."

Then he walked into No. 224. He glanced at the names under the bells, saw a single woman's name, rang her bell. A moment later, the door clicked open, he entered, walked down the hall, and knocked on Evelyn Corbin's door.

"Who is it?" came a woman's voice. "What do you want?"

"I have to do some work in your apartment," DeSalvo said.

After a moment, the door opened a few inches and Evelyn

peered out uncertainly. DeSalvo turned on his most winning smile. "There's water seeping through your windows, and I want to check for stains behind the curtains."

She let him in, apologizing for her caution. "You don't know who can be knocking on your door these days." Then she added, in an attempt at lightness, "How do I know you're not the Boston Strangler?"

"Look, if you want me to leave, I'll leave—" DeSalvo said. But he kept talking, "and I won her confidence. She was a small woman, about five feet five—she had a thirty-four-A bust. . . . I went in with her and she said she didn't have much time, she was getting ready to go to church." In the bathroom, as she was complaining of the peeling paint, he suddenly put his knife to her: "Be quiet and I won't hurt you." He ordered her into the bedroom. She began to cry. "I can't do anything—I'm under doctor's orders."

DeSalvo said, "I was going to do it to her anyway, but she was all in tears; she said she'd do it the other way." He sat on the edge of her bed, she took a pillow from the bed, put it on the floor next to the bed and kneeled on it, and it was done. "She got up . . . the next thing I know I had strangled her." He said it almost wonderingly. She had turned her back to him to replace the pillow, and he grabbed her. He tied her hands in front at the wrists with a pair of her nylon stockings. "I got on top of her, sitting on her hands. I put the pillow on top of her face so I couldn't look at her face . . . Her chin was partly showing . . . I strangled her manually." Silence, for a moment. "She did try to bounce me off. She couldn't do it, and then she didn't breathe anymore. She didn't move anymore."

"How did you keep her quiet when you tied her hands?"

"She promised not to make a sound. I told her when I left I'd tell someone she was tied up in there. 'You give me time to go,' I said." At one point, he thought he took another pair of nylon stockings from a dresser drawer and put them around her neck. "I must have cut her hands loose later—"

He left. No one paid any attention to him.

In the silence, Bottomly said, "You know, there is one you missed."

DeSalvo looked at him uncertainly. He began muttering the names again. "Brown, Graff . . . which one . . . Oh, Jesus!" He remembered who it was. "I don't want to talk about her." It was Beverly Samans, in Cambridge. She had been killed before Joann Graff and Evelyn Corbin. "I don't want to." Was it because of the brutality, Bottomly wondered? Beverly had been viciously stabbed, again and again. Death had come from these wounds, not from strangling. Yet DeSalvo had talked about Mary Brown, beaten to death.

"I just don't want to talk about it now," DeSalvo said stubbornly.

About Mary Sullivan, then? There were left only three —Beverly Samans, Mary Sullivan, and the unidentified eighty-year-old woman DeSalvo said had died of a heart attack in his arms sometime in 1962; and Mary Sullivan was the last one, the most recent one—January 4, 1964.

"I don't want to talk about her, either," DeSalvo said. Why? "I say to myself it could of been my daughter, too. Mary Sullivan—oh, that bothers me a lot." Suddenly: "I wish I was dead!"

"Albert, you must talk—"

He nodded, heavily. All right. Mary Sullivan. He knew her apartment at 44A Charles Street so well—"If you want to know, I knew every apartment on Charles Street, I been in them all, in and out, so many times in the last seven years—" It was the same as in Cambridge. New girls moving in every semester, and as the Measuring Man he'd been in every apartment house.

He knocked on Mary's door midafternoon of Saturday, January 4, 1964. Mary opened it. "She had on blue jeans, short ones, with little ragged edges on the border, and a yellow blouse." She was preparing a meal, he thought, for when she came to the door she had a little knife in her hand, "like you use for peeling potatoes. I said, 'I came up to do some work in the apartment.' She said, 'I don't know anything about it. My roommates are out.'" But he could come in and show her what had to be done.

"We went into the kitchen—it looked like she was fixing the shelves there, but I didn't get too good a look at what was in the kitchen because that's where I put the knife to her. 'Don't scream and I won't hurt you,' I said. I took her into the bedroom. There were two twin beds there with backboards. I brought her first to the bed just next to the parlor door and I tied her wrists with some long dark thing—"

"A necktie?"

"No, a scarf of some kind." He described what might well have been the red ascot found in the toilet. "I tied her feet, also." He stopped, and began to mumble. "This is what bothers me—to talk about it. I don't want to talk about it."

"You've got to talk about it."

"I know it." He described how he put a gag in her mouth, then took a mustard-colored sweater and put it over her head. "I did it so she couldn't scream. Then she said, 'It's hot under this—I can't breathe too well—' "

"She talked to you all this time?" Bottomly's voice sounded incredulous. How could she have done this with a gag in her mouth?

"Wait a second," said DeSalvo, uncertainly. "She did talk to me—I'm trying to get this thing straight."

"What did she say to you?"

He tried to remember.

"Did she plead with you, 'Don't hurt me'?" Bottomly asked.

DeSalvo remained silent, thinking. Then, with an embarrassed giggle, speaking as if to himself: "I got to tell him—I got to tell him—" Aloud: "She did talk to me. I put that thing on her face, I covered it, I know she had no gag in her mouth, I just tied her hands in front of her and then while her hands were like this here"—he demonstrated, his wrists crossed on his stomach—"I got on top of her so she could not be in any position, you know, to reach up and scratch me. . . . I . . . strangled her." His voice was dying away, but the last words were clear.

George McGrath, who had been forced to miss several earlier sessions, asked, "While she was lying on her back?"

"Yes."

"You have the gag in her mouth now?" he pursued.

"No." The word was hardly said, almost under his breath.

Bottomly: "You just have that thing over her head?"

DeSalvo sighed assent.

"She still has her clothes on?" Yes, he said. "And this is before or after you tied her feet?"

DeSalvo sighed again. "It was after." Then: "This is what I don't like to talk about." Silence. "The whole thing was . . . hands like this here"—again he demonstrated—"crossed, her feet tied right here, at ankles, right about here, her hands were tied here, and I straddled her so that her hands . . . I was sitting on them, really, because she was really fighting viciously, trying to get up . . . you know . . . for life . . ."

McGrath asked, "When did you get her clothes off, Albert? You strangled her with her clothes still on?" He said yes.

As the questioning by both men proceeded, he grew more nervous, more embarrassed. Finally he burst out, "You know—this is—I hate to confuse you people—this is what I hate to even talk about. This is killing me even to talk to you people. I'd just as soon forget the whole thing." All this was said jerkily, with nervous giggles. "But listen, here's what it is." Again he described how he had put her on the bed, placed the sweater over her head; she complained she could not breathe too well. "She was still alive when I had intercourse with her, she was alive, she allowed me to do it to her, y'understand me? I was mixed up at the time, but I did strangle her—with my two hands."

McGrath: "Face to face?"

DeSalvo demurred. "Well, no—when you say face to face—"

McGrath: "Her face was facing you, but she has the sweater over her head—"

DeSalvo: "—so I couldn't see her—"

McGrath: "—and you strangled her by using your thumbs against her—"

DeSalvo: "—throat."

McGrath: "—her Adam's apple, right? In the front?"

DeSalvo: "Yes."

He was sure of it. But he was confused—had he had intercourse with her before or after removing her clothes? He remembered taking her to the other bed, "and I do recall ejaculating over there."

Bottomly: "A second time?" DeSalvo said yes.

Slowly the full story came out. He tied her up on the first bed, using the ascot to bind her crossed wrists, ripped off most of her clothes, put the sweater over her head, had intercourse with her with the sweater over her head "so I could not see her face," strangled her, cut the ascot from her wrists with the paring knife, took the ascot—now in three parts—into the bathroom, flushed it down the toilet, returned to Mary, carried her to the second bed, removed her sweater, placed her on her back, straddled her facing her, masturbated so the semen struck her face, put the nylon stockings and blouse about her neck . . .

In the silence Bottomly managed to ask: How much time had elasped? DeSalvo was not sure. "It could have been fifteen minutes, it could have been five."

"Were you all heated up again?" Bottomly asked.

"I don't think I was ever unheated . . . It was just that a different person altogether—"

"Was it like Nina Nichols?"

"It was all the same thing, always the same feeling," DeSalvo said. He spoke with resignation in his voice. "You was there, these things were going on and the feeling after I got out of that apartment was as if it never happened. I got out and downstairs, and you could of said you saw me upstairs and as far as I was concerned, it wasn't me. I can't explain it to you any other way. It's just so unreal . . . I was there, it was done, and yet if you talked to me an hour later, or half hour later, it didn't mean nothing, it just didn't mean nothing—"

Bottomly said, "Mary Sullivan was the last one. It should be the easiest to remember in point of time but it's the hardest to remember because you don't want to remember. Isn't that right, Albert?"

"This could be possible," he said slowly. "I mean, it's just as if you were coming out of something, you understand me? This is the hardest one for me because—well, I'm realizing that these things are true, and that these things that I did do, that I have read in books about, that other people do, that I didn't think or realize I would ever do these things."

Where had he read about "these things"? McGrath asked.

In "detective books—I read a lot of sexy stuff." When? The only time he read the "sexy stuff" was when he was in jail from May 1961 to April 1962.

McGrath, too, in the sessions he had attended, had been time and again affected by a sense of unreality. Here sat De-Salvo, now leaning forward, a hand across his brow, eyes closed, industriously trying to remember—murder. On one occasion he had offered a roll of mints to both men. "Anyone want a peppermint?" he had asked.

For fourteen years McGrath had been Chief Social Investigator for the Shelden and Eleanor Glueck Research Project in Delinquency and Crime, sponsored by the Harvard Law School. In his work then and since he had interviewed virtually thousands of criminals. Albert was atypical in that he never wavered in his story. This was not true of most criminals. Questioned, they were ready to concede this point or that, if only to avoid the stress of insisting on the truth. McGrath thought that DeSalvo talked both freely and convincingly; he was not dominated by Bottomly, he did not fawn, he was not trying to please either man.

McGrath, listening, recalled his first interview with him. It had been in Bridgewater on March 8, two days after he had been appointed his guardian. Joe, Albert's oldest brother, who had been simultaneously named guardian for Albert's estate, was visiting him when McGrath arrived. The three had talked together for several hours.

Joe, short, heavyset, quick-thinking, had said, "Al used to come over to see me. He could never sit still. He always had to be going. I knew he was going off—as far as sex was concerned, I knew his problem because I got it too—we both need a lot. But," said Joe, "when I learned it got so he was carrying a knife, I knew he needed some kind of help, he was sick, he was dangerous."

McGrath had come away then with a picture of Albert DeSalvo as a man who required an unusual number of sexual experiences to be satisfied.

Now, Bottomly asked, unexpectedly, "Ever strangle anyone in Germany, Albert?"

DeSalvo shook his head.

"But you had a lot of sex exercise over there?"

DeSalvo said in a matter-of-fact voice, "Anybody did who went to Europe. That was common for any GI . . . no more than what you can make out with. In Europe there was all you wanted." Not only German girls—American girls, too.

In 1959 he and Irmgard had returned to Germany for a two-month vacation so that Irmgard could spend some time with her parents. In Germany, he robbed a number of cafes, so he had plenty of money. "I knew where they kept their cash and to me it was nothing—"

"Like taking candy from a baby?" Bottomly suggested wryly.

DeSalvo was not amused. "Irm made it a point while we were there that there'd be no sex, period. So you sure as hell know that I had my sex while I was there." He had gone about the U.S. Army post exchanges posing as a representative of the *Stars and Stripes,* selecting girls for the Army's "Best Sweetheart of All" contest. The prize was a trip to Italy. There was, of course, no such contest. He would visit the post exchanges between eight and twelve o'clock, when the girls were on duty, take their measurements, and tell them, "A man will come down and take your photograph this afternoon," adding, "If you really want to make out, I'll come down myself the first thing this afternoon and I'll make sure you get first prize." He was kept quite busy, he said. While Irmgard stayed with her parents he had driven all over Germany. After he had worked one Army area, he went to another— "I moved right to the Russian border and all the way back." He was never caught. "I was always able to spot anybody spotting me. It always came to me if I was being watched, and then I'd do nothing." He could not explain how he sensed such things.

Slowly Bottomly brought him back to Mary Sullivan. There was more that had to be told. It was not easy for DeSalvo to tell it. He squirmed uncomfortably in his chair. He struggled for words. It seemed to McGrath, as he listened, that DeSalvo had never really integrated these experiences, these murders, into his consciousness. He had kept them outside himself, and thus had been able to maintain a kind of mental health—had been able to report them as things done by someone whom he recognized was himself yet not done by himself. Now it was torture for him to relive these events: he sank back in his chair, he moved forward, he covered his face with his hands, perspiration broke out on his forehead . . . How far dare we push him, McGrath thought, before he cracks? Both McGrath and Bottomly realized they must guard against this for then it might never again be possible to interrogate him; yet they must learn as much detail as they could for purposes of verification.

Yes, said DeSalvo, finally. There was something else. He had "done something" with a broom. He did not understand why. "Still, I feel I did not insert it, at least I hope I didn't, to hurt her insides. You might say, 'What do you mean, hurt her insides? She's dead anyhow.' But it still—it's—it's to me a vicious thing."

He wore gloves. He went on reluctantly: "After I did everything to her, right, and as I put my gloves on so I'd leave no prints, so when I went by the door I wouldn't touch the door—as I was going out the broom happened to be there and I picked up the broom and did that . . ." His voice began to tremble. "Mary Sullivan was the last one. I never did it again. I never killed anyone after that. I only tied them up, I didn't hurt them . . . Once in Cambridge I was in three places in a row after that and I started to cry and I said, 'I'm sorry, I don't know why I'm here,' and I took off.

"My wife was treating me better, I was building up, you might say, my better self, the better side of me, I was very good at my job, they liked me, I got two raises . . ."

22

Through the weeks DeSalvo had been telling his story.

Why had he confessed at all? Bottomly asked. And why had he waited so long? Why had he not confessed months before, when he was seized as the Green Man?

"I trust you now," said DeSalvo, and because he did, he would tell him exactly how it was. He had read the *Record American* series by the two girls, he had seen the earlier newspaper appeal to the Strangler to turn himself in, but—"I got a wife and children. I didn't understand what was happening to me but I also knew what happens to you if these things are brought out and how you can be put away for the rest of your life." He had read a statement by Bottomly that the Strangler would be sent to a mental institution if he gave himself up, but he had also read another statement, made by Governor Peabody, who said that though he was against capital punishment he might consider the Boston Strangler "an exception." So he did nothing.

Yet the need to tell was growing all the time. Once he had been about to confess to a detective lieutenant in Cambridge. "I thought he might want to do right by me but he could be pushed against the wall by a superior, thinking of promotions," so he decided not to take the risk. "But you, Mr. Bottomly, I saw that nobody's going to push you around, so that's why I'm telling you everything."

Bottomly nodded noncommittally and DeSalvo began with his arrest in November 1964. One morning Detective Sergeant Duncan McNeill of Malden telephoned and left word with Irmgard to have him call back when he came home from work. DeSalvo did not know it but his photograph had led police to believe he was the man who had tied up and assaulted the twenty-year-old bride in Cambridge.

324

He had called back that evening. Sergeant McNeill said, "I'd like to talk to you, DeSalvo."

"About what?" Albert had asked. "Well, you come down to headquarters tomorrow at East Cambridge and we'll discuss it," McNeill said. Albert wanted to know again what it was about, and McNeill finally said, "It's about an assault on a woman."

"When he said that," DeSalvo said to Bottomly, "I looked at my wife. She was crying, sitting near me and the telephone. I knew she was crying and vomiting all day, ever since the call came that morning. I couldn't see her cry any more. She was crying her eyes out, all red—she said, 'Al, are you in trouble again?'

"I held my hand over the mouthpiece. 'Don't you worry,' I said. 'I'll take care of it.' I remembered Irm standing at the top of the stairs so many times and saying when I came home, 'Where were you?' and vomiting all day. I knew I couldn't go on any longer. I told the detective, 'Look, I'm coming down tonight.'

"He says, 'What do you mean?'

"I says, 'I'm going to come down now. Tomorrow might be too late. I want to get it all cleared up.' He didn't know what I meant, but I knew. I knew deep down this was the way it must end, I think I knew it from the very beginning. My little girl was getting bigger. I couldn't stand seeing my wife in that state . . . It just wasn't worth it. These things happened, I knew it, yet I couldn't exactly make myself believe I did it."

Bottomly asked, "Did you ever think of going to a psychiatrist?"

"I went to one in 1961," Albert replied. "It was the hardest thing to go look for help. I told him about the drive I had and he told me it's up to me. I couldn't help myself. I was the Measuring Man then. I'd go into apartments day after day. I used to know the police were right there—some of the women complained—three or four patrol cars shooting right by me, looking for me, and yet I still got out of my car and walked right in front of them and did these things, knowing they were there."

Wasn't he afraid of being caught?

"I didn't think of being caught. As the Measuring Man I wasn't really doing anything wrong. When I started, I went all through Boston, Back Bay, inside and out. I used to go up these streets so many times, I knew every apartment inside out and backwards. I'd walk in, early in the morning, there'd be three or four girls just waking up, half-awake. I'd say,

'Let's go! Wake up!' " He clapped his hands smartly. " 'I'll go down and get the doughnuts, I'll be right back, get the coffee on, girls, get the coffee on!' I'd shoot down the street, bring back half a dozen doughnuts. By the time I got back they'd have the coffee going. They'd be jumping around just scanty, or wearing baby dolls—and I was enjoying myself." He would go from one apartment to another, talk to them about modeling. "One girl would send me to another, I'd start measuring her, playing with her—soon I had her." Pause. Modestly: "I got a lot free."

He was then working the three to eleven P.M. shift at the American Biltright Rubber Company in Chelsea. When he found himself put on the seven A.M. to three P.M. shift, he was just as successful in the afternoon. "From work I'd shoot over the Mystic River Bridge, took me into Boston in five minutes. I'm not there more than an hour—I'd shoot right back, so I'm home in Malden by four. All my things were done in a matter of ten or fifteen minutes—bing! bing! All apartments, all young girls. Be there about three-ten—work that area in twenty minutes—I'd get a piece right away—be back home by quarter of four sometimes." Irmgard, he said, was keeping a close watch on him, "so I had to work fast." If he spent too much time in Boston, he would get caught in the bridge traffic going home—"and I wanted to be home before four or four-fifteen, latest."

He had been speaking animatedly. But now, as though suddenly remembering, his voice dropped. "Still, I could not stop what I was doing. This thing building up in me—all the time—I knew I was getting out of control."

"Were you ever afraid you'd hurt your wife?" Bottomly asked, thinking of the extraordinary exchange months earlier between DeSalvo and Dr. Bryan, the hypnoanalyst.

"You mean, like strangle her?" If his reference under hypnosis to Irmgard's great fear of being touched about the neck was any key to his motivation, he was not reacting here. He simply shook his head. "In her own way she was hurting me more than anything. If she'd given me the proper sex I wanted, at least treated me like a person and not degraded me all these times, I wouldn't be going out to find out if I was a man or not." Why had he not taken it out on her? Bottomly asked. Was he afraid he'd lose her?

He nodded. "Even at this moment, I love her more than anything else in this world. I'm willing to do anything to see she's well taken care of. The most important factor—I treated her too good. The worse she treated me, the more I did, the less she respected me. If she only gave me her love

. . . 'I used my sex to hurt you,' she told me. I couldn't understand why she, who I loved, treated me like dirt. She'd say, 'Don't go out at night—' For two, three years, I didn't. I stopped bowling. She once said, 'Don't ever leave me—you're the only one I know in this country.' I did everything for her." He mused silently, wretchedly.

"In 1955 Judy was born when we were at Fort Dix. My wife called me to her bed. She had what they call natural childbirth. 'The pain I went through,' she told me. 'Al, I'll kill myself if I have another baby. Promise me, Al, no more babies.' I promised her. Six weeks pass and I notice one of Judy's legs is shorter than the other, and her legs wouldn't open. Then we brought a doctor in. He told my wife—she was alone, I wasn't with her, she couldn't understand English too much—he says, 'Your daughter will never walk again in her life.' You can figure out how my wife felt. They put Judy in a frog-type splint, the doctor says, 'Take your thumbs, put them between her legs and keep massaging them.' We did this for the first two or three months until my thumbs almost went right through her body. Her skin was so raw. We kept doing this night after night, staying up, changing her diapers . . . My wife and I worked together."

But from then on, "There was no more for me. It was always Judy, always Judy, and this went on for one year, then two years. There was nothing there for me. So I cut out. My brother said to Irm, 'Al's cutting up.' The way she was treating me would hurt anyone's ego. I was like any other normal guy, trying to make out.

"I asked the doctor. 'She's so frigid,' I said. But she was afraid to have sex because we might have babies. She said, 'Our next baby might be born without arms'—like what happened to one of her girl friends. She said to me, 'If we're going to have any sex, I'll let you know.'" His voice was heavy with sarcasm. "She'll let me know! I used to think, what's wrong with me? Am I undersexed or oversexed or what? I bought some Kinsey books and read them. I wanted her to read them. She said 'I don't want to read that kind of stuff.' I said, 'Well, let's go to the doctor, let's talk this over.' But she don't want to hear nothing."

In the little room DeSalvo wrung his hands.

"How can I be all wrong, Mr. Bottomly? Even her own girl friend told Irm, 'You know damn well Al was stealing and you accepted all that money in 1961.' Irm wanted to go back to Germany when they put me in jail. Then when I came out she says, 'If you ever get in trouble again I'm taking the children and I'm leaving you and never come back.'

"It's like my mother says: 'If this woman loved you—if your father loved me like you loved your wife—even though your father did what he did to your sisters and me—I still would have forgave him and loved him. You washed the floors, you did all the work in the house, you did everything for her—that's what killed it. You were too good to her.' My mother told me that, Mr. Bottomly; can I be all wrong?"

On a Sunday morning in August Albert's mother had visited him. She was a heavyset woman, of fifty-five. From childhood poor eyesight had forced her to wear thick glasses. Now she was virtually blind, but in her son's presence attempted to hide the fact. As Albert told Bottomly later, "I tested her. You see, I *know* she's blind, but she won't let on to me. So I tested her. 'Gee, Ma,' I said, 'your hair looks beautiful. You had it fixed. How do you like mine?' She says, 'I like it the way you got it nice and short.' Is my hair short?"

"No," said Bottomly.

"But last time she was here, my hair was short, and she knew it."

They had talked together, with long periods of silence. Of her four sons, Albert had always been her favorite. He had been more attentive to her, more considerate, going out of his way to drop in to see her, even if only for a few minutes. Now she said to him, almost coaxingly, "Tell me something. You didn't hurt anybody?"

Albert, telling the story to Bottomly, said, "That's what's killing me. Her saying, 'You didn't hurt anybody.'"

He had looked at his mother sorrowfully. "Ma, where you been?"

She had said, "But it can't be you. I've been thinking back about your childhood, your growing up, how good a son you were, how good a husband you were to your wife—it can't be you. I don't think you could hurt anybody."

Albert had said, "Ma, I can't answer you, I can't answer you or anyone, but in a little while the truth will come out, and whatever it may be I've got to tell it."

His mother had shaken her head. "I'm not going to believe it's you. If you did do it, if you get the proper treatment, they'll find out how it did happen, and they'll find a reason—if you did do it. There must be a reason."

"Okay, Ma," Albert had said. He had put his arm around her. "Okay."

DeSalvo rose and paced back and forth. He dug into the pocket of his beltless, faded gray trousers and brought forth a battered wallet from which he pulled out a snapshot. It was of his daughter Judy and his son Michael—dark-haired, smiling children. "My little girl's eleven," he said. "Michael's going on seven. Some day they'll know the true story. When my daughter gets married, they'll ask, 'Who's your father? The Boston Strangler—'" He replaced the snapshot. "Don't you think I know what it means?" he said in a despairing voice. Then: "It's true, it's true. I wish it wasn't. Maybe it'll help society. Maybe they'll learn something from this—"

What would it do to his family, he asked, rhetorically. "My brother Frank, he's very immature. He said to me, 'You're all washed up.' I said, 'What do you mean? I'm not washed up. I still have to live my life in this institution.'" His sisters, Albert went on, were very concerned. "They think that I'm going to involve them. . . ."

He had not seen his father for twenty years, he said. Then they met one evening, his father took him to dinner and offered to buy him a car. Albert told him, he said, "I don't ever want to see you again. Do you think you can buy my love now?"

He had heard that his father was very concerned. "My brother came down last Sunday and told me. I said, 'Maybe this is some way God has of shooting the works to him now for what he did to his children.'" DeSalvo thought bitterly about this for a moment. Then the words came out in a rush: "I saw my father knock my mother's teeth out and then break every one of her fingers. I must have been seven. Ma was laid out under the sink—I watched it. He knocked all her teeth out. Pa was a plumber, he smashed me once across the back with a pipe. I just didn't move fast enough. He once sold me and my two sisters for nine dollars, sold us to some farmer in Maine. No one knew what happened to us. For six months Ma hunted for us and couldn't find us.

"My father—" DeSalvo spoke dully. "We used to have to stand in front of him, my brother Frank and me, every night and be beaten with his belt. I can still to this very moment tell you the color of the belt and just how long it was—two inches by 36—a belt with a big buckle on it. We used to stand in front of him every night and get beaten with that damn thing—every night, whether we did anything wrong or not. We were only in the fourth or fifth grade . . ."

Bottomly had been listening to this recital with growing horror. He could only ask now, "Was he drunk?"

"He was feeling good," DeSalvo said indifferently. "And he used to take my younger brother, Dickie, my mother will tell you this, took him, picked him right up and smashed him against the wall. My father used to go around with prostitutes in front of us . . . My sisters always had blacked eyes . . . My mother had a hard life. Six kids to bring up, and she was working all the time . . . When you're under the environment of sex all day long . . . You go up on the roof of our building and there'd be a couch up there . . . They'd give you a quarter and say, 'Beat it, kid.' . . . Always in the bedroom something being done . . .

"I'm starting to realize what I'm really involved in." He moved from one subject to another as they occurred to him. "I knew what I had to do, but I never knew the true consequences. I'm not going to back down. I told Frank, 'You tell Ma I don't care if I get the chair. I've got to go through with it. I just got to go through with it all the way.' "

Bottomly said, "You're taking a great risk." He pointed out that DeSalvo's plea in a trial would undoubtedly be not guilty by reason of insanity, but there was always the possibility that a jury would refuse to believe the defense medical testimony and find him guilty.

DeSalvo sighed. "There's no problem there because I figure, what good am I anyhow? If you're going to die for telling the truth, to hell with it. You only live once."

"Well," remarked Bottomly, "you've reached a point where you've got to get this off your chest—"

"One way or the other," DeSalvo said. "What good am I alive? If there's any way of curing me—" He knew that those with money could always buy their way out of trouble, that they could pay for medical help to cure themselves if they could be cured. But—"if the rich people live and the poor people die, then I die. There'll be other people coming along." He brooded for a moment. "What made me do it, and why? At least if the doctors find this out, it's something to give my kids. Even though I knew my father did what he did, I wanted him to love me. I want my son to love me . . . Because I think there's a lot more involved than just being a rape artist and cutting out and stealing . . . What really happened to me? This is what I can't understand."

Again he was silent, sitting at the table, chin in hand. "It's true, God knows it's all true. I wish it wasn't. I don't want to be the person who did these things. There's no rhyme or reason to it. I'm not a man who can hurt anyone—I can't do it. I'm very emotional. I break up at the least thing. I can't hurt anyone and here I'm doing the things I did . . ." Suddenly he burst out, "Thank God they had no loved ones, no children—all single women. I can be very thankful for that . . . But, still and all, a life is a life."

Later.

DeSalvo, to Bottomly: "Mr. Bottomly, how do the police feel toward this person?"

Bottomly said, "I think it's a tragedy. There's no other way to put it. It happened. You killed people. We can't undo that. You don't know why. We don't know why. Maybe the medical profession can figure it out. Maybe you can be rehabilitated."

"I'm not even looking to be free," DeSalvo said heavily.

"With your mind and ambition—you're a very intelligent fellow basically, Albert—"

"Do you know what my I.Q. is?" DeSalvo interrupted him. "I was told it's seventy."

DeSalvo was indignant. "Oh, no. It's a hundred and twenty-five, a hundred and thirty."

"With your mind and ambition you might make quite a contribution, even in an institution," Bottomly went on. Had he ever seen the film "Birdman of Alcatraz?" * DeSalvo had not, and Bottomly summarized the story of Robert Stroud, murderer of two men, sentenced to prison for life, into whose cell one day a crippled bird flew, and how he devoted the rest of his life to a study of birds, taught himself to cure them of disease, even to operate upon them, and became such an authority that he wrote a treatise used as a textbook.

DeSalvo devoured this, his eyes shining. He was all eagerness. "Mr. Bottomly, right now I shave all the old men, I wash them up—I could help these people, give them a better life. Even if I may never be released, I'll be doing something for them. I could help younger kids coming in here, seventeen, eighteen, give them the better outlook on life. Not things like teaching them how to blow a safe—I don't want to hear that kind of talk. There's a good world out there—I got off the track. Why, I don't know but I'm going to do everything to find out so some day my children won't look at me in shame and disgrace." He thought for a moment, and then in a voice reflective and surprisingly modest, said, "I think I have a fairly decent attitude towards this whole thing. I still think I can make a contribution. Many people have died for a good cause. I think these people may not have died in vain."

When Bottomly left Bridgewater that day he was, for one of the few times in his life, at a loss for words to express precisely how he felt, and what emotions swept over him.

* Based on the book, *Birdman of Alcatraz*, Thomas E. Gaddis, Random House, Inc., New York, 1955.

Could there be any doubt now? Bottomly, Tuney, DiNatale agreed: Albert was the man.

There would have to be one more session with him. And perhaps, with it, more insight into DeSalvo.

23

Little by little the word seeped out. Somehow it became known in Chelsea and nearby Malden—the first, the town in which he had grown up; the second, the town in which he had lived as a married man—that the mental patient at Bridgewater, the thirty-three-year-old laborer and father of two who claimed to be the Boston Strangler was Albert DeSalvo of 11 Florence Street Park, Malden.

Sitting in his office above the Reznik Drug Store at the corner of Broadway and Everett Street in Chelsea, Attorney Robert Sheinfeld was all but stunned. He did not know what to think. He had not seen Albert for some time but he had received a letter from him only a few months before, written from jail where Albert was awaiting trial as the Green Man. Albert was in difficulties again with the law, but there was nothing in what he had written to suggest that he was the Strangler. Or was there? Sheinfeld took the letter from Albert's file and read it again carefully. It was dated January 9, 1965. Five days later Albert was to be sent back to Bridgewater as incompetent to stand trial.

He had written:

Dear Mr. Sheinfeld,
    I feel I owe you this letter. I wanted very much that you take my case but I remembered what you told me if I ever get in trouble again don't bother you. So I have another attorney Mr. Jon A. Asgiersson, from Stoneham, my brother Joe gave me his name . . .

Well, thought Sheinfeld, Albert certainly had taken him at his word. When the police had seized him four years earlier trying to escape after failing to jimmy the door of an apartment in Cambridge, Sheinfeld had been completely out of patience. "What's the matter with you!" he had demanded. "Why did you run away from a lousy B and E? And get shot at? You could have been killed—and for what? I'm sick and tired of this. B and E, suspended sentence, put on probation, soon as probation ends, B and E again, suspended sentence, put on probation, and now this silly B and E again—" Sheinfeld, struck by a thought, had interrupted himself to ask abruptly, "This Measuring Man stuff, Albert—do you get a thrill touching these women? Is that why you do it?" Albert had denied anything like that. "Then you're not kidding me," Sheinfeld had said angrily. "It's just a front for your B and E. I've had it, Albert. You get in trouble again, don't bother me with it." Why would Albert risk death, shame himself, his wife and children, all for a petty housebreaking that might net a few dollars? Albert should know better and perhaps threatening to wash his hands of him might knock some sense into his head.

Sheinfeld read on:

> I'm not looking to get out of this trouble I am in but I am looking to be helped if I can be. I realize I am sick and have been for a long time. but I neaver knew how to ask for help. I was afriad and ashamed. how could I tell my wife I am oversexed and have a drive and urge I cannot control. even you Mr. Sheinfeld, when you had my case in 1961 in Cambridge involving all them women. you asked me if I got a thrill or feeling when I touched them. and I lyed to you and said no, because I was ashamed to admit it of my sex drive. But now its got out of hand, but still thank God I neaver got to hurt anyone.

Sheinfeld paused. Albert had written this *before* he had ever claimed to be the Strangler. Why should he now—months later—paint himself as a murderer?

> But I think the way I was going anything could have happen in time had I not been caught. I've been doing a lot of thinking—plus what the doctors have told me— that this had to come out one way or another somehow. my problem started way back in my childhood days. Mr. Sheinfeld, I want so bad to tell all I have inside me and *I have a lot*. My wife is still staying by me because she knows I am really sick and I am not lying but asking for help. Mr. Sheinfeld at Westboro State Hospital they treated me good, I saw a doctor just about every day.

They at least tried to help and find out what is really wrong or what kind of a problem a person has. I was hoping they could have sent me there. but they didn't. they sent me to Bridgewater State Hospital. At Bridgewater State Hospital Mr. Sheinfeld it's a shame all you do is to stay down there for 35 days and they send you back. I saw one doctor for about 1½ in the whole thirty-five days I was there. I filled out an answer sheet with 500 questions on it and from this they found me sane but recommend I be sent to Treatment Center. How can anyone find out in 1½ if a man is sane or not?

Mr. Sheinfeld, I no something is wrong with me. You no my family background and what my father was like and all the things he did. Mr. Sheinfeld, do you no of anyway I can be sent to a hospital where I can come clean with everything inside me. I don't care if I never come out but I want to no at least I am being helped. and maybe find out what made me be what I am and do all them bad things which I am so ashamed of. there is got to be some kind of explanation as to why this has all happen. If you could only no of the good and love I have given my wife and children. this is why she cant believe or understand why this has all happen. I tried being good and did everything to make her happy and children. Mr. Sheinfeld, the night this all happen. She cried and said Al how could you do this to me, you made me relove you all over again. So you see Mr. Sheinfeld I was trying with all my heart to be good but my drive got to bad I found myself relieving myself at least four and five times a day. it was so bad. but when I went out and did what I did that I am in here for it was so strange because it was like I was burning up inside and the feelings I was getting put me like a daze it would be like a dream I would not no where I was going but I was thinking and seeing a woman in my vision in front of me wondering what kind of a body she would have and so on. sometime before I even got anywhere I found myself sitting in the car while driving, already releaved. but in five min it came back again. I was all ready again. But when I did get a woman and she did what I asked her to after it was all over I cried and told her I was sorry please forgive me and the woman also told the police the same. they even said some of the women that they felt when I just got nexted to them, they had a feeling that I had just releaved myself because after that I just tied them up and left without even doing anything to them. its true I just put my hand on them and I was finished. and then realized again what I had done. in almost all the cases the women said more than half I didn't even touched them but tie them up and run whitch took only 3–5 min—so you see I was so build up by the time I found a woman I just got near her and I was releaved. I realize Mr. Sheinfeld that this may mean nothing to you but maybe some day someone else will come up to you with my same problem and you may be able to help him. if there is anything or in any way you can somehow help me. I'll give you my attorney I have allready told him about you but he said he would see you or call you.

Then came Asgiersson's name, address, and telephone number, printed in block letters.

I always did respect you Mr. Sheinfeld but I didn't no how to explain my problem you have always treated me better than good.

Albert DeSalvo

Then a postscript:

I went to the police station myself also Mr. Sheinfeld. I gave myself up to the police.

Sheinfeld stared again at the letter, written in a childlike hand, with its childlike misspellings, on blue-ruled school paper. When he first received it he had decided he could do nothing. Albert had hired another lawyer. It would not be proper for him to intrude himself into the case. But what *did* this letter mean? Granted, Albert had a sexual problem—his hunch *had* been right, then—but would this sort of thing make a man a murderer? And Albert had clearly written, "Thank God I neaver got to hurt anyone."

Sheinfeld could come to only one conclusion. Albert had always been terrified lest Irmgard leave him. Once he had asked the lawyer, "If a guy's insane, can his wife divorce him?" Sheinfeld, though taken aback, explained that Massachusetts law did not allow this.

There must lie the answer, thought Sheinfeld, the reason behind this entire masquerade. Albert, now locked up in Bridgewater with characters who probably knew something about the stranglings, must have thought, I'm in trouble again, if I'm insane they can't kill me, Irm can't divorce me, so I'll say these things, I'll make up this story . . .

The attorney, troubled, returned the letter to the file. If Albert proved to be the Strangler, he, Sheinfeld, would be the most flabbergasted man on earth. While he had no illusions about Albert—a petty thief, an incorrigible B and E man, an ingratiating con artist—certainly he was not a man given to violence, surely not a vicious killer, the murderer of thirteen women. As far as Sheinfeld knew, Albert had always been a perfect gentleman in the presence of women. When he had dropped into his office to make payments on his bill—even now he still owed four hundred dollars—he had always been courteous, gentle in manner, never fresh or insolent. Often there were women clients in the office. Albert's behavior at such times was above reproach. Miss Dunn, Sheinfeld's secretary, had remarked upon it, too—so likable a man, with his shy wife and lovely little girl upon whom he so obviously doted . . .

In Sheinfeld's home friends often admired an intricately carved, beautifully fashioned wooden jewel case. It was a gift from Albert. While still in the House of Correction, he had sent it to the lawyer with a note, on October 19, 1961, reading:

Dear Mr. Sheinfeld.

Sending you a package, while making my wife one I thought of you and thought maybe your wife would like one, so I went and made her one, please I'm making this out of the goodness of my heart. I learned to do so much in here. I work in the carpenter shop and learn to do so much with woods as you can see. its all done by hand buy me. also I've taken a course in math in here and doing a lot of studying not wasting my time. I'm okay, feeling fine. this is what I needed to wake me up. to bad you didn't do it the first time. you know what I mean. but I'll be okay now my wife comes up every week. you have always done me right the many talks we had together in your office, a person like you can never be forgotten. hoping this letter find you in good health.

Mr. Albert H. DeSalvo

"To bad you didn't do it the first time," Albert had written. The first time Sheinfeld defended Albert on a B and E charge was on St. Valentine's Day, 1958. Someone had broken into a Chelsea house and escaped with several silver dollars and change, some of the coins stained with red nail polish. Later that day police happened to walk into a confectionery store. There stood Albert pushing across the counter several coins stained with nail polish. He was buying a valentine for his wife and a box of candy for his little girl.

He admitted not only the burglary, but two other housebreakings that morning in which nothing had been taken. Sheinfeld made an eloquent plea. His client had served nearly ten years in the Army, he and his wife were both working, they had a crippled child, he was in debt because he had been playing the horses and numbers in an attempt to make money, but he was a good father and husband, he had learned his lesson . . . The prosecution agreed and Albert was let off with suspended sentences of one year on each of the three counts. Three years later, in 1961, when Albert was seized as the Measuring Man, Sheinfeld had told him, "The trouble with you is that you've only received suspended sentences. Maybe if you'd have had to serve thirty or sixty days on those first B and E's, you might have learned that you can't get away with such things."

Was this man a murderer? Sheinfeld could not believe it.

In Cambridge, in his basement office at the Third District Court, Robert Clifford mulled over the same question. With his boyish shock of black hair and his massive build, at forty-one Clifford looked more like a college football player than a probation officer who had behind him over fifteen years experience as a lawyer and social worker. It had been Clifford who first took Albert's history when he was arrested in 1961. Albert, sitting in a wooden chair before Clifford's desk, had affected him strangely. The man had a hangdog look: he was the eternal Sad Sack, helpless, defeated, almost apologetic for being alive—yet, when he spoke, curiously appealing. He poured his heart out to Clifford. He told him about his childhood, his family repeatedly on relief, his father going with prostitutes, beating up his mother and the children. He had burst into tears with the words, "Can you accept a man after what he's done to his family? What kind of a man is that!"

Clifford, making his notes as Albert spoke, thought, This fellow hates his father so much he doesn't even want to be a man. The world's a jungle to him where you get by only by outsmarting other people.

When Albert explained the "big kick" he got out of measuring the girls around Harvard Square, he had added, "Boy, it makes me feel powerful when I can make those girls do what I want—make them submit to me. I'm nothing in this life, Mr. Clifford. But I want to be something—"

"Did you want to be caught?"

DeSalvo's eyes lit up. "Yeah, I'd be somebody then. I'd get publicity in the papers."

He had been miserable at home, he told Clifford. "My mother was a simple girl, she got married at the age of fifteen. We used to freeze or were on welfare all the time. We never had enough to eat." When his father used to beat him, he would run away from home and live for days under the wharves in nearby East Boston. Clifford knew the East Boston docks. They were places of refuge. He had gone there often, looking for youngsters on probation. He would find them here—boys in their teens, sleeping on discarded mattresses under the wharves, boys who had run away "to get out of the heat of the kitchen, to get away from fathers always beating them up and beating up their mothers," as Clifford put it. Usually Clifford had found the mothers to be weak, masochistic women. They needed punishment and they had married the kind of man—consciously or not—who would give them punishment.

Clifford had written his report, adding the comment, "Subject is either a clever fellow or a compulsive con artist." A week later he visited the building in which Albert had grown up, an apartment house in the poorer section of Chelsea, itself a workingman's town. The moment he entered the dimly lit, cluttered interior he was assailed by a sharp, acrid odor—clothes, food, he was not sure what. Then he saw soiled clothes piled against one wall of the kitchen to within a few feet of the ceiling; beer cans were on the kitchen table, the sink was full of dirty dishes.

The only person home, apparently, was a short, heavyset man in his early thirties. He turned out to be Albert's eldest brother, Joe.

Clifford introduced himself and explained that the law required him to make a house visit to learn the family background. "You know your brother Al is in trouble—"

"He's always in trouble." Joe's voice was indifferent.

"Where's your father?"

The other stared at him coldly. "I don't know and if I did, I wouldn't tell you."

"Why?" Clifford asked.

"I don't care for him, he's never done nothing for me—" He turned away. "I got to go to work—" The interview was terminated.

Clifford glanced about, and made his notes. He checked

the welfare records. Through the years the family had been often on relief, receiving about $125 every two months. To help out, the mother had taken in sewing. Visualizing the family background, the conditions under which Albert had grown up, Clifford thought, These people have been in so much trouble they don't care anymore. The police and welfare workers have been here so often—this family has been agencied to death. There's no cohesiveness here. They're all isolated individuals, and everything in their lives is negative. They have been hit over the head for years by the old man. As they see it, everyone's against them. They live in desperation and helplessness.

Now four years later, Albert was claiming to be the Strangler.

They'd have to convince me, thought Clifford. This fellow got nothing from his family—no sense of status. He wanted desperately to be somebody. That would explain his imposture as the Strangler. Clifford thought, If Albert had struck me as a bottled-up guy—well, that would make it easier to believe he's the man. But he was fluid, everything poured out of him, nothing appeared repressed or held back . . .

Clifford read through the report he had written on Albert on March 21, 1961. No, he *can't* be, he thought.

In his chambers in Chelsea District Court, Justice John W. MacLeod, lean and vigorous in his late sixties, was in conversation with David Greenspan, his Chief Probation Officer. The rumor that Albert DeSalvo, son of Frank DeSalvo of Chelsea, was the Strangler, touched a chord of memory. Justice MacLeod had asked Greenspan to dig up the records of Frank DeSalvo, furniture mover, born May 7, 1908, Boston, son of Joseph DeSalvo, barber, and his wife Josephine. He glanced through them.

"I know this boy's father," Justice MacLeod announced. "Yes, sir. I prosecuted that man, Frank DeSalvo, in this very court. And now his son claims to be the Strangler!" The details came back to him. Nearly thirty years ago when he was a practicing attorney, he had been telephoned late one night by his father-in-law, Lieutenant Charles Grover of the Chelsea Fire Department. One of Grover's close friends in the department was Lieutenant Albert H. Roberts. Roberts' daughter Charlotte, a rather plump girl saddled with thick-lensed glasses, had married a husky young furniture mover named Frank DeSalvo, son of a Chelsea barber. She had been only fifteen at the time.

"I never could understand that marriage," Justice Mac-

Leod said. "But then Charlotte, I suppose, with those glasses, wasn't too attractive, and this fellow might have swept her off her feet— At any rate, my father-in-law telephoned to say Lieutenant Roberts had called him: his daughter had been beaten up by her husband and would I go over there. I went. I'll never forget the scene. They'd had a frightful scuffle in the living room, he'd pushed her over the divan, knocking over a lamp, they struggled on the couch, then he grabbed her hand and bent the fingers way back until they broke. She was in terrible pain." He paused, thinking of it. "That was nearly thirty years ago and I remember it."

He went through the record on Frank DeSalvo. He had been hauled into court eighteen times—five times for Non-support, brought by his wife, and five times for Assault and Battery on her—once with a revolver; and on numerous charges of B and E, Larceny, and similar offenses. He had served time in jail in 1943 and 1944. In 1944 Mrs. DeSalvo finally divorced him; a year later she remarried. In 1944 Frank DeSalvo had vanished, not to reappear in Chelsea until 1956; then he was immediately seized, brought before the court on a default warrant and ordered to pay restitution to the Chelsea Welfare Department "for its expenditure in behalf of his children." From 1956 through 1962 he managed to pay back some $1100.

Frank DeSalvo said that during the twelve years he was absent from Chelsea, he had been living in New York State with a common-law wife by whom he had had two children. When last heard of, he was known to be living with a third woman elsewhere in the state.

That was the father's record. What of the son?

Greenspan produced the folder: Albert Henry DeSalvo, born September 3, 1931, in Chelsea, third of six children. Justice MacLeod read aloud: "As a kid he snatched purses, robbed—well, specifically, on November sixth, 1943, he'd be twelve then, he and a friend beat up a newsboy and robbed him of two dollars and eighty-five cents. They attempted to blame an older boy, saying he forced them to do it, but Albert later admitted it was their own idea. He said, 'We didn't plan anything. We were just walking up the hill and saw the paper boy and robbed him. Then we split the money.' He was adjudged delinquent, the charge was reduced from Robbery to Larceny from the Person, and sentence suspended.

"Five weeks later Albert and his friend were caught breaking into a house and stealing twenty-seven dollars worth of jewelry. Albert was committed to Lyman School for Boys December twenty-ninth, 1943. His oldest brother Joseph had been there, at intervals, over a four-year period. Albert remained until paroled October twenty-sixth, 1944. That's ten months.

"At the age of thirteen years and three months Albert DeSalvo was examined by Doctor Doris Sidwell, visiting psychiatrist to this court from Massachusetts Mental Health. He was found to have a mental age of twelve years and four months. His I.Q. was ninety-three. The record shows he had tonsillitis and mumps, began school at age six, failed in the second grade, was put in a special class in the fifth grade. He told Doctor Sidwell he disliked the special class. 'They only put me in there for talking,' he said. According to this"— Justice MacLeod scanned the page—"the boy gave no one trouble in and about school. He makes a little money by 'cleaning porches and emptying and cleaning garbage pails for ladies.' At home he and his three brothers fight among themselves. He is afraid of his father. Albert comes in at four P.M. and five P.M., and his mother does not allow him out at night. He is in fair physical condition, of normal intelligence, associates with a poor type of companion, and shows great suggestibility. Doctor Sidwell, under the heading, 'Nature of the Problem,' writes: 'This boy needs adequate social supervision and redirection of his interests into supervised groups such as the Boy Scouts and the YMCA.' "

Justice MacLeod riffled through the remainder of Albert's police record. It dealt only with offenses in the Commonwealth of Massachusetts. It included his repeated B and E's, his arrest as the Measuring Man, his jail sentence, and his arrest as the Green Man. The last entries read: "Indicted by the Middlesex County Grand Jury—January, 1965, term —for Breaking and Entering and Larceny; Breaking and Entering with Intent to Commit Felony; Assault and Battery; Assault and Battery by Means of Dangerous Weapon; and Unnatural and Lascivious Act; committed February, 1965, 'until further order of the court,' to Bridgewater State Hospital."

Justice MacLeod snapped shut the file on the DeSalvos, father and son. "You know," he said, "I'd talk to that boy by the hour, right in this office, knowing as I did about his father's and mother's troubles. I liked his mother. Came from a fine Yankee family. She was shy, soft-spoken, a nice little girl, and she deserved someone worthwhile." He rose. "And now this," he said sadly. "Her boy saying he's the Strangler."

In her small clapboard house on a muddy dirt road skirting the edge of a desolate factory town within a hundred miles of Boston, Albert's mother spoke with a visitor. The little girl whom Judge MacLeod remembered was now a buxom woman who filled the rocker in which she sat. Under the coiffed blond hair, her round face with its heavy metal-rimmed spectacles was composed. Her thick-lensed glasses, so thick that her eyes were all but invisible behind them, glinted in the light that came through the Venetian blinds in the parlor window; her hands were folded in her lap. She wore a bright yellow housedress; over that, a half-apron with a scalloped edge and a gaily colored floral design. Seated next to her in the tiny parlor, his crutches leaning against his chair, was her second husband, who shall be called here Peter Khouri, an electrician. Khouri, a powerfully built man in his fifties with iron gray hair and intense black eyes, was convalescing from injuries suffered in an accident.

The visitor had seen Mr. Khouri's dark, rugged face only a few minutes before, framed in the parlor window. Because he had not wished to alarm the family, he had halted his car on the knoll of a hill some distance from the house, which was completely isolated from its neighbors, and negotiated the last hundred yards on foot. Halfway to the house he had looked up to see the face in the window: Khouri, only partly concealed by the Venetian blinds, stood there, humped forward on his crutches, his head down, peering out fiercely at him, not taking his eyes off him for an instant as he came nearer and nearer. Almost guiltily the visitor imagined what must be going through the man's mind: *It's begun. They've finally found us. This is the first of the pack, and after him all the rest—the reporters, photographers, the sensation hunters . . .* All the way to the house the visitor had felt that dark and burning gaze on him. Now Khouri sat beside his wife to help and protect her.

"No," Mrs. Khouri was saying. "I don't read the newspapers. I can't read. I haven't been able to for thirty years. I've lost my sight"—there was a little chuckle, self-conscious but undaunted—"but I can get around."

With some embarrassment her caller brought the conversation around to Albert. She knew, of course, that Albert was telling people in Bridgewater that he was the Boston Strangler.

Mrs. Khouri's face showed no change.

"I know my boy," she said. She sat, solid and impregnable. "He's supposed to have confessed but he's mental, so it can't be used against him." She would not say anything more—no, even if it dealt only with Albert's childhood, the kind of boy he'd been. The matter was in the hands of her attorney, and her visitor could speak with him.

Did she mean F. Lee Bailey?

"No, he came later."

Was it Robert Sheinfeld, then?

She shook her head. The man she referred to was Jon A. Asgiersson.

"Oh, of course," her visitor said. "Mr. Sheinfeld defended Albert in 1959—" He was going to add, "—in the St. Valentine's Day B and E," but she interrupted him.

"No," she said, very precisely. "I see you have that wrong and I want to correct you on it." At this point her husband tried to silence her, but she went on, her voice rising in pitch as though she were projecting her words to an audience of hundreds before her, an audience who could not be expected to believe and to whom the truth would have to be explained patiently again and again. "He was a boy when that happened. Another boy influenced him. He was hardly old enough to know what he was doing." And she made the announcement again patiently, giving each word the same emphasis: "I want to correct you on that because I see that you have the facts wrong."

It was clear that she referred to the attack on the newsboy, but there seemed no point in pursuing the subject.

There was silence for a moment. Moving about the kitchen, seeming lost and obviously terrified, was a tall, four-teen-year-old-girl—the daughter of this second marriage. She ventured only once into the parlor, threw a frightened glance at the visitor, and as silently slipped out again.

Mrs. Khouri spoke up. "It wouldn't be so bad, all this, if it was just my husband and myself, but it's another family concerned—we have this girl . . . I want to guard her from it. There are understanding people in the world, but there are mean people, too, who don't care."

Her husband whispered to her: "Don't talk, don't talk."

But she spoke again. "May I ask you, have you talked to any of my other sons?" The visitor said, "Yes, with Frank, the youngest." "And what did Frank say?"

He, too, had said, "See my lawyer." Her visitor did not tell her that Frank, big, burly, with the same piercing eyes as Albert, had said bitterly, standing on the sidewalk outside the small-town repair shop where he was employed, "I don't want to have anything to do with him. I don't want people to know we're related." His stepfather had had three heart attacks over what was happening—this, in addition to his terrible injuries. His mother was so overwhelmed she didn't know what to do. Yes, he supposed that sooner or later he, Frank, would be sought out; they'd want to talk to him, interview him—

He burst out, "What am I supposed to do? Run away? I've invested two hundred dollars in a Doberman pinscher—my house is bolted and the dog has the run of the place. I got to protect my wife and myself."

Almost distraught, he had turned abruptly and gone back into the shop.

Now Mr. Khouri cleared his throat. "There's nothing we can tell you—as my wife said, it's up to the lawyers." Mrs. Khouri sat, silent, her hands folded in her lap. There was so much she might have told—about herself, leaving school at fourteen in the seventh grade, fighting a futile battle against the congenital eye disease which ultimately blinded her, about her marriage to Frank DeSalvo and the home she tried to maintain for him and the six children that came, one every two years. There were so many things she did not wish to tell about the DeSalvo family, but the story of their lives had already been written in the pages of reports by social workers, welfare investigators, probation officers, psychiatrists. The violent, abusive father, who taught his children to shoplift, who abandoned his family when Albert was eight, but came back at intervals on drunken rampages to "tear up the house," to beat his sons, to rip their clothes to shreds, destroy the furniture by drilling holes in it, to smash glasses, dishes, and cupboards. One of the other sons brought into court for carnal abuse; another for fathering an illegitimate child, B and E, and larceny; a third for B and E and larceny. The mother, repeatedly assaulted after the attack that Justice MacLeod still remembered. Albert was seven. He saw it all. The elder DeSalvo reeled down the stairs. Albert ran after him and hurled a glass vase at his father; it struck him on the head just as he reached the foot of the stairs and shattered into pieces.

She did not now want to tell how she had poured out her heart to a social worker in the spring of 1944. Albert, then thirteen, was in Lyman School, with his brother Joe. She and her husband were separated, her divorce would become final July 1, but the man still gave her no peace. He was under court order to pay her twenty dollars each week for the children's care but it was never that—sometimes it was fifteen, sometimes only ten dollars. He wrote her filthy, abusive, threatening letters: he would find ways to give her less and less money; if she wanted more, he suggested obscenely, she could sell herself; she was diseased, he wrote, and he would make her pay "for neglecting the children." She had recited the catalogue of his accusations, adding resignedly, "Lies, all lies." She would get her divorce, no matter what. She had suffered too long at his hands and "I won't suffer any longer."

As for her children—she did her best to control them. She knew she wasn't very successful. Albert was not a bad boy. Now and then she'd be called to school because of some trouble he was supposed to have started "but it was always something like laughing in line—nothing serious." She felt that the other boy was really responsible for Albert's being sent to reform school; he had suggested they rob the newsboy, she said, and he thought up the idea of breaking into the house and stealing jewelry. Bad companions, she thought, probably led Joseph into trouble, too. Albert—what Albert needed was the right kind of friends. If he "got the right kind of company," she said, "he'd be an ideal boy."

The social worker who interviewed her noted on his report that husband and wife had been in the courts repeatedly, making charges and countercharges against each other. "It is difficult to discover which parent is at fault. . . . The various agencies and the courts have had considerable trouble trying to straighten the matter out. . . . There is little here for the boy—only hardship and a loose-living environment. It might be well, and only fair to the boy, were he placed in a reasonable environment for the time being, or until the parents come to realize that they have responsibility to their children."

Nothing had been done.

Now, in her home, Mrs. Khouri rose. She walked with her visitor to the door, smiled unseeingly at him, shook hands pleasantly, then closed and bolted the door.

On the second floor of Williams School, a weathered redbrick building at 62 Fifth Street, Chelsea, hurrying students filled the long corridor with their noise and chatter. Classes were changing. On the right wall, opposite the principal's office, hung a large blue-and-green pennant proclaiming the school's motto: TRUTH, HONOR, COURAGE. On the opposite wall, to one side, hung the class photographs of the nineteen-forties. Among the faces of the Class of 1948—142 boys and girls, graduates of the Junior High School—there was the smiling one of Albert DeSalvo, aged sixteen. He was older than the others, having been held back in the earlier grades, but the face was unmistakable, a youthful miniature of his police photograph: the black hair matted, almost like a wig, framing like a heavy black arch the low forehead; the nose, not so formidable but already threatening; the mouth smiling. It was a frank, open face, the smile confident, the eyes shining. Albert wore a light gray suit, a gray tie tied in a generous knot, larger, more rakish, than his fellow students.

There were teachers at Williams who had been there twenty years and more, among them Joseph A. Browne, now principal. Few recalled anything about Albert save his name. To Browne, Albert was one face in a sea of faces. Though all four DeSalvo boys—Joseph, then Albert, then Richard, then Frank, Jr.—had gone to Williams, one DeSalvo merged with the other. They had all been something of a disciplinary problem, but not so much as to stand out. No one really remembered Albert. He had passed through his classes and through his school as unnoticed and unremarked as he had passed through the streets of Boston.

Neither Justice MacLeod nor Principal Browne had in his files a copy of Albert's Army record. He had left their jurisdiction as soon as he could, for he had enlisted on September 16, 1948, three months after graduation from Williams School. He had just turned seventeen. He had been sent overseas with the United States Army of Occupation in January 1949 and assigned to the Military Police. On August 17, 1950—he had been in the service nearly two years—he refused to obey an order, was court-martialed, and fined fifty dollars. But his record from then on was excellent. He was promoted to sergeant, and received other commendations. He entered boxing competitions and emerged the middleweight Army champion in Europe. On December 5, 1953, in Germany, he married Irmgard, who lived with her parents near Frankfurt. He had met her at a dance three years before. In April 1954, he returned with his wife to the United States and was stationed at Fort Dix until February 15, 1956, when he received his honorable discharge.

Aside from his court-martial, only one other black mark was to be found against his name. This was his indictment while stationed at Fort Dix for carnal abuse, the molestation of a nine-year-old girl living in a nearby town.

The date of his alleged offense was Monday, January 3, 1955. A distraught mother had telephoned the police. That afternoon she had been preparing a roast for dinner. It was about two o'clock. She had to hurry out briefly to shop. She left behind nine-year-old Lucy and her two younger children, Billy, eight, and one-year-old Allan, asleep in the bedroom.

When she returned forty-five minutes later, Lucy told her they had had a visitor—a soldier "who said he was here for the rent." This was puzzling, for the house was their own. Lucy said, "He asked if he could come in, I said yes. He talked to Billy and me, then Billy said, 'Would you like to see my little brother?'" The soldier smiled and said he would. Billy went into the bedroom, picked up Allan, and carried him proudly into the living room. The man looked at the baby and said how cute he was. Then Billy carried Allan back to his crib. Here Lucy said, "And, Mommy, I don't like that man." "Why?" asked the mother, still unable to make sense of the incident. "Because he touched me here and here." Lucy indicated her chest and between her legs. "I said, 'Stop it,' but he said, 'I won't hurt you.'" At that point Billy had come back into the room and the man left quickly, "just like someone was chasing him."

A few hours later New Jersey State Troopers were questioning the children. Did they know what happened to boys and girls who told a lie? The two nodded soberly. Lucy repeated her story. She did not change it.

Was there anything else either could remember about the soldier? Lucy giggled. "He had a Jimmy Durante nose."

Albert might never have been seized had it not been for a woman living in another town near Fort Dix. One week earlier—Monday, December 28, 1954—Mrs. Alice B. Sloan (which is not her name) was reading in her bungalow about nine in the evening when she heard a knock on her door.

A young man stood there, dark-haired, dark-eyed, wearing a sport jacket and blue slacks. He doffed his hat. "Ma'am, did you see a prowler looking through your window?"

No, she said with some alarm. There had been reports of a prowler in the neighborhood some time before.

"Is your husband home so he can look for him?" her visitor asked. When she shook her head no, he went on, "Well, do you mind if I look around?"

"Please do, I'd appreciate it," she said nervously. The fact was that she was separated from her husband, awaiting a divorce, and she and her three small children, asleep in the rear, were alone in the house.

The man vanished. A few minutes later he was back at her door. "No—don't see him anywhere now. He was a tall fellow in a dark suit."

How had he happened to catch sight of him? she asked.

"I've been driving around the neighborhood looking for a house to rent," he said. His name was Johnson, he added, and continued pleasantly, "When will your husband be home? I'll come back with my wife."

Mrs. Sloan suddenly became suspicious.

He said, "Would you like to have my flashlight?"

"No, thank you," she said, and hurriedly closed and bolted the door. She watched from a window as he walked down the path from her bungalow and got into his car. He sat there for nearly ten minutes before driving away. Then, after another ten minutes, she saw the car return and park, and the same man, sitting at the wheel, flash his light from his car now on this bungalow, now on that. Frightened, she awakened and dressed her children and hurried with them out a back door to stay with a neighbor. She had jotted down his license number and she called the police the next morning.

The license was traced to Sergeant Albert DeSalvo, United States Army, stationed at Fort Dix. Wrightstown State Police questioned him. He had done no harm, he protested; he had seen a prowler and simply wanted to help—he had been looking for a place to rent for his wife and himself. He was permitted to go. On the following Monday came the report of Lucy's molestation by a man with a Jimmy Durante nose. Though a soldier was involved in one and a man in civilian clothes in the other, the police acted on a hunch and brought DeSalvo before Lucy and her brother. The two children immediately identified him. Albert was not flustered. Yes, he had been in their house, he said easily—he'd been looking in that area, too, for a place to rent. The children had misunderstood him to say that he had come to collect the rent. He vehemently denied Lucy's story. He had touched her on the shoulder—as one patted a little girl—but that was all.

Would he demonstrate exactly how he had touched her on the shoulder?

He refused. And on the advice of counsel, he would say no more.

Next day, January 4, 1955, he appeared in court, was released on $1,000 bail, and was subsequently indicted on a charge of Carnal Abuse by the Burlington County, New Jersey, Grand Jury. But Lucy's mother, fearful of publicity, refused to press the complaint. County Judge Cafiero ruled that all proceedings against DeSalvo "be altogether and forever stayed." The charge was nol-prossed. Accordingly, the Army took no action in the matter.

Irmgard was then pregnant with Judy, who was born at Fort Dix a few months later. Early in 1956 Albert returned to civilian life, moving with his wife and child to Chelsea. Then came St. Valentine's Day, 1958, when Albert broke into a house and stole a few dollars to buy a valentine for Irmgard and a box of candy for Judy.

Reading over the record, something about the date Albert first appeared in court in New Jersey—January 4, 1955—would strike an echo. On January 4, 1964—nine years to the day later—Albert DeSalvo would strangle nineteen-year-old Mary Sullivan.

24

On September 29, 1965, the extraordinary recital made by Albert DeSalvo came to an end. In order to convince completely the Attorney General's office that he was who he claimed to be—the Boston Strangler, the murderer of thirteen women—he would now have to force himself to describe in detail the deaths of the two victims he had repeatedly avoided discussing: the woman, about eighty, who he said died in his arms of a heart attack, and Beverly Samans.

Tuney and DiNatale, checking the death reports of aged women, had come upon a Mary Mullen, eighty-five, found dead on her sofa in her apartment on June 28, 1962. Her death, which had occurred two or three days before, had been listed as caused by heart failure. She lived alone at 1435 Commonwealth Avenue, not far from Anna Slesers, who had been strangled less than two weeks earlier.

Bottomly had brought with him at this, their last session, a number of police photographs of apartment interiors. Yes, said DeSalvo, he recognized one as the old lady's apartment—he recalled the black rocking chair, and under it, articles from her purse. "See, there's the key from her safe-deposit box—I remember dumping everything out of the purse, and that was there."

A moment before he saw the photographs, he had drawn his wavering line sketch of the apartment. Sketch and photograph complemented each other.

"I walked up to the second floor of this building, and I knocked on the door of the corner apartment. This old lady opens it—I said, 'I got to do some work in the apartment.' We went in together and sat down; I was in an armchair, she in a rocking chair. I—well, I—" He stopped, as if he had difficulty with his words.

351

"Does this bother you more than the others?" Bottomly asked.

"It all bothers me," DeSalvo said suddenly, passionately. Since the confessional mood he had struck in his last session, he spoke with much more emotion. "It's like a double nightmare, going back. She looked like my grandmother, my mother's mother . . . Last time I saw her was in Danvers,* when I came back from Germany. I went to see her with my mother. She was out of her mind, just talking . . ." His voice rose. "It does something to you, remembering how she used to make apple pies for me, she used to care for me when I was small, when my father wasn't living with us. She reminded me . . . She died in my arms, this woman—" He stopped. "Man, this is too much! I'm getting sick of it, talking about it—" He seemed on the edge of tears.

Bottomly said, "We're almost through now, Albert—"

"She got up from the rocker, turned around—she was talking nice—and I don't know what happened. All I know is my arm went around her neck. I didn't even squeeze her . . . and she went straight down. I tried to hold her; I didn't want her to fall on the floor. . . ." He said, slowly, despairingly, "It's not a dream anymore—it's true—*all these things happened!*"

Suddenly he buried his face in his hands and began to sob, unable to catch his breath. It was the first time he had broken down in the long interrogation that had now lasted several weeks. Bottomly sat quietly, watching DeSalvo, who was crying, his head cradled in his arms on the table. "I didn't mean to hurt nobody," he said brokenly, again and again. "I didn't mean to hurt nobody." Then for a moment he was silent save for his sobs.

In this silence, incredibly, music began to sound. Someone had turned on a radio in an adjoining ward, and the strains of a sentimental melody, plucked on a guitar, came filtering tinnily through to this room in which Bottomly and DeSalvo sat. The music sounded like an insane obbligato playing counterpoint to his sobs—as though it all were a Tennessee Williams play, with the music far off-stage, and DeSalvo's broken words, "I didn't mean to hurt nobody, I never wanted to hurt nobody. They all think it's a big joke, they think, 'Oh, he's trying to make money on this'—I don't want a God damn dime!" He sputtered through his tears. "I got feelings as well as anybody else. It's too much! These people . . . I stay awake, I wonder, my grandmother, my daughter . . . These

---

* Danvers State Hospital is a mental institution in Danvers, Massachusetts.

things did happen. Why? Why? Why does it have to be me?"

Bottomly said, "You've come a long way, Albert. You couldn't even talk about this before."

"I have a daughter, and I have a son and a wife, but when my children grow older, I want them to get an understanding of me . . ." He blew his nose. "I never really wanted to hurt anybody. Why didn't I do this before, and why didn't I do it after? I had these other ones the same way, the ones that followed these, and I didn't do anything more to them. What drove me to do these? There's got to be a reason. I don't think you're born like this. Why did I start? Why did I stop?"

It was not so much the shame of what people might be saying, he said, trying to control himself. It was his children. "I don't want Judy and Michael to live as I did with no father, which I know they must because they're separated from me, but I left them with love, not like my father left us. I never beat them. I just feel these things should never have happened. I want them to find out why I did these things so my name will be cleared for my children."

He dabbed at his eyes and put his handkerchief away. "I'm sorry, Mr. Bottomly," he said. "I shouldn't of acted this way—"

Bottomly said, "I'm not surprised, Albert. You've got a lot to carry. It's surprising you haven't broken down more often."

"I do it in my room," said DeSalvo.

He was able to return to the case of Mary Mullen. When she slumped to the floor, he picked her up and put her on the couch—a green couch. He knew she had died. He didn't know how he knew it but he knew it was not a faint—that it was death—and he assumed the police would think it was from natural causes. "I didn't touch her. I didn't do anything to her—she went, just like that. She passed out. If I close my eyes, as I do now, it's just like being there. I picked her up and put her on the couch and I left."

After a silence, Bottomly asked, "Albert, how did you con all these women? How did you know what to say to them?"

DeSalvo pursed his lips. "It's hard to explain—I don't know how, but the minute the door opened, if I got a glance at a crack in the ceiling, or anything—somehow, I could tell about whoever answered the door in a split second and size them up. I knew right away what she was, what I should say to her, how I should act—I had an answer for everyone who came to the door."

Was he ready, at last, to talk about Beverly Samans?

He was not, but there was no way out. Two or three days

before he found himself in Beverly's apartment in Cambridge, he said, he had been at work painting a house in Belmont. "In the cellar I opened some drawers and I found a sharp, push-button switch knife, the blade came straight out—whew!—I never saw anything like this." Without knowing why he put it in his pocket.

On a weekday morning a few days later, on his way from home, "I shot over to Cambridge." As with so many apartment houses, he knew Beverly's building well. "I'd been in it five or six times before, as the Measuring Man." He rang the bell in the vestibule, walked up, and knocked on her door. She opened it. "She was wearing a zipper-type housecoat. It seemed she was reading my lips when I talked to her."

Beverly, Bottomly recalled, was hard of hearing and always sat in the front row in her classes in order to hear the lecturer. "Oh, it was dark in her room. She didn't know me, I didn't know her. I closed the door and said, 'Don't scream, I won't hurt you . . .'" He stopped and shook his head. "Jesus, I don't want to talk about it!" Almost a scream. "I don't want to say how I did it!"

Bottomly used an approach he had not employed before. "Do you want me to come back in two or three days?"

"No—" DeSalvo expressed utter hopelessness in the monosyllable. Almost in a singsong voice, "Whether it's *today* or *tomorrow* or the *next day* I got to tell you when you come back. It just takes a minute to tell it, but it's so shocking, telling you—"

"Where did you put the knife to her? In the bathroom?"

"As a matter of fact I didn't . . . I mean, she never knew she was stabbed. We were both sitting on the bed—"

Carefully Bottomly led him back to the moment he entered Beverly's apartment and finally, haltingly, the story came out. It was quite early—about 8 A.M., Albert said—when he knocked on her door. She appeared half awake when she opened it.

Had he seen anything in the apartment other than the usual furniture?

"I'm trying to think," Albert said, after a moment, "if there was a piano." Then: "Yes, there was."

"Baby grand or upright?"

Albert wasn't sure. "But I can draw it."

On the blue-line notebook paper he drew an upright. It was the kind Beverly Samans had in the room.

"Write 'piano' next to it," Bottomly told him. Albert scrawled a *p*, then an *a*, realized it didn't look right, and stopped. Bottomly spelled it aloud for him: "P-i-a-n-o," and Albert dutifully wrote the word next to his sketch.

When Beverly—"a heavy, well-built girl"—opened the door to him he said, "I got to do some work in the apartment." She said, "Can't you come back later?" He said he could not, and she said, "Oh, well, come in and get it over with."

"I closed the door, I showed her the knife, I said, 'Don't scream and I won't hurt you. I want to make love to you—' "

She said, "I won't let you—"

"I won't have intercourse with you," he said. "I'll just play around with you and go."

She was frightened at the sight of the knife. "Promise me you won't get me pregnant, you won't rape me—"

When he said, "No, I'll just make love to you and leave—" she said, All right then, she would wash up. He followed her into the bathroom (was it a ruse so she could lock herself in there?), then out again. She lay down on the bed, he tied her wrists behind her, then put a gag in her mouth and "tied a cloth around her head over her mouth so she couldn't scream but she was still able to talk." Then he tied a blind over her eyes.

He fondled her. "Then I was going to have intercourse with her, anyway, and she began talking, 'You promised, you said you wouldn't do it to me, don't, don't, I'll get pregnant.' The words kept coming and coming, I think because she couldn't hear me saying, 'Keep quiet! Keep quiet!' I can still hear her saying, 'Don't do it—don't do that to me.' Just like hearing something over and over again. She made me feel so unclean, the way she talked to me. Everything I was doing to her, she just didn't like it. No matter what I did, she didn't like it. And she just wouldn't keep quiet. I'd do one thing, she didn't like it. I'd do another, she didn't like it. And she wouldn't shut up. I did have the knife out. I promised I wouldn't hurt her. I'd put the knife on the edge of the coffee table, the typewriter was there, she said she wouldn't scream, but she started to get loud and loud and loud . . . She was stripped naked on the bed, her hands under her—"

Bottomly interrupted. "Then she got scared?"

DeSalvo was silent.

Bottomly said, "You have to make it, Albert."

"Jesus Christ, do I have to?"

"Yes, you have to. You know that."

"Oh, God!" he said. "Her hands were tied underneath her, I put a handkerchief over her eyes so later when you found it you thought it was around her neck. It was to cover her eyes . . ." He stopped. *"I don't want to talk about it!"* Then, swiftly, "You know what happened? I stabbed her three, four times, maybe five—"

"You strangled her?"

"No. She didn't get strangled. The stuff you found around her neck, I told you . . . She was stabbed two times right over her heart. Right in the throat and neck."

"Did you have sexual relations?"

DeSalvo said he did not think so. "She kept saying, 'Don't do it! Don't do it!' She didn't want it. In other words, she was ready to do anything else. She said, 'You lied, don't do it!' She wouldn't stop screaming, trying to scream with the gag in her mouth, she kept yelling, 'You're going to do it to me, you're going to do it to me!' I was playing with her breasts, she was louder and louder, the knife was just on the corner of the table . . ."

"Are you getting ready to do it to her?" Bottomly's voice was very soft.

"It was so dark in there, so dark!" He stopped, to get control of himself. "There was a window open. I tied her up, put the gag in her mouth, closed the window, put the shade down—it made it dark, completely dark in there. . . . And I didn't see her anymore. I don't know what happened then . . . I was playing with her, she was lying right on top of the bed. She kept yelling or trying to yell . . . and I stabbed her. Once I did it once . . . I couldn't stop."

DeSalvo sat, his head down, and Bottomly realized that he was crying, not with the deep sobs that had marked him earlier but in a kind of child's intermittent weeping. "Her eyes were covered," he was saying through his tears. "I held her breast. I reached over, got the knife . . . and I stabbed her in the throat. She kept saying something. I grabbed the knife in my left hand and held the tip of her breast and I went down, two times, hard . . ." He drew a deep, shattering breath. "She moved, and next thing you know, blood all over the place—"

"Was there blood on you?"

DeSalvo shook his head.

"You jumped back?"

"I don't know that I did," DeSalvo managed to say. "After I hit her two times, nothing happened."

"Then you hit her again and again—"

DeSalvo groaned. "Jesus!"

"It's almost over," Bottomly said.

"I kept hitting her and hitting her with that damn knife," DeSalvo wept. "When I think about it now—you don't do a thing like that and forget it . . . She kept bleeding from her throat . . . I keep asking myself, Why was it about the same as Mary Brown? I stabbed her two times in the breast, too. I hit her and hit her and hit her. Why? Hard, all the time. Why did I do that? She did something to me. That's what I'm trying to tell you—"

"She refused you," Bottomly said.

"What I'm trying to tell you . . . It was just like my—"

Bottomly broke in. "She refused you and you—"

"I did that one time before, too . . . It was Irmgard. I grabbed her right by the throat, she made me feel so low, as if I was asking for something I shouldn't have, that I wanted something dirty. I wanted to kill her that night! Asking her to make love was asking a dead log to move. It was always 'Do it quick, do it fast, get it over with—' She treated me lower than an animal . . . I loved her so much, yet I hated her. I was burning up. How many nights I would lie next to her, so hot, so wanting to be loved and to love her—and she would not . . . *She* reminded me of her. 'Don't do it, don't do it!' " He paused, then with infinite bitterness: "Irmgard—*'Don't do it, it's not nice'*—Irmgard said that to me just the night before. The same way! The same way! And *she,* right through the gag she was saying, 'Don't do it, don't do it!' She was lying there, I could see everything . . . And still she talked. It wasn't the loudness to me, it was just the way she said it . . . The thing I was doing, there was nothing wrong to do it. *'Don't do it, it's not nice.'* It's not this, it's not that . . ."

On and on he went with his soliloquy. It was Beverly become Irmgard become Beverly . . .

25

Good Friday, April 8, 1966.

F. Lee Bailey, a man not easily thrown off his stride, put down his telephone, all but stunned. John Bottomly had just called to inform him that he was going to resign as Assistant Attorney General. He had had a disagreement with Attorney General Brooke over matters unrelated to the stranglings. He felt it impossible to remain in office. He was resigning as Assistant Attorney General, as Chief of the Criminal Division (a post to which he had been appointed a few months before), and as chief of the "Strangler Bureau." He was withdrawing, as well, from the Brooke-For-United-States-Senate campaign. He was returning to the private practice of law. An official announcement would be made in a few hours.

The break between Bottomly and Brooke was completely unexpected. Indeed, until a month ago Bottomly had been talked about as his running mate, as a candidate for Attorney General to succeed Brooke. His resignation would give Boston political writers material for days, but uppermost in Bailey's mind was one question: what was now to be done with Albert DeSalvo?

The past seven months since DeSalvo completed his story had been a period of legal sparring. Until today the strategy of both State and defense had been directed toward a trial. DeSalvo's case was a tremendous challenge to Bailey. He sought neither to set the man free nor to let him die in the electric chair. Rather, he wanted him placed in a hospital where doctors could study him, in the hope that society might learn what prompts the apparently senseless rape-murders that so frequently shock the country. Yet in this case, all law was reversed: it was the criminal who bore the burden of proving his guilt, and of relieving Boston of the fear that the Strangler was still about. There was no precedent for anything like this. As Bailey was to say later, "Albert was on the left bank of a river and my job was to get him to the right bank without letting him drown."

Bailey had rejected two other ways this might have been managed: presenting the case to a grand jury with the expectation that the jury would no-bill any murder indictments on grounds of insanity, or denominating Albert the Strangler and committing him to an institution for the rest of his life on the ground that the case could not be legally proved in court.

A trial was the best resolution for it would establish judicially that Albert was the Strangler. Then he could receive the required medical attention and analysis. No top-flight psychiatrist would devote himself to Albert unless he was sure that he was the Strangler. To give him such study and attention would cost tremendous amounts of money, it would take distinguished specialists who charged large fees, and it would require a long period of time. Bailey thought of Albert as a criminal research project without parallel: the man possessed virtually total recall; he was alert, intelligent, rational; he had demonstrated that he was a good hypnotic subject; and he was ready to cooperate in every way in order to learn about himself.

The procedure had already been arranged with Bottomly. Indictments for all thirteen murders were to be obtained in the three counties in which the crimes were committed and the trial was to be held in one county, probably Suffolk County, with a jury chosen from residents of the three counties. It would last from four to six weeks. Bottomly would coordinate the prosecution, conducted by the three district attorneys, as he had coordinated the search.

Now, however, Bottomly had removed himself from the picture.

Bailey's first move was to arrange a meeting with Brooke for himself, Jon Asgiersson, co-counsel, and George McGrath. Was Brooke prepared to go forward as planned? This meant, as Bailey saw it, now that Albert had carried out his part—he had told his story—that State psychiatrists would examine him to determine his sanity or insanity at the time of the murders; if insane, detectives—Donovan, Tuney, DiNatale—would take his formal confession; and indictments and trial would follow with, hopefully, a directed verdict of insanity.

Brooke was in a dilemma. Not only was there considerable doubt as to whether the State had sufficient legal evidence—for there were no witnesses to the crimes, or physical evidence linking DeSalvo to any of the murders—but there had been no criminal charges; all that existed were DeSalvo's own self-incriminating statements. There was also the fact that in this election year the case was politically dangerous. Brooke was the leading Republican candidate for the Senate seat to be relinquished by Senator Leverett Saltonstall, who had announced his retirement. The prosecution could be placed in a highly embarrassing position. Brooke, whose private polls indicated that he would be elected in November, was concerned lest he be accused of trying to make political capital out of a sensational murder case—of climbing to the Senate over the bodies of the Strangler's victims.

It seemed clear, at the meeting, that Brooke, if he moved at all, would do so very circumspectly.

Bailey pointed out that DeSalvo had told his story only because the Attorney General's office had agreed on procedures and promised to supervise the prosecution of DeSalvo's case by the three district attorneys. If Brooke left office in January without taking any action, the case would fall into the hands of Brooke's successor—and what certainty was there that the new man would carry out the original understanding on the basis of which DeSalvo had exposed himself so completely?

The meeting ended with Brooke's promise that he would explore the matter further. Perhaps, he said, he might consider appointing a special assistant—an eminent lawyer of unimpeachable reputation—to study the case and then go ahead with it as he saw fit, thus divorcing it completely from politics.

The weeks passed. No special assistant was appointed.

On May 25th a second conference was held. At the meeting Brooke suggested that the case could move forward if detectives began taking DeSalvo's formal confession. Bailey demurred. He said that months earlier Bottomly, in Brooke's presence and with Brooke's approval, had agreed "to furnish us with some evidence of Albert's mental condition" before Bailey would permit him to confess. Brooke, as Bailey later recounted it, said he did not recall this condition.

The fact was that there had been considerable discussion of this matter in the last six months, and the exact status of the understanding reached was unclear. It became apparent to Bailey that agreements made earlier with the Attorney General's office had been considerably diluted by the time Bottomly resigned. Customarily, in criminal cases the State and the defense assume an "adversary" position. What Bailey had asked for was a form of cooperation that seemed to neutralize that position. The lawyer, however, argued that in a case without precedent—one in which the defense produced the criminal—the usual ground rules had to be modified. He could not allow his client to confess unless he had some assurance that DeSalvo could do so without putting himself in the electric chair. As a defense attorney he dared not gamble on what the State's psychiatrists might say.

On this impasse the meeting ended. But just before they parted, the lawyer said to Brooke, "I still have the vehicle to try the Strangler case without risking the chair. I am considering asking for a speedy trial of Albert as the Green Man, in Middlesex County." The charges pending against him there had nothing to do with the stranglings, but the State's psychiatrists would have to testify and so their opinions would become known.

If they said Albert had been insane, Bailey would allow him to confess to the murders. If they decided he had been sane, Bailey would ask each psychiatrist, "Do you know the complete history of this man? Does your opinion take into account the fact that he killed thirteen women?" To prove this, Bailey would subpoena Bottomly to testify to what Albert had told him during the long weeks of interrogation; then he would call upon Tuney and DiNatale to testify, thus supplying the corroborative evidence they had been accumulating in the intervening months.

One way or another Bailey felt sure he would be able to denominate Albert as the Strangler without risking the chair.

Brooke was agreeable to the Green Man trial. He would ask District Attorney John J. Droney of Middlesex County to go forward on it.

Early in June Bailey filed a motion for a hearing on Albert's competency to stand trial as the Green Man.

The corroborative evidence Tuney and DiNatale had been gathering was the result of the most exhaustive scrutiny of DeSalvo's story. Since his final interrogation on September 29, 1965, the two detectives, with Sandra Irizarry at their side, had worked daily over the transcript—more than fifty hours of interviews—filling more than two thousand pages.

Their task had been the comparison of every statement of fact made by DeSalvo with every fact known about the crimes.

Under Tuney's direction a series of mimeographed score sheets were run off. Entitled "Analysis of Statements by Albert DeSalvo," each sheet was ruled into seven columns. The first was headed *Statement by DeSalvo;* the next, *True/False;* then, four columns listing sources from which these facts might have been learned by Albert, or by someone who conceivably might have fed him the information—*Newspapers; Local Police Department Reports; Crime Scene Photographs; Autopsy Report.* The seventh and last column was headed *Comments.*

Obviously, the investigators were interested in those true statements DeSalvo had made that had not appeared in, or could not have been elicited from any of the four sources. In this category his score was impressive—and grew more so as the examination continued on through the thirteen murders.

In the case of Evelyn Corbin, for example, DeSalvo had made forty-two statements of fact. Of these, thirty were found to be true, four false, and eight impossible to prove true or false (for instance: "I used the toilet. I looked in a drawer"). Twelve out of the thirty true statements were not to be found in the four sources. One had to assume that he knew these facts from having been there.

Sometimes corroborative evidence appeared in an unexpectedly dramatic fashion. DeSalvo, relating how he attacked Gertrude Gruen, the German waitress who alone of his victims escaped him, had told Bottomly that he first removed his Air Force jacket—it was warm in her apartment—and tossed it over a blue chair. Lieutenant Tuney telephoned Miss Gruen, now living in another city. Yes, the man had placed his jacket over a chair. She had told that to the police, and it had been in the newspapers, she recalled. But a *blue* chair? No. She had never owned a blue chair. The chair in her apartment in Boston had been brown.

Two weeks later Tuney received a special delivery letter from her. She must apologize. She had been rummaging among her belongings and had come across a color photograph she once took in her apartment when she had a few friends over. There was the chair, clearly visible—and unmistakably blue.

Time and again DeSalvo was found to be right. He had said there was a notebook under Beverly Samans' bed. She had probably been making out a shopping list, he thought. Both statements were true. No sources mentioned them.

DeSalvo had mentioned hearing a soft jingle of bells when he pulled open Patricia Bissette's door early that Sunday morning. He was correct about the door. It was one of the few apartment doors in Boston that opened outward, for this was a violation of the fire laws. Though he might have known about the door from his Measuring Man days, how could he know about the bells? One of Pat's friends had told Phil DiNatale that Pat had attached them to the door only a few days before her death.

Sophie Clark, DeSalvo had said, had been menstruating—
"she was just finishing," he had told Bottomly. He had torn off
the napkin and thrown it behind her TV set. Police had reported
the existence of what they called "a special article of apparel,"
but had not specified where they found it. It had in fact been
found behind the TV set.

Finally, of all the details, harmless or shocking, printable
or unprintable, one would never be forgotten by the team of
two men and one woman working so diligently on the score
sheets. DeSalvo had said Sophie's napkin was stained. He had
given the dimensions of the stain: one inch by two.

On a hot day in early June 1966, Lee Bailey visited De-
Salvo at Bridgewater. The lawyer was in excellent spirits. On
June 6 the United States Supreme Court had, based on his
appeal, reversed the conviction of his client, Dr. Sam Sheppard of Cleveland, for the murder of his wife. The following
day the Massachusetts Supreme Judicial Court had, based on
his appeal, reversed the conviction of his client, George Nassar, for the murder of Irvin Hilton. These were two enormous victories for a lawyer who had been practicing less than
six years and had only this month reached his thirty-third
birthday.

Now at last the case of his client Albert DeSalvo seemed
to be on its way to a conclusion, too. The news Bailey had
for DeSalvo was that a hearing would be held at the end of
the month on his competency to stand trial. If found competent, as Bailey expected, his trial as the Green Man most
likely would be scheduled for the fall.

Albert had been kept busy at Bridgewater. He had been
working in the kitchen, preparing breakfasts for the nurses;
he had been assisting in the dispensary, helping the orderlies
on their rounds; and he had continued his care of the old
men, giving them showers, making up their beds, and tending
to their wants.

And he had thought and thought again of his life—his
childhood, his introduction to sex, his marriage, and what
had happened after that.

On this visit, he began relating his thoughts to Bailey. (He
had already told some of this to McGrath during earlier visits.) The lawyer listened sympathetically. Albert was around
his own age. It was clear to Bailey that Albert had never before discussed himself, or his sexual guilts, with a contemporary on a man-to-man basis. Bottomly and McGrath had represented the remote and somewhat fearful authority of the
law, the doctors and psychologists the equally remote and

puzzling impersonality of medical science. He could talk to Bailey on almost a first-name basis.

He had always been a loner. He had never confided in anyone. "I was never part of the crowd," he said. He thought it might be because he never drank or smoked. His father's drunken rages had made him hate liquor. As a child he was a coward. He ran away from a fight. "I had no confidence in me—or in anyone else." He was astonished to discover, after he entered the service, how well he could fight. He had always taken good physical care of himself. Even here, at Bridgewater, he kept in condition by doing twenty-five pushups every morning, noon and night. He was proud that he had won the Middleweight Army Championship of Europe, and held it for two years. At five feet eight and a half he was smaller than many men, but he found he could drop the biggest man.

School had not been too unhappy an experience for him, except for the ten months he had been sent to Lyman School. At Williams, "I never got good marks, but the teachers liked me—I was a kind of teacher's pet, running errands, buying sandwiches for them—so I got by."

He liked to swim—and now and then, when he had a chance on neighboring farms, to ride horses. At one stage he became fascinated with bows and arrows. He went about with a friend, shooting alley cats. He never understood why he did this or what kind of a satisfaction he derived from it. He had no special feeling for cats, neither liking them nor disliking them. Bailey noted that Albert could never explain the sudden hostility that would come over him.

He stole as far back as he could remember. His father showed him when he was five how to shoplift from the five-and-ten. When Albert spoke of his father, his voice rose. His father would bring home drunks "and all kinds of things would go on in the house."

Albert did not know how far back his first sexual memory reached, but one early scene never left his mind. "I was maybe nine or ten. I was in bed, this girl was blowing me and the door opens and in walks my brother, catching us."

When he was fifteen, "a married woman—she had a kid my age—took me into her bedroom and showed me how to do every kind of sex perversion." Albert found that his participation could continue for a long time: he seemed inexhaustible, driven to seek sexual satisfaction almost without rest.

When he was sixteen, upon graduating in June 1948, from Williams School, he took a summer job as a dishwasher in a Cape Cod motel. He spent most of his spare time on the roof, from where he could look directly into some of the rooms and see couples making love. Watching, he would relieve himself by repeated masturbation. He had been an involuntary voyeur during his childhood: since puberty voyeurism had become a regular means of sexual stimulation—and fulfillment.

That September of 1948 he enlisted in the Army. He was a "spit and polish" soldier—"always the sharpest uniform, best-dressed, shoes polished, best-kept vehicles. . . . I made Colonel's Orderly twenty-seven times." This gave him time to look around for women during the day, especially soldiers' wives.

He remained in the Army from his seventeenth to his twenty-sixth year. By the time he was mustered out in February 1956, married and the father of a baby daughter, his sexual needs had brought him into conflict with the law only twice—both times in his last year in the Army, when he had been stationed at Fort Dix. The first incident was the indictment for molesting a nine-year-old girl; the second came two months later when he was arrested for disorderly conduct. Actually, he had been seized as a Peeping Tom. The charge was dropped and Albert emerged with his honorable discharge and moved to Malden with his wife and child. He was hired as a press operator by the Biltmore Rubber Company, in nearby Chelsea. Soon he had bought a car and made a down payment on the house at 11 Florence Street. He was proud of being a good provider and a good family man, home every night with his family.

But the sexual problem—his "terrible urge"—never left him. As he once told McGrath, he was driving to work one morning and as he drove he found himself having an ejaculation. He stopped his car and tried to think. "What's wrong with me? Why should this happen to me at 8 A.M. driving to work—" He never told his wife about his problem, nor did he ask for help; and when "this thing" grew worse, and he was seeking out women all the time, he feared to ask for help because it might hurt his family, or Irmgard might leave him and take the children with her. But it was with him all the time. He would come home from work "and all through dinner it was on my mind. I wanted Irmgard . . . I knew she was trying to make some excuse to avoid it. I couldn't get through dinner, it was so much on my mind." He also wanted her to make the first move—"to ask me. . . . She could never see her way clear."

One night, he turned on the TV. The program was "The Bob Cummings Show." In it the actor played a commercial photographer who hired fashion models. In one scene Cummings bustled about with a tailor's tape, measuring one strikingly beautiful girl after another who had applied to him for jobs.

Albert watched, fascinated. It was a new approach to sexual stimulation and he was never to forget it.

The Measuring Man was born then.

He had always had to get additional satisfaction outside his marriage. Although he loved Irmgard, there had always been difficulties in sex. From the very beginning he found her a little cold. But from the first he had been inordinately proud of her. Her parents were serious, respectable people who had not allowed her to go out until she reached her eighteenth birthday. Albert admired Irmgard: she had a better education, and as he told friends, "No one in her family ever even saw the inside of a jail." He felt her to be unquestionably superior to him, and he was very much the dutiful husband. She was Catholic; and though he was not, he reared the children as Catholics and took them faithfully to church. He tried to please her in every way. Yet "putting her on a pedestal" was to plague him. She "would put me down" in front of others, "make me feel like nothing" before friends. "She gave me an inferiority complex," he complained. When they argued at home, she would fling at him, "You're no better than the rest of your family." There was little she could say that was more cutting to him.

Still, he loved her very much. When he was arrested as the Measuring Man in March 1961, he was overcome with remorse. At Westborough State Hospital, where he had been sent for observation before sentence, he was in tears each time he spoke of the wrong he had done her. She looked so ill then. Once she had had to go to a hospital herself to undergo a gastrointestinal series—and it was all his fault.

"I can hardly wait to get out so I can be with her and treat her the way a wife should be treated, even if it means washing her feet," he had told the psychiatrist at Westborough.

When he finally came out of the House of Correction in April 1962, she presented him with an ultimatum. He must prove himself before she would accept him again as her husband. "I come out of jail after one year, all alone for one year in one room, and Irmgard tells me, 'I wasted a year of my life.' She puts me on probation." He could not endure it, wanting her so much, and she turning away from him. Lying next to her he felt as though he would burst. "I must learn to control my sex wants, she told me. . . . She would say I was dirty and sickening and called me an animal." She made him afraid to make love to her. "I felt less than a man in bed with her."

Yet, those last months of 1964, just before his arrest as the Green Man, she had been so wonderful to him. She gave him "so much loving, I felt no urge to go out and do those things."

She was always first in his thoughts. The night he had given himself up to the police he had said to the detectives, "Give me a couple of days to square myself—" They had let him out on $8,000 bail.

Two days later police, armed with warrants from other states, had surrounded his house and seized him—"It was foolish for me to try to get away"—but a moment of panic swept over him. Yet it really didn't matter. In those forty-eight hours he had arranged to sell his house and car, the money to go to Irmgard and the children. He had only their good interests at heart.

He knew how much Irmgard's religion meant to her. On December 16, 1965, as Christmas approached, he asked to see a Catholic priest. Bottomly arranged for Monsignor George Kerr, Chaplain of the Massachusetts House of Representatives, to visit him. Priest and patient talked together for a long time. At DeSalvo's request Monsignor Kerr wrote a long letter to Irmgard, who had gone back to Germany with the two children and was now living there under a new name. The priest wrote: Albert is in good health; he misses you and the children very much; you must prepare yourself for the fact that he has confessed to "certain unsolved crimes." He repents greatly, but he could not have continued to live with himself had he not unburdened his conscience. He hopes you will understand. He knows he will never again be a free man and he has resigned himself to that fate. He thinks constantly of you and the children, he wants very much to hear from you, and he begs you to write him, care of your sister.

Monsignor Kerr added that Albert had told him he was thinking of converting to Roman Catholicism; but he was not, as yet, ready to do it. It was something for the future.

Now, having told everything and prepared himself for whatever consequences would follow, DeSalvo waited.

The first time Bailey met DeSalvo, he thought that this could be the man, precisely because he looked so unlike what everyone had expected the Strangler to look like. Bailey had always felt that anyone looking for a monster—a Mr. Hyde—was grievously in error. Had the man been suspicious in appearance he would have been picked up long ago. They should have looked for a Dr. Jekyll—the most unlikely kind of a criminal. Albert's mild, inoffensive appearance—"sirring" everyone within sight, appearing almost apologetic for being alive—would explain why no one ever gave him a second glance.

In addition, George Nassar, whose intelligence and perception Bailey recognized, thought DeSalvo was telling the truth.

Nassar first mentioned DeSalvo to Bailey on February 10, 1965, at an Essex Superior Court hearing to determine Nassar's competency to stand trial. At a moment when they were alone, Nassar said without preface, "Mr. Bailey, how'd you like to talk to a man down at Bridgewater who says he's the Strangler?"

Bailey was not enthusiastic. "I'm not too eager to waste a visit down there to listen to some man's hallucinations," he said.

Nassar went on, "No, I think he's the guy. If he *was* the Strangler, could he tell his story and earn enough from it to support his family the rest of their lives?"

"I doubt it," said Bailey. "Because telling it would put him in the electric chair. In order to tell his story he'd have to expose it, which means making a public confession. That could be thrown into the grand jury and result in an indictment for murder."

Nassar digested this soberly. Bailey asked, "Who is the man?"

Nassar said it was an inmate named Albert DeSalvo. He had asked Nassar to ask Bailey if he would want to defend him.

Bailey said, "I don't doubt there are a lot of fellows at Bridgewater ready to claim they're the Strangler."

Nassar went on seriously, "I've done a lot of talking to him and I'm almost convinced. Why don't you talk to him yourself?"

Well, said Bailey, he would ask to see him "next time I'm down in Bridgewater."

Nassar, originally sent to Bridgewater on January 18 for observation, was returned after the hearing for additional study, and Bailey went on to other matters.

A week later, the lawyer received a call from Dr. Ames Robey, Medical Director at Bridgewater. A patient named Albert DeSalvo, said Dr. Robey, had written him requesting that he please notify Mr. Bailey that he would like to see him. After another week passed, a Joseph DeSalvo left a telephone message with Bailey's secretary: his brother, Albert, a patient at Bridgewater, wanted to consult him. Would he please come down to Bridgewater and talk to him?

Bailey had been too busy. But on March 4 he had to talk to Nassar about his forthcoming trial. He decided he would see DeSalvo at Bridgewater at the same time. Although Bailey had read about the stranglings he knew few details. Before driving down he talked with Lieutenant Donovan, asking him for "half-questions" to pose to a man who might turn out to be a good suspect.

Thereafter, the lawyer, armed with half a dozen key words "to throw at the man"—words such as "belt," "ascot," "bottle"—saw DeSalvo for the first time on March 4. That afternoon he telephoned Donovan and gave him DeSalvo's responses. Donovan was impressed. Two days later Bailey visited DeSalvo again at Bridgewater and this time recorded a long statement from him about the stranglings.

Until the full story came out—that DeSalvo had made three requests to see him—Bailey knew he would be criticized for his unorthodox approach to the case. Lawyers, after all, had been known to solicit business at Bridgewater. He knew, too, that many would think of the affair as a hoax or a publicity stunt, which would make him even more suspect. Finally, he was not unaware of the political implications that could be drawn from the fact that he approached Boston police, rather than the Attorney General's office, with his information. Bailey's explanation later was that he knew Donovan, and he did not know Bottomly; more importantly, he assumed that Donovan's Homicide Bureau would possess more details than the Attorney General's office, which had entered the scene only after the stranglings were over.

What Bailey had not anticipated was that it would fall upon him, a defense attorney, to prove that DeSalvo was the Strangler. "We found ourselves before a really unbelievable situation. It was up to us to prove he was the right man—and to do it without giving the State a single piece of legal evidence. Albert had to get by that electric chair. He had to get by it thirteen times."

The Middlesex County Courthouse in East Cambridge, a stone's throw from the bleak wooden terminal in which the Boston trolleys make their last stop, is a massive red brick building imbued with New England solidity. Here, on the last day of June 1966, in a square, old-fashioned courtroom on the second floor, Albert DeSalvo made his first public appearance since he had been committed to Bridgewater as mentally ill on February 4, 1965.

The occasion was a hearing to determine his competency to stand trial as the Green Man. Perhaps thirty persons were in the courtroom, among them virtually all the principal actors in the story of the Boston Strangler.

John Bottomly, now no longer Assistant Attorney General, but still deeply involved in these closing chapters of the unique case, was present. Sitting in the rear of the court, watching the proceedings yet taking no part in them, he still felt a twinge of concern. He had wanted so badly to carry the case through to a conclusion. "I'm sorry I had to leave it undone," he told a friend. "Yet it was being undone, anyway." A month before his resignation he had sent a memorandum to Brooke recommending the steps necessary to conclude the Strangler case. Brooke, he said, had not replied; nor had he been able to get any decision to go ahead when he brought the matter up again, he said.

The police who had lived with the stranglings from the very first one on June 14, 1962—more than four years ago—were present. Lieutenant John Donovan, Chief of Homicide, Lieutenant Edward Sherry, and the three remaining members of Bottomly's original "Strangler Bureau": Lieutenant Andrew Tuney, Detective Phillip DiNatale, and their assistant, Sandra Irizarry. As for the others, Special Officer James Mellon was now carrying out police duties in suburban Roxbury; Officer Steve Delaney had left the force and was employed in a private detective agency; and Jane Downey, who had worked so zealously with Sandra to compile the casebooks of each strangling, had long since returned to the Eminent Domain division.

On the witness benches, awaiting their call to testify, were the psychiatrists: Dr. Robert Ross Mezer and Dr. Samuel Tartakoff (private practitioners who had examined DeSalvo during his internment at Bridgewater these past eighteen months) and Dr. Robey.

At the defense table were F. Lee Bailey, his assistant Charles Burnim, and Jon Asgiersson, DeSalvo's co-counsel; opposite them sat Donald L. Conn, Assistant District Attorney of Middlesex County. George McGrath, until recently DeSalvo's guardian, was not present: he was in New York, the newly appointed Corrections Commissioner of the city.

No member of DeSalvo's family was present.

In the center of the room in the square prisoner's box, raised about three feet off the floor, his back to the audience, his face toward the empty bench and the waiting lawyers, sat DeSalvo. Ten feet behind him sat two ponderous, khaki-clad men, who almost took up the space of four, with their bellies overflowing their broad leather belts. The two faces were surprisingly alike—rugged, rough-hewn, and having an outdoors look that sharply contrasted with the faces of the lawyers, psychiatrists, and reporters. These were prison guards from Bridgewater. They had brought DeSalvo, in manacles, from the State Hospital this morning; a few hours later they would return him there in the same fashion.

Standing almost at DeSalvo's elbows, on either side of the prisoner's box, were two uniformed bailiffs, alert and watchful. They seemed altogether unnecessary. Albert sat quietly, sedate as a minister in a neatly pressed blue suit, a white shirt with widespread collar, and a generous knot in his blue tie—the same knot he tied the day he posed, aged sixteen, for his graduation photograph at Williams School. Now and then, waiting for the proceedings to begin, he touched his chin nervously with the thumb and forefinger of his right hand—a massive hand for a man his size—or allowed a quick smile to flash over his face. With the smile, the narrow small face dominated by the long nose suddenly lit up with an unexpected charm: seeing Albert's smile, one understood many things.

It was an extraordinary session that was about to begin in the stifling courtroom. Every person present knew that the man before them was Albert DeSalvo, the Boston Strangler. But not once was the word "strangling" to be used. There were to be references to "certain crimes," there were to be allusions to DeSalvo's "past history," but at no time would anything more explicit be said. In the eyes of the law he was Albert DeSalvo, the Green Man, about to be judged as to his competency to stand trial on indictments charging armed robbery, assault, and indecent and lascivious acts—but not murder.

Almost unnoticed, a white-haired clerk rose and began his "Hear Ye! Hear Ye!", concluding with a fervent, "God bless the Commonwealth of Massachusetts." Everyone stood up as Judge Horace J. Cahill, elderly, pink-faced, bespectacled, and stern in his black robes, entered and took his place on the bench.

First, Dr. Mezer and Dr. Tartakoff testified that DeSalvo suffered from a commitable mental disease but could stand trial. Dr. Mezer described it as "chronic undifferentiated schizophrenia" which "would make it difficult for him to accept the world of reality as most people know it." Dr. Tartakoff had characterized him as a "sociopath with dangerous tendencies"; that is, "an individual who from early life has shown deviations from what are usually considered normal patterns of behavior, thinking, and emotional reactions."

There was a bustle in the room when the last psychiatrist to testify, Dr. Robey, took the stand. It had been his diagnosis that originally resulted in DeSalvo's commitment. A tall, long-legged, partially bald man with a boyish, eager face, he brought with him a copy of DeSalvo's medical record at Bridgewater.

He differed sharply as to Albert's competence. The man suffered from "schizophrenic reaction, chronic undifferentiated type"—a type that "also has very extensive signs of sexual deviation." And he added:

"My opinion is that I cannot—repeat—cannot consider him competent to stand trial." He had seen DeSalvo at Bridgewater, he said, "vacillate back and forth, sometimes appearing strictly sociopathic; at other times almost like an acute anxiety hysteric; at other times appearing much more obsessive and compulsive; again appearing very close to wild overt psychosis." He had seen DeSalvo "when he appeared to be almost very much what we refer to as in a homosexual panic, or sexual panic of some sort."

At this DeSalvo reddened and shook his head emphatically.

How would DeSalvo act under stress of a trial, Conn asked.

"He could become more overtly paranoid and indulge in an outburst," Dr. Robey said. He might also become violent. Under Conn's questioning, he went on to say that he considered DeSalvo a "compulsive confessor." He added, "He has a real need, because of his underlying illness, to prove to himself and to others his own importance."

Bailey began a lengthy cross-examination. Dr. Robey knew, of course, that DeSalvo said he had faked his hallucinations, because he thought he would be sent to Bridgewater and be released soon after. Dr. Robey repeated his conviction that Albert had not been faking.

As for understanding the charges pending against him, Dr. Robey felt that DeSalvo might "intellectually know" them but—"Emotionally, I am not so sure. . . ." In such patients one often found the "emotional awareness of the significance is lost or distorted."

Dr. Robey also felt that under the stress of cross-examination, DeSalvo would be "in such a state that he would not be making sense."

Bailey asked: "To your knowledge, has he been in circumstances of great stress?"

"No."

"He has not?"

"No," repeated Dr. Robey, firmly.

The lawyer's voice suddenly rang out: "Are you aware that he has been the subject of the most gigantic homicide investigation in the history of the Commonwealth?"

There was a sudden hush in the court. It was the first reference to the fact everyone knew and no one mentioned—Albert's other identity. This was to happen four more times: the testimony walking up the hill to this sensational fact and then walking back down away from it. All were aware—the judge, the psychiatrists, the attorneys, and Albert DeSalvo himself—of his rights, his dangers, and their obligation to say nothing that would infringe on those rights or open the door to those dangers.

Dr. Robey said quietly, "Yes." Bailey did not pursue the question but asked if it was not a fact that DeSalvo refused to cooperate with him.

No, said Dr. Robey.

Wasn't it a fact, Bailey went on, that DeSalvo decided not to cooperate with him after he learned that Dr. Robey had written a letter containing "confidential information" about him to a writer named Gerold Frank?

Dr. Robey recalled writing to Mr. Frank who, he said, had been originally referred to him by Assistant Attorney General Bottomly. He did not remember the letter's contents, however.

Bailey showed him a copy of the letter, dated August 4, 1965. "Yes," said Dr. Robey with a smile, after reading it. It was his letter. Judge Cahill ordered it entered as Exhibit 1. Bailey revealed that another inmate of Bridgewater had rifled Dr. Robey's files, come upon a carbon of the letter, and had shown it to Albert. In the letter Dr. Robey wrote, in part, that he still considered Albert incompetent to stand trial, and described him as "paranoid."

Was it not a fact, asked Bailey, that from then on DeSalvo refused to tell Dr. Robey anything about himself, that "he has never consented to discuss and has, in fact, not discussed certain crimes under investigation of which you are well aware—serious crimes?"

It was the second reference to the other Albert DeSalvo.

Dr. Robey said no, Albert would say he did not want to talk about himself "and then he would proceed to tell you a great deal about himself," but then he agreed that Albert had not discussed the other crimes with him.

Then Bailey stated that DeSalvo had discussed these crimes with other psychiatrists.

The cross-examination moved on to other subjects.

Now Albert DeSalvo stood in the witness stand, almost at attention, his hands at his sides, and Bailey, speaking quietly, began to lead him through a catechism:

"Albert, have you understood the proceedings that have gone on today, do you think?"

"Yes, sir."

"Have you heard the testimony of the doctors?"

"Yes, sir."

"Do you feel you are ready to go to trial?"

"Yes, sir."

"Have you ever had any doubts at all about what your defense would be if these cases were called to trial?"

"I have never had any doubts as to what my defense would be because I'm doing only what is right, no matter what the consequences may be. I am fully aware of these."

"Now, Albert, do you wish further treatment by psychiatrists?"

"What I always asked for was medical help, and I haven't yet received any."

"Are you concerned about going to prison?"

"No, sir. I am concerned about being helped. If not, what is the good of living?"

"Would you rather be in Walpole Prison or Bridgewater?"

"I prefer not to be in any prison. I prefer to be in the hospital where I can at least get some type of treatment."

Bailey led him into the subject of his treatment at Bridgewater. DeSalvo said instead of medical attention, "when I came into the institution, I was first brought up to what they call the 'F' ward for highly violent patients. I was stripped naked, sat in a chair. There were four or five officers sitting watching television, while the other inmates were screaming and running around and doing things. They had me sitting there naked, asking me certain questions—unethical questions." He paused. "They told me, 'If you're not crazy now, you will be when we get through with you.'"

Bailey asked, "Albert, are you concerned about the possibility of conviction?"

"Yes, sir, I am concerned."

"Do you realize there is a risk that you might be convicted?"

"Yes."

"Are you willing to assume that risk in order to have this matter thrashed out?"

"Yes, sir, I am."

The third reference to Albert's other identity came when Conn, cross-examining him, asked, "Do you fully understand the possible penalties for the crimes under which you are currently indicted in this county?" And when DeSalvo said yes, went on, "Do you fully understand the implications of your past conduct? Do you understand what can happen to you, sir, as a result of what you have done?" Yes, said DeSalvo, again.

The fourth time came in a series of questions by Conn: "You indicated, Mr. DeSalvo, that you made certain disclosures to Assistant Attorney General John Bottomly. Did you have such interviews?"

"Yes, sir."

"And during the course of these interviews, you made certain disclosures to Mr. Bottomly?"

Judge Cahill interrupted. "That is characterizing it, indicating that it was something out of the ordinary. He is protected on that on the advice of counsel."

"Yes, your Honor," said Conn. And went on: "There were certain conditions spelled out before you talked to him?"

That was right.

"Can you give us the gist of these conditions?"

"Well," said Albert. He sought for words. "My attorney explained that he would have certain high officials talk to me and prove that the person involved in these things is just not shooting blanks—and who would be in a position to verify that these are true facts. I was told that under the conditions anything I said would never be held against me."

Conn: "And what was the information going to be used for? Were you told? To prove that in such—"

Bailey had stood up, but Judge Cahill broke in. "You are getting close—"

"I know," said Conn.

Judge Cahill repeated his words warningly: "You are getting closer—"

Bailey spoke. "Your Honor, this is a little difficult for the defendant. I will stipulate that the information was to be used for the benefit of the doctors in determining whether or not this man's history was fact or delusion."

Judge Cahill sat back. "All right. Let it go at that."

Conn asked, Did DeSalvo know what his defense would be?

Yes, he said. Not guilty by reason of insanity.

"Do you feel that you are sick?"

"I feel that I am in a mental condition."

How long did he think he had been in this "mental condition"?

DeSalvo spoke softly, now and then gesturing with his hands at his sides—turning them, palms up, as if seeking to find words. "I feel that it could have started from my childhood and erupted more violently during the later stages of my life. I have reexamined my own background many many times, having time; and after thinking this all over, I said, 'What good is my life now?' I have to do what I think is right, no matter what happens. So long as the truth is revealed, so society will somehow understand it—"

"What do you mean by 'right'? What is 'right' for you?" Conn asked.

Outside, there was a sudden rat-a-tat-tat of jackhammers pounding on a construction job. DeSalvo waited. The June heat was oppressive—and became more so when Judge Cahill ordered the windows closed and even the fans turned off so DeSalvo's words could be heard above the outside noise. Life seemed stilled in a haze of heat that had settled in the huge, high-ceilinged courtroom with its dark-stained chairs and benches, and its four square chandeliers. Only DeSalvo's thin boy's voice and the small impersonal clicking of the stenotypist's machine could be heard.

"I feel that what is right is to tell the truth, and if to tell the truth is going to hurt me. . . ." He gestured resignedly. "Well, that's the chance. I am willing to take the risk because if I have to be punished in any way, then these are the penalties I must accept." He paused. "I have got to live with myself. I have got to do what I feel is right, no matter what may happen to me."

"This is something you *have* to do?" pursued Conn. His accusing gaze seemed even more relentless. Was the State, perhaps, attempting to prove him incompetent, suggesting that DeSalvo labored under a compulsion to confess?

"No, it is not something I have to do," DeSalvo said. "It's very hard to explain. It's something inside you, that once in your life you have got to do what is right."

"And what is right, Mr. DeSalvo, even though it hurts your wife and children, whom you love, is to tell the truth?"

Yes, said DeSalvo.

"And to tell what you have done in the past?"

It was the final reference.

Albert began to lift his hands again, then dropped them.

"I feel that I couldn't live with myself. . . . I wish to in my own way to release everything that is inside me, the truth. And whatever may be the consequences, I will accept because I have always from the very beginning wanted to tell the truth."

Ten days later Judge Cahill found Albert DeSalvo competent. On July 11, 1966, he was brought before Judge George P. Ponte in the same courthouse. He pleaded not guilty. Assistant District Attorney Conn recommended that DeSalvo be remanded without bail to Bridgewater, for trial—as the Green Man—at a later date to be agreed upon.

Lee Bailey moved close to the bench and said, "Your Honor, though this man is charged with other offenses, he has committed thirteen homicides. I agree that Bridgewater State Hospital is the best place for him."

The two massive guards took DeSalvo into custody again.

Albert DeSalvo, the Boston Strangler, had still not—legally—been in a courtroom.

Today DeSalvo, awaiting treatment—"perhaps the doctors can cut out the corner of my brain that made me do those things"—continues his duties at Bridgewater, caring for senile patients, shaving the old men, feeding them when they are unable to feed themselves.

Four years had passed since Anna Slesers was found dead by her son in the hallway of her small apartment at 77 Gainsborough Street and one of the most exhaustive manhunts of modern times began. Thirteen women had died, hundreds more had been assaulted, and one of the most civilized of cities had been terrorized by a single man, pathologically criminal and cunning.

It is unlikely now that Albert DeSalvo, the man responsible for all this, will ever stand trial as the Boston Strangler—but it is clear that he will never be free again.

But no matter what direction is taken by the law and those who act in its behalf—determined to protect the rights of society, yet equally determined to protect the rights of the individual—the story of the Boston stranglings has ended.

AFTERWORD

Shortly after midnight on Friday, February 24, 1967, Albert DeSalvo broke out of Bridgewater with two other patients, George W. Harrison, 33, a burglar, and Frederick E. Erickson, 41, a convicted wife-killer.

It was an extraordinary epilogue to an extraordinary story. DeSalvo's escape came little more than a month after he stood trial as the Green Man. It had been a brief trial, beginning January 10 and ending on January 18. The charges against him were breaking and entering, assault and battery, armed burglary, and "unnatural and lascivious acts" against four women in four Boston suburbs—charges that had nothing to do with the stranglings.

As the reader knows, it had been F. Lee Bailey's hope to win a verdict of not guilty of the Green Man charges by reason of insanity, and as proof of DeSalvo's insanity, to put into evidence at this trial the long confession DeSalvo had made to Bottomly and McGrath. Bailey then planned to have Phil DiNatale corroborate DeSalvo's confession by reporting how the Attorney General's Strangler Bureau had checked out detail after detail of his story and found these "to square with the facts."

But Bailey failed. The bench, acting on objections of Assistant District Attorney Conn, refused to allow any evidence relating to the stranglings. Neither Bottomly nor DiNatale were allowed to testify. These crimes, the judge ruled, were not before the court. Nevertheless Bailey continued this line of defense, taking repeated exception to the court's rulings. Two defense psychiatrists characterized DeSalvo as a severe schizophrenic of the paranoid type; they were permitted to testify that he had admitted to them that he was the Strangler, and had told of the "undescribable compulsion" that came over him when he strangled. The judge explained that he admitted this testimony "solely as part of the history" the defendant had given the psychiatrists but that "it is not substantive evidence of the commission of any crime." And when

378

he finally charged the jury, he ordered them to purge from their minds DeSalvo's story of the stranglings. "He is not on trial in this court for homicide," he asserted.

Psychiatrists for the State, while agreeing that DeSalvo was mentally ill and dangerous, contended that he knew right from wrong and at the time he committed the Green Man assaults had not been laboring under an "irresistible impulse" —the mark of insanity.

On January 18, after deliberating less than four hours, the all-male jury found DeSalvo guilty as charged. He was sentenced to life imprisonment for armed robbery, to be served after he completed a nine-to-ten-year sentence on the other charges.

"Massachusetts has burned another witch," Bailey declared bitterly. It was his first defeat in a series of sensational court victories, including the acquittals of Dr. Samuel Sheppard in Cleveland in November and Dr. Carl Coppolino in Freehold, New Jersey, a month later. What had happened, he said, was not the fault of the jury, but of Massachusetts' archaic laws on criminal insanity. He would appeal the case to the Massachusetts Supreme Court.

DeSalvo was returned to Bridgewater State Hospital pending the result of the appeal. And it was from here, five weeks later, that he escaped with his two companions.

His breakout launched one of the most intensive manhunts in history. Hysteria swept the entire eastern seaboard, heightened by minute-to-minute coverage by television, radio, and newspapers. The Royal Canadian Mounted Police, the FBI, border patrols, and customs officials were enlisted in the search. Boston itself was on the edge of panic; this was the nightmare of only a few years ago suddenly come upon them again. Many women living alone moved into hotels; none of the Strangler's victims had lived in a hotel. Sons and daughters began checking on the safety of their mothers living alone; there was a rush to buy locks and door chains; women actually feared to emerge on the streets.

Thousands of police spread through the city, checking every vacant house in which DeSalvo might be hiding. Police in cruisers drove up and down the streets, scanning pedestrians —perhaps the man who had maintained such invisibility all through the search for the Strangler was at this very moment sauntering down the street. Police dogs and helicopters were brought into the search. Wild rumors circulated: he was seen in Boston, in Baltimore, in Pittsburgh, in Dayton; he was enroute to New York, enroute to Mexico, enroute to Canada, seeking a plastic surgeon to change his features; he was aboard a ship bound for a hideout abroad; he was flying to Germany where his wife and children now lived.

Thirty-six hours after he broke out, at the height of the hysteria, he quietly gave himself up in Lynn, Massachusetts, a few miles from Bridgewater.

Why had he escaped?

It was "to dramatize his situation," Bailey said, after talking with his client. The lawyer told of a conversation with DeSalvo weeks before, immediately after the trial. DeSalvo had been deeply dejected by the verdict. He had hoped to be found insane, which would have relieved him of the responsibility for his crimes; he had hoped to have psychiatric treatment so he would know why he had done what he had done, and perhaps even be cured. Now, it seemed to him, there was no hope; he would simply "rot in jail" the rest of his life.

"I can walk out of this place anytime I want to," he told Bailey. "What would happen if I did?"

"They'd set up the biggest manhunt in history, and chances are that some trigger-happy cop or citizen would kill you."

"Maybe that'd be the best thing that could happen," DeSalvo said heavily.

Bailey shook his head. He felt confident they would win their appeal. Then DeSalvo could be tried again, under more modern insanity laws, laws more in accord with what psychiatry had discovered about mental illness in recent years. Under such laws, Bailey said, he was certain DeSalvo would be found insane.

But DeSalvo brooded. The only way he could be assured of psychiatric help was if he was accepted as the Boston Strangler; the Commonwealth, he felt, had not carried out its promises to him—it had not allowed proof that he was the Strangler. If, however, he did escape, and a tremendous manhunt got under way, wouldn't that prove it? Certainly no such search would be organized if he were simply the Green Man.

So—as he was to tell Bailey later—he decided to break out.

It was a comparatively easy escape. Bridgewater had never been a place of maximum security. "We are keeping murderers in a hen-coop," Superintendent Gaughan said afterwards.

As DeSalvo told the story, Harrison and Erickson had begun to plan their own escape months before. They had invited DeSalvo to join them. He had refused, then. Now, having lost his case, he agreed and took over the plans. He had been helping a locksmith repair his lock, and in the process, made himself a key, he said. It was reported, however, that a gun, a blank key, and hacksaw blades were smuggled in to him. Whatever the case, when the time for the escape came, the three men left rolled blankets and pillows in their cots, simulating the outlines of their bodies. They waited for a moment between cell checks. DeSalvo, key in hand, stuck his arm through the large peephole in the door of his cell, unlocked his door, then unlocked the doors of Harrison and Erickson, whose cells were on either side of his on the third floor. The men climbed down an elevator shaft under construction; then, using pieces of scaffolding they found, they climbed a twenty-foot wall, dropped into a snow-covered field, and ran across it to a main road.

DeSalvo left a note on his bunk addressed to Superintendent Gaughan. Its text was not made public, but in it DeSalvo said, in substance, that he was escaping to dramatize his situation, to call attention to the bad conditions in Bridgewater; that he was sorry to embarrass Gaughan by this act but wanted him to know that he did not intend to hurt anybody, felt no hostility toward anybody.

The three stole a car in the town of Bridgewater and drove off toward Boston. On the way Harrison and Erickson proposed that they should break into a house, rob it, and then hold the family hostage. They had read about this in the newspapers and had been intrigued. DeSalvo vetoed the idea. "We're not going to hurt nobody," he said. They had reached the town of Everett when their car began to stall; they managed to nurse the motor until they rolled into a deserted service station. There the motor simply stopped. They abandoned the car—it was still before dawn—and Albert telephoned his brother, Joseph, 37, who lived nearby. As Joseph told police later, Albert, sounding "very excited," asked him to meet him at the service station. Joseph first thought it was all a joke, that Albert was calling him from Bridgewater. But he decided to go to the scene anyway. When he arrived, he said, he was surprised to see the other two men. Albert told him he'd also telephoned their younger brother, Richard, in Chelsea, and Richard was waiting there with a change of clothes for him.

The four drove in Joseph's car to Chelsea, where Richard supplied Albert with a pair of trousers, a sweater, and a jacket. (When Albert broke out he was wearing prison attire of gray denim slacks and shirt, the latter bearing the telltale initials MCI, for Massachusetts Correctional Institute, and over the shirt, a mackinaw.)

381

Now the five drove to a rapid-transit station in Charlestown, where Harrison and Erickson were dropped off. Once on their own, Harrison and Erickson made their way to Waltham. They started drinking steadily. On Friday night, thirteen hours after their escape, they drunkenly turned themselves in to an attorney, Martin Fay, who met them in a Waltham bar and drove them back to Bridgewater—a hair-raising drive during which Harrison at one point tried to throw himself out of the car.

Meanwhile, the three brothers drove back to Chelsea, because Richard had to go to work. Then Joseph drove Albert to Lynn. Here Albert got out, saying that he knew this area well. It was about 8 A.M. The two brothers parted. Joseph later said that he gave Albert $150 and a pair of eyeglasses, then drove home, on the way tossing Albert's prison clothing into a Good Will Industries deposit can at a shopping center. (Police later found the clothes there.)

Albert, alone, fortified with pep pills he had stolen from the dispensary at Bridgewater, spent the rest of that day riding buses and listening to news of the search on a small transistor radio he carried with him. He had one narrow escape, he said later. He was waiting for a bus when a policeman accosted him. "Hey, are you DeSalvo?" he demanded. And DeSalvo, with that presence of mind which had always marked him in emergencies, retorted, "Of course not. My name's Johnson—" He pointed to a nearby apartment building. "I live right upstairs there—check with my wife, if you want—she's home."

The policeman walked away.

Late that night he slipped into the cellar of a three-story wooden house at 785 Western Ave. It was about 2:30 A.M. when he carefully pushed open the door, which had a broken lock. It creaked. Two floors above, Arthur Vincent, 37, and his sister, Mrs. Simone Fedas, watching a late movie on TV, heard the sound. Was someone trying to break into a neighboring liquor store? they wondered. They investigated briefly, saw nothing, and returned to their TV set.

DeSalvo later said he knew there was a woman in the house —he had seen her name on the bell—and was proud that he had done nothing; that he had harmed no one, as he had promised. He slept on newspapers and rags in the cellar that night. In a bin he found a sailor's uniform—it belonged to Vincent's nephew who had been discharged from the Navy half a dozen years before—and tried it on. It turned out to be not a bad fit. DeSalvo was wearing brown shoes, an odd com-

382

bination with a sailor's uniform, but nothing could be done about it.

On his transistor radio he heard that the Boston *Record-American* had announced a reward of $5,000 for him, dead or alive; then, later, that Bailey, in South Carolina where he was involved in another case, had offered a reward of $10,000 for him, alive, obviously fearing that the newspaper's offer might lead someone to shoot him on sight. The lawyer broadcast a plea to DeSalvo to turn himself in. The appeal was repeated every few hours by Charles Burnim, Bailey's assistant.

By 2:40 that Saturday afternoon DeSalvo, cold, tired, and hungry, decided to respond to his lawyer's plea and give himself up. Wearing the Navy uniform, he slipped out of the cellar, to see a searching patrol pass by; he turned up his collar and walked a few hundred feet to Simon's Clothing Store on Western Avenue—a huge, rambling place—and asked a clerk, Frederick Waldron, "Can I use your telephone?"

Waldron was a social-work supervisor who worked Saturdays in the store. His first thought was, *That face . . .* He motioned to James Trelegan, the manager. The two men had the same thought. Could this sailor be DeSalvo? The man's face had been on the front page of every newspaper.

Waldron spoke up. "Sorry, we don't have a pay station here."

DeSalvo blurted out, "This is an emergency. I got to call F. Lee, and I don't have any change."

F. Lee could only mean F. Lee Bailey—DeSalvo's attorney.

Waldron pointed to a telephone on a counter, and while DeSalvo made his call, Trelegan strolled to the rear of the store, notified the owner, J. B. Simon, and immediately called Lynn police on another telephone.

DeSalvo rang Bailey's office. The call was taken by Andrew Tuney. Tuney, who as a Detective Lieutenant in the State Police had been in charge of the Attorney General's Strangler Bureau, had subsequently given up his position to become the owner of Bailey's investigative agency, and now directed the firm's pre-trial investigations. He had been waiting at the telephone in hope that DeSalvo would respond to the broadcast plea.

He recognized DeSalvo's voice at once. "Call the police off," he was saying. "I'm ready to come in."

"Where are you, Albert?" Tuney asked.

"I'm in Lynn," came the reply. DeSalvo gave him the address of the store.

"Stay right where you are until we get there," Tuney told

383

him, and hurriedly left for Lynn with several of Bailey's other associates.

Meanwhile Trelegan's whispered call—an urgent "DeSalvo's here!—I'm not fooling!"—had sent Lynn police racing to the scene.

DeSalvo put down the phone and turned to find Trelegan emerging from the rear. He rubbed his hand over his nose. Might he have a cup of coffee? "Come along," said Trelegan, and led him to another part of the shop where a coffee pot stood on an electric grill.

Just before they sat down to the coffee, Trelegan took a chance.

"Are you DeSalvo?" he asked.

The sailor did not seem surprised. "I'm DeSalvo."

"Mind if I frisk you?"

"Not at all," DeSalvo said mildly, even raising his arms to make it easier for Trelegan.

At this point Lynn police arrived, guns in hand, far ahead of Bailey's associates, who were driving in from Boston.

"You DeSalvo?" he was asked again. And again he admitted his identity. Witnesses said he seemed relieved.

Minutes later, at police headquarters, DeSalvo told reporters, "I didn't bother nobody and I never will. I didn't mean no harm to nobody." He had broken out, he said, "to bring back to the attention of the public that a man has a mental illness, and hires a lawyer, and no one does anything about it."

So ended the bizarre epilogue to the story of the Boston Strangler. For thirty-six hours New England and the entire eastern seaboard had experienced a return to the hysteria that existed at the time of the stranglings. DeSalvo's escape led to a series of investigations, not only into the apparent lack of security at Bridgewater but also into living conditions in the ancient, overcrowded institution. If his purpose had been to call his position to public attention, there was no question that DeSalvo had succeeded.

385

position of body when found, 32
strangulation by human hands, 31
Davis, Nancy, 237, 238
Davis, Tommy, Detective, 100, 105, 112, 122, 132
Day, Doris, actress, 103
"Decoration" on necks or other parts of victims, 258
see also (under name of individual victim), Position of body when found; Sexual assault upon
Decorator Fabrics, Inc., 16
Delaney, Stephen, Metropolitan Police Officer, 95, 123, 125, 146, 178, 186, 187, 188, 191, 192, 193, 194, 195, 196, 197, 198, 199, 226, 230, 233, 234, 284, 370
Delmore, Patricia, 87, 136, 177, 188, 199, 203, 204, 205, 226, 227
Demented man as Strangler, 98
theory of Suffolk County Medical Examiner, 46-47
see also Insane person or persons; Madman theory
Dennisport cottage, of friends of Mary Sullivan, 201, 226
Denver suburb of Northglen, 248
Department of Legal Medicine, Harvard University, 46
Derry, New Hampshire, 15
DeSalvo, Albert, confessed Boston Strangler, 239-44, 247-54, 255-60, 262, 263, 264, 265, 266, 281, 284-307, 308-32, 333-57, 358-77
Army background of, 286, 287
Army record of, 286, 322, 347, 349, 365
as "B and E" man, 256, 295, 311, 334, 337, 338, 342, 343, 344, 349
brutality of father of, 329, 330, 339
Dictaphone confession of, 253, 259
hypnoanalysis of, 268-75, 281
Interrogation of, by George McGrath, 319-21
Interrogation of, by J. S. Bottomly, 285, 286-98
second session, 298-306
third session, 308, 309, 311, 312, 313, 314, 315, 316, 317-32
I.Q. of, 331, 342

letter from, to attorney Sheinfeld, 333-34
letter from, to wife, Irmgard, 275-77
list of confessed assaults by, 243, 253
list of charges against, by Commonwealth of Massachusetts, 342
mental condition of, diagnosed, 371, 372
middleweight Army boxing champion in Europe, 347, 364
note and gift to attorney Sheinfeld, 337
offenses of, while stationed at Fort Dix, 347, 348
physical description of, 286
facial characteristics, 287, 348, 349
voice quality, 287
police record of, 341, 342
previous police record of, 240-41
sex exploits of in Germany, 321
telegram to, from attorney Bailey, 259-60
war record of, 286
ward mate of George Nassar, 250, 251, 253, 259, 262
see also "Green Man" and "Measuring Man"
DeSalvo, Charlotte, mother of Albert DeSalvo, 329-30, 340, 341
thick glasses of, 328, 340
name (through second marriage), Mrs. Peter Khouri, 342, 343, 344, 345, 346
DeSalvo, Dickie, brother of Albert DeSalvo, 329
DeSalvo, Frank, Sr., father of Albert DeSalvo, 329, 330, 339, 345
police record of, 340, 341
DeSalvo, Frank, youngest brother of Albert DeSalvo, 249, 250, 329, 344, 345
DeSalvo, Irene, sister of Albert DeSalvo, 242
DeSalvo, Irmgard, wife of Albert DeSalvo, 242, 243, 244, 247, 248, 249, 250, 252, 253, 259, 264, 265, 274, 275, 299, 306, 313, 322, 324, 325, 326, 327, 328, 335, 336, 337, 347, 349, 365, 366, 367
letter to, from husband, 275-77